Contributors

Audrey Knippa, MS, MPH, RN, CNE
Nursing Education Coordinator and
  Content Project Leader

Sheryl Sommer, PhD, MSN, RN
Director, Nursing Curriculum and
  Education Services

Brenda Ball, MEd, BSN, RN
Nursing Education Specialist

Lois Churchill, MN, RN
Nursing Education Specialist

Carrie B. Elkins, DHSc, MSN, PHCNS, BC
Nursing Education Specialist

Mary Jane Janowski, MA, BSN, RN
Nursing Resource Specialist

Karin Roberts, PhD, MSN, RN, CNE
Nursing Education Coordinator

Mendy G. Wright, DNP, MSN, RN
Nursing Education Specialist

Derek Prater, MS Journalism
Lead Product Developer and Editorial Project Leader

Erika A. Archer, BS Education, Foreign Language
Product Developer

Johanna Barnes, BA Journalism
Product Developer

Chris Crawford, BS Journalism
Product Developer

Hilary E. Groninger, BS Journalism
Product Developer

Megan E. Herre, BS Journalism
Product Developer

Amanda Lehman, BA English
Product Developer

Joanna Shindler, BA Journalism
Product Developer

Brant L. Stacy, BS Journalism, BA English
Product Developer

Consultants

Susan Adcock, MS, RN

Claire Creamer, MS, RN, CPNP

Penny Fauber, PhD, RN

Terri Lemon, MSN, RN

Gale P. Sewell, MSN, RN, CNE

INTELLECTUAL PROPERTY NOTICE

IMPORTANT NOTICE TO THE READER

USER'S GUIDE

Welcome to the Assessment Technologies Institute® RN Nursing Care of Children Review Module Edition 8.0. The mission of ATI's Content Mastery Series® review modules is to provide user-friendly compendiums of nursing knowledge that will:

- Help you locate important information quickly.

- Assist in your remediation efforts.

- Provide exercises for applying your nursing knowledge.

- Facilitate your entry into the nursing profession as a newly licensed RN.

Organization

This review module is organized into units covering the foundations of nursing care of children, nursing care of children with system disorders, and nursing care of children with special needs. Chapters within these units conform to one of four organizing principles for presenting the content:

- Nursing concepts

- Growth and development

- Procedures

- Systems disorders

Nursing concepts chapters begin with an overview describing the central concept and its relevance to nursing. Subordinate themes are covered in outline form to demonstrate relationships and present the information in a clear, succinct manner.

Growth and development chapters cover expected growth and development, including physical and psychosocial development and age-appropriate activities, and health promotion, including immunizations, health screenings, nutrition, and injury prevention.

Procedures chapters include an overview describing the procedure(s) covered in the chapter. These chapters will provide you with nursing knowledge relevant to each procedure, including indications, interpretations of findings, client outcomes, nursing actions, and complications.

Systems disorders chapters include an overview describing the disorder(s) and/or disease process. These chapters may provide information on health promotion and disease prevention before addressing assessments, including risk factors, subjective data, and objective data. Next, you will focus on collaborative care, including nursing care, medications, interdisciplinary care, therapeutic procedures, surgical interventions, care after discharge, and client outcomes. Finally, you will find complications related to the disorder, along with nursing actions in response to those complications.

Application Exercises

Questions are provided at the end of each chapter so you can practice applying your knowledge. The Application Exercises include both NCLEX-style questions, such as multiple-choice and multiple-select items, and questions that ask you to apply your knowledge in other formats, such as short-answer and matching items. After the Application Exercises, an answer key is provided, along with rationales for the answers.

NCLEX® Connections

To prepare for the NCLEX-RN, it is important for you to understand how the content in this review module is connected to the NCLEX-RN test plan. You can find information on the detailed test plan at the National Council of State Boards of Nursing's Web site: https://www.ncsbn.org/. When reviewing content in this review module, regularly ask yourself, "How does this content fit into the test plan, and what types of questions related to this content should I expect?"

To help you in this process, we've included NCLEX Connections at the beginning of sections and units and with each question in the Application Exercises Answer Keys. The NCLEX Connections at the beginning of sections and units will point out areas of the detailed test plan that relate to the content within the section or unit. The NCLEX Connections attached to the Application Exercises Answer Keys will demonstrate how each exercise fits within the detailed content outline.

These NCLEX Connections will help you understand how the detailed content outline is organized, starting with major client needs categories and subcategories and followed by related content areas and tasks. The major client needs categories are:

- Safe and Effective Care Environment
  - Management of Care
  - Safety and Infection Control
- Health Promotion and Maintenance
- Psychosocial Integrity
- Physiological Integrity
  - Basic Care and Comfort
  - Pharmacological and Parenteral Therapies
  - Reduction of Risk Potential
  - Physiological Adaptation

An NCLEX Connection might, for example, alert you that content within a unit is related to:

- Physiological Adaptation
  - Alterations in Body Systems
    - Identify signs, symptoms, and incubation periods of infectious diseases.

Icons

Icons are used throughout the review module to draw your attention to particular areas. Keep an eye out for these icons:

 This icon indicates an Overview, or introduction, to a particular subject matter. Descriptions and categories will typically be found in an Overview.

 This icon is used for the Application Exercises and the Application Exercises Answer Keys.

This icon is used for NCLEX connections.

 This icon is used for content related to safety. When you see this icon, take note of safety concerns or steps that nurses can take to ensure client safety and a safe environment.

This icon indicates that a media supplement, such as a graphic, an animation, or a video, is available. If you have an electronic copy of the review module, this icon will appear alongside clickable links to media supplements. If you have a hardcopy version of the review module, visit www.atitesting.com for details on how to access these features.

Feedback

ATI welcomes feedback regarding this review module. Please provide comments to: comments@atitesting.com.

Table of Contents

Unit 3   Nursing Care of Children With Special Needs

UNIT 1: FOUNDATIONS OF NURSING CARE OF CHILDREN

Section: Perspectives of Nursing Care of Children

- Family-Centered Nursing Care
- Physical Assessment Findings
- Health Promotion of the Infant (Birth to 1 Year)
- Health Promotion of the Toddler (1 to 3 Years)
- Health Promotion of the Preschooler (3 to 6 Years)
- Health Promotion of the School-Age Child (6 to 12 Years)
- Health Promotion of the Adolescent (12 to 20 Years)

NCLEX® CONNECTIONS

When reviewing the chapters in this section, keep in mind the relevant sections of the NCLEX® outline, in particular:

CLIENT NEEDS: SAFETY AND INFECTION CONTROL

Relevant topics/tasks include:
- Accident/Injury Prevention
  - Identify and facilitate correct use of infant and child car seats.

CLIENT NEEDS: HEALTH PROMOTION AND MAINTENANCE

Relevant topics/tasks include:
- Aging Process
  - Provide care and education that meets the special needs of the infant client 1 month to 1 year.
- Developmental Stages and Transitions
  - Provide education to clients/staff members about expected age-related changes and age-specific growth and development.
- Health and Wellness
  - Identify precautions and contraindications to immunizations.
- Techniques of Physical Assessment
  - Choose physical assessment equipment and techniques appropriate for the client.

UNIT 1	FOUNDATIONS OF NURSING CARE OF CHILDREN
Section	Perspectives of Nursing Care of Children
Chapter 1	Family-Centered Nursing Care

Overview

- Families are groups that should remain constant in children's lives.

- Family is defined as what an individual considers it to be.

- Positive family relationships are characterized by parent-child interactions that show mutual warmth and respect.

- Family-centered nursing care includes:

  - Agreed upon partnerships between families of children, nurses, and health care providers, in which the families and children benefit.

  - Respecting cultural diversity and incorporating cultural views in the plan of care.

  - Understanding growth and developmental needs of children and their families.

  - Treating children and their families as clients.

  - Working with all types of families.

  - Collaborating with families regarding hospitalization, home, and community resources.

  - Allowing families to serve as experts regarding their children's health conditions, usual behaviors in different situations, and routine needs.

- Promoting family-centered care

  - Nurses should perform comprehensive family assessments to identify strengths and weaknesses of families.

  - Nurses should pay close attention when family members state that a child "isn't acting right" or has other concerns.

  - Children's opinions should be considered when providing care.

Family Composition

TYPE	MEMBERS
Nuclear family	Two parents and their children (biologic, adoptive, step, foster)
Traditional nuclear family	Married couple and their biologic children (only full brothers and sisters)
Single-parent family	One parent and one or more children
Blended family (also called reconstituted)	At least one stepparent, stepsibling, or half sibling
Extended family	At least one parent, one or more children, and other individuals either related or not related
Gay/Lesbian family	Two members of the same sex that have a common-law tie and may or may not have children
Foster family	A child or children that have been placed in an approved living environment away from the family of origin – usually with one or two parents
Binuclear family	Parents that have terminated spousal roles but continue their parenting roles
Communal family	Individuals that share common ownership of property and goods and exchange services without monetary consideration

- Changes That Occur With the Birth (or Adoption) of the First Child
    - Parents' sense of self and how families work
    - Division of labor and roles within the relationships of couples
    - Relationships with grandparents
    - Work relationships

Parenting Styles

TYPE	DESCRIPTION	EXAMPLE
Dictatorial or authoritarian	• Parents try to control the child's behaviors and attitudes through unquestioned rules and expectations.	• The child may not watch television on school nights.
Permissive or laissez-faire	• Parents exert little or no control over the child's behaviors.	• The child may watch television whenever he wants to watch it.

TYPE	DESCRIPTION	EXAMPLE
Democratic or authoritative	<ul><li>Parents direct the child's behavior by setting rules and explaining the reason for each rule setting.</li><li>Parents negatively reinforce deviations from the rules.</li></ul>	<ul><li>The children may watch television for an hour if her homework is completed.</li><li>The privilege is taken away but may be reinstated based on new guidelines.</li></ul>

- Positive Parental Influences

    o Parents have good mental health.

    o Structure and routine is maintained in the household.

    o Parents engage in activities with the child.

    o There is communication that validates the child's feelings.

    o The child is monitored for safety with special consideration for his developmental needs.

- Guidelines for Promoting Healthy Behavior in Children

    o Set realistic limits and expectations based on the developmental level of the child.

    o Validate the child's feelings.

    o Provide reinforcement for appropriate behavior.

    o Focus on the child's behavior when disciplining the child.

Family Assessment

- Genogram – Medical history for parents, siblings, aunts, uncles, and grandparents

- Structure – Members in the family (mother, father, son)

- Developmental tasks – Tasks a family works on as the child grows (parents with a school-age child helping her to develop peer relations)

- Family functions/roles – Ways in which family members interact with each other (mother being the disciplinarian)

- Family stressors – Events that cause stress (illness of a child)

Client Outcomes

- The family will provide a safe environments for all family members.

CHAPTER 1: FAMILY-CENTERED NURSING CARE

 Application Exercises

1. A nurse is caring for a 5-year-old child who has autism and lives with her mother, two brothers, and grandmother. Which of the following describes this family's composition?

    A. Nuclear family

    B. Blended family

    C. Extended family

    D. Gay/Lesbian family

2. A nurse is caring for several children. Match each of the following parenting styles to the parental statement that most reflects that style.

_____	Democratic	A. "Your curfew is 10 p.m. You know that."
_____	Dictatorial	B. "As long as you have your homework done, I don't care when you come home."
_____	Permissive	C. "Tonight is a school night, so you need to come home by 10 p.m."

3. A nurse is performing family assessment. Which of the following should the nurse include? (Select all that apply.)

    _____ Genogram

    _____ Structure

    _____ Child's physical growth

    _____ Developmental tasks

    _____ Family functions/roles

    _____ Family stressors

CHAPTER 1: FAMILY-CENTERED NURSING CARE

 Application Exercises Answer Key

1. A nurse is caring for a 5-year-old child who has autism and lives with her mother, two brothers, and grandmother. Which of the following describes this family's composition?

    A. Nuclear family

    B. Blended family

    C. Extended family

    D. Gay/Lesbian family

An extended family includes one or more parents, one or more children, and other family members, such as a grandmother. A nuclear family includes two parents and their children. A blended family includes at least one stepparent, stepsibling, and/or half sibling. A gay/lesbian family includes a common-law tie between two members of the same sex who may or may not have children.

NCLEX® Connection: Safety and Infection Control, Developmental Stages and Transitions

2. A nurse is caring for several children. Match each of the following parenting styles to the parental statement that most reflects that style.

C	Democratic	A. "Your curfew is 10 p.m. You know that."
A	Dictatorial	B. "As long as you have your homework done, I don't care when you come home."
B	Permissive	C. "Tonight is a school night, so you need to come home by 10 p.m."

NCLEX® Connection: Safety and Infection Control, Developmental Stages and Transitions

3. A nurse is performing family assessment. Which of the following should the nurse include? (Select all that apply.)

X	**Genogram**
X	**Structure**
	Child's physical growth
X	**Developmental tasks**
X	**Family functions/roles**
X	**Family stressors**

Genogram, structure, developmental tasks, family functions/roles, and family stressors should all be included in a family assessment. The child's physical growth is part of that child's individual assessment.

NCLEX® Connection: Safety and Infection Control, Developmental Stages and Transitions

UNIT 1	FOUNDATIONS OF NURSING CARE OF CHILDREN
Section	Perspectives of Nursing Care of Children
Chapter 2	Physical Assessment Findings

Overview

- Perform examinations in nonthreatening environments.

- Alter exams to accommodate children's developmental needs.

- Observe behaviors that signal children's readiness to cooperate.

- Involve children and family members in examinations Adolescents may prefer to be examined without family members present.

- Praise children for cooperation during exams.

Nursing Considerations

- Keep the room warm and well lit.

- Distract the child when bringing equipment that can be perceived as threatening into the room.

- Provide privacy.

- Tell the child, using age-appropriate language, what to expect as the physical exam is being performed.

- Examine the child in a secure, comfortable position. For example, a toddler may sit on a parent's lap if desired.

- Proceed to examine the child in an organized sequence when possible.

- Encourage the child and/or family to ask questions during physical exams.

Expected Vital Signs

- Temperature

    o Birth to 1 year (axillary) – 36.5 to 37.2 ° C (97.7 to 98.9° F)

    o 1 to 12 years (oral) – 36.7 to 37.7° C (98.1 to 99.9° F)

    o 12 years and older (oral) – 36.6 to 36.7° C (97.8 to 98.0° F)

- Pulse

    o   Birth to 1 week – 100 to 160/min with brief fluctuations above and below this range, depending on activity level (crying, sleeping)

    o   1 week to 3 months – 100 to 220/min

    o   3 months to 2 years – 80 to 150/min

    o   2 to 12 years – 70 to 110/min

    o   12 years and older – 50 to 90/min

- Respirations

    o   Newborn – 30 to 60/min with short periods of apnea (less than 15 seconds)

    o   Newborn to 1 year – 30/min

    o   1 to 2 years – 25 to 30/min

    o   2 to 6 years – 21 to 24/min

    o   6 to 12 years – 19 to 21/min

    o   12 years and older – 16 to 18/min

- Blood Pressure

    o   Age, height, and gender all influence blood pressure readings. Readings should be compared with standard measurements (The National High Blood Pressure Program tables).

    o   Infants – 60 to 80 mm Hg systolic and 40 to 50 mm Hg diastolic

    o   The following chart provides examples of expected ranges of blood pressure by age and gender.

AGE	GIRLS		BOYS	
	SYSTOLIC (MM HG)	DIASTOLIC (MM HG)	SYSTOLIC (MM HG)	DIASTOLIC (MM HG)
1 year	97 to 107	53 to 60	94 to 106	50 to 59
3 years	100 to 110	61 to 68	100 to 113	59 to 67
6 years	104 to 114	67 to 75	105 to 117	67 to 76
10 years	112 to 122	73 to 80	110 to 123	73 to 82
16 years	122 to 132	79 to 86	125 to 138	79 to 87

Expected Physical Assessment Findings

- General Appearance

    o   Appears undistressed

    o   Appears clean and well-kept

- Muscle tone
  - Limp posture with extension of the extremities is expected.
  - Erect head posture is expected in infants after 4 months of age.
- Has no body odors
- Makes eye contact when addressed (except infants)
- Follows simple commands as age appropriate
- Uses speech, language, and motor skills spontaneously
- Growth – Growth can be evaluated using weight, height, body mass index (BMI), and head circumference. Growth charts are tools that can be used to assess the overall health of a child. To see growth charts by age and gender, visit the Web site for the Centers for Disease Control and prevention (http://www.cdc.gov).

- Skin, Hair, and Nails
  - Skin
    - Skin color may show normal variations based on race and ethnicity.
    - Temperature should be warm or slightly cool to the touch.
    - Skin turgor should demonstrate brisk elasticity with adequate hydration.
    - Skin texture should be smooth and slightly dry.
    - Lesions are not normal findings.
    - Skin folds should be symmetric.
  - Hair
    - Hair should be evenly distributed, smooth, and strong.
    - Children approaching adolescence should be assessed for the presence of secondary hair growth.
  - Nails
    - Pink over the nail bed and white at the tips
    - Smooth and firm (but slightly flexible in infants)
    - No clubbing
- Lymph nodes should be nonpalpable, but lymph nodes that are small, palpable, nontender, and mobile in children may still be considered normal.
- Head and Neck
  - Head
    - The shape of the head should be symmetric.
    - Fontanels should be flat. The posterior fontanel usually closes between 2 and 3 months of age, and the anterior fontanel usually closes between 12 and 18 months of age.

- Face
  - Symmetric appearance and movement
  - Proportional features
- Neck
  - Short in infants
  - No palpable masses
  - Midline trachea
  - Full range of motion present whether assessed actively or passively

- Eyes
  - Visual acuity – May be difficult to assess in children under 3 years of age
    - Visual acuity in infants can be assessed by holding an object in front of the eyes and checking to see if the infant is able to fix on the object and follow it.
    - Older children should be tested using a Snellen chart or symbol chart.
  - Color vision should be assessed using the Ishihara color test. The child should be able to correctly identify shapes.
  - Peripheral visual fields should be:
    - Upward 50°
    - Downward 70°
    - Nasally 60°
    - Temporally 90°
  - Extraocular movements may not be symmetric in newborns.
    - Corneal light reflex should be symmetric.
    - Cover/uncover test should demonstrate equal movement of the eyes. The presence of strabismus should be further evaluated in children between 4 and 6 years of age.
    - Six cardinal fields of gaze should demonstrate no nystagmus.
  - Eyebrows should be symmetric and evenly distributed from the inner to the outer canthus.
  - Eyelids should close completely and open to allow the lower border and most of the upper portion of the iris to be seen.
  - Eyelashes should curve outward and be evenly distributed with no inflammation around any of the hair follicles.
  - Conjunctiva
    - Palpebral is pink.
    - Bulbar is transparent.

- o   Lacrimal apparatus is without excessive tearing, redness, or discharge.

- o   Sclera should be white.

- o   Corneas should be clear.

- o   Pupils should be:

  - ▪   Round

  - ▪   Equal in size

  - ▪   Reactive to light

  - ▪   Accommodating (can be tested in older children)

- o   Irises should be round with the permanent color manifesting around 6 to 12 months of age.

- **Internal Exam**

  - o   Red reflex should be present in infants.

  - o   Arteries, veins, optic discs, and maculas may be visualized in older children and adolescents.

- **Ears**

  - o   Alignment

    - ▪   The top of the auricles should meet in an imaginary horizontal line that extends from the outer canthus of the eye.

  - o   External ear

    - ▪   The external ear should be free of lesions and nontender.

    - ▪   The ear canal should be free of foreign bodies or discharge.

    - ▪   Cerumen is an expected finding.

  - o   Internal ear

    - ▪   In infants, pull the pinna down and back to visualize the tympanic membrane.

    - ▪   In children older than 3 years of age, pull the pinna up and back to visualize.

    - ▪   The tympanic membrane should be pearly gray.

    - ▪   The light reflex should be visible.

    - ▪   Umbo (tip of the malleolus) and manubrium (long process or handle) are the bony landmarks that should be visible.

    - ▪   The ear canal should be pink with fine hairs.

- - Hearing
    - Newborns should have intact acoustic blink reflexes to sudden sounds.
    - Infants should turn toward sounds.
    - Older children can be screened by whispering a word from behind to see if they can identify the word.
- Nose
  - The position should be midline.
  - Patency should be present for each nostril without excessive flaring.
  - Internal structures
    - The septum is midline and intact.
    - The mucosa is deep pink and moist with no discharge.
  - Smell can be assessed in older children.
- Mouth and Throat
  - Lips
    - Darker pigmented than facial skin
    - Smooth, soft, and moist
  - Gums
    - Coral pink
    - Tight against the teeth
  - Mucous membranes
    - Without lesions
    - Moist and pink
  - Tongue
    - Infants may have white coatings on their tongues from milk that can be easily removed. Oral candidiasis coating is not easily removed.
    - Children and adolescents should have pink, symmetric tongues that they are able to move beyond their lips.
  - Teeth
    - Infants should have 6 to 8 teeth by 1 year of age.
    - Children and adolescents should have teeth that are white and smooth, with 20 deciduous and 32 permanent teeth.
  - Hard and soft palates – Intact, firm, and concave
  - Uvula – Intact and moves with vocalization

- o Tonsils
  - Infants – May not be able to visualize
  - Children – Barely visible to prominent, same color as surrounding mucosa, deep crevices that hold food particles
- o Speech
  - Infants – Strong cry
  - Children and adolescents – Clear and articulate
- Thorax and Lungs
  - o Chest shape
    - Infants – Shape is almost circular with anteroposterior diameter equaling the transverse or lateral diameter.
    - Children and adolescents – The transverse diameter to anteroposterior diameter changes to 2:1.
  - o Ribs and sternum – More soft and flexible in infants, symmetric, and smooth with no protrusions or bulges
  - o Movement – Symmetric, no retractions
    - Infants – Irregular rhythms are common.
    - Children younger than 7 – More abdominal movement is seen during respirations.
  - o Breath sounds
    - Infants – Harsher and easier to hear than in adults; harder to differentiate between upper versus lower respiratory sounds
    - Children and adolescents – Vesicular sounds heard over the lung fields
  - o Breasts
    - Newborns – Breasts may be enlarged during the first several months.
    - Children and adolescents – Nipples and areolas are darker pigmented and symmetric.
    - Females – Breasts typically develop between 10 to 14 years of age. The breasts should appear asymmetric, have no masses, and be palpable.
    - Males may develop a firm, approximately 2-cm area of breast tissue or gynecomastia.

- Circulatory System

  - Heart sounds – S_1 and S_2 heart sounds should be clear and crisp. S_1 is louder at the apex of the heart. S_2 is louder near the base of the heart. Sinus arrhythmias that are associated with respirations are common. Physiologic splitting of S_2 and S_3 heart sounds are expected findings in children.

  - Pulses

    - Infants – Brachial, temporal, and femoral pulses should be palpable, full, and localized.

    - Children and adolescents – Pulse locations and expected findings are the same as those in adults.

- Abdomen – Without tenderness, no guarding. Peristaltic waves may be visible in thinner children.

  - Shape – Symmetric and without protrusions around the umbilicus

    - Infants and toddlers have rounded abdomens.

    - Children and adolescents should have flat abdomens.

  - Bowel sounds should be heard every 5 to 30 seconds.

  - Descending colon – Cylindric mass that is possibly palpable in the lower left quadrant due to the presence of stool

- Musculoskeletal System

  - Length, position, and size are symmetric.

  - Joints – Stable and symmetric with full range of motion and no crepitus or redness

  - Spine

    - Infants – Spines should be without dimples or tufts of hair. They should be midline with an overall C-shaped lateral curve.

    - Toddlers appear squat with short legs and protuberant abdomens.

    - Preschoolers appear more erect than toddlers.

    - Children should develop the cervical, thoracic, and lumbar curvatures like that of adults.

    - Adolescents should remain midline (no scoliosis noted).

  - Gait

    - Toddlers and young children – A bowlegged or knock-knee appearance is a common finding. Feet should face forward while walking.

    - Older children and adolescents – A steady gait should be noted with even wear on the soles of shoes.

- Neurologic System

REFLEX	EXPECTED FINDING	EXPECTED AGE
Sucking and rooting reflexes	• Elicited by stroking an infant's cheek or the edge of an infant's mouth o The infant turns her head toward the side that is touched and starts to suck.	Birth to 4 months
Palmar grasp	• Elicited by placing an object in an infant's palm o The infant grasps the object.	Birth to 6 months
Plantar grasp	• Elicited by touching the sole of an infant's foot o The infant's toes curl downward.	Birth to 8 months
Moro reflex (startle)	• Elicited by striking a flat surface an infant is lying on or by allowing the head and trunk of an infant in a semi-sitting position to fall backward to an angle of at least 30° o The infant's arms and legs symmetrically extend and then abduct while her fingers spread to form a C shape.	Birth to 4 months
Tonic neck reflex (fencer position)	• Elicited by turning an infant's head to one side o The infant extends the arm and leg on that side and flexes the arm and leg on the opposite side.	Birth to 3 to 4 months
Babinski reflex	• Elicited by stroking the outer edge of the sole of an infant's foot up toward the toes o The infant's toes fan upward and out.	Birth to 1 year

REFLEX	EXPECTED FINDING	EXPECTED AGE
Stepping	• Elicited by holding an infant upright with his feet touching a flat surface ○ The infant makes stepping movements.	Birth to 4 weeks

CRANIAL NERVES		
CRANIAL NERVE	EXPECTED FINDINGS INFANTS	EXPECTED FINDINGS CHILDREN/ADOLESCENTS
I Olfactory	• Difficult to test	• Identifies smells through each nostril individually
II Optic	• Looks at face and tracks with eyes	• Has intact visual acuity, peripheral vision, and color vision
III Oculomotor	• Blinks in response to light • Has pupils that are reactive to light	• Has no nystagmus and PERRLA is intact
IV Trochlear	• Looks at face and tracks with eyes	• Has the ability to look down and in with eyes
V Trigeminal	• Has rooting and sucking reflexes	• Is able to clench teeth together • Detects touch on face with eyes closed
VI Abducens	• Looks at face and tracks with eyes	• Is able to see laterally with eyes
VII Facial	• Has symmetric facial movements	• Has the ability to differentiate between salty and sweet on tongue • Has symmetric facial movements
VIII Acoustic	• Tracks a sound • Blinks in response to a loud noise	• Does not experience vertigo • Has intact hearing
IX Glossopharyngeal	• Has an intact gag reflex	• Has an intact gag reflex • Is able to taste sour sensations on back of tongue

    RN NURSING CARE OF CHILDREN

| | CRANIAL NERVES | |
CRANIAL NERVE	EXPECTED FINDINGS INFANTS	EXPECTED FINDINGS CHILDREN/ADOLESCENTS
X Vagus	• Has no difficulties swallowing	• Speech clear, no difficulties swallowing
XI Spinal Accessory	• Moves shoulders symmetrically	• Has equal strength of shoulder shrug against examiner's hands
XII Hypoglossal	• Has no difficulties swallowing • Opens mouth when nares are occluded	• Has a tongue that is midline • Is able to move tongue in all directions with equal strength against tongue blade resistance

- ○ Deep tendon reflexes should demonstrate the following:
  - ■ Partial flexion of the lower arm at the biceps tendon
  - ■ Partial extension of the lower arm at the triceps tendon
  - ■ Partial extension of the lower leg at the patellar tendon
  - ■ Plantar flexion of the foot at the Achilles tendon
- ○ Cerebellar function (children and adolescents)
  - ■ Finger to nose test – Rapid coordinated movements
  - ■ Heel to shin test – Able to run the heel of one foot down the shin of the other leg while standing
  - ■ Romberg test – Able to stand with slight swaying while eyes are closed
- ○ Language, cognition, and fine and gross motor development can be screened using a standardized tool such as the Denver Developmental Screening Test – Revised (Denver II). Referrals for further evaluation should not be based solely on results of one tool, but on a combination of data collected from psychosocial and medical histories and a physical examination.

- • Genitalia
  - ○ Male
    - ■ Hair distribution is diamond shaped after puberty in adolescent males. No pubic hair is noted in infants and small children.
    - ■ Penis
      - □ Penis should appear straight.
      - □ Urethral meatus should be at the tip of the penis.
      - □ Foreskin may not be retractable in infants and small children.
      - □ Enlargement of the penis occurs during adolescence.

- Scrotum
    - The scrotum hangs separately from the penis.
    - The skin on the scrotum has a rugated appearance and is loose.
    - The left testicle hangs slighter lower than the right.
    - The inguinal canal should be absent of swelling.
    - During puberty, the testes and scrotum enlarge with darker scrotal skin.
- Female
    - Hair distribution over the mons pubis should be documented in terms of amount and location during puberty. Hair should appear in an inverted triangle. No pubic hair should be noted in infants or small children.
    - Labia – Symmetric, without lesions, moist on the inner aspects
    - Clitoris – Small, without bruising or edema
    - Urethral meatus – Slit-like in appearance with no discharge
    - Vaginal orifice – The hymen may be absent, or it may completely or partially cover the vaginal opening prior to sexual intercourse.
- Anus – Surrounding skin should be intact with sphincter tightening noted if the anus is touched. Routine rectal exams are not done with the pediatric population.

CHAPTER 2: PHYSICAL ASSESSMENT FINDINGS

(A) Application Exercises

1. A nurse is caring for a child who is more than 3 years of age. List five basic assessments that the nurse should include in the child's physical assessment.

2. By what age should the anterior fontanel be closed?

　　A. 2 weeks

　　B. 6 months

　　C. 10 months

　　D. 18 months

3. A nurse is caring for a 9-month-old infant. Rank the following assessments in the order in which the nurse should perform them.

　　_____　Axillary temperature

　　_____　Respiratory rate

　　_____　Weight

　　_____　Heart rate

4. Match each of the following reflexes with the correct response.

_____ Rooting reflex	A. When the infant's head is turned to the side, he extends his arm and leg on that side and flexes the arm and leg on the opposite side
_____ Palmar grasp	B. Arms and legs extend when the infant is startled by a loud noise.
_____ Plantar grasp	C. The head is turned to the side when the infant's cheek or mouth is touched.
_____ Moro reflex (startle)	D. The infant grasps an object when his palm is touched.
_____ Asymmetric tonic neck reflex	E. The infant's toes curl downward when the sole of his foot is touched.

5. A nurse is caring for a 14-year-old adolescent client. Match the cranial nerve with the expected finding.

_____	Olfactory	A. No vertigo is present.
_____	Optic	B. The tongue is midline.
_____	Oculomotor	C. No nystagmus is present.
_____	Trochlear	D. The adolescent has symmetric facial movements.
_____	Trigeminal	E. The adolescent has clear speech.
_____	Abducens	F. The adolescent is able to clench her teeth together.
_____	Facial	G. Visual acuity is intact.
_____	Acoustic	H. The gag reflex is intact.
_____	Glossopharyngeal	I. Both shoulders have equal strength.
_____	Vagus	J. The adolescent is able to look laterally with eyes.
_____	Spinal Accessory	K. The adolescent can individually identify smells through each nostril.
_____	Hypoglossal	L. The adolescent is able to look down with both eyes.

CHAPTER 2: PHYSICAL ASSESSMENT FINDINGS

 Application Exercises Answer Key

1. A nurse is caring for a child who is more than 3 years of age. List five basic assessments that the nurse should include in the child's physical assessment.

   Height, weight, temperature, respiratory rate, heart rate, and blood pressure

    NCLEX® Connection: Reduction of Risk Potential, System Specific Assessment

2. By what age should the anterior fontanel be closed?

   A. 2 weeks

   B. 6 months

   C. 10 months

   D. 18 months

   The posterior fontanel usually closes by 2 to 3 months, and the anterior fontanel usually closes by 18 months.

    NCLEX® Connection: Safety and Infection Control, Developmental Stages and Transitions

3. A nurse is caring for a 9-month-old infant. Rank the following assessments in the order in which the nurse should perform them.

   4   Axillary temperature

   1   Respiratory rate

   3   Weight

   2   Heart rate

   A physical examination should be performed on a child starting with the least invasive procedure and should progress towards the most invasive procedure. Assessing the respiratory rate is the least invasive, followed by the heart rate, which requires touching the child with a stethoscope, followed by the weight, which requires picking up the child and placing him on a scale, followed by obtaining an axillary temperature.

    NCLEX® Connection: Reduction of Risk Potential, System Specific Assessment

4. Match each of the following reflexes with the correct response.

__C__	Rooting reflex	A. When the infant's head is turned to the side, he extends his arm and leg on that side and flexes the arm and leg on the opposite side
__D__	Palmar grasp	B. Arms and legs extend when the infant is startled by a loud noise.
__E__	Plantar grasp	C. The head is turned to the side when the infant's cheek or mouth is touched.
__B__	Moro reflex (startle)	D. The infant grasps an object when his palm is touched.
__A__	Asymmetric tonic neck reflex	E. The infant's toes curl downward when the sole of his foot is touched.

(N) **NCLEX® Connection: Safety and Infection Control, Developmental Stages and Transitions**

5. A nurse is caring for a 14-year-old adolescent client. Match the cranial nerve with the expected finding.

__K__	Olfactory	A. No vertigo is present.
__G__	Optic	B. The tongue is midline.
__C__	Oculomotor	C. No nystagmus is present.
__L__	Trochlear	D. The adolescent has symmetric facial movements.
__F__	Trigeminal	E. The adolescent has clear speech.
__J__	Abducens	F. The adolescent is able to clench her teeth together.
__D__	Facial	G. Visual acuity is intact.
__A__	Acoustic	H. The gag reflex is intact.
__H__	Glossopharyngeal	I. Both shoulders have equal strength.
__E__	Vagus	J. The adolescent is able to look laterally with eyes.
__I__	Spinal Accessory	K. The adolescent can individually identify smells through each nostril.
__B__	Hypoglossal	L. The adolescent is able to look down with both eyes.

(N) **NCLEX® Connection: Safety and Infection Control, Developmental Stages and Transitions**

UNIT 1	FOUNDATIONS OF NURSING CARE OF CHILDREN
Section	Perspectives of Nursing Care of Children
Chapter 3	Health Promotion of the Infant (Birth to 1 Year)

Expected Growth and Development

- Physical Development

    - The infant's posterior fontanel closes by 2 to 3 months of age.

    - The infant's anterior fontanel closes by 12 to 18 months of age.

    - Weight, height, and head circumference measurements are used to track the size of infants.

        - Weight – Infants gain approximately 150 to 210 g (about 5 to 7 oz) per week the first 6 months of age. Infants triple their birth weights by the end of the first year of life.

        - Height – Infants grow approximately 2.5 cm (1 in) per month the first 6 months of age, and then approximately 1.25 cm (0.5 in) per month for the next 6 months.

        - Head circumference – The circumference of infants' heads increases approximately 1.5 cm (0.6 in) per month for the first 6 months of life, and then approximately 0.5 cm (0.2 in) between 6 and 12 months of age.

    - Dentition – Six to eight teeth should erupt in infants' mouths by the end of the first year of age.

        - Teething pain can be eased using cold teething rings, over-the-counter teething gels, or acetaminophen (Tylenol) and/or ibuprofen (Advil). Ibuprofen should be used only in infants over the age of 6 months.

        - Clean infants' teeth using cool, wet washcloths.

        - Bottles should not be given to infants when they are falling asleep. This will help to avoid prolonged exposure to milk or juice that can cause dental caries (bottle mouth syndrome).

AGE	GROSS MOTOR SKILLS	FINE MOTOR SKILLS
1 month	Demonstrates head lag	• Has a grasp reflex
2 months	Lifts head off mattress	• Holds hands in an open position
3 months	Raises head and shoulders off mattress	• No longer has a grasp reflex • Keeps hands loosely open
4 months	Rolls from back to side	• Places objects in mouth

AGE	GROSS MOTOR SKILLS	FINE MOTOR SKILLS
5 months	Rolls from front to back	• Uses palmar grasp dominantly
6 months	Rolls from back to front	• Holds bottle
7 months	Bears full weight on feet	• Moves objects from hand to hand
8 months	Sits unsupported	• Begins using pincer grasp
9 months	Pulls to a standing position	• Has a crude pincer grasp
10 months	Changes from a prone to a sitting position	• Grasps rattle by its handle
11 months	Walks while holding on to something	• Places objects into a container
12 months	Sits down from a standing position without assistance	• Tries to build a two-block tower without success

 View Media Supplement: Fine and Gross Motor Development (Video)

- Cognitive Development

  - Piaget – Sensorimotor stage (birth to 24 months)

    - There are three things that occur during this time: separation, object permanence, and mental representation.

      - Separation is when infants learn to separate themselves from other objects in the environment.

      - Object permanence is the process by which infants know that an object still exists when it is hidden from view. This occurs at approximately 9 months of age.

      - Mental representation is the recognition of symbols.

  - Language

    - Vocalizes with cooing noises

    - Responds to noises

    - Turns head to the sound of a rattle

    - Laughs and squeals

    - Pronounces single-syllable words

    - Begins speaking two-word phrases and progresses to speaking three-word phrases

- Psychosocial Development

  - The stage of psychosocial development for infants, according to Erikson, is trust versus mistrust.

  - The infants trust that their feeding, comfort, stimulation, and caring needs will be met.

- ○ Social development is initially influenced by infants' reflexive behaviors and includes attachment, separation, recognition/anxiety, and stranger fear.

    - Attachment is seen when infants begin to bond with their parents. This development is seen within the first month, but it actually begins before birth. The process is enhanced when infants and parents are in good health, have positive feeding experiences, and receive adequate rest.

    - Separation recognition occurs during the first year as infants learn physical boundaries from other people. Learning how to respond to people in their environments is the next phase of development. Positive interactions with parents, siblings, and other caregivers help to establish trust.

    - Separation anxiety develops between 4 and 8 months of age. Infants will protest loudly when separated from parents, which can cause considerable anxiety for parents.

    - Stranger fear becomes evident between 6 and 8 months of age, when infants are less likely to accept strangers.

  - ○ Self-Concept Development

    - By the end of the first year, infants will be able to distinguish themselves as being separate from their parents.

  - ○ Body-Image Changes

    - Infants will discover that their mouths are pleasure producers (Freud – oral stage).

    - Hands and feet are seen as objects of play.

    - Infants discover that smiling causes others to react.

- • Age-Appropriate Activities

  - ○ Infants will have short attention spans and will not interact with other children during play (solitary play). Appropriate toys and activities that stimulate the senses and encourage development include:

    - Rattles

    - Mobiles

    - Teething toys

    - Nesting toys

    - Playing pat-a-cake

    - Playing with balls

    - Reading books

Health Promotion

- Immunizations

  - 2010 Centers for Disease Control and Prevention (CDC) immunization recommendations for healthy infants less than 12 months of age (http://www.cdc.gov) include:

    - Birth – Hepatitis B (Hep B)

    - 2 months – Diphtheria and tetanus toxoids and pertussis (DTaP), rotavirus vaccine (RV), inactivated poliovirus (IPV), *Haemophilus influenzae* type B (Hib), pneumococcal vaccine (PCV), and Hep B

    - 4 months – DTaP, RV, IPV, Hib, PVC

    - 6 months – DTaP, IPV (6 to 18 months), PVC, and Hep B (6 to 12 months); RotaTeq, an alternative formulation for RV, requires 3 doses that must be completed by 32 weeks of age.

    - 6 to 12 months – Seasonal influenza vaccination yearly; the trivalent inactivated influenza vaccine (TIV) is available as an intramuscular injection.

- Nutrition

  - Feeding alternatives

    - Breastfeeding provides a complete diet for infants during the first 6 months of life and is recommended by health care providers.

    - Iron-fortified formula is an acceptable alternative to breast milk. Cows' milk is not recommended.

  - Solids can be introduced between 4 and 6 months of age.

    - Indicators for readiness include interest in solid foods, voluntary control of the head and trunk, and hunger less than 4 hr after vigorous nursing or intake of 8 oz of formula.

    - Iron-fortified rice cereal should be offered first.

    - New foods should be introduced one at a time, over a 5- to 7-day period to observe for signs of allergy or intolerance, which may include fussiness, rash, vomiting, diarrhea, and constipation. Vegetables or fruits are first started between 6 and 8 months of age. After both have been introduced, meats may be added.

    - Milk, eggs, wheat, citrus fruits, peanuts, peanut butter, and honey should be delayed until the first year of life.

    - Breast milk/formula should be decreased as intake of solid foods increases.

    - Table foods that are cooked, chopped, and unseasoned are appropriate by 9 months of age.

    - Appropriate finger foods include ripe bananas; toast strips; graham crackers; cheese cubes; noodles; and peeled chunks of apples, pears, or peaches.

    - Parents should be encouraged to use iron-enriched foods after infants are 6 months of age.

- ○ Weaning can be accomplished when infants are able to drink from cups with handles (sometime after 6 months).
  - ■ One feeding may be replaced with breast milk or formula in a cup with handles.
  - ■ Bedtime feedings are the last to be replaced.
- ● Injury Prevention
  - ○ Aspiration of foreign objects
    - ■ Small objects that can become lodged in the throat (grapes, coins, candy) should be avoided.
    - ■ Age-appropriate toys should be provided.
    - ■ Clothing should be checked for safety hazards (loose buttons)
  - ○ Bodily harm
    - ■ Sharp objects should be kept out of reach.
    - ■ Infants should be kept away from heavy objects that can be pulled down onto them.
    - ■ Infants should not be left unattended with any animals present.
    - ■ Infant should be monitored for shaken baby syndrome.
  - ○ Burns
    - ■ The temperature of bath water should be checked.
    - ■ Thermostats on hot water heaters should be turned down.
    - ■ Working smoke detectors should be kept in the home.
    - ■ Handles of pots and pans should be kept turned to the back of stoves.
    - ■ Sunscreen should be used when infants will be exposed to the sun.
    - ■ Electrical outlets should be covered.
  - ○ Drowning
    - ■ Infants should not be left unattended in bathtubs.
  - ○ Falls
    - ■ Crib mattresses should be kept in the lowest position possible with the rails all the way up.
    - ■ Restraints should be used in infant seats.
    - ■ Infant seats should be placed on the ground or floor if used outside of the car, and they should not be left unattended or on elevated surfaces.
    - ■ Safety gates should be used across stairs.
  - ○ Poisoning
    - ■ Exposure to lead paint should be avoided.
    - ■ Toxins and plants should be kept out of reach.

- Safety locks should be kept on cabinets with cleaners and other household chemicals.
- The phone number for a poison control center should be kept near the phone.
- Medications should be kept in childproof containers, away from the reach of infants.
- A working carbon monoxide detector should be kept in the home.

○ Motor-vehicle injuries

- Infants should be placed in approved rear-facing car seats in the back seat, preferably in the middle, (away from air bags and side impact). Infants should be in rear-facing car seats for the first year of life and until they weigh 9.1 kg (20 lb). It is recommended to have infants ride rear facing until they have reached the weight limit allowed for the car seat (as long as the top of the infant's head does not extend above the top of the seat back). In addition, a five-point harness or T-shield should be part of a convertible restraint.

○ Suffocation

- Plastic bags should be avoided.
- Balloons should be kept away from infants.
- Crib mattresses should fit snugly.
- Crib slats should be no farther apart than 6 cm (2.4 in).
- Crib mobiles or crib gyms should be removed by 4 to 5 months of age.
- Pillows should be kept out of the crib.
- Infants should be placed on their backs for sleep.
- Toys with small parts should be kept out of reach.
- Drawstrings should be removed from jackets and other clothing.

CHAPTER 3: HEALTH PROMOTION OF THE INFANT (BIRTH TO 1 YEAR)

 Application Exercises

1. The mother of an infant asks the nurse when she can expect her infant to begin walking. What gross motor skills should the infant develop before he begins walking?

2. The mother of an infant tells the nurse that her infant makes many sounds. What should the nurse tell the mother about the language development of the infant?

3. A nurse is caring for a 4-month-old infant? Which of the following immunizations should the infant be given? (Select all that apply.)

_____ Measles, mumps, rubella (MMR)

_____ *Haemophilus influenzae* type B (Hib)

_____ Polio (IPV)

_____ Diphtheria and tetanus toxoids and pertussis (DTaP)

_____ Pneumonococcal vaccine (PCV)

_____ Varicella

_____ Rotavirus vaccine (RV)

4. A nurse is caring for an infant who will soon eat solid foods. The nurse should inform the parents that which of the following foods should be introduced into an infant's diet first?

A. Strained yellow vegetables

B. Iron-fortified cereals

C. Puréed fruits

D. Whole milk

CHAPTER 3: HEALTH PROMOTION OF THE INFANT (BIRTH TO 1 YEAR)

 Application Exercises Answer Key

1. The mother of an infant asks the nurse when she can expect her infant to begin walking. What gross motor skills should the infant develop before he begins walking?

Getting up to a sitting position and sitting alone

Pulling up to a standing position

Standing holding on and/or standing alone

Development is cephalocaudal; therefore, before the infant can walk, he must develop the skills of sitting and standing.

 NCLEX® Connection: Safety and Infection Control, Developmental Stages and Transitions

2. The mother of an infant tells the nurse that her infant makes many sounds. What should the nurse tell the mother about the language development of the infant?

The infant will first respond to noises and turn her head toward the sound. As she grows she will vocalize cooing sounds, such as "ooos" and "aahs," laugh and squeal, pronounce single-syllable words, and then begin to speak two and then three-word phrases.

 NCLEX® Connection: Safety and Infection Control, Developmental Stages and Transitions

3. A nurse is caring for a 4-month-old infant? Which of the following immunizations should the infant be given? (Select all that apply.)

_____	Measles, mumps, rubella (MMR)
__X__	**_Haemophilus influenzae_ type B (Hib)**
__X__	**Polio (IPV)**
__X__	**Diphtheria and tetanus toxoids and pertussis (DTaP)**
__X__	**Pneumonococcal vaccine (PCV)**
_____	Varicella
__X__	**Rotavirus vaccine (RV)**

Hib, IPIV, DTaP, PVC, and RV are all given at 4 months of age. MMR and varicella are not recommended by the CDC until the child is at least 12 months old.

 NCLEX® Connection: Health Promotion and Maintenance, Health Promotion/Disease Prevention

4. A nurse is caring for an infant who will soon eat solid foods. The nurse should inform the parents that which of the following foods should be introduced into an infant's diet first?

    A. Strained yellow vegetables

    B. Iron-fortified cereals

    C. Puréed fruits

    D. Whole milk

Cereal is the first solid food introduced to an infant. Maternal iron stores in the infant begin to diminish around 4 months; therefore, iron-fortified cereal should be used. Puréed yellow vegetables are introduced, followed by puréed fruits. Whole milk should not be given until after the first year of life.

NCLEX® Connection: Basic Care and Comfort, Nutrition and Oral Hydration

UNIT 1	FOUNDATIONS OF NURSING CARE OF CHILDREN
Section	Perspectives of Nursing Care of Children
Chapter 4	Health Promotion of the Toddler (1 to 3 years)

Expected Growth and Development

- Physical Development

  - Anterior fontanels close by 18 months of age.

  - Weight – At 30 months of age, toddlers should weigh four times their birth weights.

  - Height – Toddlers grow about 7.5 cm (3 in) per year.

AGE	GROSS MOTOR SKILLS	FINE MOTOR SKILLS
15 months	• Walks without help • Creeps up stairs	• Uses a cup well • Builds a tower of two blocks
18 months	• Assumes a standing position	• Manages a spoon without rotation • Turns pages in a book, two or three at a time
2 years	• Walks up and down stairs	• Builds a tower of six or seven blocks
2.5 years	• Jumps in place with both feet • Stands on one foot momentarily	• Draws circles • Has good hand-finger coordination

- Cognitive Development

  - Piaget – The sensorimotor stage transitions to the preoperational stage.

    - The concept of object permanence is fully developed.

    - Toddlers have and demonstrate memories of events that relate to them.

    - Domestic mimicry (playing house) is evident.

    - Preoperational thought does not allow for toddlers to understand other viewpoints, but it does allow them to symbolize objects and people to imitate previously seen activities.

  - Language

    - Language increases to about 400 words with toddlers speaking in two- to three-word phrases.

- Psychosocial Development

    o The stage of psychosocial development for toddlers, according to Erikson, is autonomy versus shame and doubt.

        ▪ Independence is paramount for toddlers, who are attempting to do everything for themselves.

        ▪ Separation anxiety continues to occur when parents leave toddlers.

    o Moral Development

        ▪ Moral development is closely associated with cognitive development.

        ▪ Egocentric – Toddlers are unable to see things from the perspectives of others; they can only view things from their personal points of view.

        ▪ Punishment and obedience orientation begin with a sense that good behavior is rewarded and bad behavior is punished.

    o Self-Concept Development

        ▪ Toddlers progressively see themselves as separate from their parents and increase their explorations away from them.

    o Body-Image Changes

        ▪ Toddlers appreciate the usefulness of various body parts.

        ▪ Toddlers will develop gender identity by 3 years of age.

- Age-Appropriate Activities

    o Solitary play evolves into parallel play, in which toddlers observe other children and then may engage in activities nearby.

    o Appropriate activities

        ▪ Filling and emptying containers

        ▪ Playing with blocks

        ▪ Looking at books

        ▪ Playing with toys that can be pushed and pulled

        ▪ Tossing balls

    o Temper tantrums result when toddlers are frustrated with restrictions on independence. Providing consistent, age-appropriate expectations helps toddlers to work through frustration.

    o Toilet training can begin when it is recognized that toddlers have the sensation of needing to urinate or defecate. Parents should demonstrate patience and consistency in toilet training. Nighttime control may develop last of all.

    o Discipline should be consistent with well-defined boundaries that are established to develop appropriate social behavior.

Health Promotion

- Immunizations

    o 2010 Centers for Disease Control and Prevention (CDC) immunization recommendations for healthy toddlers 12 months to 3 years of age (http://www.cdc.gov) include:

        ▪ 12 to 15 months – Inactivated poliovirus (IPV) (6 to 18 months); *Haemophilus influenzae* type B (Hib); pneumococcal vaccine (PCV); measles, mumps, and rubella (MMR); and varicella

        ▪ 12 to 23 months – Hepatitis A (Hep A), given in two doses at least 6 months apart

        ▪ 15 to 18 months – Diphtheria and tetanus toxoids and pertussis (DTaP)

        ▪ 12 to 36 months – Yearly seasonal trivalent inactivated influenza vaccine (TIV); the live, attenuated influenza vaccine (LAIV) by nasal spray (at 2 years of age)

- Nutrition

    o Toddlers are generally picky eaters who will repeatedly request their favorite foods.

    o Toddlers should consume 24 to 30 oz of milk per day, and they may switch from drinking whole milk to drinking low-fat milk (2% fat) at 2 years of age.

    o Juice consumption should be limited to 4 to 6 oz per day.

    o Food serving size should be 1 tbsp for each year of age.

    o Exposure to a new food may need to occur 8 to 15 times before toddlers develop an acceptance of it.

    o If there is a family history of allergy, then cows' milk, chocolate, citrus fruits, egg whites, seafood, and nut butters may be gradually introduced while monitoring for reactions.

    o Toddlers generally prefer finger foods because of increasing autonomy.

    o Regular meal times and nutritious snacks best meet nutrient needs.

    o Snacks or desserts that are high in sugar, fat, or sodium should be avoided.

    o Foods that are potential choking hazards (nuts, grapes, hot dogs, peanut butter, raw carrots, tough meats, popcorn) should be avoided.

    o Adult supervision should always be provided during snack and mealtimes.

    o Foods should be cut into small, bite-size pieces to make them easier to swallow and to prevent choking.

    o Toddlers should not be allowed to engage in drinking or eating during play activities or while lying down.

    o Parents should follow dietary recommendations outlined by the United States Department of Agriculture (http://www.mypyramid.gov).

- Injury Prevention
  - Aspiration of foreign objects
    - Small objects (grapes, coins, candy) that can become lodged in the throat should be avoided.
    - Toys that have small parts should be kept out of reach.
    - Age-appropriate toys should be provided.
    - Clothing should be checked for safety hazards (loose buttons).
    - Balloons should be kept away from toddlers.
  - Bodily harm
    - Sharp objects should be kept out of reach.
    - Firearms should be kept in locked boxes or cabinets.
    - Toddlers should not be left unattended with any animals present.
    - Toddlers should be taught stranger safety.
  - Burns
    - The temperature of bath water should be checked.
    - Thermostats on hot water heaters should be turned down.
    - Working smoke detectors should be kept in the home.
    - Pot handles should be turned toward the back of the stove.
    - Electrical outlets should be covered.
    - Toddler should wear sunscreen when outside.
  - Drowning
    - Toddlers should not be left unattended in bathtubs.
    - Toilet lids should be kept closed.
    - Toddlers should be closely supervised when near pools or any other body of water.
    - Toddlers should be taught to swim.
  - Falls
    - Doors and windows should be kept locked.
    - Crib mattresses should be kept in the lowest position with the rails all the way up.
    - Safety gates should be used across stairs.

- ○ Motor-vehicles injuries
  - ■ Approved car seats should be used in the back seats of cars (away from air bags).
  - ■ Toddlers should be in approved rear-facing car seats in the back seat until they weigh 9.1 kg (20 lb). Toddlers may then sit in approved forward-facing car seats in the back seat. Toddlers may usually remain in car seats until 4 years of age and/or 40 lb.
- ○ Poisoning
  - ■ Exposure to lead paint should be avoided.
  - ■ Safety locks should be placed on cabinets that contain cleaners and other chemicals.
  - ■ The phone number for a poison control center should be kept near the phone.
  - ■ Medications should be kept in childproof containers, away from the reach of toddlers.
  - ■ A working carbon monoxide detector should be placed in the home.
- ○ Suffocation
  - ■ Plastic bags should be avoided.
  - ■ Crib mattresses should fit tightly.
  - ■ Crib slats should be no farther apart than 6 cm (2.4 in).
  - ■ Pillows should be kept out of cribs.
  - ■ Drawstrings should be removed from jackets and other clothing.

CHAPTER 4: HEALTH PROMOTION OF THE TODDLER (1 TO 3 YEARS)

 Application Exercises

1. A nurse is caring for several children. List the immunizations the nurse should give for children in each of the age groups listed below.

> 12 to 15 months
>
> 12 to 23 months
>
> 15 to 18 months
>
> 12 to 36 months

2. A parent of a 20-month-old toddler is concerned about how often the toddler gets hurt. The nurse should inform the parent that toddlers are prone to accidents for what reasons?

3. The father of a 17-month-old toddler is frustrated with the toddler's behavior. The father tells the nurse that the toddler is "bad," but he doesn't know how to make the toddler behave better. Which of the following responses is appropriate?

> A. "Allow your child to learn by trial and error."
>
> B. "Consistently enforce well-defined limits."
>
> C. "Reward your child's good behavior, but ignore the bad behaviors."
>
> D. "Punish your child when he behaves badly."

4. A 13-month-old toddler is being discharged from the hospital. Which of the following potential health risks should the nurse address with the parents? (Select all that apply.)

> _____ Elevated cholesterol levels
>
> _____ Poisoning
>
> _____ Peer pressure
>
> _____ Burns
>
> _____ Falls

5. The parents of a 14-month-old toddler want to know why their daughter has not been responsive to toilet training. The toddler is standing by herself but still crawls for locomotion. Her vocabulary is developing, but she does not seem to understand what it means to "go potty." The nurse should inform the parents that the toddler needs to develop what skills before she is able to achieve toilet training?

CHAPTER 4: HEALTH PROMOTION OF THE TODDLER (1 TO 3 YEARS)

 Application Exercises Answer Key

1. A nurse is caring for several children. List the immunizations the nurse should give for children in each of the age groups listed below.

    12 to 15 months – **IPV (6 to 18 months), Hib, PCV, MMR, and varicella**

    12 to 23 months – **Hep A, given in two doses at least 6 months apart**

    15 to 18 months – **DTaP**

    12 to 36 months – **Yearly seasonal TIV**

 NCLEX® Connection: Health Promotion and Maintenance, Health Promotion/Disease Prevention

2. A parent of a 20-month-old toddler is concerned about how often the toddler gets hurt. The nurse should inform the parent that toddlers are prone to accidents for what reasons?

Toddlers are still developing their fine and gross motor skills, while at the same time trying to exert their independence through movement. Developmental tasks include developing autonomy, wanting to try things alone, wanting to explore more of the world away from parents, walking well, and beginning to run and climb.

 NCLEX® Connection: Health Promotion and Maintenance, Developmental Stages and Transitions

3. The father of a 17-month-old toddler is frustrated with the toddler's behavior. The father tells the nurse that the toddler is "bad," but he doesn't know how to make the toddler behave better. Which of the following responses is appropriate?

    A. "Allow your child to learn by trial and error."

    B. "Consistently enforce well-defined limits."

    C. "Reward your child's good behavior, but ignore the bad behaviors."

    D. "Punish your child when he behaves badly."

Toddlers need to have consistent boundaries enforced for discipline to be effective. Behavior should not be enforced with only rewards or only punishments. Trial and error lacks consistent boundaries and may allow the toddler to experience unhealthy consequences.

 NCLEX® Connection: Health Promotion and Maintenance, Developmental Stages and Transitions

4. A 13-month-old toddler is being discharged from the hospital. Which of the following potential health risks should the nurse address with the parents? (Select all that apply.)

_____ Elevated cholesterol levels

__X__ **Poisoning**

_____ Peer pressure

__X__ **Burns**

__X__ **Falls**

Poisoning, burns, and falls are all potential risks for this age group because the child is gaining independence and becoming more curious. Elevated cholesterol levels may become an issue during adolescence. Peer pressure usually begins during the school-age years, becoming more of a risk during adolescence.

 NCLEX® Connection: Health Promotion and Maintenance, Aging Process

5. The parents of a 14-month-old toddler want to know why their daughter has not been responsive to toilet training. The toddler is standing by herself but still crawls for locomotion. Her vocabulary is developing, but she does not seem to understand what it means to "go potty." The nurse should inform the parents that the toddler needs to develop what skills before she is able to achieve toilet training?

Voluntary control of anal and urethral sphincters

Gross motor skills of sitting, walking, and squatting

Fine motor skills for removing clothing

Communication skills to indicate toileting need

Cognitive skills to follow directions

The ability to recognize the urge for toileting

 NCLEX® Connection: Health Promotion and Maintenance, Developmental Stages and Transitions

UNIT 1	FOUNDATIONS OF NURSING CARE OF CHILDREN
Section	Perspectives of Nursing Care of Children
Chapter 5	Health Promotion of the Preschooler (3 to 6 years)

Expected Growth and Development

- Physical Development

    o   Weight – Preschoolers should gain about 2 to 3 kg (4.5 to 6.5 lb) per year.

    o   Height – Preschoolers should grow about 6.2 to 7.5 cm (2.5 to 3 inches) per year.

    o   Preschoolers' bodies evolve away from the characteristically unsteady wide stances and protruding abdomens of toddlers, into a more graceful, posturally erect, and sturdy physicality.

    o   Fine and gross motor skills

    ■   Preschoolers should show improvement in fine motor skills, which will be displayed by activities like copying figures on paper and dressing independently.

AGE	GROSS MOTOR SKILLS
3 years	• Rides a tricycle • Jumps off bottom step • Stands on one foot for a few seconds
4 years	• Skips and hops on one foot • Throws a ball overhead
5 years	• Jumps rope • Walks backward with heel to toe • Moves up and down stairs easily

- Cognitive Development

    o   Piaget – Preschoolers are still in the preoperational phase of cognitive development. They participate in preconceptual thought (from 2 to 4 years of age) and intuitive thought (from 4 to 7 years of age).

- Preconceptual thought – Preschoolers make judgments based on visual appearances. Misconceptions in thinking during this stage include:
  - Artificialism – Everything is made by humans.
  - Animism – Inanimate objects are alive.
  - Imminent justice – A universal code exists that determines law and order.
- Intuitive thought – Preschoolers can classify information, and they become aware of cause-and-effect relationships.

  ○ Time – Preschoolers begin to understand the concepts of the past, present, and future. By the end of the preschool years, children may comprehend days of the week.

  ○ Language – The vocabulary of preschoolers continues to increase. Preschoolers can speak in sentences and identify colors, and they enjoy talking.

- Psychosocial Development

  ○ The stage of psychosocial development for preschoolers, according to Erikson, is initiative versus guilt.

  - Preschoolers may take on many new experiences, despite not having all of the physical abilities necessary to be successful at everything. Guilt may occur when preschoolers are unable to accomplish a task and believe they have misbehaved. Guiding preschoolers to attempt activities within their capabilities while setting limits is appropriate.

  ○ Moral Development

  - Preschoolers continue in the good-bad orientation of the toddler years, but they begin to understand behaviors in terms of what is socially acceptable.

  ○ Self-Concept Development

  - Preschooler feels good about themselves with regard to mastering skills that allow independence (dressing, feeding). During stress, insecurity, or illness, preschoolers may regress to previous immature behaviors or develop habits (nose picking, bedwetting, thumb sucking).

  ○ Body-Image Changes

  - Mistaken perceptions of reality coupled with misconceptions in thinking lead to active fantasies and fears. The greatest fear is that of bodily harm, resulting in fear of the dark or animals.

  - Sex-role identification is occurring.

  ○ Social Development

  - Preschoolers generally do not exhibit stranger anxiety and have less separation anxiety. However, prolonged separation, such as during hospitalization, can provoke anxiety. Favorite toys and appropriate play should be used to help ease preschoolers' fears.

  - Pretend play is healthy and allows preschoolers to determine the difference between reality and fantasy.

- o Sleep disturbances frequently occur during early childhood, and problems range from difficulties going to bed to night tremors. Advise parents to:

    - Assess whether or not the bedtime is too early if preschoolers are still taking naps. On average, preschoolers need about 12 hr of sleep per day. Some still require a daytime nap.

    - Keep a consistent bedtime routine.

    - Use a night-light.

    - Reassure preschoolers who have been frightened, but avoid allowing preschoolers to sleep with their parents.

- Age-Appropriate Activities

    - o Parallel play shifts to associative play during the preschool years. Play is not highly organized, but cooperation does exist between children. Appropriate activities include:

        - Playing ball

        - Putting puzzles together

        - Riding tricycles

        - Playing pretend and dress-up activities

        - Role playing

        - Painting

        - Sewing cards and beads

        - Reading books

Health Promotion

- Immunizations

    - o The 2010 Centers for Disease Control (CDC) immunization recommendations for healthy preschoolers 3 to 6 years of age (http://www.cdc.gov) include:

        - 4 to 6 years – Diphtheria and tetanus toxoids and pertussis (DTaP); measles, mumps, and rubella (MMR); varicella; and inactivated poliovirus (IPV)

        - 36 to 59 months – Yearly seasonal influenza vaccine; trivalent inactivated influenza vaccine (TIV); or live, attenuated influenza vaccine (LAIV) by nasal spray

- Health Screenings

    - o Vision screening is routinely done in the preschool population as part of the prekindergarten physical exam. Visual impairments such as myopia and amblyopia can be detected and treated before poor visual acuity impairs learning.

- Nutrition

    - o Preschoolers consume about half the amount of energy that adults do (1,800 kcal).

    - o Picky eating may remain a behavior in preschoolers, but often by 5 years of age they become more willing to sample different foods.

- Preschoolers need 13 to 19 g/day of complete protein in addition to adequate calcium, iron, folate, and vitamins A and C.
- Parents need to ensure that preschoolers are receiving a balance of nutrients.
  - Healthy food recommendations are posted by the United States Department of Agriculture (http://www.mypyramid.gov).
- Injury Prevention
  - Bodily harm
    - Firearms should be kept in locked cabinets or containers.
    - Preschoolers should be taught stranger safety.
    - Preschoolers should be taught to wear protective equipment (helmet, pads).
  - Burns
    - Thermostats should be turned down on hot water heaters.
    - Working smoke detectors should be kept in the home.
    - Preschoolers should have sunscreen applied when outside.
  - Drowning
    - Preschoolers should not be left unattended in bathtubs.
    - Preschoolers should be closely supervised when near the pool or any other body of water.
    - Preschoolers should be taught to swim.
  - Motor-vehicle injuries
    - Preschoolers should sit in approved forward-facing car seats in the back seat away from airbags. Usually preschoolers may remain in car seats until 4 years of age and/or 40 lb. When preschoolers have outgrown car seats, booster seats in the back seat should be used. Children should be restrained in car seats or booster chairs until adult seat belts fit correctly. Laws may vary from state to state and requirements may be up to a weight of 80 lb and a height of 4 feet 9 inches, which is when adult seat belts will most likely fit correctly.
  - Poisoning
    - Exposure to lead paint should be avoided.
    - Plants should be kept out of reach.
    - Safety locks should be placed on cabinets with cleaners and other chemicals.
    - The phone number for a poison control center should be kept near the phone.
    - Medications should be kept in childproof containers, out of reach of preschoolers.
    - A working carbon monoxide detector should be placed in the home.

CHAPTER 5: HEALTH PROMOTION OF THE PRESCHOOLER (3 TO 6 YEARS)

(A) Application Exercises

1. A nurse is providing nutritional teaching to a group of parents whose children attend a local day care. Which of the following is an effective way to encourage good nutritional habits for a preschooler?

    A. Offer snacks if the child does not like what is served.

    B. Serve nutritious foods that all family members will eat.

    C. Allow the child to eat only what she asks for.

    D. Insist that the child eat all of the food that is served to her.

2. A parent tells a nurse at a well-child visit that his 4-year-old son is always talking about someone named George. The parent tells the nurse that the family does not even know anyone named George. The child tells his parents about George's escapades, such as climbing onto the counter to raid the cookie jar. What explanation should the nurse give to the parent about his son's behavior?

3. The parents of a preschooler are worried because their child has so much trouble going to sleep at night. Which of the following are strategies the nurse should recommend to help the preschooler go to sleep? (Select all that apply.)

    _____ Let the child fall asleep in another room.

    _____ Place a night-light in the child's room.

    _____ Keep a regular bedtime schedule.

    _____ Insist the child take a nap to make up for lost nighttime sleep.

    _____ Read a bedtime story to the child.

    _____ Allow the child to play quietly in her room.

4. A nurse is caring for a preschooler who has previously been kept up to date on immunizations. What immunizations should the preschooler receive?

5. A nurse is performing a vision screening for a preschooler. The nurse knows that vision screening is done on the preschool child to detect and possibly treat _____ and _____.

CHAPTER 5: HEALTH PROMOTION OF THE PRESCHOOLER (3 TO 6 YEARS)

 Application Exercises Answer Key

1. A nurse is providing nutritional teaching to a group of parents whose children attend a local day care. Which of the following is an effective way to encourage good nutritional habits for a preschooler?

 A. Offer snacks if the child does not like what is served.

 B. Serve nutritious foods that all family members will eat.

 C. Allow the child to eat only what she asks for.

 D. Insist that the child eat all of the food that is served to her.

 Preschoolers learn by example. Seeing family members eat healthy foods will encourage them to do the same. Offering snacks as alternatives and allowing the child to eat only what she asks for will not promote good nutritional habits. Insisting that the child eat all of the food served even if she is no longer hungry can lead to feelings of guilt and overeating.

 NCLEX® Connection: Basic Care and Comfort, Nutrition and Oral Hydration

2. A parent tells a nurse at a well-child visit that his 4-year-old son is always talking about someone named George. The parent tells the nurse that the family does not even know anyone named George. The child tells his parents about George's escapades, such as climbing onto the counter to raid the cookie jar. What explanation should the nurse give to the parent about his son's behavior?

 George is most likely an imaginary friend or playmate. Imaginary playmates help children in many ways. When the child is lonely, an imaginary playmate can be a companion. An imaginary friend also experiments with things that the child is afraid of trying.

 NCLEX® Connection: Health Promotion and Maintenance, Aging Process

3. The parents of a preschooler are worried because their child has so much trouble going to sleep at night. Which of the following are strategies the nurse should recommend to help the preschooler go to sleep? (Select all that apply.)

 _____ Let the child fall asleep in another room.

 __X__ Place a night-light in the child's room.

 __X__ Keep a regular bedtime schedule.

 _____ Insist the child take a nap to make up for lost nighttime sleep.

 __X__ Read a bedtime story to the child.

 __X__ Allow the child to play quietly in her room.

 Various strategies can be used to help a preschool child go to sleep. Placing a night-light in her room will provide some light for reassurance. Reading a bedtime story and/or allowing the child to play quietly before sleep can help to calm the child down. Keeping a regular bedtime schedule is also important for regulating sleep-wake cycles. It is best if the child learns to fall asleep in her own room. If the child still needs an afternoon nap, it might be necessary to make the bedtime later.

 NCLEX® Connection: Health Promotion and Maintenance, Developmental Stages and Transitions

4. A nurse is caring for a preschooler who has previously been kept up to date on immunizations. What immunizations should the preschooler receive?

Diphtheria and tetanus toxoids and pertussis (DTaP)

Inactivated poliovirus (IPV)

Measles, mumps, and rubella (MMR)

Varicella

Yearly seasonal trivalent inactivated influenza vaccine (TIV) for preschoolers 36 to 59 months of age

 NCLEX® Connection: Health Promotion and Maintenance, Health Promotion/Disease Prevention

5. A nurse is performing a vision screening for a preschooler. The nurse knows that vision screening is done on the preschool child to detect and possibly treat _____ and _____.

Myopia and amblyopia are two visual impairments that may be detected during screening of the preschool child.

 NCLEX® Connection: Health Promotion and Maintenance, Health Screening

UNIT 1	FOUNDATIONS OF NURSING CARE OF CHILDREN
Section	Perspectives of Nursing Care of Children
Chapter 6	Health Promotion of the School-Age Child (6 to 12 Years)

Expected Growth and Development

- Physical Development
  - Weight – School-age children will gain about 2 to 4 kg (4.4 to 8.8 lb) per year.
    - Weight gain typically occurs between 9 and 12 years of age (girls from 9 to 12 and boys from 10 to 12 years of age).
  - Height – School-age children will grow about 5 cm (2 inches) per year.
    - Changes in height usually occur after 10 to 12 years of age for girls and 12 to 14 years of age for boys (after the period of weight gain).
  - Changes related to puberty begin to appear in females.
    - Budding of breasts
    - Appearance of pubic hair
    - Onset of menarche
  - Changes related to puberty begin to appear in males.
    - Enlargement of testicles with changes in the scrotum (increased looseness)
    - Appearance of pubic hair
  - Permanent teeth erupt.
  - Visual acuity improves to 20/20.
  - Auditory acuity and sense of touch is fully developed.
  - Fine and gross motor development
    - During the school-age years, coordination continues to improve.
- Cognitive Development
  - Piaget – Concrete operations
    - Sees weight and volume as unchanging
    - Understands simple analogies
    - Understands time (days, seasons)
    - Classifies more complex information

- Understands various emotions
- Becomes self-motivated
- Is able to solve problems

  o Language

  - Defines many words and understands rules of grammar
  - Understands that a word may have multiple meanings

- Psychosocial Development

  o The stage of psychosocial development for school-age children, according to Erikson, is industry versus inferiority.

  - A sense of industry is achieved through advancements in learning.
  - School-age children are motivated by tasks that increase self-worth.
  - Fears of ridicule by peers and teachers over school-related issues are common. Some children manifest nervous behaviors (nail biting) to deal with the stress.

  o Moral Development

  - Early on, school-age children may not understand the reasoning behind many rules and may try to find ways around them. Instrumental exchange ("I'll help you if you help me") is in place. Children want to make the best deal, and they do not really consider elements of loyalty, gratitude, or justice as they make decisions.
  - In the latter part of the school-age years, children move into a law-and-order orientation with more emphasis placed on justice being administered.

  o Self-Concept Development

  - School-age children strive to develop a healthy self-respect by finding out in what areas they excel.
  - School-age children need parents to encourage them regarding educational or extracurricular successes.

  o Body-Image Changes

  - This is the age at which solidification of body image occurs.
  - Curiosity about sexuality should be addressed with education regarding sexual development and the reproductive process.
  - School-age children are more modest than preschoolers and place more emphasis on privacy issues.

  o Social Development

  - Peer groups play an important part in social development. Peer pressure begins to take effect.
  - Friendships begin to form between same-gender peers. This is the time period when clubs and best friends are popular.

- Children prefer the company of same-gender companions.
- Most relationships come from school associations.
- Children may rival same-gender parents.
- Conformity becomes evident.

- Age-Appropriate Activities
  - Competitive and cooperative play is predominant.
  - Children from 6 to 9 years of age
    - Play simple board and number games.
    - Play hopscotch.
    - Jump rope.
    - Collect rocks, stamps, cards, coins, or stuffed animals.
    - Ride bicycles.
    - Build simple models.
    - Join organized sports (for skill building).
  - Children from 9 to 12 years of age
    - Make crafts.
    - Build models.
    - Collect things/engage in hobbies.
    - Solve jigsaw puzzles.
    - Play board and card games.
    - Join organized competitive sports.

Health Promotion

- Immunizations
  - 2010 Centers for Disease Control and Prevention (CDC) immunization recommendations for healthy school-age children 6 to 12 years of age (http://www.cdc.gov) include:
    - If not given between 4 and 5 years of age, children should receive the following vaccines by 6 years of age – Diphtheria and tetanus toxoids and pertussis (DTaP); inactivated poliovirus (IPV); measles, mumps, and rubella (MMR); and varicella
    - Yearly seasonal influenza vaccine – Trivalent inactivated influenza vaccine (TIV) or live, attenuated influenza vaccine (LAIV) by nasal spray
    - 11 to 12 years – Tetanus and diphtheria toxoids and pertussis vaccine (Tdap), human papillomavirus vaccine (HPV2) in three doses (for females), and HPV4 (for males)

- Health Screenings

  o Scoliosis – School-age children should be screened for scoliosis by examining for a lateral curvature of the spine before and during growth spurts. Screening may take place at schools or at a health care facilities.

 View Media Supplement: Scoliosis Screening (Video)

- Nutrition

  o By the end of the school-age years, children should be eating adult proportions of food. They need quality nutritious snacks.

  o Obesity is an increasing concern of this age group that predisposes children to low self-esteem, diabetes, heart disease, and high blood pressure. Advise parents to:

    - Avoid using food as a reward.

    - Emphasize physical activity.

    - Ensure that a balanced diet is consumed. Recommendations posted by the United States Department of Agriculture may be found on the Web (http://www.mypyramid.gov).

    - Teach children to make healthy food selections for meals and snacks.

    - Avoid eating fast-food frequently.

    - Avoid skipping meals.

  o Dental health

    - Brush daily.

    - Floss daily.

    - Have regular checkups.

    - Have regular fluoride treatments.

- Injury Prevention

  o Bodily harm

    - Firearms should be kept in locked cabinets or boxes.

    - Children should not be allowed to use trampolines.

    - Safe play areas should be identified.

    - Stranger safety should be taught.

    - Children should be taught to wear helmets and/or pads when rollerblading, skateboarding, bicycling, riding scooters, skiing, and snowboarding.

- o Burns
    - Children should be taught fire safety and potential burn hazards.
    - Working smoke detectors should be kept in the home.
    - Children should use sunscreen when outside.
- o Drowning
    - Children should be supervised when swimming or when near a body of water.
    - Children should be taught to swim.
- o Motor-vehicle injuries
    - Children should be restrained in car seats or booster chairs until adult seat belts fit correctly. Laws may vary from state to state and requirements may be up to a weight of 36.3 kg (80 lb) and a height of 4 feet 9 inches, which is when adult seat belts will most likely fit correctly. Properly fitting adult seat belts should have the lap belt laying across the upper thighs and the shoulder belt fitting across the chest.
    - Children less than 13 years of age are safest in the back seat.
- o Poisoning/Substance abuse
    - Cleaners or chemicals should be kept in locked cabinets or out of reach of younger children.
    - Children should be taught to say "no" to illegal drugs and alcohol.

CHAPTER 6: HEALTH PROMOTION OF THE SCHOOL-AGE CHILD (6 TO 12 YEARS)

 Application Exercises

1. A nurse is teaching a class about pubertal changes in girls. One of the children asks a question about when development appears. Number the following changes in the order they occur.

　　_____　Menarche

　　_____　Breast buds

　　_____　Appearance of pubic hair

2. The mother of a 9-year-old child reports that her son develops stomach cramping every Sunday night before school. How can the nurse assist this parent and child?

3. A nurse is caring for a child who has just turned 11 years of age. What immunizations should the child receive before she turns 12?

4. A nurse is teaching a course about safety during the school-age years. Which of the following information should the nurse include in the course? (Select all that apply.)

　　_____　Keeping stair gates closed

　　_____　Wearing helmets when riding bicycles or skateboarding

　　_____　Playing safely on trampolines

　　_____　Implementing firearm safety

　　_____　Wearing seat belts

5. A nurse is teaching the parents of a school-age child about maintaining a healthy diet. Identify three strategies that the nurse may include in the teaching about decreasing the risk for obesity.

CHAPTER 6: HEALTH PROMOTION OF THE SCHOOL-AGE CHILD (6 TO 12 YEARS)

 Application Exercises Answer Key

1. A nurse is teaching a class about pubertal changes in girls. One of the children asks a question about when development appears. Number the following changes in the order they occur.

   __3__ Menarche

   __1__ Breast buds

   __2__ Appearance of pubic hair

 NCLEX® Connection: Reduction of Risk Potential, System Specific Assessment

2. The mother of a 9-year-old child reports that her son develops stomach cramping every Sunday night before school. How can the nurse assist this parent and child?

   The nurse can explore with the child's mother possible reasons for this behavior. The child may be experiencing difficulties with academics, peers, and/or teachers. The nurse can give the mother guidance as to how to talk with her child. Follow-up may be necessary to determine the need for referrals for additional help for the child.

 NCLEX® Connection: Health Promotion and Maintenance, Developmental Stages and Transitions

3. A nurse is caring for a child who has just turned 11 years of age. What immunizations should the child receive before she turns 12?

   Tetanus and diphtheria toxoids and pertussis vaccine (Tdap)

   Human papillomavirus vaccine (HPV) in 3 doses

   Meningococcal vaccine (MCV4)

   Yearly influenza vaccine – Trivalent inactivated influenza vaccine (TIV) or live, attenuated influenza vaccine (LAIV) by nasal spray

 NCLEX® Connection: Health Promotion and Maintenance, Health and Wellness

4. A nurse is teaching a course about safety during the school-age years. Which of the following information should the nurse include in the course? (Select all that apply.)

	Keeping stair gates closed
X	**Wearing helmets when riding bicycles or skateboarding**
	Playing safely on trampolines
X	**Implementing firearm safety**
X	**Wearing seat belts**

School-age children are active and need to take precautions, such as wearing seat belts when in the car and wearing helmets and pads when skateboarding or bicycling. School-age children are also able to understand rules for firearm safety. There is no safe play on trampolines. School-age children are coordinated enough to climb and descend stairs.

 NCLEX® Connection: Safety and Infection Control, Accident/Injury Prevention

5. A nurse is teaching the parents of a school-age child about maintaining a healthy diet. Identify three strategies that the nurse may include in the teaching about decreasing the risk for obesity.

Avoid or reduce fast-food meals.

Encourage physical activities.

Do not use food as a reward.

Provide nutritious meals.

 NCLEX® Connection: Physiological Adaptation, Alterations in Body Systems

UNIT 1	FOUNDATIONS OF NURSING CARE OF CHILDREN
Section	Perspectives of Nursing Care of Children
Chapter 7	Health Promotion of the Adolescent (12 to 20 Years)

Expected Growth and Development

- Physical Development

  o The final 20% to 25% of height is achieved during puberty.

  o Acne may appear during adolescence.

  o Girls may cease to grow at about 2 to 2.5 years after the onset of menarche. They will grow 5 to 20 cm (2 to 8 in) and gain 7 to 25 kg (15.5 to 55 lb).

  o Boys tend to stop growing at around 18 to 20 years of age. They will grow 10 to 30 cm (4 to 12 inches) and gain 7 to 30 kg (15.5 to 66 lb).

  o In girls, sexual maturation occurs in the following order:

    ▪ Appearance of breast buds

    ▪ Growth of pubic hair (although some girls may have hair growth prior to breast bud development)

    ▪ Onset of menstruation

  o In males, sexual maturation occurs in the following order:

    ▪ Increase in the size of the testes and scrotum

    ▪ Appearance of pubic hair

    ▪ Rapid growth of genitalia

    ▪ Growth of axillary hair.

    ▪ Appearance of downy hair on upper lip

    ▪ Change in voice

  o Sleep habits change with puberty due to increased metabolism and rapid growth during the adolescent years. Changes are characterized by staying up late, sleeping in later in the morning, and perhaps sleeping longer than was done during the school-age years.

- Cognitive Development

  o Piaget – Formal operations

    ▪ Capable of thinking at an adult level

    ▪ Able to think abstractly and deal with principles

    ▪ Capable of evaluating the quality of their own thinking

- Able to maintain attention for longer periods of time
- Highly imaginative and idealistic
- Capable of making decisions through logical operations
- Future oriented
- Capable of using deductive reasoning
- Able to understand how the actions of an individual influence others

  o Language

- Adolescents develop jargon within their peer groups. They are able to communicate one way with peer groups and another way with adults or teachers. Development of communication skills is essential for adolescents.

- Psychosocial Development

  o The psychosocial development stage of adolescents, according to Erikson, is identity versus role confusion.

- Adolescents develop a sense of personal identity that is influenced by expectations of their families.

  □ Group identity – Adolescents may become part of a peer group that greatly influences behavior.

  o Vocationally – Adolescents solidify work habits and plan for future college and careers.

  o Sexually – There is increased interest in the opposite gender.

  o Health perceptions – Adolescents may view themselves as invincible to bad outcomes of risky behaviors.

  o Moral Development

- Conventional law and order – Rules are not seen as absolutes. Each situation needs to be looked at, and perhaps the rules will need to be adjusted. Not all adolescents attain this level of moral development during these years.

  o Self-Concept Development

- A healthy self-concept is developed by having healthy relationships with peers, family, and teachers. Identifying a skill or talent helps maintain a healthy self-concept. Participation in sports, hobbies, or the community can have a positive outcome.

  o Body-Image Changes

- Adolescents seem particularly concerned with the body images portrayed by the media. Changes that occur during puberty result in comparisons between individual adolescents and their surrounding peer groups. Parents also give their input as to hair styles, dress, and activities. Adolescents may require help if depression or eating disorders result due to poor body image.

- ○ Social Development

  - ■ Peer relationships develop. These relationships act as a support system for adolescents.

  - ■ Best-friend relationships are more stable and longer lasting than they were in previous years.

  - ■ Parent-child relationships change to allow a greater sense of independence.

- Age-Appropriate Activities

  - ○ Nonviolent video games

  - ○ Nonviolent music

  - ○ Sports

  - ○ Caring for a pet

  - ○ Career-training programs

  - ○ Reading

  - ○ Social events (going to the movies, school dances)

Health Promotion

- Immunizations

  - ○ 2010 Centers for Disease Control (CDC) recommendations for healthy adolescents 12 to 20 years of age (http://cdc.gov) include the following vaccines if not given at age 11 to 12 – Tetanus and diphtheria toxoids and pertussis vaccine (Tdap); meningococcal (MCV4); human papillomavirus vaccine (HPV2 series for females and HPV4) series for males; and yearly influenza vaccine (trivalent inactivated influenza vaccine [TIV] or live, attenuated influenza vaccine [LAIV] by nasal spray)

- Health Screenings

  - ○ Scoliosis – Screenings for scoliosis should continue during the adolescent years. These screenings should include an examination for a lateral curvature of the spine before and during growth spurts. Screenings may take place at school or at a health care facility.

- Nutrition

  - ○ Rapid growth and high metabolism require increases in quality nutrients. Nutrients that tend to be deficient during this stage of life are iron, calcium, and vitamins A and C.

  - ○ Eating disorders commonly develop during adolescence (more prevalent in girls than in boys) due to a fear of being overweight, fad diets, and/or the desire to maintain control over some aspect of life. Eating disorders include anorexia nervosa, bulimia nervosa, and obesity.

- o Advise parents to:
  - ■ Avoid using food as a reward.
  - ■ Emphasize physical activity.
  - ■ Ensure that a balanced diet is consumed. Healthy food recommendations are posted by the United States Department of Agriculture (http://www.mypyramid.gov).
  - ■ Teach children to make healthy food selections for meals and snacks.
- o Dental health
  - ■ Brush daily.
  - ■ Floss daily.
  - ■ Have regular checkups.
  - ■ Have regular fluoride treatments.
- • Injury Prevention
  - o Bodily harm
    - ■ Keep firearms in a locked cabinet or box.
    - ■ Teach proper use of sporting equipment prior to use.
    - ■ Insist on helmet use and/or pads when rollerblading, skateboarding, bicycling, riding scooters, skiing, and snowboarding.
    - ■ Avoid trampolines.
    - ■ Be aware of changes in mood. Monitor for self-harm in adolescents who are at risk. Watch for:
      - □ Poor school performance
      - □ Lack of interest in things that were of interest to the adolescent in the past
      - □ Social isolation
      - □ Disturbances in sleep or appetite
      - □ Expression of suicidal thoughts
  - o Burns
    - ■ Teach fire safety.
    - ■ Apply sunscreen when outside.
  - o Drowning
    - ■ Teach adolescents to swim.
    - ■ Teach adolescents not to swim alone.

- o Motor-vehicle injuries
  - Encourage attendance at drivers' education courses. Emphasize the need for adherence to seat belt use.
  - Insist on helmet use with bicycles, motorcycles, skateboards, roller blades, and snowboards.
  - Discourage use of cell phones while driving and enforce laws regarding use.
  - Teach the dangers of combining substance abuse with driving.
  - Role model desired behavior.
- o Substance abuse
  - Monitor for signs of substance abuse in adolescents who are at risk.
  - Teach adolescents to say "no" to illegal drugs and alcohol.
  - Present a no-tolerance attitude.
- o Sexually transmitted diseases (STDs)
  - Provide education and resources for treatment.
- o Pregnancy prevention
  - Provide education.

CHAPTER 7: HEALTH PROMOTION OF THE ADOLESCENT (12 TO 20 YEARS)

 Application Exercises

1. A nurse is teaching a class about sexual maturation in males. Identify the order in which sexual maturation changes occur in males by numbering the changes from 1 to 6.

   _____ The voice changes.

   _____ Pubic hair appears.

   _____ Size of testes increases.

   _____ Downy hair appears on the upper lip.

   _____ Axillary hair grows.

   _____ Rapid growth of genitalia occurs.

2. A nurse in a clinic is assessing an adolescent. The adolescent's mother is concerned about her daughter's sleep habits. The nurse should inform the mother that sleep habits change with puberty due to _____ and _____.

3. A nurse is caring for an adolescent client. The nurse should recognize that the adolescent is likely to take risks because

   A. he is incapable of thinking at an adult level.

   B. he sees himself as invincible to bad outcomes.

   C. he has a short attention span.

   D. he shows no respect for the rules.

4. A nurse is caring for an adolescent whose parent is concerned that he may be depressed. Identify five behavioral changes the nurse should mention that may indicate the adolescent is socially isolated or depressed.

CHAPTER 7: HEALTH PROMOTION OF THE ADOLESCENT (12 TO 20 YEARS)

 Application Exercises Answer Key

1. A nurse is teaching a class about sexual maturation in males. Identify the order in which sexual maturation changes occur in males by numbering the changes from 1 to 6.

   6 The voice changes.

   2 Pubic hair appears.

   1 Size of testes increases.

   5 Downy hair appears on the upper lip.

   4 Axillary hair grows.

   3 Rapid growth of genitalia occurs.

    NCLEX® Connection: Reduction of Risk Potential, System Specific Assessment

2. A nurse in a clinic is assessing an adolescent. The adolescent's mother is concerned about her daughter's sleep habits. The nurse should inform the mother that sleep habits change with puberty due to _____ and _____.

   Increased metabolism, rapid growth

    NCLEX® Connection: Health Promotion and Maintenance, Aging Process

3. A nurse is caring for an adolescent client. The nurse should recognize that the adolescent is likely to take risks because

   A. he is incapable of thinking at an adult level.

   B. he sees himself as invincible to bad outcomes.

   C. he has a short attention span.

   D. he shows no respect for the rules.

   Adolescents may be able to recite the consequences of their behavior, but they believe that they are invincible; therefore, they believe the consequences will not happen. Adolescents have longer attention spans than younger children and they are capable of thinking at adult levels. Although rules are not seen as absolute for some adolescents, they may still have respect for the rules.

    NCLEX® Connection: Health Promotion and Maintenance, Developmental Stages and Transitions

4. A nurse is caring for an adolescent whose parent is concerned that he may be depressed. Identify five behavioral changes the nurse should mention that may indicate the adolescent is socially isolated or depressed.

Poor school performance

Lack of interest in things that were of interest to the adolescent in the past

Lack of interaction with others

Disturbances in sleep or appetite

Expression of suicidal thoughts

Ⓝ NCLEX® Connection: Health Promotion and Maintenance, Developmental Stages and Transitions

UNIT 1: FOUNDATIONS OF NURSING CARE OF CHILDREN

Section: Special Considerations of Nursing Care of Children

- Safe Administration of Medication
- Pain Management
- Hospitalization, Illness, and Play
- Death and Dying

NCLEX® CONNECTIONS

When reviewing the chapters in this section, keep in mind the relevant sections of the NCLEX® outline, in particular:

CLIENT NEEDS: PSYCHOSOCIAL INTEGRITY

Relevant topics/tasks include:
- End-of-Life Care
  - Recognize the need for and provide psychosocial support to family/caregiver.
- Family Dynamics
  - Recognize the impact of illness/disease on individual/family lifestyle.
- Grief and Loss
  - Evaluate the client's coping and fears related to grief and loss.

CLIENT NEEDS: BASIC CARE AND COMFORT

Relevant topics/tasks include:
- Nonpharmacological Comfort Interventions
  - Assess the client's need for pain management and intervene as needed using non-pharmacological comfort measures.

CLIENT NEEDS: PHARMACOLOGICAL AND PARENTERAL THERAPIES

Relevant topics/tasks include:
- Dosage Calculation
  - Perform calculations needed for medication administration.
- Medication Administration
  - Educate the client about medications.
- Pharmacological Pain Management
  - Administer and document pharmacological pain management appropriate for the client's age and diagnoses.

UNIT 1	FOUNDATIONS OF NURSING CARE OF CHILDREN
Section	Special Considerations of Nursing Care of Children
Chapter 8	Safe Administration of Medication

Overview

- Organ system immaturity affects drug sensitivity in infants and children.

- Variations

  - Newborns and young infants may have intense and prolonged responses to medications.

  - In comparison to adults, medications administered by IM injection are absorbed more slowly in newborns, but faster in infants.

  - A limited protein-binding capacity may lead to high concentrations of free drugs.

  - Newborns are highly sensitive to medications that affect the CNS and are metabolized by the liver.

  - Newborns have limited renal excretion abilities. Therefore, they must have reduced dosages of medications that are eliminated by the renal system.

  - Starting at 1 year of age, children's pharmacokinetic responses to medication will start to be similar to those of adults, with the exception of faster metabolism until age 12.

- Pediatric dosages are based on body weight, body surface area (BSA), and maturation of body organs.

- Nurses should be particularly alert when administering medications to children due to the high risk for medication error.

  - Adult medication forms and concentrations may require dilution, calculation, preparation, and administration of very small doses. Certain medications should be double checked by another nurse. Nurses should be aware of those medications and follow facility policies on administration.

Six Rights of Safe Medication Administration

- Right client – Verify the client's identification each time a medication is administered.

    - The Joint Commission requires that two client identifiers be used when administering medications. Acceptable identifiers include the client's name, an assigned identification number, a telephone number, a birth date, or another person-specific identifier. Infants and young children cannot be relied upon to identify themselves. Young children may answer to any name that is called. A parent or guardian can be asked to identify an infant or young child.

- Right medication – Correctly interpret the medication prescription (verify completeness and clarity). Read the label three times: when container is selected, when removing dose from container, and when container is replaced. Leave unit-dose medication in its package until administration.

- Right dose – Calculate the correct medication dose. Check medication reference to ensure the dose is within usual range. Have a second nurse check if unsure or if facility policy requires it. Use a cutting device to break a scored tablet.

- Right time – Administer the medication on time to maintain consistent therapeutic blood levels. It is generally acceptable to give the medication 0.5 hr before or after the scheduled time. However, refer to the medication reference or facility policy for exceptions. PRN medications should not be given sooner than the interval specified by the primary care provider.

- Right route – Select the correct preparation for the prescribed route (otic versus ophthalmic, topical ointment, or drops). Understand how to safely and correctly administer the medication. Administer injections only from preparations designed for parenteral use. If the route is not designated, or if a specified route is not recommended, contact the health care provider for clarification.

- Right documentation – Immediately record pertinent information, including the client's response to the medication.

Factors Influencing Medication Administration

- Organ system immaturity is the greatest factor that affects medication response in children.

- Psychosocial variables affecting medication responses in children

    - Health-illness beliefs of the child and family

    - Previous experiences with medications

    - Knowledge base

    - Cultural beliefs

    - Developmental stage

    - Social support/financial status

Assessment

- Medication and food allergies

- Medication dose appropriate for child's weight

- Child's ability to cooperate with medication administration

- Tissue and skin integrity when administering IM and topical medications

- IV patency when administering IV medications

Nursing Interventions

- Administration of Oral Medications

  ○ Consider the oral route as the preferred route for children and milliliters (mL) as the preferred measurement (5 mL = 1 tsp, 30 mL = 1 oz).

  ○ Use plastic, needleless syringes for measurement and administration of small doses of medications.

  ○ To ensure that the total dose is given, use only a small amount of liquid or soft food when mixing medications.

  ○ Do not crush enteric-coated or time-released tablets. Divide tablets only if scored.

  ○ Strategies for administering oral medications to infants

    ▪ Do not mix a medication with formula because the infant may not take all of the formula, which will result in the infant not receiving the full dose of medication. This may also alter the taste of the formula, which may cause the infant to refuse to drink it in the future.

    ▪ Hold the infant in a semi-upright or semi-Fowler's position to prevent aspiration.

    ▪ Use a medicine cup once the infant is able to drink from a cup.

    ▪ Place the medication into nipples from which the infant can suck.

  ○ Administering oral medications via a feeding tube or a gastrostomy tube

    ▪ Check tube placement before administering any medication.

    ▪ Use liquid forms of medications.

    ▪ Check the compatibility of medications before mixing.

    ▪ Do not mix medications with enteral feedings.

    ▪ Flush the tubing with warm water before and after each medication. Amount of flush solution depends on the length and gauge of tubing. Determine this amount, which is usually 1.5 times the tubing volume, before administering medication.

- Rectal Medication Administration

  o This route is used as a substitute for oral administration (for a child with nausea/vomiting or difficult oral administration).

  o Acetaminophen (Tylenol), sedatives, morphine, and some antiemetics are available in suppository form.

  o Cut the suppository lengthwise for partial dosing due to the irregular shaping of the suppository.

  o Insert suppository with the apex (pointed end) entering first, then gently push beyond rectal sphincter and hold the buttocks together until the urge to expel has passed (5 to 10 min).

- Other Medication Administration Routes

  o Optic, otic, and nasal administration

    ■ Procedures for these routes are similar to adult administration.

    ■ Pull the auricle down and back when instilling otic solutions for children up to 3 years of age. Pull the auricle up and back for older children.

    ■ Strategies to gain the child's cooperation

      □ Allow the parent to be present. The parent may also hold the child.

      □ Warm otic solutions to room temperature before instilling.

      □ Hyperextend the child's neck for nasal medication administration to prevent the medication from sliding down into the child's throat.

- Subcutaneous (SQ) and Intradermal Medication Administration

  o These administration techniques are very similar for children and adults.

  o Strategies to decrease pain

    ■ Apply a eutectic mixture of local anesthetics (EMLA) in the form of a cream or disk 60 min prior to injection.

    ■ Use an appropriately sized needle.

    ■ Change the needle if used to puncture the rubber top of a vial.

    ■ Ensure that the amount of medication injected is appropriate for the child's muscle size (approximately 0.5 mL in infants and 2.0 mL in children).

SUBCUTANEOUS	INTRADERMAL

• Insert the needle at a 90° angle, or a 45° angle for a child with minimal subcutaneous tissue.
• Sites
  ○ Upper arm (lateral aspect, center third),
  ○ Abdomen (avoid umbilicus)
  ○ Anterior thigh (center third)
• Common uses
  ○ Insulin administration
  ○ Allergy desensitization
  ○ Hormone replacement
  ○ Immunizations
	• Insert the needle at a 15° angle, injecting the medication to form a bleb (a small bubble) just beneath the surface of the skin.
	• The intradermal site is the inside surface of the forearm, not the medial surface.
	• Common uses
	  ○ Local anesthetic
	  ○ Tuberculosis (TB) skin testing
	  ○ Allergy testing

- Intramuscular (IM) Medication Administration

  ○ Strategies to decrease pain

    ▪ Apply a eutectic mixture of local anesthetics (EMLA) in the form of a cream or disk a minimum of 60 min, preferably 2 to 2.5 hr, prior to injection.

    ▪ Change needle if used to puncture the rubber top of a vial.

    ▪ Use the smallest gauge possible.

  ○ Considerations when selecting a site

    ▪ Medication amount, viscosity, and type

    ▪ Muscle mass, condition, access of site, and potential for contamination

    ▪ Treatment course frequency and number of injections

    ▪ Ability to obtain proper positioning of the child

  ○ General considerations for IM medication administration

    ▪ The vastus lateralis site is usually the recommended site for infants and children less than 2 years of age (it can accommodate fluid 0.5 mL for infants to 2.0 mL for children).

    ▪ After age 2, the ventral gluteal site can be used (it can accommodate fluid up to 2 mL).

    ▪ The deltoid site has a smaller muscle mass and can only accommodate up to 0.5 mL in infants and 1 mL in children.

 View Media Supplement: Pediatric IM Injections (Video)

SITE	NEEDLE SIZES	POSITIONS	COMMENTS
Vastus Lateralis	• 22 to 25 gauge • 0.625 to 1 inch • 0.5 mL for infants to 2.0 mL for children	• Supine • Side lying • Sitting	• Recommended site for infants and children less than 2 years of age • May be used for toddlers and older children
Ventrogluteal	• 22 to 25 gauge • 0.625 to 1 inch • 2.0 mL for children	• Supine • Side lying • Prone	• Can be used for children ages 2 and older • Less painful than vastus lateralis • Free of any nerves or blood vessels
Deltoid	• 22 to 25 gauge • 0.625 to 1 inch • 0.5 mL for infants to 1.0 mL for children	• Supine • Side lying • Sitting	• Not as painful as vastus lateralis • Less local side effects than with vastus lateralis • Should not be used in infants/children with underdeveloped muscles • If muscle size is appropriate, it may be used for immunization of toddlers and children

- Intravenous (IV) Medication Administration
  - Peripheral venous access devices
    - Use for continuous and intermittent IV medication administration.
    - A child who requires short-term therapy may be discharged with a peripheral line that is maintained by a home health care nurse.
  - Central venous access devices (VADs)
    - Long-term central VADs may be tunneled or implanted infusion ports.
    - If a child is to go home with a VAD, discharge instructions should include how to prepare and inject medication, flush the line, and perform dressing changes.
    - Short-term, or nontunneled, catheters are inserted into large veins and are used in acute care, emergency situations and intensive care units.
    - Peripherally inserted central catheters (PICCs) are used for short- to moderate-length therapy. PICCs are the least costly and have the fewest incidences of complications

CHAPTER 8: SAFE ADMINISTRATION OF MEDICATION

 Application Exercises

1. A nurse is preparing to administer medications to an infant. Which of the following should the nurse consider? (Select all that apply.)

_____ Prolonged responses to medications

_____ Decreased absorption of topical medications

_____ Increased sensitivity to medications affecting the CNS

_____ Increased serum protein-binding sites

_____ Limited renal excretion

2. A nurse is preparing to administer an immunization to an infant. Which of the following should the nurse select as an appropriate site?

A. Deltoid

B. Ventrogluteal

C. Vastus lateralis

D. Dorsogluteal

3. List three interventions that a nurse may use to decrease the risk of medication errors when administering a medication to a child. Explain each intervention.

4. When instilling an otic solution into a child's ear, the nurse should pull the auricle _____ and ____.

CHAPTER 8: SAFE ADMINISTRATION OF MEDICATION

 Application Exercises Answer Key

1. A nurse is preparing to administer medications to an infant. Which of the following should the nurse consider? (Select all that apply.)

   X   **Prolonged responses to medications**

          Decreased absorption of topical medications

   X   **Increased sensitivity to medications affecting the CNS**

          Increased serum protein-binding sites

   X   **Limited renal excretion**

   Due to organ system immaturity, infants have prolonged responses to medications, increased sensitivity to medications affecting the CNS, and limited renal excretion. Absorption of topical medications is increased, and there are decreased serum protein-binding sites.

 NCLEX® Connection: Health Promotion and Maintenance, Aging Process

2. A nurse is preparing to administer an immunization to an infant. Which of the following should the nurse select as an appropriate site?

   A. Deltoid

   B. Ventrogluteal

   C. Vastus lateralis

   D. Dorsogluteal

   The vastus lateralis is the most developed muscle in the infant; therefore, it is the site of choice for administering IM injections in infants.

 NCLEX® Connection: Health Promotion and Maintenance, Aging Process

3. List three interventions that a nurse may use to decrease the risk of medication errors when administering a medication to a child. Explain each intervention.

INTERVENTION	RATIONALE
Have a second nurse verify dosage calculation.	Adult medication forms may be used, which will require calculation of very small doses.
Obtain accurate weight of child.	Dosages are usually based on weight or body surface area.
Mix the medication with a small amount of liquid or soft food.	If the medication is mixed in a large amount of liquid or food, the child may refuse to finish the dose.

 NCLEX® Connection: Safety and Infection Control, Accident/Injury Prevention

4. When instilling an otic solution into a child's ear, the nurse should pull the auricle _____ and ____.

Down, back

Pulling the auricle down and back, instead of up and back (as would be done in an adult), will help open the ear canal and facilitate administration of the medication. This method straightens the child's ear canal, making it easier to instill the otic solution.

 NCLEX® Connection: Health Promotion and Maintenance, Aging Process

UNIT 1	FOUNDATIONS OF NURSING CARE OF CHILDREN
Section	Special Considerations of Nursing Care of Children
Chapter 9	Pain Management

Overview

- Assessment of pain in children is complex and challenging.

- Children have a right to adequate assessment and management of pain. The nurse's role is to advocate for the child and family and educate about proper pain management.

- Pain is whatever the child says it is, and it exists whenever the child says it does. The child's report of pain is the most reliable diagnostic measurement of pain. Behavioral measures are also used to evaluate pain.

- The type of pain children experience includes procedure-related pain, operative and trauma-associated pain, and/or acute and chronic pain from illness or injury.

- Pain assessments should be performed and recorded frequently by the nurse, and pain may be considered the fifth vital sign.

- The effectiveness of treatment should be evaluated in a timely manner (15 min after IV pain medication administration, 30 min after IM pain medication, 30 to 60 min after oral medication administration and nonpharmacologic therapies).

  o Assessment is more difficult to determine in infants and young children because they lack the verbal skills to state how severe the pain is. Older children and adolescents are able to self-report information about what they are experiencing.

  o Behaviors in a child with pain can vary from immobility and stillness to restlessness and constant mobility.

  o Changes in blood pressure, pulse, and respiratory rate are temporary physiologic changes associated with the pain. Initially, elevated vital signs will return to normal despite the persistence of pain.

  o Children from 3 to 7 years of age may comprehend how to use a pain rating scale, and self-report using pain scales may be useful with children over 7 years of age. However, each child's ability should be assessed. Verification with parents will validate assessment. Often, parents may indicate that the child is experiencing pain, and the nurse should be attuned to this report.

- Proper pain management includes the use of pharmacological and nonpharmacological pain management therapies, such as guided imagery.

- Children receiving opioid medications need to be monitored closely for respiratory depression.

Influential Factors

- Age can influence how pain is perceived and how it can be communicated.

- Fatigue, anxiety, and fear can increase sensitivity to pain.

- Genetic sensitivity can increase or decrease the amount of pain tolerated.

- Cognitive impairment may impact a child's ability to report pain or report it accurately.

- Prior experiences can increase or decrease sensitivity depending on whether or not adequate relief was obtained, especially in older children and adolescents.

- Family and friends may decrease sensitivity to pain by staying with the child.

- Culture may influence how a child expresses pain or the meaning given to it.

Nursing Assessment

 View Media Supplement: Pain Assessment in Children (Video)

- Subjective data may be obtained using a symptom analysis. A nurse should adapt questions to the appropriate developmental level of the child.

SYMPTOMS	QUESTIONS TO ASK
• Location is described using anatomical terminology and landmarks.	• "Where is your pain?" • "Does it hurt anywhere else?" • "Can you point to where it hurts?"
• Quality refers to how the pain feels. • Feelings of pain include: sharp, dull, aching, burning, stabbing, pounding, throbbing, shooting, gnawing, tender, heavy, tight, tiring, exhausting, sickening, terrifying, torturing, nagging, annoying, intense, and/or unbearable.	• "What does the pain feel like?" • "Is the pain throbbing, burning, or stabbing?"

• Intensity, strength, and severity are measures of the pain. Pain assessment tools (description scale, number rating scale) can be used to:
  o Measure pain.
  o Monitor pain.
  o Evaluate effectiveness of interventions.
	• "Can you rate your pain on a scale of 0 to 10?"
	• "How much pain do you have now?"
	• "What is the worst/best the pain has been?"

SYMPTOMS	QUESTIONS TO ASK
• The timing of pain includes the onset, duration, and frequency. ○ This may be difficult for a child to understand. An older child or adolescent may have a better understanding of time.	• "When did the pain start?" • "How long does the pain last?" • "How often does the pain occur?" • "Is the pain constant or intermittent?"
• Setting has to do with where the child is or what he is doing when the pain occurs.	• "Where are you when you feel pain?" • "What are you doing when you feel pain?"
• Associated symptoms may include fatigue, depression, nausea, and anxiety, and they should be noted.	• "Do you feel tired or sad when you are in pain?"
• Aggravating/relieving factors are things that make the pain feel better or worse.	• "What makes the pain better?" • "What makes the pain worse?"

- • Objective Data

  - ○ Behaviors complement self-report and assist in pain assessment of children who are unable to verbalize their feelings.

    - ■ Facial expressions (grimace, wrinkled forehead) and body movements (restlessness, pacing, guarding)

    - ■ Moaning and crying

    - ■ Decreased attention span

  - ○ Physiologic measures of blood pressure, pulse, and respiratory rate will be temporarily increased by acute pain. Eventually, increased vital signs will return to normal despite the persistence of pain. Therefore, physiologic indicators may not be an accurate measure of pain over time.

  - ○ Common pain scale

PAIN ASSESSMENT TOOL	FORM OF EVALUATION	AGE OF CHILD

CRIES Neonatal Postoperative Scale	• Pain rated on a scale of 0 to 10
	• Behavior indicators
	  ○ Crying
	  ○ Changes in vital signs
	  ○ Changes in expression
	  ○ Altered sleeping patterns
		32 weeks of gestation to 20 weeks of life

PAIN ASSESSMENT TOOL	FORM OF EVALUATION	AGE OF CHILD

Faces, Legs, Activity, Cry, and Consolability (FLACC) Postoperative Pain Tool	• Behavior indicators
	  ○ Facial expressions
	  ○ Position of legs
	  ○ Activity
	  ○ Crying
	  ○ Ability to be consoled
		2 months to 7 years

FACES Pain Rating Scale	• Rating scale uses drawings of happy and sad faces to depict levels of pain.	3 years and older
Visual Analog Scale (VAS)	• Pain is rated on a scale of 0 to 10. • Child points to the number that best describes the pain he is experiencing.	7 years and older (may be effective with children as young as 4.5 years)

Noncommunicating Children's Pain Checklist	• Pain is rated on a scale of 0 to 18.
	• Behavior indicators
	  ○ Vocalization
	  ○ Socialization
	  ○ Facial expressions
	  ○ Activity level
	  ○ Movement of extremities
	  ○ Physiologic changes
		3 to 18 years of age (for children with or without cognitive impairments)

Nursing Interventions

- Interventions should be determined in conjunction with the family and child. Severity of the pain will also guide the choice of treatment.

- Pharmacological measures

  - Give medications routinely versus PRN (as needed) to manage pain that is expected to last for an extended period of time.

  - Use caution when administering medications to newborns less than 2 to 3 months of age because of immature liver function.

- o Combine adjuvant medications (steroids, antidepressants, sedatives, antianxiety medications, muscle relaxants, anticonvulsants) with other analgesics.
- o Use nonopioid and opioid medications.
  - ▪ Acetaminophen (Tylenol) and NSAIDs are acceptable for mild to moderate pain.
  - ▪ Opioids are acceptable for moderate to severe pain. Medications used include morphine sulfate, oxycodone (OxyContin), and fentanyl (Duragesic).
  - ▪ Combining a nonopioid and an opioid medication treats pain peripherally and centrally. This offers greater analgesia with less adverse effects (respiratory depression, constipation, nausea).
- (S) • Appropriate Routes

ROUTE	NURSING IMPLICATIONS
Oral	• The oral medication route is preferred due to its convenience, cost, and ability to maintain steady blood levels. • Oral medications take 1 to 2 hr to reach peak analgesic effects. Therefore, these medications are not suited for children experiencing pain that requires rapid relief or pain that is fluctuating in nature.
Topical/transdermal	• One type of topical/transdermal medication is a eutectic mixture of local anesthetics (EMLA), which contains equal quantities of lidocaine and prilocaine in the form of a cream or disk. o Use EMLA for any procedure in which the skin will be punctured (IV insertion, biopsy) 60 min prior to a superficial puncture and 2 hr prior to a deep puncture. o Place an occlusive dressing over the cream after application. o Prior to the procedure, remove the dressing or disk and clean the skin. An indication of an adequate response is reddened or blanched skin. o Demonstrate to the child that the skin is not sensitive by tapping or scratching lightly. o Instruct parents to apply EMLA at home prior to coming to a health care facility for the procedure. • Fentanyl o Use for children older than 12 years of age. o Use to provide continuous pain control. It has an onset of 12 to 24 hr and a duration of 72 hr. o Use an immediate-release opioid for breakthrough pain. o Treat respiratory depression with naloxone (Narcan).
Continuous intravenous (IV)	• Use continuous intravenous (IV) medication administration to provide stable blood levels.

ROUTE	NURSING IMPLICATIONS
Patient-controlled analgesia (PCA)	• Use a PCA to control pain from injury and chronic conditions. • Administer morphine, fentanyl, and hydromorphone (Dilaudid) via PCA. • Allow child to control PCA if appropriate. • Designate one family member or one nurse to control PCA.

- Nonpharmacological Measures

   o   Positioning

   o   Teaching breathing and relaxation techniques

   o   Splinting

   o   Maintaining a calm environment (low noise, reduced lighting)

   o   Providing ice to swollen or injured area

   o   Offering warm blankets

   o   Assisting with guided imagery

   o   Offering distractions (video games, cartoons, videos)

   o   Providing comfort with physical contact (holding, rocking)

   o   Administering sucrose pacifiers for infants during procedures.

CHAPTER 9: PAIN MANAGEMENT

 Application Exercises

1. A 10-year-old child has just had an appendectomy following a ruptured appendix. A nurse is monitoring the child's response to antibiotics, postoperative healing, and pain control. Which of the following tools is appropriate for assessing the child's pain?

    A. FLACC Postoperative Pain Tool

    B. FACES Pain Rating Scale

    C. CRIES Neonatal Postoperative Scale

    D. Visual Analogue Scale

2. For which of the following children should a nurse use the child's behavior, rather than a self-report, as an indication of pain?

    A. 2 year old

    B. 8 year old

    C. 12 year old

    D. 16 year old

3. Which of the following are appropriate nonpharmacological pain management techniques for a nurse to use with a 5-year-old child who has a fractured femur? (Select all that apply.)

    _____ Relaxation techniques

    _____ Distraction

    _____ Guided imagery

    _____ Holding or rocking

    _____ Positioning

4. A nurse is caring for an adolescent client who has a long-leg cast applied following surgical repair of a fractured leg. The first night in the hospital, the client states, "My leg hurts really badly." The next action the nurse should take is to

    A. obtain more information about the characteristics of the pain.

    B. give the adolescent a dose of pain medication as prescribed.

    C. reassure the adolescent that the pain will diminish in a few days.

    D. distract the adolescent by turning on the television.

RN NURSING CARE OF CHILDREN   79

CHAPTER 9: PAIN MANAGEMENT

 Application Exercises Answer Key

1. A 10-year-old child has just had an appendectomy following a ruptured appendix. A nurse is monitoring the child's response to antibiotics, postoperative healing, and pain control. Which of the following tools is appropriate for assessing the child's pain?

    A. FLACC Postoperative Pain Tool

    B. FACES Pain Rating Scale

    C. CRIES Neonatal Postoperative Scale

    D. Visual Analogue Scale

The visual analogue scale is appropriate for this child. The FLACC Postoperative Pain Tool is used for infants and children up to 7 years of age, the FACES Pain Rating Scale is appropriate for early childhood, and CRIES Neonatal Postoperative Scale is used for newborns and young infants.

 NCLEX® Connection: Reduction of Risk Potential, System Specific Assessment

2. For which of the following children should a nurse use the child's behavior, rather than a self-report, as an indication of pain?

    A. 2 year old

    B. 8 year old

    C. 12 year old

    D. 16 year old

A 2-year-old child is not able to verbalize pain. However, this child may exhibit signs of distress such as crying, irritability, and restlessness. The older children should be able to report the pain experienced.

 NCLEX® Connection: Reductions of Risk Potential, System Specific Assessment

3. Which of the following are appropriate nonpharmacological pain management techniques for a nurse to use with a 5-year-old child who has a fractured femur? (Select all that apply.)

    _____ Relaxation techniques

    __X__ **Distraction**

    _____ Guided imagery

    __X__ **Holding or rocking**

    __X__ **Positioning**

Distraction (coloring, watching television, playing with toys), holding or rocking, and positioning are all appropriate nonpharmacological pain management techniques for a 5-year-old child. This child will not be able to practice relaxation techniques or follow guided imagery.

 NCLEX® Connection: Physiological Adaptation, Alterations in Body Systems

4. A nurse is caring for an adolescent client who has a long-leg cast applied following surgical repair of a fractured leg. The first night in the hospital, the client states, "My leg hurts really badly." The next action the nurse should take is to

A. obtain more information about the characteristics of the pain.

B. give the adolescent a dose of pain medication as prescribed.

C. reassure the adolescent that the pain will diminish in a few days.

D. distract the adolescent by turning on the television.

According to the nursing process, the first action the nurse should take is to gather more information regarding the adolescent's report of pain. Administering pain medication, reassuring the adolescent, and providing distraction are all appropriate actions, but none of them is the first action the nurse should take.

Ⓝ NCLEX® Connection: Reductions of Risk Potential, System Specific Assessment

UNIT 1	FOUNDATIONS OF NURSING CARE OF CHILDREN
Section	Special Considerations of Nursing Care of Children
Chapter 10	Hospitalization, Illness, and Play

Overview

- A nurse is likely to encounter children who are ill and/or hospitalized. When caring for these children, it is important to know what play activities are considered appropriate.

HOSPITALIZATION AND ILLNESS

Overview

- Families and children may experience major stress related to hospitalization. The nurse should be alert to signs of stress and intervene as appropriate.

- Families should be considered clients when children are ill.

- Separation anxiety during hospitalization manifests in three behavioral responses:

  o Protest (screaming)

  o Despair (developmental regression)

  o Detachment (lack of interaction with unfamiliar people)

- Each child's understanding of illnesses and hospitalization is dependent on the child's stage of development and cognitive ability.

Impact Based on Development

AGE	LEVEL OF UNDERSTANDING	IMPACT OF HOSPITALIZATION
Infant	• Inability to describe symptoms and follow directions • Lack of understanding for the need of therapeutic procedures	• Experiences stranger anxiety between 6 to 18 months of age • Displays physical behaviors as expressions of discomfort due to inability to verbalize • May experience sleep deprivation due to strange noises, monitoring devices, and procedures

AGE	LEVEL OF UNDERSTANDING	IMPACT OF HOSPITALIZATION
Toddler	• Limited ability to describe symptoms • Poorly developed sense of body image and boundaries • Limited understanding for the need for therapeutic procedures • Limited ability to follow directions	• Experiences separation anxiety • May exhibit an intense reaction to any type of procedure due to the intrusion of boundaries
Preschooler	• Limited understanding of the cause of illness but knows what illness feels like • Limited ability to describe symptoms • Fears related to magical thinking • Ability to understand cause and effect inhibited by concrete thinking	• May experience separation anxiety • May harbor fears of bodily harm • May believe illness and hospitalization are a punishment
School-age child	• Beginning awareness of body functioning • Ability to describe pain symptoms • Increasing ability to understand cause and effect	• Fears loss of control • Seeks information as a way to maintain a sense of control • May sense when not being told the truth • May experience stress related to separation from peers and regular routine
Adolescent	• Increasing ability to understand cause and effect • Perceptions of illness severity are based on the degree of body-image changes	• Develops body-image disturbance • Attempts to maintain composure but is embarrassed about losing control • Experiences feelings of isolation from peers • Worries about outcome and impact on school/activities • May not adhere to treatments/medication regimen due to peer influence

Family Responses

- Fear and guilt regarding not bringing the child in for care earlier

- Frustration due to the perceived inability to care for the child

- Altered family roles

- Worry regarding finances if work is missed .

- Worry regarding care of other children within the household

- Fear related to lack of knowledge regarding illness or treatments

Assessment

- Child's and family's understanding of the illness or the reason for hospitalization

- Stressors unique to the child and family (needs of other children in the family, socioeconomic situation, health of other extended family members)

- Past experiences with hospitalization and illness

- Developmental level and needs of child/family

- Parenting role and the family's perception of role changes

- Support available to the child/family

Nursing Interventions

- Teach the child and family what to expect during hospitalization.

- Encourage parents or family members to stay with the child during the hospital experience to reduce the stress.

- Attempt to maintain routine as much as possible.

AGE-RELATED INTERVENTIONS	
AGE	INTERVENTIONS
Infant	• Place infants whose parents are not in attendance close to nursing stations so that their needs may be quickly met. • Provide consistency in assigning caregivers.
Toddler	• Encourage parents to provide routine care for the child, such as changing diapers and feeding the child. • Encourage the child's autonomy by giving the child appropriate choices. • Provide consistency in assigning caregivers.

AGE-RELATED INTERVENTIONS	
AGE	INTERVENTIONS
Preschooler	• Explain all procedures using simple, clear language. Avoid medical jargon and terms that can be misinterpreted by the child. • Encourage the child's independence by letting the child provide self-care. • Encourage the child to express feelings. • Validate the child's fears and concerns. • Provide toys that allow for emotional expression, such as a pounding board to release feelings of protest. • Provide consistency in assigning caregivers. • Give choices when possible, such as "Do you want your medicine in a cup or a spoon?" • Allow younger children to handle equipment if it is safe.
School-age	• Provide factual information. • Encourage the child to express feelings. • Try to maintain a normal routine for long hospitalizations, including time for school work. • Encourage contact with peer group.
Adolescent	• Provide factual information. • Include the adolescent in the planning of care to relieve feelings of powerlessness and lack of control. • Encourage contact with peer group.

View Media Supplement: Interventions for Hospitalization (Video)

PLAY

 Overview

- Play allows children to express feelings and fears.

- Play facilitates mastery of developmental stages and assists in the development of problem solving abilities.

- Play allows children to learn socially acceptable behaviors.

- Play activities should be specific to each child's stage of development.

- Play can be used to teach children.

- Play is a means of protection from everyday stressors.

Content of Play

- Social affective – Taking pleasure in relationships

- Sense-pleasure – Objects in the environment catching the child's attention

- Skill – Demonstrating new abilities

- Unoccupied behavior – Focusing attention on something of interest

- Dramatic – Pretending and fantasizing

- Games – Imitative, formal, or competitive

Social Character of Play

- Onlooker – The child observing others

- Solitary – The child playing alone

- Parallel – Children playing independently but among other children, which is characteristic of toddlers

- Associative – Children playing together without organization, which is characteristic of preschoolers

- Cooperative play – Organized playing in groups, which is characteristic of school-age children

Functions of Play

- Play helps in the development of the following types of skills:

  o Intellectual

  o Sensorimotor

  o Social

    ▪ Self-awareness

    ▪ Creativity

    ▪ Therapeutic and moral values

Play Activities Related to Age

- Infants

  o Birth to 3 months – Visual and auditory stimuli

  o 3 to 6 months – Noise-making objects and soft toys

  o 6 to 9 months – Teething toys and social interaction

  o 9 to 12 months – Large blocks, toys that pop apart, and push-and-pull toys

- Toddlers
  - Cloth books
  - Large crayons and paper
  - Push-and-pull toys
  - Tricycles
  - Balls
  - Puzzles with large pieces
  - Educational television
  - Videos for children
- Preschoolers
  - Associative, imitative, and imaginative play
  - Drawing, painting, riding a tricycle, swimming, jumping, and running
  - Educational television and videos
- School-age children
  - Games that can be played alone or with another person
  - Team sports
  - Musical instruments
  - Arts and crafts
  - Collections
- Adolescents
  - Team sports
  - School activities
  - Reading and listening to music
  - Peer interactions

Therapeutic Play

- Makes use of dolls and/or stuffed animals
- Encourages the acting out of feelings of fear, anger, hostility, and sadness
- Enables the child to learn coping strategies in a safe environment
- Assists in gaining cooperation for medical treatment

Assessment

- Developmental level of the child
- Motor skills
- Level of activity tolerance
- Child's preferences

Nursing Interventions

- Select activities that enhance development.
- Observe the child's play for clues to the child's fears or anxieties.
- Encourage parents to bring one favorite toy from home.
- Use dolls and/or stuffed animals to demonstrate a procedure before it is done.
- Provide play opportunities that meet the child's level of activity tolerance.
- Allow the child to go to the play room if able.
- Encourage the adolescent's peers to visit.

CHAPTER 10: HOSPITALIZATION, ILLNESS, AND PLAY

 Application Exercises

1. An 18-month-old child is admitted to the hospital for pneumonia. The child is in a mist tent with 24% O_2 and has an IV of dextrose 5% in 0.9% sodium chloride at 45 mL/hr infusing in his right arm. Which of the following are stressors that the nurse may expect this child and family to experience? (Select all that apply.)

_____ Strange environment

_____ Lack of control

_____ Fear of bodily harm

_____ Concern about body image

_____ Separation anxiety

2. Match the following behaviors to the stages of separation anxiety.

_____ Protest   A. Withdrawal and quietness

_____ Despair   B. Lack of protest when parents leave

_____ Detachment   C. Crying

3. List several issues that a nurse may expect an adolescent who is hospitalized to experience.

4. Match the following play activities with the appropriate ages.

_____ Watching black-and-white mobiles   A. 1 to 3 years

_____ Playing peek-a-boo   B. 3 to 6 months

_____ Holding a soft rattle   C. Birth to 3 months

_____ Playing with cloth books   D. 9 to 12 months

_____ Banging large block   E. 6 to 9 months

5. In which of the following activities should a nurse expect an adolescent to participate? (Select all that apply.)

_____ Playing video games with peers

_____ Playing in groups without structure

_____ Participating in school sports

_____ Drawing or coloring

_____ Reading or listening to music

_____ Creating art projects

CHAPTER 10: HOSPITALIZATION, ILLNESS, AND PLAY

 Application Exercises Answer Key

1. An 18-month-old child is admitted to the hospital for pneumonia. The child is in a mist tent with 24% O_2 and has an IV of dextrose 5% in 0.9% sodium chloride at 45 mL/hr infusing in his right arm. Which of the following are stressors that the nurse may expect this child and family to experience? (Select all that apply.)

__X__	**Strange environment**
__X__	**Lack of control**
_____	Fear of bodily harm
_____	Concern about body image
__X__	**Separation anxiety**

Strange environment, lack of control, and separation anxiety are stressors toddlers experience during hospitalization. Toddlers are developing a sense of autonomy, so lack of control and a strange environment are threatening. Fear of bodily harm occurs with preschoolers, and concern about body image is associated with adolescents.

 NCLEX® Connection: Health Promotion and Maintenance, Developmental Stages and Transitions

2. Match the following behaviors to the stages of separation anxiety.

__C__	Protest	A. Withdrawal and quietness
__A__	Despair	B. Lack of protest when parents leave
__B__	Detachment	C. Crying

 NCLEX® Connection: Health Promotion and Maintenance, Developmental Stages and Transitions

3. List several issues that a nurse may expect an adolescent who is hospitalized to experience.

Feelings of isolation, especially from peers

Worries regarding the outcome of the illness and how it may affect activities and school

Noncompliance with treatment regimen if it interferes with activities or makes the adolescent appear different

Concerns about body image

 NCLEX® Connection: Health Promotion and Maintenance, Developmental Stages and Transitions

4. Match the following play activities with the appropriate ages.

C	Watching black-and-white mobiles	A. 1 to 3 years
E	Playing peek-a-boo	B. 3 to 6 months
B	Holding a soft rattle	C. Birth to 3 months
A	Playing with cloth books	D. 9 to 12 months
D	Banging large block	E. 6 to 9 months

NCLEX® Connection: Health Promotion and Maintenance, Aging Process

5. In which of the following activities should a nurse expect an adolescent to participate? (Select all that apply.)

X	**Playing video games with peers**
_____	Playing in groups without structure
X	**Getting involved in school sports**
_____	Drawing or coloring
X	**Reading or listening to music**
_____	Creating art projects

Peers are very important to adolescents. Therefore, the adolescent is likely to participate in any activity that includes peers, such as playing video games and team sports. Reading and listening to music are also activities an adolescent may participate in. Unstructured play, drawing, and coloring are more appropriate for preschoolers. School-age children enjoy completing art projects.

NCLEX® Connection: Health Promotion and Maintenance, Aging Process

UNIT 1	FOUNDATIONS OF NURSING CARE OF CHILDREN
Section	Special Considerations of Nursing Care of Children

Chapter 11   Death and Dying

Overview

- The death of a child may be traumatic and devastating for a family.

- Parental grief may last a lifetime, place stress on marital relations, and impact a parent's ability to assist siblings in dealing with their grief.

- Children, regardless of age, will experience grief and loss, which is expressed sporadically through behavior and play and is present for a long period of time. Grief in children is expressed and dealt with in an individual manner. Children who have sustained the loss of siblings may experience physical symptoms (sleep disturbances, depression) or may display behaviors like trying to be perfect or acting out for attention.

- Dysfunctional grief is a type of complicated grief that persists for more than a year after the loss. This type of grief presents with the following characteristics: intense and prolonged feelings of loneliness, emptiness, and yearnings; distractive thoughts; an inability to sleep; lowered self-esteem; and loss of interest in daily activities.

- Family-centered care is required to meet the needs of each individual family member who is experiencing grief.

- Palliative care (end-of-life care)

  ○ Palliative care is a multidisciplinary approach that focuses on the process of dying rather than prolonging life in cases in which cures are no longer possible.

  ○ Pain control, symptom management, and support of the child and family must be given top priority in the terminal stages of illness.

  ○ Palliative care uses education, support, and honest communication to foster a therapeutic environment.

- End-of-life decisions require honest information regarding prognosis, disease progression, treatment options, and the impact of the treatments. These decisions are made during a highly stressful time. It is important that all health care personnel are aware of the child and family's decisions.

- Nurses may experience personal grief when caring for children with whom they have developed rapport and intimacy. A debriefing of the entire staff by professional grief/mental health counselors may be indicated.

RN NURSING CARE OF CHILDREN

Factors Influencing Loss, Grief, and Coping Ability

- Interpersonal relationships and social support networks

- Type and significance of loss

- Culture and ethnicity

- Spiritual and religious beliefs and practices

- Prior experience with loss

- Socioeconomic status

- Current stage of development

AGE	RELEVANT FACTORS
Infants/Toddlers (birth to 3 years)	• Have little to no concept of death • Have egocentric thinking that prevents them from understanding death (toddlers) • Mirror parental emotions (sadness, anger, depression, anxiety) • React in response to the changes brought about by being in the hospital (change of routine, painful procedures, immobilization, less independence, separation from family) • May regress to an earlier stage of behavior
Preschool children (3 to 6 years)	• Have egocentric thinking • Have magical thinking that allows them to believe that their thoughts can cause an event such as death (As a result, they may feel guilty and shameful.) • Interpret separation from parents as punishment for bad behavior • View dying as temporary because they have no concept of time and because the dead person may still have attributes of the living (sleeping, eating, breathing)
School-age children (6 to 12 years)	• Start to respond to logical or factual explanations • Begin to have an adult concept of death (inevitable, irreversible, universal), which generally applies to school-age children who are older (9 to 12 years) • Experience fear of the disease process, the death process, the unknown, and loss of control ○ Fear is often displayed through uncooperative behavior. • May be curious about funeral services and what happens to the body after death

AGE	RELEVANT FACTORS
Adolescents (12 to 20 years)	• May have an adult-like concept of death • May have difficulty accepting death because they are discovering who they are, establishing an identity, and dealing with issues of puberty • Rely more on their peers rather than the influence of their parents, which may cause the reality of a serious illness to cause adolescents to feel isolated. • May be unable to relate to peers and communicate with their parents • May become more stressed by changes in physical appearance from the medications or illness than the prospect of death • May experience guilt and shame

- Factors that may increase the family's potential for dysfunctional grieving following the death of a child include:

  o Lack of a support system

  o Presence of poor coping skills

  o Association of violence or suicide with the death of the child

  o Sudden and unexpected death of the child

  o Lack of hope or presence of pre-existing mental health issues

Assessment

- Knowledge regarding diagnosis, prognosis, and care

- Perceptions and desires regarding diagnosis, prognosis, and care

- Nutritional status, as well as growth and development patterns

- Activity and energy level of the child

- Parents' wishes regarding the child's end-of-life care

- Presence of a do-not-resuscitate (DNR) order

- Family coping and available support

- The stage of grief the child and family are experiencing

- Symptoms of normal grief, which may include:

  o Feelings of sadness, denial, anxiety, and/or yearning

  o Feelings of guilt and/or anger toward the deceased

  o Somatic reports of chest pain, palpitations, headaches, nausea, changes in sleep patterns, or fatigue

  o Experience of hearing the deceased person's voice

Nursing Interventions

- Care for terminally ill children.

CARE	FOCUS
Hospital care	• The child cannot be managed at home (the family does not want or is not able to provide necessary care, the child requires intensive nursing care).
Home care	• A home care agency nurse provides assessments, treatments, medications, supplies, and equipment under the direction of the health care provider.
Hospice care	• The psychological, spiritual, physical, and social needs of the child and family will be managed. • Family members providing most of the care with support from the hospice team. • Priority is given to pain and symptom control. • Support to the family will continue post death. Family needs will be addressed after death occurs.

- Allow an opportunity for anticipatory grieving, which impacts the way a family will cope with the death of a child.

- Offer primary nursing.

- Offer strategies specific to developmental level.

AGE GROUP	DEVELOPMENTAL APPROACH
Infants and toddlers	• Encourage parents to stay with the child. • Attempt to maintain a normal environment.
Preschoolers	• Encourage parents to stay with the child. • Communicate with the child in honest, simple terms. • Be aware of medical jargon that may frighten the child.
School-age children	• Encourage parents to stay with the child. • Use language that is clear regarding the disease, medications, procedures, and expectations. • Encourage self-care to promote independence and self-esteem. • Allow participation in plans for funeral services.
Adolescents	• Be honest and respectful when communicating. • Encourage self-care to promote independence and self-esteem. • Allow participation in plans for funeral services. • Encourage parents or other family members to stay with the adolescent.

- Palliative Care

  o Consider the child, siblings, and parents as the units of care.

  o Provide an environment that is as close to being like home as possible.

  o Consult with the child and family for desired measures.

  o Respect the family's cultural and religious preferences and rituals.

  o Provide and clarify information and explanations.

  o Encourage physical contact; address feelings; and show concern, empathy, and support.

  o Provide comfort measures (warmth, quiet, noise control, dry linens).

  o Provide adequate nutrition and hydration.

  o Control pain.

    - Give medications on a regular schedule.

    - Treat breakthrough pain.

    - Increase doses as necessary to control pain.

    - Encourage use of relaxation, imagery, and distraction to help manage pain.

- Care for grieving families during the dying process.

  o Provide information to the child and family about the disease, medications, procedures, and expected events.

  o Encourage and support parents to participate in caring for the child.

  o Encourage parents to remain near the child as much as possible.

  o Encourage the child's independence and control as developmentally and physically appropriate.

  o Allow for visitation of family and friends as desired.

  o Emphasize open, honest communication among the child, family, and health care team.

  o Provide support to the child and family with decision-making.

  o Provide opportunities for the child and family to ask questions.

  o Assist the child with completion of unfinished tasks.

  o Assist parents to cope with their feelings and help them to understand the child's behaviors.

  o Use books, movies, art, music, and play therapy to stimulate discussions and provide an outlet for emotions.

  o Provide and encourage professional support and guidance from a trusted member of the health care team.

  o Remain neutral and accepting.

o   Give reassurance that the child is not in pain and that all efforts are being made to maintain comfort and support of the child's life.

o   Recognize and support the individual differences of grieving. Advise families that each member may react differently on any given day.

o   Give families privacy, unlimited time, and opportunities for any cultural or religious rituals. Respect the family's decisions regarding care of the child.

o   Encourage discussion of special memories and people, reading of favorite books, providing favorite toys/objects, physical contact, sibling visits, and continued verbal communication, even if the child seems unconscious.

o   After death, validate the loss.

- The nurse should express his own feelings of loss and sadness to someone who can offer support.

- Issues and decisions to be addressed at the time of death include the following:

  □   Organ and/or tissue donation if applicable

  □   Autopsy

  □   Viewing of the body

  □   Sibling's attendance at the funeral

CHAPTER 11: DEATH AND DYING

 Application Exercises

1. Which of the following nursing interventions is appropriate when working with a school-age child who has a terminal disease?

    A. Give factual explanations of the disease, medications, and procedures.

    B. Perform all care for the child.

    C. Tell the child that everything will be okay.

    D. Reinforce that being in the hospital is not a punishment for her behavior.

2. Match the age group with the expected behavior regarding grieving and death.

_____	Preschoolers	A. Interpret separation from parents as punishment for bad behavior
_____	Toddlers	B. Mirror parent's emotions
_____	School-age children	C. Become more stressed by changes in physical appearance from the medications or illness than from the prospect of death
_____	Adolescents	D. Often display fear through uncooperative behavior

3. Identify interventions that a nurse should use when providing support to a child and family during the dying process.

CHAPTER 11: DEATH AND DYING

 Application Exercises Answer Key

1. Which of the following nursing interventions is appropriate when working with a school-age child who has a terminal disease?

   A. Give factual explanations of the disease, medications, and procedures.

   B. Perform all care for the child.

   C. Tell the child that everything will be okay.

   D. Reinforce that being in the hospital is not a punishment for her behavior.

   School-age children should be given factual information. It is important for the school-age child to maintain some level of participation in self-care to maintain independence and self-esteem. Telling the child that everything will be okay is giving false reassurance and will not help the child develop trust in the caregiver. Preschoolers who think that actions can cause bad things to happen.

   NCLEX® Connection: Psychosocial Integrity, Grief and Loss

2. Match the age group with the expected behavior regarding grieving and death.

A	Preschoolers	A. Interpret separation from parents as punishment for bad behavior
B	Toddlers	B. Mirror parent's emotions
D	School-age children	C. Become more stressed by changes in physical appearance from the medications or illness than from the prospect of death
C	Adolescents	D. Often display fear through uncooperative behavior

   NCLEX® Connection: Psychosocial Integrity, Grief and Loss

3. Identify interventions that a nurse should use when providing support to a child and family during the dying process.

   Establish rapport and develop a therapeutic relationship with the child and family.

   Schedule time for the child and family to have uninterrupted time together.

   Provide factual information and answer questions directly and honestly.

   Make a referral for professional support and counseling if indicated.

   Assess and monitor pain frequently. Ensure that adequate pain management is provided.

   NCLEX® Connection: Psychosocial Integrity, End of Life Care

UNIT 2: NURSING CARE OF CHILDREN WITH SYSTEM DISORDERS

Section: Neurosensory Disorders

- Meningitis and Reye Syndrome
- Seizures
- Head Injury
- Visual and Hearing Impairments

NCLEX® CONNECTIONS

When reviewing the chapters in this section, keep in mind the relevant sections of the NCLEX® outline, in particular:

CLIENT NEEDS: PHARMACOLOGICAL AND PARENTERAL THERAPIES

Relevant topics/tasks include:

- Adverse Effects/ Contraindications/Side Effects/Interactions
  - Notify the provider of side effects, adverse effects, and contraindications of medications and parenteral therapy.
- Expected Actions/Outcomes
  - Evaluate the therapeutic effect of medications.

CLIENT NEEDS: HEALTH PROMOTION & MAINTENANCE

Relevant topics/tasks include:

- Diagnostic Tests
  - Evaluate the results of diagnostic testing and intervene as needed.
- Potential for Alterations in Body Systems
  - Compare current client data to baseline client data.
- Potential for Complications of Diagnostic Tests/ Treatments/Procedures
  - Use precautions to prevent injury and/ or complications associated with a procedure or diagnosis.

CLIENT NEEDS: PHYSIOLOGICAL ADAPTATION

Relevant topics/tasks include:

- Alterations in Body Systems
  - Provide care to the client who has experienced a seizure.
- Illness Management
  - Evaluate the effectiveness of the treatment regimen for a client with an acute or chronic diagnosis.
- Unexpected Response to Therapies
  - Assess the client for an unexpected adverse response to therapy.

UNIT 2	NURSING CARE OF CHILDREN WITH SYSTEM DISORDERS
Section	Neurosensory Disorders
Chapter 12	Meningitis and Reye Syndrome

Overview

- Meningitis is an inflammation of the meninges, which are the membranes that protect the brain and spinal cord.

- Reye syndrome is a life-threatening disease that leads to multisystem failure.

- Meningitis and Reye syndrome have similar symptoms and are both often preceded by viral infections. Therefore, testing may be necessary to differentiate between the two.

MENINGITIS

Overview

- Viral or aseptic, meningitis usually requires only supportive care for recovery.

- Bacterial, or septic, meningitis is a contagious infection. The prognosis depends on how quickly care is initiated.

Assessment

- Risk Factors

  - Viral Meningitis

    - Viral illnesses (mumps, measles, herpes)

  - Bacterial Meningitis

    - Upper respiratory infections (otitis media, tonsillitis) caused by bacterial agents (*Neisseria meningitides* [meningococcal], *Streptococcus pneumonia* [pneumococcal], *Haemophilus influenzae, Escherichia coli*)

    - Immunosuppression

    - Injuries that provide direct access to cerebrospinal fluid (skull fracture, penetrating head wound)

    - Overcrowded living conditions

- Subjective Data
  - The child may report photophobia or headache.
  - Parents may report that the child is irritable, has vomited, and is drowsy.
- Objective Data
  - Physical Assessment Findings
    - Newborns
      - No illness is present at birth, but it progresses within a few days.
      - Clinical signs may be vague and difficult to diagnose.
        - ‣ Poor muscle tone, weak cry, and poor feeding
        - ‣ Fever or hypothermia
      - Nuchal rigidity is not usually present.
      - Bulging fontanels are a late sign.
    - 2 months to 2 years
      - Seizures with a high-pitched cry
      - Fever and irritability
      - Bulging fontanels
      - Possible nuchal rigidity
      - Poor feeding
      - Vomiting
      - Brudzinski's and Kernig's signs do not assist with the diagnosis.
    - 2 years through adolescence
      - Seizures (often initial sign)
      - Nuchal rigidity
      - Positive Brudzinski's sign (flexion of extremities occurring with deliberate flexion of the child's neck)
      - Positive Kernig's sign (resistance to extension of the child's leg from a flexed position)

View Media Supplement:
- Brudzinski's Sign (Image)
- Kernig's Sign (Image)

- Fever and chills
- Headache
- Vomiting
- Photophobia

- □ Irritability and restlessness that may progress to drowsiness, delirium, stupor, and coma

- □ Petechia or purpuric type rash (seen with meningococcal infection)

- □ Involvement of joints (seen with meningococcal and *Haemophilus influenza*)

- □ Chronic draining ear (seen with pneumococcal infection)

○ Laboratory Tests

- ■ Perform a blood culture and sensitivity test to identify an appropriate broad-spectrum antibiotic.

- ■ Complete blood counts should be taken.

- ■ Cerebrospinal fluid (CSF) should be collected.

  - □ Results indicative of meningitis

    - ▸ CSF that appears cloudy (bacterial) or clear (viral)

    - ▸ Elevated WBC

    - ▸ Elevated protein levels

    - ▸ Decreased glucose (bacterial)

    - ▸ Elevated CSF pressure

○ Diagnostic Procedures

- ■ CSF analysis

  - □ This is the best diagnostic test for meningitis.

  - □ The collection of CSF with a lumbar puncture (performed by a health care provider)

  - □ Nursing Actions

    - ▸ Have the child empty his bladder if appropriate.

    - ▸ Place the child in the fetal position and assist in maintaining the position. Older children may be placed in the sitting position.

    - ▸ Administer sedatives as prescribed.

    - ▸ Apply a eutectic mixture of local anesthetics (EMLA), which contains equal quantities of lidocaine and prilocaine, over the area between L3 and L5 60 min prior to the procedure.

    - ▸ Appropriately label the three test tubes of CSF and deliver them to the laboratory.

    - ▸ Monitor the site for hematoma and/or infection.

  - □ Client Education

    - ▸ Encouage the child to remain in bed for 4 to 8 hr in a flat position to prevent leakage and a resulting spinal headache. This may not be possible for infants, toddlers, or preschoolers.

- CT scan or MRI
    - These may be performed to identify increased intracranial pressure (ICP) and/or an abscess.
    - Nursing Actions
        - Assist with positioning.
        - Administer sedatives as prescribed.

Collaborative Care

- Nursing Care

    - The presence of petechia or a purpuric-type rash requires immediate medical attention.

    - Isolate the child as soon as meningitis is suspected.

    - Initiate and maintain isolation precautions (droplet precautions) per facility protocol. This requires a private room or a room with cohorts, the wearing of a surgical mask within 3 feet of the child, appropriate hand hygiene, and the use of designated equipment, such as blood pressure cuff and thermometer. Continue for 24 hr after the first antibiotic has been administered.

    - Continue frequent monitoring of vital signs, urine output, fluid status, pain level, neurologic status, and head circumference (for infants).

    - Initiate IV fluids to maintain hydration. Continue fluid and electrolyte replacement as indicated by laboratory values.

    - Maintain NPO status if the child has a decreased level of consciousness. As the child's condition improves, advance to clear liquids and then to a diet that the child can tolerate.

    - Decrease environmental stimuli.
        - Provide for a quiet environment.
        - Minimize the child's exposure to bright light (natural and electric).

    - Provide comfort.
        - Keep the child's room cool.
        - Position the child without a pillow and slightly elevate the head of the bed. The child may prefer a side-lying position to take pressure off his neck.

    - Maintain safety (keep the bed in a low position, take seizure precautions).

    - Keep the family informed of the child's condition.

- Medications
  - Antibiotics
    - Administer for bacterial infections via an IV route. Length of therapy is determined by the child's condition and CSF results (normal blood glucose levels, negative culture). Therapy may last as long as 10 days.
    - Nursing Considerations
      - Assess for allergies.
    - Client Education
      - Provide support for the child and family.
      - Educate the family about the need to complete the entire course of medication.
  - Corticosteroids – Dexamethasone (Decadron)
    - Administer to prevent neurologic complications.
    - Nursing Considerations
      - Assess for effectiveness of medication.
    - Client Education
      - Provide support for the child and family.
      - Educate on the administration of the medication and side effects that may occur.
  - Anticonvulsants – Phenytoin (Dilantin)
    - Prophylaxis for seizures
    - Nursing Considerations
      - Assess for effectiveness of the medication.
      - Monitor therapeutic medication levels.
    - Client Education
      - Educate about the need to administer the medication on schedule.
  - Analgesics
    - Nonopioids should be used to avoid masking changes in the level of consciousness.
    - Nursing Considerations
      - Monitor respiratory status.
      - Monitor level of consciousness.
    - Client Education
      - Provide support for the child and family.

- Care After Discharge

  - Client Education

    - Early and complete treatment should be provided for upper respiratory infections.

    - Encourage parents to maintain appropriate immunizations for the child. Children should receive the *Haemophilus influenza* Type B vaccine (Hib) and the pneumococcal conjugate vaccine (PCV) at 2, 4, and 6 months of age, then again between 12 and 15 months of age.

- Client Outcomes

  - The child will experience minimal neurologic deficits.

Complications

- Increased ICP

  - Could lead to brain damage

  - Nursing Actions

    - Monitor for signs of increased intracranial pressure.

      - Infants – Bulging or tense fontanels, increased head circumference, high-pitched cry, distended scalp veins, irritability, bradycardia, and respiratory changes

      - Children – Increased irritability, headache, nausea, vomiting, diplopia, seizures, bradycardia, and respiratory changes

    - Provide interventions to reduce ICP (positioning, avoidance of coughing, straining, and bright lights, environmental stimuli).

REYE SYNDROME

Overview

- Reye syndrome primarily affects the liver and brain, causing:

  - Liver dysfunction

    - Bleeding and poor blood clotting

  - Cerebral edema (with increased intracranial pressure).

    - Lethargy progressing to coma

    - Potential for cerebral herniation

  - Hypoglycemia

  - Shock

- Reye syndrome has been mistaken for a variety of other disorders, including encephalitis, meningitis, poisoning, sudden infant death syndrome (SIDS), diabetes mellitus, and psychiatric illness.

- The prognosis for Reye syndrome is best with early recognition and treatment.

Assessment

- Risk Factors

  o The cause of Reye syndrome is unknown. However, research has revealed an association between using aspirin (salicylate) products for treating viral infections and the development of Reye syndrome.

  o Peak incidence occurs in January, February, and March. The symptoms most often appear at the end of a viral illness (viral upper respiratory infection, varicella) but may occur earlier in the illness.

- Subjective Data

  o History of recent viral illness or recent use of aspirin.

- Objective Data

  o Physical Assessment Findings

    ▪ Reye syndrome presents in five clinical stages. Each stage contains intensified signs and symptoms of the previous stage.

STAGE	MANIFESTATIONS
I	• Lethargy • Vomiting • Anorexia • Early liver dysfunction • Brisk pupillary reaction • Ability to follow commands
II	• Confusion/disorientation/delirium • Combativeness • Hyperventilation • Hyperactive reflexes • Sluggish pupillary response • Response to painful stimuli
III	• Coma • Seizures • Flexion rigidity

STAGE	MANIFESTATIONS
IV	• Deeper coma • Extension rigidity • Fixed, large pupils, and loss of corneal reflexes • Brainstem dysfunction • Minimal liver dysfunction
V	• Hypotonia • Seizures • Respiratory arrest • Absence of liver dysfunction

- Laboratory Tests

  - Liver enzymes (alanine aminotransferase [ALT], aspartate aminotransferase [AST]) – Elevated

  - Serum ammonia level – Elevated

  - Serum electrolytes – altered due to cerebral edema and liver changes

  - Serum blood glucose – Hypoglycemia

  - CBC may indicate low Hgb, Hct, and platelets.

  - Coagulation times may be extended.

- Diagnostic Procedures

  - Liver biopsy

    - A liver biopsy consists of taking a piece of liver tissue, via a large-bore needle, and sending this tissue to the pathology department. Care should be taken to ensure that the child's clotting studies are within normal limits prior to the procedure.

    - Nursing Actions

      ▸ Maintain NPO status prior to the procedure.

      ▸ Monitor for hemorrhage postprocedure.

      ▸ Assess vital signs frequently postprocedure.

    - Client Education

      ▸ Encourage the parents to limit the child's postprocedure activities to decrease the risk of hemorrhage.

  - Cerebrospinal fluid (CSF) analysis

    - A lumbar puncture should be performed to collect CSF and rule out meningitis as a cause of symptoms (performed by a provider, usually a physician)

Collaborative Care

- Nursing Care

    o Maintain hydration.

        ■ Administer IV fluids as prescribed.

        ■ Maintain accurate I&O.

        ■ Insert indwelling urinary catheter as ordered.

    o Position the child.

        ■ Avoid extreme flexion, extension, or rotation.

        ■ Maintain the head in a midline neutral position.

        ■ Keep the head of the bed elevated 30°.

    o Monitor appropriateness of coagulation.

        ■ Note unexplained or prolonged bleeding.

        ■ Apply pressure after procedures.

        ■ Prepare to administer vitamin K.

    o Monitor pain status and response to painful stimuli. Administer pain medications when appropriate.

    o Insert a nasogastric tube as ordered.

    o Assist with intubation and maintain a ventilator if required.

    o Take seizure precautions.

    o Keep the family informed of the child's status.

    o Provide private time for the family to be with the child if death is imminent.

    o Contact support for the family.

- Medications

    o Osmotic diuretic – Mannitol (Osmitrol)

        ■ To decrease cerebral swelling, administer as prescribed.

        ■ Nursing Considerations

            □ Monitor the child for increased intracranial pressure.

    o Insulin

        ■ Administer to increase glucose metabolism.

        ■ Nursing Considerations

            □ Monitor blood glucose levels prior to insulin administration and periodically.

- Client Education
  - Provide support for the child.

- Interdisciplinary Care

  - The child who has neurologic deficits post-Reye syndrome will require interventions from other members of the health care team. Occupational therapy and physical therapy may be needed to help the child adapt to neurologic deficits. A dietician may also be needed to assist in maintaining adequate nutrition.

- Care After Discharge

  - Client Education

    - Teach parents to avoid giving salicylates for pain or fever in children.

    - Teach parents to read labels of over-the-counter medications to check for the presence of salicylates.

- Client Outcomes

  - The child will experience minimal neurologic deficits.

Complications

- Neurologic Sequelae

  - Neurologic complications may include speech and/or hearing impairment, cerebral palsy, paralysis, and/or developmental delays based on the length and severity of illness.

  - Nursing Actions

    - Explain the child's condition and needs to the family.

  - Client Education

    - Help the family identify support services for home care.

- Death

  - Nursing Actions

    - Support the family in grief.

    - Contact spiritual support as appropriate.

CHAPTER 12: MENINGITIS AND REYE SYNDROME

(A) Application Exercises

Scenario: A mother brings her 3-year-old child to the emergency department. Four days ago, the child was diagnosed with otitis media. Now the mother says her child is lethargic and cries constantly when held. The child vomited 3 hr ago.

1. What interventions should the nurse anticipate after assessing the child?

2. When performing the initial assessment, the nurse found that when the child's head was flexed, his knees and hips also flexed. The nurse should document this finding as

    A. Kernig's sign.

    B. Nuchal rigidity.

    C. Brudzinski's sign.

    D. Cushing's reflex.

3. The child grimaces when the light is on in the room. Which of the following interventions should the nurse implement to minimize photophobia?

    A. Avoid using the television.

    B. Keep the volume down on the radio.

    C. Bandage both eyes temporarily.

    D. Elevate the head of the bed.

4. Which of the following vaccines should a nurse administer to protect an infant from bacterial meningitis? (Select all that apply.)

    _____ Inactivated polio vaccine (IPV)

    _____ Pneumococcal conjugate vaccine (PVC)

    _____ Diphtheria and tetanus toxoids and acellular pertussis vaccine (DTaP)

    _____ *Haemophilus influenzae* type B vaccine (Hib)

    _____ Trivalent inactivated influenza vaccine (TIV)

5. A child is admitted with possible Reye syndrome. The nurse should recognize that which of the following factors in the child's health history supports this diagnosis?

    A. Recent history of urinary tract infection

    B. Recent history of bacterial otitis media

    C. Recent episode of gastroenteritis

    D. Recent episode of *Haemophilus influenzae* meningitis

6. Which of the following manifestations are indicative of stage II of Reye syndrome? (Select all that apply.)

    _____   Coma

    _____   Fixed pupils

    _____   Hyperventilation

    _____   Combativeness

    _____   Hyperactive deep-tendon reflexes

CHAPTER 12: MENINGITIS AND REYE SYNDROME

 Application Exercises Answer Key

Scenario: A mother brings her 3-year-old child to the emergency department. Four days ago, the child was diagnosed with otitis media. Now the mother says her child is lethargic and cries constantly when held. The child vomited 3 hr ago.

1. What interventions should the nurse anticipate after assessing the child?

> **After the assessment, the nurse should suspect meningitis; therefore, droplet isolation precautions should be initiated by placing the child in a private room, wearing a mask when within 3 feet of the child, performing frequent hand hygiene, and designating personal equipment for the child. The nurse should also be prepared to initiate IV access and to assist with performance of a lumbar puncture.**

 NCLEX® Connection: Safety and Infection Control, Standard/Transmission-Based/Other Precautions

2. When performing the initial assessment, the nurse found that when the child's head was flexed, his knees and hips also flexed. The nurse should document this finding as

> A. Kernig's sign.
>
> B. Nuchal rigidity.
>
> **C. Brudzinski's sign.**
>
> D. Cushing's reflex.

> **Brudzinski's sign is the flexion of the hips and knees when the child's head is purposefully flexed. Kernig's sign is the pain associated with extending the knee when the hip is flexed. Nuchal rigidity is resistance of the neck to passive range of motion. Cushing's reflex is a late neurologic sign of increased intracranial pressure in which there is increased blood pressure with widened pulse pressure and bradycardia.**

NCLEX® Connection: Reduction of Risk Potential, System Specific Assessment

3. The child grimaces when the light is on in the room. Which of the following interventions should the nurse implement to minimize photophobia?

A. Avoid using the television.

B. Keep the volume down on the radio.

C. Bandage both eyes temporarily.

D. Elevate the head of the bed.

Photophobia is an abnormal sensitivity to light. Keeping the television off will minimize light exposure. Regulating the volume of sounds will not affect light sensitivity. Bandaging both eyes is not an appropriate intervention for a 3-year-old child. Elevating the head of the bed is an effective comfort measure for the child with meningitis, but it has no effect on photophobia.

 NCLEX® Connection: Physiological Adaptation, Infectious Disease

4. Which of the following vaccines should a nurse administer to protect an infant from bacterial meningitis? (Select all that apply.)

	Inactivated polio vaccine (IPV)
X	**Pneumococcal conjugate vaccine (PVC)**
	Diphtheria and tetanus toxoids and acellular pertussis vaccine (DTaP)
X	*Haemophilus influenzae* **type B vaccine (Hib)**
	Trivalent inactivated influenza vaccine (TIV)

Immunizing infants beginning at 2 months of age with Hib and PCV protects them from common types of bacterial meningitis. IPV, DTaP, and TIV vaccines will not prevent bacterial meningitis.

 NCLEX® Connection: Health Promotion and Maintenance, Health Promotion/Disease Prevention

5. A child is admitted with possible Reye syndrome. The nurse should recognize that which of the following factors in the child's health history supports this diagnosis?

A. Recent history of urinary tract infection

B. Recent history of bacterial otitis media

C. Recent episode of gastroenteritis

D. Recent episode of *Haemophilus influenzae* meningitis

Gastroenteritis is the only recent illness mentioned that is related to a viral episode. The other choices are caused by bacterial infections.

 NCLEX® Connection: Physiological Adaptation, Infectious Disease

6. Which of the following manifestations are indicative of stage II of Reye syndrome? (Select all that apply.)

_____ Coma

_____ Fixed pupils

__X__ **Hyperventilation**

__X__ **Combativeness**

__X__ **Hyperactive deep-tendon reflexes**

Stage II symptoms include confusion/disorientation/delirium, combativeness, hyperventilation, hyperactive reflexes, sluggish pupillary response, and an ability to respond to painful stimuli. Coma and fixed pupils are symptoms in later stages of Reye syndrome.

(N) NCLEX® Connection: Physiological Adaptation, Infectious Disease

UNIT 2	NURSING CARE OF CHILDREN WITH SYSTEM DISORDERS
Section	Neurosensory Disorders

Chapter 13	Seizures

Overview

- Seizures are abrupt, abnormal, excessive, and uncontrolled electrical discharges of neurons within the brain that may cause alterations in level of consciousness and/or changes in motor and sensory abilities and/or behavior. Seizures can be abrupt in nature or slow and insidious in onset.

- Epilepsy is the term used to define the medical disorder characterized by chronic, recurring abnormal brain electrical activity.

- The three major categories of seizures include generalized, partial (focal/local), and unclassified (idiopathic).

Assessment

- Risk Factors

    o Genetic predisposition

    o Acute febrile state, particularly among infants and children under the age of 2

    o Head trauma

    o Cerebral edema

    o Abrupt cessation of antiepileptic medications (AEDs)

    o Infection

    o Metabolic disorders, such as hypoglycemia or hyperglycemia

    o Exposure to toxins, such as lead and insecticides

    o Brain tumor

    o Hypoxia

    o Acute drug and alcohol withdrawal

    o Fluid and electrolyte imbalances

    o Triggering factors

        ▪ Increased physical activity

        ▪ Excessive stress

- Overwhelming fatigue
- Acute alcohol ingestion
- Exposure to flashing lights
- Specific substances such as alcohol, caffeine, cocaine, aerosols, and glue products

- Subjective and Objective Data

  o Generalized

  - Tonic-clonic seizure (previously referred to as grand mal)
    - It may begin with an aura (alteration in vision, smell, or emotional feeling).
    - It begins with a 10 to 20 second tonic episode (stiffening of muscles) and loss of consciousness.
    - A 1 to 2 min clonic episode (rhythmic jerking of the extremities) follows a tonic episode.
    - Breathing may stop during the tonic phase and become irregular during the clonic phase.
    - Cyanosis may accompany breathing irregularities.
    - Biting of the cheek or tongue may occur during the clonic phase.
    - Incontinence may also accompany the seizure.
    - A period of confusion and sleepiness follows the seizure during the postictal phase.

  - Tonic seizure
    - Only the tonic phase is experienced.
    - It usually last only a few seconds.
    - Loss of conscious does not occur.
    - Tonic seizures are much less common than tonic-clonic seizures.

  - Clonic seizure
    - Only the clonic phase is experienced.
    - Fatigue does not usually follow the seizure.
    - Clonic seizures are much less common than tonic-clonic seizures.

  - Absence seizure
    - Absence seizures are most common in children.
    - It consists of a loss of consciousness that lasts seconds.
    - Blank staring is associated with this type of seizure.
    - Baseline neurologic function is resumed after the seizure, with no apparent sequela.

- Myoclonic seizure
  - It consists of brief jerking or stiffening of the extremities.
  - It may be symmetric or asymmetric.
  - It lasts for seconds.
- Atonic or akinetic seizure
  - Muscle tone is lost for a few seconds.
  - A period of confusion follows.
  - Loss of muscle tone frequently results in falling.
- Partial (focal/local)
  - Complex partial seizure
    - It has associated automatisms (behaviors that the child is unaware of, such as lip smacking or picking at clothes).
    - A loss of consciousness that lasts for several minutes occurs.
    - Amnesia may occur immediately prior to and after the seizure.
  - Simple partial seizure
    - Consciousness is maintained throughout the event.
    - Seizure activity may consist of unusual sensations, a sense of déjà vu, autonomic abnormalities (changes in heart rate and abnormal flushing, unilateral abnormal extremity movements, pain, offensive smell).
- Unclassified (idiopathic)
  - These seizures do not fit into other categories; they account for half of all seizure activity and occur for no known reason.
- Laboratory Tests
  - Laboratory tests should include alcohol and illicit drug levels and screens for the presence of excessive toxins, if suspected. In addition, cerebrospinal fluid may be obtained for analysis.
- Diagnostic Procedures
  - Electroencephalogram (EEG)
    - An EEG records electrical activity and may identify the origin of seizure activity.
    - Nursing Actions
      - Administer sedatives as prescribed.
      - Assist with positioning.

□ Client Education

▸ Abstain from caffeine for several hours prior to the procedure.

▸ Wash hair before (no oils or sprays) and after (to remove electrode glue) the procedure.

▸ Inform the child that he may be asked to take deep breaths and/or exposed to flashes of light during the procedure.

▸ If prescribed, instruct parent to withhold sleep prior to test.

▷ Inform the child that he may be allowed to sleep during the test. Sleep may be withheld prior to test and may be induced during the test.

▸ Inform the child that the test will not be painful.

■ Magnetic resonance imaging (MRI), CT imaging/computed axial tomography (CAT) scan, positron emission tomography (PET) scan, and skull x-rays may all be used to identify or rule out potential causes of seizures.

Collaborative Care

- Nursing Care

  o During a seizure

    ■ Protect the child from injury (move furniture away, hold head in lap if on the floor).

    ■ Position the child to provide a patent airway.

    ■ Be prepared to suction oral secretions.

    ■ Turn the child to the side (decreases risk of aspiration).

    ■ Loosen restrictive clothing.

    ■ Do not attempt to restrain the child.

    ■ Do not attempt to open the jaw or insert an airway during seizure activity (this may damage teeth, lips, or tongue). Do not use padded tongue blades.

  o Post Seizure

    ■ Maintain the child in a side-lying position to prevent aspiration and to facilitate drainage of oral secretions.

    ■ Check vital signs.

    ■ Assess for injuries

    ■ Perform neurologic checks.

    ■ Allow the child to rest if necessary.

    ■ Reorient and calm the child (she may be agitated or confused).

    ■ Institute seizure precautions, including placing the bed in the lowest position and padding the side rails to prevent future injury.

- Encourage the child to describe the period before, during, and after the seizure activity.

- Determine if the child experienced an aura, which may indicate the origin of seizure in the brain.

- Try to determine the possible trigger, such as fatigue or stress.

- Document the onset and duration of seizure and client findings/observations prior to, during, and following the seizure (level of consciousness, apnea, cyanosis, motor activity, incontinence).

- Medications

  ○ Antiepileptic drugs (AEDs) – Diazepam (Valium), phenytoin (Dilantin), carbamazepine (Tegretol), valproic acid (Depakene) and fosphenytoin sodium (Cerebyx)

    - Seizure control

    - Nursing Considerations

      □ Monitor therapeutic serum medication levels.

    - Client Education

      □ Medications should be taken at the same time every day to enhance effectiveness.

      □ Be aware of medication and food interactions that are specific to each medication.

- Interdisciplinary Care

  ○ The school nurse should be involved in providing for the child's safety in the school setting. This may include implementation of an individualized education plan or another specialized program.

- Surgical Interventions

  ○ Vagal nerve stimulator

    - This procedure is performed under general anesthesia.

    - The device is implanted into the left chest wall. It is connected to an electrode that is placed at the left vagus nerve. The device is then programmed to administer intermittent vagal nerve stimulation at a rate specific to the child's needs.

    - In addition to routine stimulation, the child may initiate vagal nerve stimulation by holding a magnet over the implantable device at the onset of seizure activity. This will either abort the seizure or lessen its severity.

    - Client Education

      □ Educate the child/family about the importance of periodic laboratory testing to monitor AED levels.

      □ Encourage medication adherence.

□ Inform the child about possible medication interactions (decreased effectiveness of oral contraceptives).

□ Encourage the child to wear a medical alert bracelet or necklace at all times.

□ Refer the family to the state's Department of Motor Vehicles to determine laws regarding driving for clients with seizure disorders.

- Client Outcomes

  ○ The child will experience a decreased incidence of seizures.

  ○ The child will be compliant with the medication regimen.

Complications

- Status epilepticus

  ○ Status epilepticus is prolonged seizure activity that lasts longer than 30 min or continuous seizure activity in which the child does not enter a postictal phase. This acute condition requires immediate treatment to prevent loss of brain function, which may become permanent.

  ○ Nursing Actions

    ▪ Maintain airway, provide oxygen, establish IV access, perform ECG monitoring, and monitor pulse oximetry and ABG results.

    ▪ As prescribed, administer a loading dose of diazepam (Valium) or lorazepam (Ativan) followed by a continuous infusion of phenytoin (Dilantin) or fosphenytoin sodium (Cerebyx).

  ○ Client Education

    ▪ Provide support for the family.

CHAPTER 13: SEIZURES

 Application Exercises

1. A child is admitted for a surgical procedure. The child has a seizure disorder and says that he is feeling "odd." The parent says that he thinks the child is about to have a seizure. Which of the following nursing interventions should be implemented for this child? (Select all that apply.)

_____ Provide privacy.

_____ Ease the child to the floor if standing.

_____ Move furniture away from the child.

_____ Loosen the child's clothing.

_____ Insert a padded tongue blade.

_____ Restrain the child.

2. Which of the following is the priority intervention a nurse should take when caring for a child who just experienced a generalized seizure?

A. Keep the child in a side-lying position.

B. Take the child's vital signs.

C. Reorient the child to the environment.

D. Check the child for injuries.

3. A nurse is providing teaching regarding an electroencephalogram (EEG) that is scheduled for the next day. Which of the following instructions should the nurse provide to the parents?

A. "Be sure your child does not drink beverages with caffeine on the morning of the procedure."

B. "Do not wash your child's hair the night before the procedure."

C. "Withhold all fluid and foods the morning of the procedure."

D. "Give your child an analgesic the night before the procedure."

CHAPTER 13: SEIZURES

 Application Exercises Answer Key

1. A child is admitted for a surgical procedure. The child has a seizure disorder and says that he is feeling "odd." The parent says that he thinks the child is about to have a seizure. Which of the following nursing interventions should be implemented for this child? (Select all that apply.)

__X__	**Provide privacy.**
__X__	**Ease the child to the floor if standing.**
__X__	**Move furniture away from the child.**
__X__	**Loosen the child's clothing.**
_____	Insert a padded tongue blade.
_____	Restrain the child.

Privacy should be afforded the child if possible. The child should then be eased to the floor to prevent falling. If there is any furniture close by, it should be moved away from the child to prevent injury. The child's clothing should be loosened. To prevent injury, nothing should be placed in the child's mouth, and the child should not be restrained during a seizure.

 NCLEX® Connection: Safety and Infection Control, Injury Prevention

2. Which of the following is the priority intervention a nurse should take when caring for a child who just experienced a generalized seizure?

A. Keep the child in a side-lying position.

B. Take the child's vital signs.

C. Reorient the child to the environment.

D. Check the child for injuries.

The greatest risk for the child is aspiration. Therefore, the priority intervention during the postictal phase is to keep the child in a side-lying position so secretions can drain from the mouth. The other interventions are important, but they are not the priority at this time.

 NCLEX® Connection: Physiological Adaptation, Medical Emergencies

3. A nurse is providing teaching regarding an electroencephalogram (EEG) that is scheduled for the next day. Which of the following instructions should the nurse provide to the parents?

   A. "Be sure your child does not drink beverages with caffeine on the morning of the procedure."

   B. "Do not wash your child's hair the night before the procedure."

   C. "Withhold all fluid and foods the morning of the procedure."

   D. "Give your child an analgesic the night before the procedure."

   Products that contain caffeine should be avoided for several hours prior to the EEG, but decaffeinated products and foods may be consumed. Hair should be washed prior to the procedure. The test will not be painful, so analgesia is not necessary

   (N) NCLEX® Connection: Reduction of Risk Potential, Therapeutic Procedures

UNIT 2	NURSING CARE OF CHILDREN WITH SYSTEM DISORDERS
Section	Neurosensory Disorders
Chapter 14	Head Injury

Overview

- Head injuries can be classified as open (skull integrity is compromised – penetrating trauma) or closed (skull integrity is maintained – blunt trauma). Head injuries are also classified as mild, moderate, or severe, depending upon Glasgow Coma Scale (GCS) ratings and length of loss of consciousness.

- Open head injuries pose a high risk for infection.

- Skull fractures are often accompanied by brain injury. Damage to brain tissue may be the result of decreased oxygen supply, direct impact from the skull fracture, or an instrument that caused the trauma. The glucose levels in the brain are negatively affected, resulting in an alteration in neurologic synaptic ability.

- Head injuries may or may not be associated with hemorrhage (epidural, subdural, and intracerebral). Cerebrospinal fluid leakage is also possible. Any collection of fluid or foreign object that occupies space within the confines of the skull poses a risk for cerebral edema, cerebral hypoxia, and brain herniation.

- Cervical spine injury should always be suspected when head injury occurs and must be ruled out prior to removing any devices used to stabilize the cervical spine.

Health Promotion and Disease Prevention

- Wear helmets when skate boarding, riding a bike or motorcycle, skiing, playing football, and participating in any other sport that may lead to head injury. Helmets that are appropriate for the sport should be worn.

- Wear seat belts when driving or riding in a car.

- Avoid dangerous activities (riding a bicycle at night without a light, driving faster than the speed limit or while under the influence of alcohol or drugs).

Assessment

- Risk Factors

  o Lack of supervision

  o Poor/absent safety practices

  o Improper use of safety devices (helmets, seat belts)

- Subjective Data

  o History of events leading up to the injury, including any reports of dizziness, headache, diplopia, and/or vomiting

  o Amnesia (loss of memory) before or after injury

  o Alcohol or drug ingestion

- Objective Data

  o Physical Assessment Findings

    ▪ Loss of consciousness – The length of time the client is unconscious is significant.

    ▪ Signs of increased intracranial pressure (ICP) and brainstem involvement

      □ Severe headache

      □ Deteriorating level of consciousness, restlessness, irritability, and agitation

      □ Dilated and fixed, constricted and fixed, slow to react, or nonreactive pupils

      □ Alteration in breathing pattern, such as deep, fast, and intermittent gasping respirations

      □ Abnormal posturing

        ▸ Decorticate (dysfunction of the cerebral cortex) – Demonstrates the arms, wrists, and fingers flexed and bent inward onto the chest and the legs extended and adducted

        ▸ Decerebrate (dysfunction at the midbrain) – Demonstrates a backward arching of the head and arms with legs rigidly extended and toes pointing downward

        (M) View Media Supplement:
        - Decorticate Posturing (Image)
        - Decerebrate Posturing (Image)

        ▸ Flaccidity – Demonstrates no muscle tone

      □ A child who is comatose and has asymmetric pupils or one pupil that is dilated and nonreactive is a medical emergency.

      □ Cushing's reflex is a late sign characterized by severe hypertension with widening pulse pressure (systolic – diastolic) and bradycardia.

    ▪ Cerebrospinal fluid (CSF) leakage from the nose and ears

      □ A sample of fluid that makes a yellow stain (halo sign) surrounded by blood on a paper towel and tests positive for glucose indicates CSF leakage.

- Seizure activity
- Other signs
  - Difficulty waking up
  - Odd behavior
  - Visual disturbances, such as double or blurred vision
  - Uncoordinated movements and difficulty walking
  - Bulging fontanels and inconsolable crying (in infants)
- Glasgow Coma Scale (GCS)
  - GCS scores of 8 or less are associated with severe head injury and coma.
  - GCS scores between 9 and 12 indicate moderate head injury.
  - GCS scores of 13 or greater reflect minor head trauma.
  - Laboratory Tests
    - Arterial blood gases (ABGs)
    - Alcohol level and drug screen
    - CBC with differential
  - Diagnostic Procedures
    - Cervical spine films
      - Rule out cervical spine injury.
    - Computerized tomography (CT) and/or magnetic resonance imaging (MRI) of head and/or neck
      - May be performed with and without contrast if indicated
    - Measurement of ICP
      - The expected reference range is 10 to 15 mm Hg.
      - Client Education
        - Provide support to the child and family.

Collaborative Care

- Nursing Care
  - Ensure the child's spine is stabilized until spinal cord injury is ruled out.
  - Monitor the child's vital signs, level of consciousness, pupils, ICP, motor activity, sensory perception, and verbal responses at frequent intervals. Use the Glasgow Coma Scale as indicated.
  - Maintain a patent airway. Provide mechanical ventilation as indicated.
  - Administer oxygen as indicated to maintain an oxygen saturation level greater than 95%.

- ○ Hyperventilate the child to keep the $PaCO_2$ between 30 and 35 mm Hg (this reduces cerebral blood flow).

- ○ Maintain c-spine stability if indicated.

- ○ Implement actions that will decrease ICP.

  - ▪ Keep the head of the bed elevated to 30°, which will also promote venous drainage.

  - ▪ Avoid extreme flexion, extension, or rotation of the head and maintain in midline neutral position.

  - ▪ Keep the child's body in alignment, avoiding hip flexion/extension.

  - ▪ Minimize endotracheal or oral suctioning.

  - ▪ Instruct the child to avoid coughing and blowing her nose, because these activities increase ICP.

- ○ Restrain extremities as indicated to prevent pulling on tubes.

- ○ Implement measures to prevent complications of immobility (turn every 2 hr, maintain footboard and splints). Specialty beds may be used.

- ○ Insert and maintain an indwelling urinary catheter.

- ○ Administer stool softener to prevent straining (Valsalva maneuver).

- ○ Report to the provider the presence of CSF from nose or ears.

- ○ Provide a calm, restful environment (limit visitors, minimize noise).

- ○ Use energy conservation measures. Alternate activities with rest periods.

- ○ Implement seizure precautions.

- ○ Monitor fluid and electrolyte values and osmolarity to detect changes in sodium regulation, the onset of diabetes insipidus, or severe hypovolemia.

- ○ Provide adequate fluids to maintain cerebral perfusion. When a large amount of IV fluids is ordered, monitor the child carefully for excess fluid volume, which may increase ICP.

- ○ Maintain the child's safety (side rails up, padded side rails, call light within reach).

- ○ Provide nutritional support (total parenteral nutrition, enteral nutrition).

- ○ Maintain ongoing communication with the child.

- ○ Instruct the family on effective ways to communicate with the child (touching, talking, assisting with care as appropriate).

- Medications
  - Corticosteroids – Dexamethasone (Decadron) and methylprednisolone (Solu-Medrol)
    - Decrease cerebral edema
    - Nursing Considerations
      - Monitor for signs of infection.
  - Mannitol (Osmitrol)
    - Osmotic diuretic used to treat cerebral edema
    - Nursing Considerations
      - Administer intravenously to treat acute cerebral edema.
      - Insert an indwelling urinary catheter to monitor fluid status and renal function.
  - Phenytoin (Dilantin)
    - Used to prevent or treat seizures that may occur
    - Nursing Considerations
      - Monitor therapeutic medication levels.
      - Check for medication interactions.
  - Analgesics – Morphine sulfate and fentanyl citrate (Sublimaze)
    - Control pain and restlessness.
    - Nursing Considerations
      - Use opioids if the child is receiving ventilation.
      - Avoid the use of opioids due to their CNS depressant effect that will make neurologic assessment difficult.
- Interdisciplinary Care
  - Care for the child who has a head injury should include professionals from other disciplines as indicated. These may include physical, occupational, recreational and/or speech therapists.
  - Social services should be contacted to provide links to social service agencies and schools.
  - Rehabilitation facilities are frequently used to compress the time required to recover from a head injury and support re-emergence into society.

- Surgical Interventions
  - Craniotomy
    - A craniotomy is removal of nonviable brain tissue that allows for expansion and/or removal of epidural or subdural hematomas. It involves drilling a burr hole or creating a bone flap to permit access to the affected area.
    - Nursing Actions
      - Initially, care will focus on the prevention of complications, maximizing cerebral function, and supporting other physiologic systems to include mechanical ventilation and parenteral nutrition.
      - Postoperative treatment will depend upon the neurologic status of the child after surgery.
- Client Outcomes
  - The child will experience minimal neurologic deficits.
  - The child will be able to perform ADLs independently or with assistive devices.
  - The child will be able to ambulate independently or with assistive devices.

Complications

- Brain Herniation
  - Downward shift of brain tissue due to cerebral edema
  - Clinical signs include fixed, dilated pupils; deteriorating level of consciousness; Cheyne-Stokes respirations; hemodynamic instability; and abnormal posturing.
  - With treatment, severe neurologic impairment usually persists.
  - Nursing Actions
    - This situation should be prevented before treatment is needed.
    - Close monitoring of the child's vital signs and neurologic status will allow early reporting of changes in the Glasgow Coma Scale score, an increase in the blood pressure, and alterations in respiratory pattern and effort.
    - Early treatment of increased ICP should be implemented.
    - Emergent treatment includes administration of mannitol (Osmitrol) and possible surgical (debulking) treatment.
  - Client Education
    - Family members should be frequently apprised of the health status of the child.
    - The decision to surgically treat brain herniation is made in the presence of a critical situation.
    - Social service workers and/or pastoral personnel may be helpful to support the family while reinforcing the medical situation.

CHAPTER 14: HEAD INJURY

 Application Exercises

1. A nurse is caring for a child who was recently admitted to the emergency department after a motor-vehicle crash. The child is unresponsive, has spontaneous respirations of 22/min, and has a laceration on the forehead that is bleeding. Which of the following is the priority nursing action at this time?

    A. Keep the neck stabilized.

    B. Insert a nasogastric tube.

    C. Obtain vital signs.

    D. Establish IV access.

2. An adolescent client who has a gunshot wound to the head is being admitted to the critical care unit from the emergency department. Which of the following assessment findings are indicative of increased intracranial pressure? (Select all that apply.)

    _____ Report of headache

    _____ Dilated pupils

    _____ Generalized rash

    _____ Deep, fast respirations

    _____ Abdominal pain

3. A child who has a closed head injury is experiencing increased intracranial pressure. Which of the following actions should the nurse take to decrease the potential for raising the intracranial pressure? (Select all that apply.)

    _____ Suction the endotracheal tube every 2 hr.

    _____ Provide hyperventilation.

    _____ Use two pillows to elevate the head.

    _____ Administer a stool softener.

    _____ Maintain body alignment.

CHAPTER 14: HEAD INJURY

 Application Exercises Answer Key

1. A nurse is caring for a child who was recently admitted to the emergency department after a motor-vehicle crash. The child is unresponsive, has spontaneous respirations of 22/min, and has a laceration on the forehead that is bleeding. Which of the following is the priority nursing action at this time?

   A. Keep the neck stabilized.

   B. Insert a nasogastric tube.

   C. Obtain vital signs.

   D. Establish IV access.

   The greatest risk to the child is further cervical injury. Therefore, the priority intervention is for the nurse to keep the neck stabilized until cervical injury can be ruled out. Inserting a nasogastric tube, obtaining vital signs, and establishing IV access are important, but none of them is the priority action.

    NCLEX® Connection: Physiological Adaptation, Medical Emergencies

2. An adolescent client who has a gunshot wound to the head is being admitted to the critical care unit from the emergency department. Which of the following assessment findings are indicative of increased intracranial pressure? (Select all that apply.)

__X__	**Report of headache**
__X__	**Dilated pupils**
_____	Generalized rash
__X__	**Deep, fast respirations**
_____	Abdominal pain

   Headache, dilated (or pinpoint) pupils, and deep, fast respirations are findings related to increased intracranial pressure. Generalized rash and abdominal pain are not signs of increased intracranial pressure.

    NCLEX® Connection: Physiological Adaptation, Medical Emergencies

3. A child who has a closed head injury is experiencing increased intracranial pressure. Which of the following actions should the nurse take to decrease the potential for raising the intracranial pressure? (Select all that apply.)

_____ Suction the endotracheal tube every 2 hr.

__X__ **Provide hyperventilation.**

_____ Use two pillows to elevate the head.

__X__ **Administer a stool softener.**

__X__ **Maintain body alignment.**

Hyperventilating the child will prevent hypercarbia, which can cause vasodilation with a secondary increase in intracranial pressure. Administration of a stool softener will decrease the need to bear down during bowel movements. This is necessary because bearing down can increase intracranial pressure. Maintaining body alignment will prevent increased ICP, and pillows should be avoided because they may cause hyperflexion of the child's neck. Suctioning should not be performed routinely, but on an as needed basis.

NCLEX® Connection: Physiological Adaptation, Medical Emergencies

UNIT 2	NURSING CARE OF CHILDREN WITH SYSTEM DISORDERS
Section	Neurosensory Disorders
Chapter 15	Visual and Hearing Impairments

 Overview

- Sensory impairments in children most commonly affect the eyes and ears. Adequate vision and hearing are necessary for normal growth and development. Therefore, it is important to identify any impairments early in life.

VISUAL IMPAIRMENTS

 Overview

- Common types of visual impairment in children include strabismus (misalignment of eyes), refractive errors (nearsightedness, farsightedness, astigmatism), and amblyopia (decreased acuity in one eye).

- Children may also experience cataracts and glaucoma.

Health Promotion and Disease Prevention

- Encourage the family to work with the child's school to meet educational needs.

Assessment

- Risk Factors

  o Visual impairment may result from prenatal or postnatal infections, retinopathy of prematurity, trauma, or chronic illnesses (such as sickle cell anemia or juvenile rheumatoid arthritis).

- Subjective and Objective Data

  o Visual screening using age-appropriate tools (E Snellen chart used for children who cannot read, alphabet Snellen chart used for children who can read)

     View Media Supplement: Vision and Hearing Screening (Video)

  o Visual acuity of 20/70 to 20/200 is considered partially sighted or school vision.

  o Visual acuity of 20/200 or less and/or a visual field of 20° or less in the better eye is considered legal blindness, which has legal implications for the child's care.

VISUAL IMPAIRMENT	SYMPTOMS
Myopia (nearsightedness)	• Sees close objects clearly, but not objects in the distance • Headaches and dizziness • Eye rubbing • Difficulty reading • Clumsiness (frequently walking into objects) • Poor school performance
Hyperopia (farsightedness)	• Sees distant objects clearly, but not objects that are close • Normal vision until about age 7 • The child is usually able to accommodate.
Astigmatism	• Uneven vision in which only parts of letters on a page may be seen • Headache and vertigo • The appearance of normal vision because tilting the head enables all letters to be seen
Strabismus	• Misaligned eyes • Frowning or squinting • Difficulty seeing print clearly • One eye closed to enable better vision • Head tilted to one side • Headache, dizziness, diplopia, photophobia, and crossed eyes
Amblyopia (lazy eye)	• Reduced visual acuity in one eye

Collaborative Care

- Nursing Care

  o Maintain normal to bright lighting for the child when reading, writing, or participating in any activity that requires close vision.

  o Identify safety hazards.

  o Provide information regarding laser surgery for clients who have myopia, hyperopia, or astigmatism.

  o Inform the child and family about corrective measures.

    ▪ Myopia may be corrected with biconcave lenses that help focus light rays on the retina.

    ▪ Hyperopia may be corrected using convex lenses that help focus light rays on the retina.

    ▪ Astigmatism may be corrected with a special lens to correct refractive errors.

    ▪ Strabismus may be corrected with eye exercises or patching of the strong eye.

- Surgical Interventions

  o Surgical repair of strabismus

    - Increases visual stimulation to the weaker eye

    - Nursing Actions

      □ Provide preoperative teaching using age-appropriate teaching methods, such as puppets or dolls for preschoolers.

      □ Ensure that parents understand procedure.

      □ Apply antibiotic ointment to the affected eye for 2 to 3 days.

    - Client Education

      □ Provide support for the child and family.

      □ Encourage adherence to follow-up visits.

- Client Outcomes

  o The child will maintain visual acuity.

  o The child will be free of injury.

HEARING IMPAIRMENTS

Overview

- Hearing impairments affect the ability to clearly process linguistic sounds and impact speech.

Health Promotion and Disease Prevention

- Help families identify community resources for children who are hearing impaired.

- Teach children and families to avoid further damage and hearing loss.

  o Avoid exposing children to hazardous noise.

  o Encourage children to wear ear protection if loud environmental noise cannot be avoided.

Assessment

- Risk Factors

  o Hearing defects may be caused by a variety of conditions, including anatomic malformation, maternal ingestion of toxic substances during pregnancy, perinatal asphyxia, perinatal infection, chronic ear infection, and/or ototoxic medications.

  o Hearing defects are associated with chronic conditions such as Down syndrome and/or cerebral palsy.

    - Conductive losses involve interference of sound transmission, which may result from otitis media, external ear infection, foreign bodies or excessive ear wax.

- Sensorineural losses involve interference of the transmission along the nerve pathways, which may result from congenital defects or secondary to acquired conditions (infection, ototoxic medication, exposure to constant noise – as in a NICU).
- Central auditory imperception involves all other hearing losses (aphasia, agnosia [inability to interpret sounds]).

Subjective and Objective Data

- Infants
    - Lack of startle reflex
    - Failure to respond to noise
    - Absence of vocalization
    - Delayed verbal development
- Older children
    - Speaking in monotone
    - Need for repeated conversation
    - Speaking loudly for situation

Collaborative Care

- Nursing Care
    - Use an interpreter when working with a child who is hearing impaired. Always remember to talk to the child, not the interpreter.
    - Assess gait/balance for instability.
    - Adjust environment for physiologic symptoms.
    - Identify safety hazards.
    - Use a hearing aid for conductive loss.
- Client Outcomes
    - The child will learn strategies to communicate effectively.
    - The child will remain free of injury.

Complications

- Delayed growth and development
    - Visual and hearing impairments may prevent the child from appropriate speech and motor development. Identifying the impairment early may minimize this.
    - Nursing Actions
        - Encourage self-care and optimal independence.
    - Client Education
        - Assist the family to obtain and access appropriate assistive devices.

CHAPTER 15: VISUAL AND HEARING IMPAIRMENTS

 Application Exercises

1. A school health nurse is performing a vision clinic for kindergarten children. The nurse has set up an area to use the E Snellen vision chart to conduct visual assessments. Why should the nurse use the E Snellen chart to test vision in kindergarten children?

2. While observing a classroom of students, a school nurse makes several observations about one of the children. Which of the following signs are indicative of strabismus? (Select all that apply.)

   _____ Laying the head down beside the work and writing

   _____ Moving the head around over the work and squinting

   _____ Covering one eye while reading

   _____ Positioning the work farther away from the eyes

   _____ Blinking frequently

3. The parents of a 7-year-old child who has strabismus are trying to help their child with school work. Which of the following strategies will assist the child to complete homework? (Select all that apply.)

   _____ Perform the work on a computer.

   _____ Work at a desk, and use a well-placed desk lamp.

   _____ Do the work immediately after school.

   _____ Ensure that distractions are minimal.

   _____ Read the assignment to the child without letting him see the paper.

4. A mother is talking to a community health nurse about her child's hearing. The mother tells the nurse that her child was fine until about 2 days ago when the child said he had constant "tickling" in his right ear and was unable to hear out of it. The nurse suspects conductive hearing loss. Which of the following factors are causes of conductive hearing loss? (Select all that apply.)

   _____ Congenital nerve damage in the inner ear

   _____ A foreign body lodged in the ear canal

   _____ Otitis media

   _____ External ear canal infection

   _____ Exposure to noise from explosion

   _____ Excess ear wax

CHAPTER 15: VISUAL AND HEARING IMPAIRMENTS

 Application Exercises Answer Key

1. A school health nurse is performing a vision clinic for kindergarten children. The nurse has set up an area to use the E Snellen vision chart to conduct visual assessments. Why should the nurse use the E Snellen chart to test vision in kindergarten children?

> **A kindergarten student may or may not be able to distinguish the letters of the alphabet yet. However, all kindergarten students should be able to distinguish directions by pointing after brief instructions from the nurse.**

 NCLEX® Connection: Reduction of Risk Potential, System Specific Assessment

2. While observing a classroom of students, a school nurse makes several observations about one of the children. Which of the following signs are indicative of strabismus? (Select all that apply.)

_____	Laying the head down beside the work and writing
__X__	**Moving the head around over the work and squinting**
__X__	**Covering one eye while reading**
_____	Positioning the work farther away from the eyes
_____	Blinking frequently

> **The child that has strabismus attempts to minimize the double vision that is occurring. The best way to do this is by squinting. This will allow the objects to focus into one another. The child might also cover one eye so that the object is only seen once. Laying the head down beside the work while writing and positioning the work farther away from the eyes have no significance for the child that has strabismus. Frequent blinking is a sign of myopia (nearsightedness).**

 NCLEX® Connection: Reduction of Risk Potential, System Specific Assessment

3. The parents of a 7-year-old child who has strabismus are trying to help their child with school work. Which of the following strategies will assist the child to complete homework? (Select all that apply.)

_____	Perform the work on a computer.
__X__	**Work at a desk, and use a well-placed desk lamp.**
_____	Do the work immediately after school.
__X__	**Ensure that distractions are minimal.**
_____	Read the assignment to the child without letting him see the paper.

> **It is important for the child to have bright lighting and minimal distractions when doing school work. The child needs time to rest his eyes from reading for a period of time after school. Performing the work using a computer may cause eye strain. Reading the assignment might be helpful, but it is important for the child to see the assignment.**

 NCLEX® Connection: Psychosocial Integrity, Alterations in Body System

4. A mother is talking to a community health nurse about her child's hearing. The mother tells the nurse that her child was fine until about 2 days ago when the child said he had constant "tickling" in his right ear and was unable to hear out of it. The nurse suspects conductive hearing loss. Which of the following factors are causes of conductive hearing loss? (Select all that apply.)

_____	Congenital nerve damage in the inner ear
X	**A foreign body lodged in the ear canal**
X	**Otitis media**
X	**External ear canal infection**
_____	Exposure to noise from explosion
X	**Excess ear wax**

A foreign body, a middle ear infection, an external ear canal infection, and excess ear way may all cause conductive hearing loss. Congenital nerve damage in the inner ear and exposure to loud noise are both causes of sensorineural hearing loss.

Ⓝ NCLEX® Connection: Reduction of Risk Potential, System Specific Assessment

UNIT 2: NURSING CARE OF CHILDREN WITH SYSTEM DISORDERS

Section: Respiratory Disorders

- Oxygen and Inhalation Therapy
- Acute and Infectious Respiratory Illnesses
- Asthma
- Cystic Fibrosis

NCLEX® CONNECTIONS

When reviewing the chapters in this section, keep in mind the relevant sections of the NCLEX® outline, in particular:

CLIENT NEEDS: SAFETY AND INFECTION CONTROL	CLIENT NEEDS: REDUCTION OF RISK POTENTIAL	CLIENT NEEDS: PHYSIOLOGICAL ADAPTATION
Relevant topics/tasks include:	Relevant topics/tasks include:	Relevant topics/tasks include:
• Standard Precautions/ Transmission-Based Precautions/Surgical Asepsis	• Diagnostic Tests	• Alterations in Body Systems
○ Understand communicable diseases and the modes of organism transmission.	○ Evaluate the results of diagnostic testing and intervene as needed.	○ Provide pulmonary hygiene.
	• Laboratory Values	• Illness Management
	○ Identify laboratory values for ABGs, BUN, cholesterol, glucose, hematocrit, hemoglobin, glycosylated hemoglobin, platelets, potassium, sodium, WBC, creatinine, PT, PTT and APTT, INR.	○ Manage the care of a client with impaired ventilation/ oxygenation.
	• Potential for Alterations in Body Systems	• Pathophysiology
	○ Identify the client's potential for aspiration.	○ Identify pathophysiology related to an acute or chronic condition.

UNIT 2	NURSING CARE OF CHILDREN WITH SYSTEM DISORDERS
Section	Respiratory Disorders
Chapter 16	Oxygen and Inhalation Therapy

Overview

- Oxygen is used to maintain adequate cellular oxygenation. It is used in the treatment of many acute and chronic respiratory problems (hypoxemia, cystic fibrosis, asthma). Supplemental oxygen may be delivered using a variety of methods, depending on individual circumstances.

- Pulse oximetry is used to monitor the effectiveness of inhalation therapies.

- Common treatment methods for children with respiratory issues (acute or chronic)

  o Nebulized aerosol therapy

  o Metered-dose inhaler (MDI) or dry powder inhaler (DPI)

  o Chest physiotherapy (CPT)

  o Oxygen therapy

  o Suctioning

  o Artificial Airways

Pulse Oximetry

- This is a noninvasive measurement of the oxygen saturation of the blood.

- A pulse oximeter is a device that is operated by a battery or electricity and has a sensor probe that is attached securely to the child's fingertip, toe, bridge of nose, earlobe, or forehead with a clip or band.

- A pulse oximeter measures arterial oxygen saturation (SaO_2) via a wave of infrared light that measures light absorption by oxygenated and deoxygenated hemoglobin in arterial blood. SaO_2 and SpO_2 are used interchangeably.

- Indications

  o Pulse oximetry is used for a variety of situations in which quick assessments of a child's respiratory status are needed.

- ○ Client Presentation
  - Children who present with the following signs and symptoms will benefit from pulse oximetry:
    - □ Increased work of breathing
    - □ Wheezing
    - □ Coughing
    - □ Cyanosis
- Interpretation of Findings
  - ○ The expected reference range for SaO_2 is 95% to 100%. Acceptable levels may range from 91 to 100%. Some illnesses may allow for an SaO_2 of 85% to 89%.
  - ○ Results less than 91% require nursing intervention to assist the child to regain normal SaO_2 levels. An SaO_2 of less than 86% is a life-threatening emergency. The lower the SaO_2 level, the less accurate the value.
- Preprocedure
  - ○ Nursing Actions
    - Perform hand hygiene and provide privacy.
    - Find an appropriate probe site. The probe site must be dry and have adequate circulation.
    - Be sure the child is in a comfortable position and that the arm is supported if a finger is used as a probe site.
- Intraprocedure
  - ○ Nursing Actions
    - Apply the sensor probe to the site.
    - Press the power switch on the oximeter.
    - Note the pulse reading and compare it with the child's radial pulse. Any discrepancy warrants further assessment.
    - Allow time for the readout to stabilize, then record the value as the oxygen saturation.
    - Remove the probe, turn off the oximeter, and store it appropriately.
    - If continuous monitoring is required, make sure the alarms are set for a low and a high limit, the alarms are functioning, and the sound is audible. Assess the condition of the skin under the probe every 4 hr, and move the sensor every 24 hr if indicated.
- Postprocedure
  - ○ Nursing Actions
    - Document the findings and report abnormal findings to the health care provider.

- If a child's SaO_2 is less than 90% (indicating hypoxemia):
  - Confirm that the sensor probe is properly placed.
  - Confirm that the oxygen delivery system is functioning and that the child is receiving prescribed oxygen levels.
  - Place the child in a semi-Fowler's or Fowler's position to maximize ventilation.
  - Encourage deep breathing.
  - Report significant findings to the health care provider.
  - Remain with the child and provide emotional support to decrease anxiety.

Nebulized Aerosol Therapy

- The process of nebulization breaks up medications (bronchodilators, mucolytic agents) into minute particles that are then dispersed throughout the respiratory tract. These droplets are much finer than those created by inhalers.

  - Medication may be given through a hand-held nebulizer that is held by the child. The hand-held nebulizer is a small machine that changes a medication solution into a mist.

- Indications

  - Diagnoses

    - Respiratory conditions that necessitate bronchodilators or corticosteroids

- Desired Therapeutic Outcomes

  - The child will maintain a patent airway.

  - The child will maintain an oxygen saturation of 95% to 100%

- Nursing Actions

  - Preparation of the Client

    - Instruct the child and family that the treatment may take 10 to 15 min.

    - Determine if the child is able to hold the mouthpiece or if a mask should be used.

    - Perform a preprocedure assessment, including vital signs.

    - Pour the medication into the small container and attach the device to an air or oxygen source.

  - Ongoing Care

    - Encourage the child to take slow, deep breaths through an open mouth.

    - Monitor the child during the treatment.

    - Assess vital signs, oxygen saturation, and lung sounds at the completion of treatment.

    - Inform the family that a portable device may be rented for home use.

- Complications
  - Tachycardia
    - Nursing Actions
      - Assess the child's cardiac status.
      - Stop the medication.
    - Client Education
      - Inform the parents that the child may experience jitteriness or an increased heart rate during the treatment.

Metered-Dose Inhaler (MDI) or Dry Powder Inhaler (DPI)

- These are hand-held devices that allow children to self-administer medications on an intermittent basis.

- Indications
  - Diagnoses
    - Respiratory conditions that necessitate bronchodilators or corticosteroids

- Desired Therapeutic Outcomes
  - The child will maintain a patent airway.
  - The child will maintain an oxygen saturation of 95% to 100%.

- Nursing Actions
  - Provide instructions to the child and parents for use of an MDI.

  > **(M) View Media Supplement:** Metered-Dose Inhaler (Animation)

    - Remove the cap from the inhaler.
    - Shake the inhaler five to six times.
    - Hold the inhaler with the mouthpiece at the bottom.
    - Hold the inhaler with the thumb near the mouthpiece and the index and middle fingers at the top.
    - Hold the inhaler approximately 2 to 4 cm (1 to 2 in) away from the front of the mouth.
    - Take a deep breath and then exhale.
    - Tilt the head back slightly, and press the inhaler. While pressing the inhaler, begin a slow, deep breath that lasts for 3 to 5 seconds to facilitate delivery to the air passages.
    - Hold the breath for 10 seconds to allow the medication to deposit in the airways.

- ■ Take the inhaler out of the mouth and slowly exhale through pursed lips.

- ■ Resume normal breathing.

o Instruct the child to use a spacer to keep the medication in the device longer, thereby increasing the amount of medication delivered to the lungs and decreasing the amount of the medication in the oropharynx.

- ■ If a spacer is used, instruct the child to:

  - □ Remove the covers from the mouthpieces of the inhaler and of the spacer

  - □ Insert the MDI into the end of the spacer.

  - □ Shake the inhaler five to six times.

  - □ Exhale completely and then close the mouth around the spacer mouthpiece

  - □ Continue as with an MDI.

o Provide instructions to the child and parents for the use of a DPI.

- ■ Do not shake the device.

- ■ Take the cover off the mouthpiece.

- ■ Follow the directions of the manufacturer, such as turning the wheel of the inhaler, for preparing the medication.

- ■ Exhale completely.

- ■ Place the mouthpiece between the lips and take a deep breath through the mouth.

- ■ Hold breath for 5 to 10 seconds.

- ■ Take the inhaler out of the mouth and slowly exhale through pursed lips.

- ■ Resume normal breathing.

o If more than one puff is prescribed, instruct the child to wait the length of time directed before administering the second puff.

o Instruct the child to remove the canister and rinse the inhaler, cap, and spacer once a day with warm running water. Instruct the child to dry the inhaler before using it again.

- • Complications

  - o Fungal infections

    - ■ Fungal infections of the oral cavity may occur with corticosteroid use.

    - ■ Nursing Actions

      - □ Administer cool liquids.

    - ■ Client Education

      - □ Instruct the child and parents to clean the MDI and spacer after each use and to have the child rinse his mouth and gargle with warm water after administration.

Chest Physiotherapy (CPT)

- Chest physiotherapy is the use of a set of techniques that include percussion, vibration, and postural drainage. Gravity and positioning loosen respiratory secretions and move them into the central airways where they can be removed by coughing or suctioning to promote removal of excessive secretions from specific areas of the lungs.

- Indications

  - Client Presentation

    - Thick secretions with an inability to clear the airway

    - Contraindication – Decreased cardiac reserves, pulmonary embolism, or increased intracranial pressure

- Desired Therapeutic Outcomes

  - The child will maintain a patent airway.

  - The child will maintain an oxygen saturation of 95% to 100%.

- Preprocedure

  - Nursing Actions

    - Schedule treatments 1 hr before meals or 2 hr after meals and at bedtime to decrease the likelihood of vomiting or aspirating.

    - Administer a bronchodilator medication or nebulizer treatment 30 min to 1 hr prior to postural drainage if prescribed.

    - Offer the child an emesis basin and facial tissues

- Intraprocedure

  - Nursing Actions

    - Perform hand hygiene, provide privacy, and explain the procedure to the child and parents.

    - Ensure proper positioning of the child to promote drainage of specific areas of the lungs.

      - Apical sections of the upper lobes – Fowler's position

      - Posterior sections of the upper lobes – Side-lying position

      - Right lobe – On the left side with a pillow under the chest wall

      - Left lobe – Trendelenburg position

    - Apply manual percussion by using cupped hand or a special device to clap rhythmically on the chest wall to break up secretions.

    - Place hands on the affected area, tense hand and arm muscles, and move the heel of the hands to create vibrations as the child exhales to help remove secretions. Have the client cough after each set of vibrations.

- ■ Have the child remain in each postural drainage position for 10 to 15 min to allow time for percussion, vibration, and postural drainage.
- ■ Discontinue the procedure if the child reports faintness or dizziness.

- Postprocedure
  - o Nursing Actions
    - ■ Perform lung auscultation and assess the amount, color, and character of the expectorated secretions.
    - ■ Document interventions and repeat the procedure as prescribed (typically 2 to 3 times per day).

- Complications
  - o Hypoxia
    - ■ Decrease in SaO_2
    - ■ Nursing Actions
      - □ Monitor respiratory status during the procedure.
      - □ Discontinue the procedure if the child experiences dyspnea.

Oxygen Therapy

- Oxygen therapy increases the oxygen concentration of the air that is being breathed.
  - o Humidification of oxygen will moisten the airways, which promotes loosening and mobilization of pulmonary secretions and prevents drying and injury of respiratory structures.

- Indications
  - o Diagnoses
    - ■ Hypoxemia
      - □ Hypoxemia develops when there is an inadequate level of oxygen in the blood. Hypovolemia, hypoventilation, and interruption of arterial flow can lead to hypoxemia.

EARLY SIGNS	LATE SIGNS
• Tachypnea	• Confusion and stupor
• Tachycardia	• Cyanosis of skin and mucous membranes
• Restlessness	• Bradypnea
• Pallor of the skin and mucous membranes	• Bradycardia
• Elevated blood pressure	• Hypotension
• Symptoms of respiratory distress (use of accessory muscles, nasal flaring, tracheal tugging, adventitious lung sounds)	• Cardiac dysrhythmias

- Desired Therapeutic Outcomes

  o The child will maintain a patent airway.

  o The child will maintain an SaO$_2$ of 95% to 100%.

- Nursing Actions

  o Preparation of the Client

    ■ Warm oxygen to prevent hypothermia.

    ■ Use a calm, nonthreatening approach.

    ■ Explain all procedures to the child and parents.

    ■ Place the child in a semi-Fowler's or Fowler's position to facilitate breathing and to promote chest expansion.

    ■ Ensure that all equipment is working properly.

  o Ongoing Care

    ■ Provide oxygen therapy at the lowest liter flow that will correct hypoxemia.

    ■ Assess/monitor lung sounds and respiratory rate, rhythm, and effort to determine the child's need for supplemental oxygen.

      □ Signs and symptoms of hypoxemia are shortness of breath, anxiety, tachypnea, tachycardia, restlessness, pallor or cyanosis of skin and/or mucous membranes, adventitious breath sounds, and confusion.

      □ Signs and symptoms of hypercarbia (elevated levels of CO_2) are restlessness, hypertension, and headache.

    ■ Do not allow oxygen to blow directly onto the faces of infants.

    ■ Change linens and clothing frequently.

    ■ Monitor temperature for hypothermia.

    ■ Avoid placing toys that could induce sparks in the tent.

    ■ Assess/monitor oxygenation status with pulse oximetry and arterial blood gases (ABGs).

    ■ Apply the oxygen delivery device prescribed.

    ■ Promote good oral hygiene and provide as needed.

    ■ Promote turning, coughing, deep breathing, and use of incentive spirometry and suctioning.

    ■ Promote rest and decrease environmental stimuli.

    ■ Provide emotional support for children who appear anxious.

    ■ Assess nutritional status and provide supplements as prescribed.

    ■ Assess/monitor the child's skin integrity. Provide moisture and pressure-relief devices as indicated.

    ■ Assess/monitor and document the child's response to oxygen therapy.

- Titrate oxygen to maintain the prescribed oxygen saturation.
- Discontinue oxygen gradually.

DELIVERY SYSTEM	NURSING IMPLICATIONS
Oxygen hood – Small plastic hood that fits over the infant's head	• Use a minimum flow rate of 4 to 5 L/min to prevent carbon dioxide buildup. • Ensure that the child's neck, chin, or shoulders do not rub against the hood. • Secure a pulse oximeter to the child for continuous SaO_2 monitoring.
Oxygen tent – Large plastic tent that fits over the crib or bed and can provide oxygen and humidity if prescribed	• Use oxygen tents for children older than 2 to 3 months. • Set the tent on a high flow rate to flood the tent with oxygen. Then, adjust flow meter to the desired amount prior to placing the child into the tent. Repeat if the tent has been opened for an extended period of time. • An oxygen level greater than 30% to 50% FiO_2 is hard to maintain, especially if the child is restless in bed. • Keep the tent around the perimeter of the bed. • Plan care to minimize how often the tent is opened. • Monitor the temperature inside the tent to ensure that it is appropriate. • Use plastic or vinyl toys, avoiding soft toys and toys that are mechanical or electrical. • Keep the child warm and dry.
Nasal cannula – Disposable plastic tube with two prongs for insertion into the nostrils that delivers an oxygen concentrations of 24% to 40% FiO_2 at a flow rate of 1 to 6 L/min	• Nasal cannulas are safe, easy to apply, and well tolerated. • The child is able to eat, talk, and ambulate while wearing a cannula. • Cannulas may be used by infants and older children who are cooperative. • Assess the patency of the nares. • Ensure that the prongs fit in the nares properly. • A nasal cannula may cause skin breakdown and dry mucous membranes. • Supply the child with a water-soluble gel if the nares are dry. • Provide humidification for flow rates greater than 4 L/min. • Prongs can become dislodged easily; therefore, monitor the child frequently.
Pediatric face mask – Pediatric-size mask that covers the child's nose and mouth	• Face masks are not tolerated well by children. • Cooperation may be gained from an older child by giving an explanation of the need for therapy.

- Complications
  - Combustion
    - Oxygen is combustible.
    - Nursing Actions
      - Place "No Smoking" or "Oxygen in Use" signs to alert others of the fire hazard.
      - Know where the closest fire extinguisher is located.
      - Have the child wear a cotton gown, because synthetics or wools may create sparks of static electricity.
      - Ensure that all electric devices (razors and heating pads) are in working condition.
      - Ensure that all electric machinery (monitors, suction machines) are well grounded.
      - Avoid toys that may induce a spark.
      - Do not use volatile, flammable materials (alcohol, acetone) near children who are receiving oxygen.
    - Client Education
      - Educate the child and others about the fire hazards of smoking with oxygen use.
  - Oxygen toxicity
    - Oxygen toxicity may result from high concentrations of oxygen (typically 50%), long duration of oxygen therapy (typically greater than 24 to 48 hr), and the child's degree of lung disease.
      - Signs and symptoms include a nonproductive cough, substernal pain, nasal stuffiness, nausea and vomiting, fatigue, headache, sore throat, and hypoventilation.
    - Nursing Actions
      - Use the lowest level of oxygen necessary to maintain an adequate SaO_2.
      - Monitor ABGs and notify the health care provider if SaO_2 levels rise outside of the expected reference range.
      - Use of an oxygen mask with continuous positive airway pressure (CPAP), bilevel positive airway pressure (BiPAP), or positive end-expiratory pressure (PEEP) while a child is on a mechanical ventilator may decrease the amount of oxygen needed.
      - Decrease the amount of oxygen gradually.

Suctioning

- Suctioning can be accomplished orally, nasally, or endotracheally.

- Indications

  - Diagnosis

    - Hypoxemia

  - Client Presentation

    - Early signs of hypoxemia (restlessness, tachypnea, tachycardia, decreased SaO_2 levels, adventitious breath sounds, visualization of secretions, cyanosis, absence of spontaneous cough)

- Desired Therapeutic Outcomes

  - The child will maintain a patent airway.

  - The child will maintain an SaO_2 of 95% to 100%.

- Endotracheal suctioning (ETS)

  - Preprocedure

    - Nursing Actions

      - Perform hand hygiene, provide privacy, and explain the procedure to the child.

      - Don the required personal protective equipment.

      - Assist the child to a high-Fowler's or Fowler's position for suctioning if possible.

      - Perform ETS through a tracheostomy or an endotracheal tube. Obtain a suction catheter with an outer diameter of no more than 1 cm (0.5 in) of the internal diameter of the endotracheal tube.

      - Ask for assistance if necessary.

      - Hyperoxygenate the child using a bag-valve-mask (BVM) resuscitator or specialized ventilator function with an FiO_2 of 100%.

      - Obtain baseline breath sounds and vital signs, including oxygen saturation (SaO_2) by pulse oximeter. Oxygen saturation may be monitored continually during the procedure.

  - Intraprocedure

    - Nursing Actions

      - Open the sterile suction package using surgical aseptic technique.

      - Place the sterile drape or towel on the child's chest.

      - Set up the container, touching only the outside.

      - Pour approximately 100 mL of sterile water or 0.9% sodium chloride (NaCl) into the container.

▫ Don sterile gloves.

    ▸ Use the clean/nondominant hand to hold the connecting tube; this glove protects the nurse.

    ▸ Use the sterile/dominant hand to hold the sterile catheter; this glove protects the child.

▫ Connect the suction catheter to the wall unit's tubing.

▫ Set the suction pressure to no higher than 110 mm Hg for children, and 95 mm Hg for infants. Use the lowest amount of pressure possible.

▫ Test the suction setup by aspirating sterile water/0.9% NaCl solution from the cup. If the unit is operating properly, continue with the procedure.

▫ Remove the bag or ventilator from the tracheostomy or endotracheal tube and insert the catheter into the lumen of the airway. Advance the catheter until resistance is met. The catheter should reach the level of the carina (location of bifurcation into the mainstem bronchi).

▫ Pull the catheter back 0.5 cm (0.2 in) prior to applying suction to prevent mucosal damage.

▫ Apply suction intermittently by covering and releasing the suction port with the thumb for 5 seconds at a time.

▫ Apply suction only while withdrawing the catheter and rotating it with the thumb and forefinger.

▫ Limit each suction attempt to no longer than 5 seconds to avoid hypoxemia and the vagal response. Limit suctioning to two to three attempts.

▫ Reattach the BVM or ventilator and supply the child with 100% inspired oxygen.

▫ Clear the catheter and tubing.

▫ Allow time, usually 30 to 60 seconds, for the child to recover between sessions.

▫ Repeat as necessary.

▫ Once suctioning is complete, clear the suction tubing by aspirating sterile water/0.9% NaCl solution.

○ Postprocedure

   ■ Nursing Actions

     ▫ Document the child's response.

● Complications

○ Hypoxia

   ■ A decrease in SaO_2 or cyanosis

   ■ Nursing Actions

     ▫ Stop the procedure.

     ▫ Limit each suction attempt to no longer than 10 to 15 seconds.

- □ Limit suctioning to two to three attempts.

- □ Allow the child 30 to 60 seconds for recovery between suction passes.

- □ Hyperoxygenate the child before and after each suctioning pass.

Artificial Airways

- A tracheotomy is a sterile surgical incision into the trachea through the skin and muscles for the purpose of establishing an airway.

- A tracheotomy can be performed as an emergency procedure or as a scheduled surgical procedure.

- A tracheostomy is the stoma/opening that results from a tracheotomy to provide and secure a patent airway. A tracheostomy can be permanent or temporary.

- Artificial airways can be placed orotracheally, nasotracheally, or through a tracheostomy to assist with respiration.

  - ○ Pediatric tracheostomy tubes made of plastic have a more acute angle than adult tubes. Pediatric tracheostomy tubes soften with body temperature to shape to the contour of the child's trachea. No inner cannula is necessary, because this material resists the accumulation of dried secretions.

  - ○ Pediatric tubes made of metal have an inner cannula. These tubes have a decreased risk of causing an allergic reaction.

- Indications

  - ○ Client Presentation

    - ■ Indications for artificial airways include artificial ventilation and obstruction of the upper airway.

- Desired Therapeutic Outcomes

  - ○ The child will maintain a patent airway.

  - ○ The child will maintain an oxygen saturation of 95% to 100%.

- Nursing Actions

  - ○ Preparation of the Client

    - ■ Children younger than 8 years of age must use an uncuffed endotracheal tube.

  - ○ Ongoing Care

    - ■ Assess/Monitor

      - □ Oxygenation, ventilation (respiratory rate, effort, SaO_2), and vital signs hourly

      - □ Thickness, quantity, odor, and color of mucous secretions

      - □ The stoma and the skin surrounding the stoma for signs of inflammation or infection (redness, swelling, or drainage)

- Provide adequate humidification and hydration to thin secretions and decrease the risk of mucus plugging.

- Do not suction routinely, because this may cause mucosal damage, bleeding, and bronchospasm.

- Assess/monitor the need for suctioning. Suction on a PRN basis when assessment findings indicate the need to do so (audible/noisy secretions, crackles, restlessness, tachypnea, tachycardia, and mucus in the airway).

- Maintain surgical aseptic technique when suctioning to prevent infection.

- Provide emotional support to the child and parents.

- Give frequent oral care, usually every 2 hr.

- For cuffed tubes, keep the pressure below 20 mm Hg to reduce the risk of tracheal necrosis due to prolonged compression of tracheal capillaries.

- Provide tracheostomy care every 8 hr.

  □ If necessary, suction the tracheostomy tube using sterile suctioning supplies.

  □ Remove old dressings and excess secretions.

  □ Apply the oxygen source loosely if the child's oxygen saturation level decreases during the procedure.

  □ Use cotton-tipped applicators and gauze pads to clean the exposed outer cannula surfaces. Begin with half-strength (mixed with sterile 0.9% NaCl) or full strength hydrogen peroxide followed by 0.9% NaCl. Clean in a circular motion from stoma site outward.

  □ Use surgical aseptic technique to remove and clean the inner cannula (use half-strength or full strength hydrogen peroxide to clean the cannula and sterile 0.9% NaCl to rinse it). Replace the inner cannula if it is disposable.

  □ Clean the stoma site and then the tracheostomy plate with half-strength or full strength hydrogen peroxide followed by sterile 0.9% NaCl.

  □ Place split dressing that are 4 inches by 4 inches around the tracheostomy.

  □ Change tracheostomy ties if they are soiled. Secure new ties in place before removing soiled ones to prevent accidental decannulation.

  □ If a knot is needed, tie a square knot that is visible on the side of the neck. Check that one or two fingers fit between the tie tape and the neck.

  □ Document the type and amount of secretions, the general condition of the stoma and surrounding skin, the child's response to the procedure, and any teaching or learning.

- Change nondisposable tracheostomy tubes every 6 to 8 weeks or per protocol.

- Reposition the client every 2 hr to prevent atelectasis and pneumonia.

- ○ Client Education.

    - ■ Provide discharge teaching regarding the following:

        - □ Tracheostomy care

        - □ Signs and symptoms that the family should immediately report to the health care provider (signs of infection or copious secretions)

        - □ Ways to achieve good nutrition

- ● Complications

    - ○ Accidental decannulation

        - ■ Accidental decannulation in the first 72 hr after surgery is an emergency because the tracheostomy tract has not matured and replacement may be difficult.

        - ■ Nursing Actions

            - □ Always have an additional staff member present when moving the tube or during any situation in which decannulation may occur.

        - ■ Client Education

            - □ When caring for the tube at home, have a second tube on hand to use as a replacement in the event of dislodgement.

            - □ Have scissors available to cut the old strings in an emergency.

    - ○ Occlusion

        - ■ Occlusion is a situation in which the tube is clogged with secretions and prevents adequate air exchange.

        - ■ Nursing Actions

            - □ Maintain a patent airway with suctioning.

        - ■ Client Education

            - □ Instruct the parents about the need to suction to prevent occlusion.

CHAPTER 16: OXYGEN AND INHALATION THERAPY

 Application Exercises

1. Match each oxygen administration and/or inhalation therapy with the appropriate child, based on age and disorder.

_____	Oxygen provided via a nasal cannula	A. An infant born with a congenital heart defect
_____	Mist/oxygen tent	B. An active toddler with pneumonia
_____	Plastic oxygen hood over the head	C. A school-age child with an asthma exacerbation
_____	Oxygen administered via a face mask or nasal cannula	D. An adolescent who is postoperative following a reduction of a fractured left femur

2. Nursing interventions for a child receiving inhalation therapy in an oxygen tent include which of the following?

    A. Tuck the tent snugly around the bottom perimeter of the bed.

    B. Keep the top of the tent closed or covered.

    C. Allow soft toys, such as stuffed animals, inside the tent.

    D. Once the prescribed temperature is set, do not readjust.

3. When assessing a child removed from an oxygen tent, a nurse should recognize that which of the following findings is an early indication of hypoxemia?

    A. Nonproductive cough

    B. Hypoventilation

    C. Nasal flaring

    D. Nasal stuffiness

CHAPTER 16: OXYGEN AND INHALATION THERAPY

 Application Exercises Answer Key

1. Match each oxygen administration and/or inhalation therapy with the appropriate child, based on age and disorder.

    __D__   Oxygen provided via a nasal cannula

    __B__   Mist/oxygen tent

    __A__   Plastic oxygen hood over the head

    __C__   Oxygen administered via a face mask or nasal cannula

A. An infant born with a congenital heart defect

B. An active toddler with pneumonia

C. A school-age child with an asthma exacerbation

D. An adolescent who is postoperative following a reduction of a fractured left femur

> The most effective way to deliver oxygen to an infant is using a plastic oxygen hood. The toddler should be placed in a mist/oxygen tent, allowing him to play and move around without being restricted. The school-age child may be able to tolerate a face mask and should be encouraged to do so until her condition improves. The adolescent should be able to comply with directions given to maintain oxygen administration via nasal cannula.

 NCLEX® Connection: Reduction of Risk Potential, Therapeutic Procedures

2. Nursing interventions for a child receiving inhalation therapy in an oxygen tent include which of the following?

A. Tuck the tent snugly around the bottom perimeter of the bed.

B. Keep the top of the tent closed or covered.

C. Allow soft toys, such as stuffed animals, inside the tent.

D. Once the prescribed temperature is set, do not readjust.

> To prevent oxygen loss from the tent, it should be snuggly tucked in around the perimeter of the bed. Oxygen is not lost if the top of the tent is open, because oxygen is heavier than air and is more concentrated toward the bottom of the tent. Soft toys, such as stuffed animals, absorb moisture and are difficult to keep dry in the humidified tent. Also, toys that are mechanical or electronic can be a source of sparks; therefore, they are a potential fire hazard. Vinyl or plastic toys that do not absorb moisture are better options. The temperature inside the tent will need to be frequently assessed and should be readjusted as often as needed to maintain an optimal temperature.

 NCLEX® Connection: Reduction of Risk Potential, Therapeutic Procedures

3. When assessing a child removed from an oxygen tent, a nurse should recognize that which of the following findings is an early indication of hypoxemia?

   A. Nonproductive cough

   B. Hypoventilation

   C. Nasal flaring

   D. Nasal stuffiness

   Early signs of hypoxemia include tachypnea, tachycardia, restlessness, pallor of the skin and mucous membranes, elevated blood pressure, and symptoms of respiratory distress, such as nasal flaring and use of accessory muscles. Nonproductive cough, hypoventilation, and nasal stuffiness are signs and symptoms of oxygen toxicity. Other signs of oxygen toxicity include substernal pain, nausea and vomiting, fatigue, headache, and sore throat.

   Ⓝ NCLEX® Connection: Reduction of Risk Potential, Potential for Complications of Diagnostic Tests/Treatments/Procedures

UNIT 2	NURSING CARE OF CHILDREN WITH SYSTEM DISORDERS
Section	Respiratory Disorders

Chapter 17   Acute and Infectious Respiratory Illnesses

Overview

- ○   Acute and infectious respiratory illnesses that are prevalent in children include tonsillitis, nasopharyngitis, pharyngitis, croup syndromes, bacterial tracheitis, bronchitis, bronchiolitis, allergic rhinitis, and pneumonia.

TONSILLITIS AND TONSILLECTOMY

Overview

- Tonsils are masses of lymph-type tissue found in the pharyngeal area. They filter pathogenic organisms (viral and bacterial), which helps to protect the respiratory and gastrointestinal tracts. In addition, they contribute to antibody formation.

- Palatine tonsils are located on both sides of the oropharynx. These are the tonsils removed during a tonsillectomy.

- Other tonsils are the pharyngeal tonsils, also known as the adenoids. These are removed during an adenoidectomy.

- Tonsils are highly vascular, which helps them to perform their function of protecting against infection because foreign materials, such as viral or bacterial organisms, enter the body through the mouth.

- In some instances, enlarged tonsils can block the nose and throat. This can interfere with normal breathing, nasal and sinus drainage, sleeping, swallowing, and speaking.

- Enlarged tonsils can also disrupt the normal functioning of the eustachian tube, which can impede hearing.

- Acute tonsillitis occurs when the tonsils become inflamed and reddened. Small patches of yellowish pus also may become visible. Acute tonsillitis may become chronic.

Assessment

- Risk Factors

  - ○   Exposure to a viral or bacterial agent

  - ○   Immature immune systems (found in younger children)

- Subjective Data

  - Reports of sore throat with difficulty swallowing

  - History of otitis media and hearing difficulties

- Objective Data

  - Physical Assessment Findings

    - Mouth odor

    - Mouth breathing

    - Snoring

    - Nasal qualities in the voice

    - Fever

    - Tonsil inflammation with redness and edema

  - Laboratory Tests

    - Throat culture for group A β-hemolytic streptococci (GABHS)

    - Preoperative CBC to assess for anemia and infection

Collaborative Care

- Nursing Care

  - Tonsillitis

    - Provide symptomatic treatment for viral tonsillitis (rest, cool fluids, warm salt-water gargles).

    - Administer antibiotic therapy for bacterial tonsillitis.

- Medications

  - Antipyretics – Acetaminophen (Tylenol)

    - Antipyretics decrease fever.

    - Nursing Considerations

      - Be aware of allergies.

    - Client Education

      - Teach appropriate dosing for acetaminophen.

  - Antibiotics – Amoxicillin (Amoxil)

    - Nursing Considerations

      - Be aware of allergies.

    - Client Education

      - Teach parents to administer antibiotics for the full course of treatment.

○ Analgesics – Acetaminophen (Tylenol) and codeine

- Nursing Considerations

  □ Provide pain control on a regular schedule.

  □ Monitor for side effects.

- Client Education

  □ Teach the family to monitor for side effects.

  □ Teach the child and family the proper dosing to prevent overdose.

- Therapeutic Procedures

  ○ Tonsillectomy

    - Nursing Actions

      □ Preoperatively

        ‣ Encourage the use of warm salt-water gargles and throat lozenges.

        ‣ Encourage fluid intake and monitor hydration status of the child (until required NPO status).

      □ Postoperatively

NURSING CONSIDERATION	NURSING ACTIONS
Positioning	• Position the child on his side to facilitate drainage. • Elevate the head of the child's bed when he is fully awake.
Assessment	• Assess the child for signs of bleeding, which include frequent swallowing, clearing the throat, restlessness, bright red emesis, tachycardia, and/or pallor. • Assess the child's airway and vital signs. • Monitor the child for any difficulty breathing related to oral secretions, edema, and/or bleeding.
Comfort measures	• Provide an ice collar and analgesics. • Keep the child's throat moist. • Administer pain medication on a regular schedule.
Diet	• Encourage clear liquids and fluids after a return of the gag reflex, avoiding red-colored liquids and milk-based foods initially. • Advance the child's diet with soft, bland foods.
Instruction	• Discourage coughing, throat clearing, and nose blowing in order to protect the surgical site. • Refrain from placing pointed objects in the back of the mouth. • Alert parents that there may be clots or blood-tinged mucus in vomitus.

- Client Education

  □ Instruct the family to notify the health care provider if signs of bleeding occur.

  □ Encourage the child to rest.

- Care After Discharge

  o Client Education

  - Instruct the parents to contact the provider if the child experiences difficulty breathing, bright red bleeding, lack of oral intake, an increase in pain, and/or any signs of infection.

  - Tell the parents to ensure that the child does not put anything sharp (ice-cream stick, straw, any pointed object) into her mouth.

  - Teach the parents to administer pain medications for discomfort.

  - Encourage fluid intake and diet advancement to a soft diet with no spicy foods or hard, sharp foods like corn chips.

  - Instruct the child and family to limit strenuous activity and physical play with no swimming for 2 weeks.

  - Instruct the child and family that full recovery usually occurs within 10 days to 2 weeks.

- Client Outcomes

  o The child will recover from surgery without complications, such as hemorrhage.

Complications

- Hemorrhage

  o Nursing Actions

  - Use a good light source and possibly a tongue depressor to directly observe the child's throat.

  - Assess the child for signs of bleeding (tachycardia, repeated swallowing and clearing of throat, hemoptysis). Hypotension is a late sign of shock.

  - Contact the provider immediately if there is any indication of bleeding.

  o Client Education

  - Instruct the family to report signs of bleeding (frequent swallowing, clearing the throat, restlessness, bright red emesis, tachycardia, pallor).

- Chronic infection

  ○ Chronically infected tonsils may pose a potential threat to other parts of the body. Some children who have tonsillitis frequently may develop other diseases, such as rheumatic fever and kidney infection.

  ○ Client Education

    ▪ Instruct the family to seek medical attention when the child presents with symptoms of tonsillitis.

COMMON RESPIRATORY ILLNESSES

Overview

- Disorders can affect both the upper (nasopharynx, pharynx, larynx, and upper part of the trachea) and lower (lower trachea, mainstem bronchi, segmental bronchi, subsegmental bronchioles, terminal bronchioles, and alveoli) respiratory tracts.

- Infections of the respiratory tract may affect more than one area.

- Infectious agents include Group A β-hemolytic streptococci (GABHS), respiratory syncytial virus (RSV), *Haemophilus influenzae*, *Streptococcus pneumoniae*, and *Mycoplasma pneumoniae*.

Assessment

- Risk Factors

  ○ Age

    ▪ Infants between 3 and 6 months of age are at an increased risk due to the decrease of maternal antibodies acquired at birth and the lack of antibody protection.

    ▪ Viral infections are more common in toddlers and preschoolers. The incidence of these infections decreases by age 5.

    ▪ GABHS and *Mycoplasma pneumoniae* infection rates increase after age 5.

    ▪ Certain viral agents can cause serious illness during infancy, but will only cause a mild illness in older children.

  ○ Anatomy

    ▪ A short, narrow airway can become easily obstructed with mucus or edema.

    ▪ A short respiratory tract allows infections to travel quickly to the lower airways.

    ▪ Infants and young children have small surface areas for gas exchange.

    ▪ Infectious agents have easy access to the middle ear through the short and open eustachian tubes of infants and young children.

- ○ Decreased resistance due to:
    - ▪ Compromised immune system
    - ▪ Anemia
    - ▪ Nutritional deficiencies
    - ▪ Allergies
    - ▪ Chronic medical conditions (asthma, cystic fibrosis, congenital heart disease)
    - ▪ Exposure to second-hand smoke
- ○ Seasonal variables
    - ▪ Children with asthma have a greater incidence of respiratory infections during cold weather.
    - ▪ RSV and other common respiratory infections are more common during the winter and spring.
    - ▪ Infections caused by *Mycoplasma pneumoniae* are more frequent during autumn and early winter.
- Subjective Data
    - ○ Nursing history that includes recent infections, medications taken, immunization status, and family coping
    - ○ Reports of sore throat, decreased activity level, chest pain, fatigue, difficulty breathing, shortness of breath, and decreased appetite
- Objective Data
    - ○ Physical Assessment Findings

RESPIRATORY ILLNESS	SIGNS/SYMPTOMS
• Nasopharyngitis (common cold) ○ Self-limiting virus that persists for 7 to 10 days	• Nasal inflammation, rhinorrhea, cough, dry throat, sneezing, and nasal qualities heard in voice • Fever, decreased appetite, and irritability
• Pharyngitis (strep throat) ○ Caused by GABHS	• Inflamed throat with exudate, pain with swallowing • Headache, fever, and abdominal pain • Cervical lymphadenopathy • Truncal, axillary, and perineal rash
• Bacterial tracheitis ○ Infection of the lining of the trachea	• Thick, purulent drainage from the trachea that can obstruct the airway and cause respiratory distress

RESPIRATORY ILLNESS	SIGNS/SYMPTOMS
• Bronchitis (tracheobronchitis) ○ Associated with an upper respiratory infection (URI) and inflammation of large airways ○ Self-limiting and requires symptomatic relief	• Persistent cough as a result of inflammation
• Bronchiolitis ○ Mostly caused by the respiratory syncytial virus (RSV) ○ Primarily affects the bronchi and bronchioles ○ Occurs at the bronchiolar level	• Rhinorrhea – Pharyngitis, intermittent fever, cough, and wheezing • Coughing that progresses toward wheezing, increased respiratory rate, nasal flaring, retractions, and cyanosis
• Allergic rhinitis ○ Caused by seasonal reaction to allergens most often in the autumn or spring	• Watery rhinorrhea; nasal congestion; itchiness of the nose, eyes, and pharynx; itchy, watery eyes; nasal quality of the voice; dry, scratchy throat; snoring; poor sleep leading to poor performance in school; and fatigue
• Pneumonia (RSV, *Streptococcus pneumoniae*, *Haemophilus influenzae*, *Mycoplasma pneumoniae*)	• High fever • Cough that may be unproductive or productive of white sputum • Retractions and nasal flaring • Rapid, shallow respirations • Chest pain • Adventitious breath sounds (rhonchi, crackles) • Pale color that progresses to cyanosis • Irritability, anxiety, agitation, and fatigue • Abdominal pain, diarrhea, lack of appetite, and vomiting • Sudden onset, usually following a viral infection (bacterial pneumonia)

RESPIRATORY ILLNESS	SIGNS/SYMPTOMS
Croup Syndromes	

• Bacterial epiglottitis (acute supraglottitis)
  ○ Medical emergency
  ○ Caused by *Haemophilus influenzae*
	• Sitting with chin pointing out, mouth opened, and tongue protruding
	• Drooling
	• Anxiety with respiratory distress
	• Absence of spontaneous coughing
	• Dysphonia (hoarseness or difficulty speaking)
	• Dysphagia (difficulty swallowing)
	• Inspiratory stridor (noisy inspirations)
	• Sore throat, high fever, and restlessness

• Acute laryngitis ○ Self-limiting viral infection	• Hoarseness as the only symptom
• Acute laryngotracheobronchitis ○ Causative agents include RSV, influenza A and B, and *Mycoplasma pneumoniae*	• Low-grade fever, restlessness, hoarseness, barky cough, inspiratory stridor, and retractions
• Acute spasmodic laryngitis ○ Self-limiting illness that may result from allergens	• Barky cough, restlessness, difficulty breathing, hoarseness, and nighttime episodes of laryngeal obstruction

    ○ Laboratory Tests

        ■ Throat culture for GABHS

        ■ Blood samples

            □ Elevated serum antistreptolysin-O (ASO) titer

            □ Elevated C-reactive protein (CRP) or sedimentation rate in response to an inflammatory reaction

        ■ CBC to assess for anemia and infection

        ■ Sputum culture and sensitivity to detect infection

- o Diagnostic Procedures
  - ■ Collection of direct aspiration of nasal secretions
    - □ The secretions are collected for immunofluorescence analysis to detect RSV. One to 3 mL of NS is instilled into one of the child's nostrils. The fluid is then aspirated for evaluation.
    - □ Nursing Actions
      - ‣ Place the child in a supine position.
      - ‣ Use a sterile syringe without a needle.
    - □ Client Education
      - ‣ Caregivers should be educated about the potential need for isolation, dependent on the results of laboratory tests.
  - ■ Chest x-ray
    - □ Identifies infiltration in pneumonia
    - □ Nursing Actions
      - ‣ Ensure the child is positioned correctly to avoid the need for a repeat x-ray.
    - □ Client Education
      - ‣ Inform adolescents of childbearing age of the need for confirmation of nonpregnant status.

Collaborative Care

- • Nursing Care
  - o Closely monitor progression of illness and ensuing respiratory distress. Observe for increased heart and respiratory rate, retractions, nasal flaring, and restlessness.
  - o Make emergency equipment for intubation readily accessible.
  - o Do not attempt to use a tongue depressor or take a throat culture if epiglottis is suspected.
  - o Use oxygen and high humidity for infants and young children with hoods or tents.
  - o Use postural drainage and/or chest physiotherapy (CPT) to help mobilize and remove fluid from the lungs.
  - o Maintain adequate hydration by offering preferred fluids at frequent intervals. Administer IV fluids as prescribed.
  - o Allow for the child to be held in an upright position.

- Medications
  - Epinephrine
    - Administer for vasoconstriction of submucosa and to decrease edema.
    - Nursing Considerations
      - Administer via a nebulizer (racemic epinephrine).
      - Observe the child for 3 hr after administration of medication.
    - Client Education
      - Inform the child that she may feel an acceleration in heart rate during the administration of this medication.
  - Corticosteroids – Dexamethasone (Decadron) and budesonide (Rhinocort)
    - Administer to decrease inflammation.
    - Nursing Considerations
      - Administer orally via nebulizer or IV route.
    - Client Education
      - Assist the child to rinse his mouth after nebulizer treatment.
  - Antipyretics – Acetaminophen (Tylenol)
    - Administer to decrease fever.
    - Nursing Considerations
      - Be aware of allergies.
    - Client Education
      - Educate the client about the proper dose of medication.
  - Mild analgesic
    - Administer to decrease pain.
    - Nursing Considerations
      - Monitor for safety while using analgesics.
    - Client Education
      - Advise the parents of proper dosing and safety considerations.
  - Antibiotics
    - Administer to treat bacterial infection.
    - Nursing Considerations
      - Be aware of allergies.
    - Client Education
      - Advise parents that the child should finish the full course of antibiotics.

- Care After Discharge

  o Use a cool-air vaporizer to provide humidity.

  o Rest during febrile illness.

  o Maintain adequate fluid intake. Infants may be given commercially prepared oral rehydration solutions, and older children may be given sports drinks.

  o Limit use of nose drops or sprays to 3 days to prevent rebound congestion.

  o Apply an ice bag or heating pad to the neck to decrease pain from enlarged cervical nodes.

  o Administer medications using accurate dosages and appropriate time intervals.

  o Develop strategies to decrease the spread of infection. Strategies include performing good hand hygiene; covering the nose and mouth with tissues when sneezing and coughing; properly disposing of tissues; not sharing cups, eating utensils, and towels; and keeping infected children from contact with children who are well.

  o Seek further medical attention for the child if symptoms worsen or respiratory distress occurs.

- Client Outcomes

  o The child and family will adhere to the medication regimen.

  o The child will be free of infection.

Complications

- Airway Obstruction

  o May result from progression of respiratory infectious process or foreign body aspiration

  o Nursing Actions

    ■ Ensure proper body alignment. Position the child (prone, semiprone, side lying) to promote lung expansion, prevent gas exchange, and prevent aspiration.

    ■ Perform suctioning of airways if indicated, limiting each attempt to 5 seconds.

    ■ Do not examine the child's throat with a tongue blade or take a throat culture if epiglottitis is suspected.

    ■ Administer medications as prescribed to include epinephrine and corticosteroids.

    ■ Carry out CPT.

- Assist the child to deep breathe with the use of a splint, and expectorate sputum.
- Ensure availability of emergency equipment.
  - ○ Client Education
    - Instruct parents to keep small objects away from children.
    - Instruct parents to identify respiratory distress (increased heart and respiratory rate, nasal flaring, chest retractions, increased restlessness) and to seek medical attention.

CHAPTER 17: ACUTE AND INFECTIOUS RESPIRATORY ILLNESSES

(A) Application Exercises

1. Which of the following is a function of the tonsils?

    A. Contribute to the functioning of the eustachian tube.

    B. Filter and protect against invading pathogens.

    C. Play a role in the formation of antigens.

    D. Promote nasal and sinus drainage.

2. List several examples of diversionary activities that are appropriate for a nurse to provide to a school-age child following a tonsillectomy.

3. A nurse is caring for a child who is in the postoperative period following a tonsillectomy. When assessing the child, the nurse should recognize which of the following findings as consistent with postoperative bleeding?

    A. Hgb of 11.6 and Hct of 37%

    B. Inflamed and reddened throat

    C. Frequent swallowing and clearing of the throat

    D. Blood-tinged mucus

4. Which of the following nursing interventions should be included in the postoperative care for a child following a tonsillectomy?

    A. Encourage the child to blow her nose gently to clear the sinuses.

    B. Notify the provider if clots or blood-tinged mucus are observed in emesis.

    C. Avoid red-colored liquids and milk-based foods initially.

    D. Position the child supine during the initial postoperative period.

5. A nurse is assessing a child who is suspected to have bacterial epiglottitis. Which of the following manifestations support the suspected illness? (Select all that apply.)

    _____ Hoarseness and difficulty speaking

    _____ Difficulty swallowing

    _____ Low-grade fever

    _____ Drooling

    _____ Dry, barking cough

    _____ Stridor

CHAPTER 17: ACUTE AND INFECTIOUS RESPIRATORY ILLNESSES

 Application Exercises Answer Key

1. Which of the following is a function of the tonsils?

    A. Contribute to the functioning of the eustachian tube.

    B. Filter and protect against invading pathogens.

    C. Play a role in the formation of antigens.

    D. Promote nasal and sinus drainage.

    Tonsils are masses of lymph-type tissue found in the pharyngeal area. The primary role of tonsils is to filter pathogenic organisms (viral and bacterial) to protect the respiratory and gastrointestinal tracts. They do not contribute to the functioning of the eustachian tube, nor do they promote nasal and sinus drainage. The tonsils contribute to the formation of antibodies, not antigens.

 NCLEX® Connection: Physiological Adaptation, Pathophysiology

2. List several examples of diversionary activities that are appropriate for a nurse to provide to a school-age child following a tonsillectomy.

    Watch a movie.

    Play a board game.

    Put a puzzle together.

    Play cards.

    Read a book.

    Visit with a friend/family member.

    Color a picture.

    Play a video game.

    Make a craft.

 NCLEX® Connection: Health Promotion and Maintenance, Aging Process

3. A nurse is caring for a child who is in the postoperative period following a tonsillectomy. When assessing the child, the nurse should recognize which of the following findings as consistent with postoperative bleeding?

    A. Hgb of 11.6 and Hct of 37%

    B. Inflamed and reddened throat

    C. Frequent swallowing and clearing of the throat

    D. Blood-tinged mucus

Signs of bleeding include frequent swallowing, clearing of the throat, restlessness, bright red emesis, tachycardia, and pallor. The Hgb and Hct are within the expected reference range. An inflamed and reddened throat and some blood-tinged mucus are also expected findings.

 NCLEX® Connection: Reduction of Risk Potential, Complications of Diagnostic Tests/ Treatments/Procedures

4. Which of the following nursing interventions should be included in the postoperative care for a child following a tonsillectomy?

    A. Encourage the child to blow her nose gently to clear the sinuses.

    B. Notify the provider if clots or blood-tinged mucus are observed in emesis.

    C. Avoid red-colored liquids and milk-based foods initially.

    D. Position the child supine during the initial postoperative period.

Following a tonsillectomy clear liquids and fluids should be encouraged after a return of the gag reflex. Red-colored liquids and milk-based foods should be avoided initially, and then the diet should be advanced with soft, bland foods. Discourage the child from coughing, throat clearing, and nose blowing in order to protect the surgical site. Position the child on her side to facilitate drainage, or elevate the head of the child's bed when he is fully awake. Alert the parents that there may be clots or blood-tinged mucus in vomitus.

 NCLEX® Connection: Reduction of Risk Potential, Complications of Diagnostic Tests/ Treatments/Procedures

5. A nurse is assessing a child who is suspected to have bacterial epiglottitis. Which of the following manifestations support the suspected illness? (Select all that apply.)

__X__	**Hoarseness and difficulty speaking**
__X__	**Difficulty swallowing**
_____	Low-grade fever
__X__	**Drooling**
_____	Dry, barking cough
__X__	**Stridor**

A child who is ill with epiglottitis typically exhibits dysphonia (hoarseness or difficulty speaking), dysphagia (difficulty swallowing), and drooling. Inspiratory stridor (noisy inspirations) is also common. The child usually has a high fever, not a low-grade fever, and a cough is not present.

 NCLEX® Connection: Reduction of Risk Potential, System Specific Assessment

UNIT 2	NURSING CARE OF CHILDREN WITH SYSTEM DISORDERS
Section	Respiratory Disorders
Chapter 18	Asthma

Overview

- Asthma is a chronic inflammatory disorder of the airways that results in intermittent and reversible airflow obstruction of the bronchioles.

- The obstruction occurs either by inflammation or airway hyper-responsiveness.

- The cause of asthma is unknown.

- Manifestations of asthma

  ○ Mucosal edema

  ○ Bronchoconstriction

  ○ Excessive secretion production

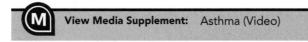
View Media Supplement: Asthma (Video)

- Asthma diagnoses are based on symptoms and classified into one of the following four categories.

  ○ Mild intermittent – Symptoms occur less than twice a week.

  ○ Mild persistent – Symptoms occur more than twice a week, but not daily.

  ○ Moderate persistent – Daily symptoms occur in conjunction with exacerbations twice a week.

  ○ Severe persistent – Symptoms occur continually, along with frequent exacerbations that limit the child's physical activity and quality of life.

Assessment

- Risk Factors

  ▪ Young children are more susceptible to infections.

  ▪ The presence of second hand smoke increases the risk for asthma.

- Subjective Data

  - Anxiety

  - Stress

  - Chest tightness

  - History regarding current and previous asthma exacerbations

    - Onset and duration

    - Precipitating factors (stress, exercise, exposure to irritant)

    - Changes in medication regimen

    - Medications that relieve symptoms

    - Other medications taken

    - Self-care methods used to relieve symptoms

- Objective Data

  - Physical Assessment Findings

    - Dyspnea

    - Coughing

    - Wheezing

    - Mucus production

    - Use of accessory muscles

    - Poor oxygen saturation (low SaO_2)

    - Tachycardia and premature ventricular contractions (PVCs)

  - Laboratory Tests

    - ABGs

      - Hypoxemia (decreased PaO_2 of less than 80 mm Hg)

      - Hypocarbia (decreased $PaCO_2$ of less than 35 mm Hg early in attack)

      - Hypercarbia (increased $PaCO_2$ of greater than 45 mm Hg later in attack)

    - Sputum cultures

      - Bacteria may be present, indicating infection.

- o Diagnostic Procedures
  - Pulmonary function tests (PFTs) are the most accurate tests for diagnosing asthma and its severity.
    - Forced vital capacity (FVC) is the volume of air exhaled from full inhalation to full exhalation.
    - Forced expiratory volume (FEV_1) is the volume of air able to be blown out as quickly as possible during the first second of a forceful exhalation after inhaling fully.
    - Peak expiratory flow rate (PEFR), measured using a peak expiratory flow meter (PEFM), is the maximum airflow exhaled forcefully in 1 second.
    - A decrease in FEV_1 or PEFR by 15% to 20% below the expected value is common in children with asthma. An increase in these values by 12% following the administration of bronchodilators is diagnostic for asthma.
  - A chest x-ray is used to diagnose changes in chest structure over time.
    - Nursing Actions
      - ▸ Prepare the child for the procedure.
    - Client Education
      - ▸ Provide support for the family.

Collaborative Care

- Nursing Care
  - o Assess airway patency, respiratory rate, symmetry, effort, and use of accessory muscles.
  - o Assess breath sounds in all lung fields. Lung sounds may be diminished.
  - o Monitor for shortness of breath, dyspnea, and audible wheezing. An absence of wheezing may indicate severe constriction of the alveoli.
  - o Check ABGs, SaO_2, CBC, and chest x-ray results.
  - o Position the child to maximize ventilation (high-Fowler's).
  - o Administer oxygen therapy as prescribed.
  - o Initiate and maintain IV access.
  - o Maintain a calm and reassuring demeanor.
  - o Encourage appropriate vaccinations and prompt medical attention for infections.

- Medications

  o Bronchodilators (inhalers)

    - Short-acting beta$_2$ agonists (albuterol [Proventil], terbutaline [Brethine]) provide rapid relief for acute asthma attacks.

    - Cholinergic antagonists (anticholinergic medications), such as ipratropium (Atrovent), block the parasympathetic nervous system, providing relief of acute bronchospasms.

    - Nursing Considerations

      □ Instruct the child and family in the proper use of MDI, DPI, or nebulizer.

      □ Watch the child for tremors and tachycardia when he is taking albuterol.

      □ Observe the child for dry mouth when he is taking ipratropium.

    - Client Education

      □ Encourage older children who are taking ipratropium to suck on hard candies to help with dry mouth.

      □ Instruct the child to take a bronchodilator inhaler 5 min prior to an anti-inflammatory inhaler to promote bronchodilation and increased absorption of medication.

  o Antiinflammatory agents

    - Antiinflammatory agents decrease airway inflammation for long-term management.

    - Corticosteroids (fluticasone [Flovent] and prednisone [Deltasone])

    - Leukotriene modifiers (montelukast [Singulair]), mast cell stabilizers (cromolyn sodium [Intal]), and monoclonal antibodies (omalizumab [Xolair])

    - Nursing Considerations

      □ Watch the child for decreased immunity function.

      □ Monitor the child for hyperglycemia.

      □ Advise the child to report black, tarry stools.

      □ Observe the child for fluid retention and weight gain, which may be common.

      □ Observe the child's throat and mouth for aphthous (cold sore) lesions

    - Client Education

      □ Encourage the child to drink plenty of fluids to promote hydration.

      □ Encourage the child to take a glucocorticosteroid (prednisone [Deltasone]) with food.

      □ Instruct the child to rinse her mouth or gargle with warm saltwater after the use of an inhaler.

      □ Instruct the child and family to watch for redness, sores, or white patches in the mouth, and report them to the provider.

- Interdisciplinary Care

    o Respiratory services should be consulted for inhalers and breathing treatments.

    o Nutritional services may be contacted for weight loss or gain related to medications or diagnosis.

    o Rehabilitation care may be consulted if the child has prolonged weakness and needs assistance with increasing level of activity.

- Care After Discharge

    o Client Education

        ▪ Instruct the child how to recognize and avoid triggering agents, such as:

            □ Smoke

            □ Dust

            □ Mold

            □ Sudden weather changes (especially warm to cold)

            □ Seasonal allergens (grass, tree and weed pollens)

            □ Animal dander

            □ Stress

        ▪ Instruct the child how to properly self-administer medications (nebulizers and inhalers).

        ▪ Educate the child and family regarding infection prevention techniques.

            □ Promote good nutrition.

            □ Reinforce importance of good hand hygiene.

        ▪ Encourage prompt medical attention for infections.

        ▪ Stress the importance of keeping immunizations, including seasonal influenza and pneumonia vaccines, up to date.

        ▪ Encourage regular exercise as part of asthma therapy.

            □ Promotes ventilation and perfusion

            □ Maintains cardiac health

            □ Enhances skeletal muscle strength

        ▪ Children may require medication before exercise.

- Client Outcomes

    o The child will be able to maintain adequate gas exchange.

    o The child will prevent acute attacks.

    o The child will have relief of symptoms.

    o The child will adhere to the medication regimen.

Complications

- Respiratory failure

  o Persistent hypoxemia related to asthma can lead to respiratory failure.

  o Nursing Actions

    - Monitor oxygenation levels and acid-base balance.

    - Prepare for intubation and mechanical ventilation as indicated.

- Status asthmaticus

  o A life-threatening episode of airway obstruction that is often unresponsive to common treatment

  o Symptoms include wheezing, labored breathing, use of accessory muscles, distended neck veins, and risk for cardiac and/or respiratory arrest.

  o Nursing Actions

    - Prepare for emergency intubation.

    - Administer humidified oxygen.

    - Administer three nebulizer treatments of a beta$_2$-agonist, 20 to 30 min apart. Ipratropium bromide may be added to the nebulizer to increase bronchodilation.

    - Obtain IV access.

    - Monitor ABGs and serum electrolytes.

    - Administer corticosteroid (oral, IM, IV).

    - Other therapies may include:

      □ Magnesium sulfate via IV or by inhalation, which results in smooth muscle relaxation and decreases inflammation.

      □ Heliox via nonrebreathing face mask.

      □ Ketamine (Ketalar) via IV.

    - Prepare the child for admission for continued follow-up.

CHAPTER 18: ASTHMA

 Application Exercises

1. Which of the following parameters indicate deterioration in a child's respiratory status? (Select all that apply.)

    _____ SaO$_2$ 95%

    _____ Wheezing

    _____ Retraction of sternal muscles

    _____ Warm extremities

    _____ Premature ventricular complexes (PVCs)

    _____ Respiratory rate of 34/min

    _____ Anxiety

2. Two hours after arriving in a medical-surgical unit, a child develops dyspnea. The child's SaO$_2$ is 91%, and the child is exhibiting audible wheezing and use of accessory muscles. Which of the following medications should the nurse expect to administer?

    A. Fluticasone (Flovent)

    B. Montelukast (Singulair)

    C. Cromolyn sodium (Intal)

    D. Albuterol (Proventil)

3. A child is exhibiting suspected clinical manifestations of asthma. The mother asks the nurse what tests will be necessary to diagnose her child. Which of the following diagnostic procedures should the nurse tell the mother is used to diagnose asthma?

    A. Arterial blood gases (ABGs)

    B. Chest x-ray

    C. Pulmonary function tests (PFTs)

    D. Allergy tests

CHAPTER 18: ASTHMA

(A) Application Exercises Answer Key

1. Which of the following parameters indicate deterioration in a child's respiratory status? (Select all that apply.)

_____ SaO$_2$ 95%

___X___ **Wheezing**

___X___ **Retraction of sternal muscles**

_____ Warm extremities

___X___ **Premature ventricular complexes (PVCs)**

___X___ **Respiratory rate of 34/min**

___X___ **Anxiety**

Wheezing, retraction of sternal muscles, PVCs, respiratory rate of 34/min, and anxiety are all related to the child's declining respiratory status. Warm extremities along with an SaO$_2$ of 95% are expected findings that do not indicate distress.

(N) NCLEX® Connection: Reduction of Risk Potential, System Specific Assessment

2. Two hours after arriving in a medical-surgical unit, a child develops dyspnea. The child's SaO$_2$ is 91%, and the child is exhibiting audible wheezing and use of accessory muscles. Which of the following medications should the nurse expect to administer?

A. Fluticasone (Flovent)

B. Montelukast (Singulair)

C. Cromolyn sodium (Intal)

D. Albuterol (Proventil)

Albuterol is a beta$_2$-agonist agent that is used for relief of acute symptoms. Fluticasone is a glucocorticoid agent that is used for long-term anti-inflammatory effects, montelukast is a leukotriene modifier that is used for long-term management of asthma. Cromolyn sodium is a mast cell stabilizer that is used for prophylaxis of asthma.

(N) NCLEX® Connection: Pharmacological and Parenteral Therapies, Pharmacological Agents/ Actions

3. A child is exhibiting suspected clinical manifestations of asthma. The mother asks the nurse what tests will be necessary to diagnose her child. Which of the following diagnostic procedures should the nurse tell the mother is used to diagnose asthma?

    A. Arterial blood gases (ABGs)

    B. Chest x-ray

    C. Pulmonary function tests (PFTs)

    D. Allergy tests

PFTs are used for diagnosing asthma and its severity. ABGs, allergy tests, and chest x-rays are all diagnostic procedures that will contribute to the assessment of the child with asthma, but they do not provide a diagnosis.

NCLEX® Connection: Reduction of Risk Potential, Diagnostic Tests

Overview

- Cystic fibrosis is a dysfunction of the exocrine glands that causes the glands to produce thick, tenacious mucus.

- Major organs affected are the lungs, pancreas, small intestine, and liver.

- Abnormally thick mucus leads to mechanical obstruction of organs, which alters their functions.

- Sweat and salivary glands excrete excessive electrolytes, specifically sodium and chloride.

Assessment

- Risk Factors

    o Cystic fibrosis is hereditary and transmitted as an autosomal recessive trait. Thus, both parents must be carriers of the gene.

- Subjective Data

    o History of chronic respiratory infections

- Objective Data

    o Physical Assessment Findings

        ▪ Meconium ileus at birth manifested as distention of the abdomen, vomiting (may be bile-stained), and inability to pass stool

        ▪ Absence of pancreatic enzymes

        ▪ Respiratory findings

            □ Fatigue

            □ Chronic cough

            □ Thick, yellow-grey mucus

            □ Positive sputum culture (*Pseudomonas aeruginosa*, *Haemophilus influenzae*)

            □ Fever

            □ Shortness of breath, dyspnea, and wheezing

□ Cyanosis

□ Difficulty exhaling air, resulting in hyperinflation of the lungs

□ Barrel-shaped chest

□ Clubbing of the fingers and toes

■ Gastrointestinal findings

□ Large, loose, fatty, sticky, foul-smelling stools

□ Impaired digestion

□ Failure to gain weight

□ Delayed growth patterns

□ Distended abdomen

□ Thin arms and legs

□ Atrophy of buttocks and thighs

■ Integumentary findings

□ Sweat, tears, and saliva are abnormally salty

■ Endocrine and reproductive system findings

□ Delayed puberty

□ Viscous cervical mucus

□ Decreased or absent sperm

o Laboratory Tests

■ A sweat chloride test should be used to measure the amount of chloride in skin sweat. A normal chloride concentration of sweat is less than 40 mEq/L. Values of greater than 40 mEq/L in infants are suggestive of cystic fibrosis, and values greater than 60 mEq/L in children indicate the presence of cystic fibrosis.

■ A stool analysis can indicate the presence of steatorrhea (undigested fat) and azotorrhea (foul-smelling from protein).

■ Sputum culture and sensitivity can detect infection.

o Diagnostic Procedures

■ Blood glucose – Hyperglycemia related to insulin resistance or deficiency

■ Chest x-ray

□ May indicate diffuse atelectasis and obstructive emphysema

□ Nursing Actions

▸ Ensure that the child is properly positioned for the procedure to avoid the need to repeat the x-ray.

- Abdominal x-ray
  - Detect meconium ileus
  - Nursing Actions
    - Ensure that the child is properly positioned for the procedure to avoid the need to repeat the x-ray.

Collaborative Care

- Nursing Care
  - Give respiratory treatments to include aerosol therapy, chest physiotherapy, breathing exercises, and assistance with coughing/expectoration of secretions.
  - Perform CPT 1 hr before meals or 2 hr after meals if possible.
  - Use oxygen with caution to prevent oxygen narcosis.
  - Promote adequate nutritional intake, and provide pancreatic enzymes at meals and with snacks.
  - Encourage adequate fluid and salt intake.
  - Provide meticulous skin care and oral hygiene.
  - Administer antibiotics through a central venous access port.
- Medications
  - Hypoglycemic agents
    - Nursing Considerations
      - Monitor blood glucose levels and administer hypoglycemic agents as prescribed.
  - Bronchodilators (inhalers)
    - Short-acting beta$_2$-agonists, such as albuterol (Proventil), provide rapid relief.
    - Cholinergic antagonists (anticholinergics), such as ipratropium (Atrovent), block the parasympathetic nervous system, providing relief of acute bronchospasms.
    - Nursing Considerations
      - Instruct the child and family in the proper use of an MDI, DPI, or nebulizer.
      - Monitor the child for tremors and tachycardia when he is taking albuterol.
      - Observe the child for dry mouth when taking ipratropium.
    - Client Education
      - Encourage older children to suck on hard candies to help dry mouth while taking ipratropium.

- o Antibiotics
  - Antibiotics are used to treat bacterial infections.
  - Nursing Considerations
    - □ Be aware of allergies.
  - Client Education
    - □ Advise parents that the child should finish the full course of antibiotics.
- o Dornase alfa (Pulmozyme)
  - Decreases the viscosity of mucus and improves lung function
  - Nursing Considerations
    - □ Monitor the child for improvement in PFTs
  - Client Education
    - □ Instruct the child in the use of a nebulizer.
    - □ Instruct the child to use once daily.
- o Pancreatic enzymes – Pancrelipase (Pancrease)
  - Used to treat pancreatic insufficiency associated with cystic fibrosis
  - Nursing Considerations
    - □ Capsules should be given with all meals.
    - □ Capsules can be swallowed whole or sprinkled on food.

- Interdisciplinary Care
  - o Respiratory therapy, social services, and dieticians may be involved in the care of the child who has cystic fibrosis.

- Care After Discharge
  - o Ensure that the family has information regarding access to medical equipment.
  - o Provide teaching about equipment prior to discharge.
  - o Instruct the family in ways to provide CPT and breathing exercises. For example, a child can stand on her head by using a large, cushioned chair placed against a wall.
  - o Promote regular primary care provider visits.
  - o Emphasize the need for up-to-date immunizations with the addition of an initial seasonal influenza vaccine at 6 months of age and then yearly.
  - o Promote regular physical activity.
  - o Encourage the family to participate in a support group and use community resources.

- Client Outcomes
  - o The child will maintain respiratory function and adequate growth and development for the condition.
  - o The child will remain free from infection.

Complications

- Respiratory Complications

  o Children who have cystic fibrosis are at increased risk for hospitalization related to pulmonary complications (respiratory infection, acute respiratory distress).

  o Nursing Actions

    ▪ Promptly treat respiratory infections with antibiotic therapy.

    ▪ Provide pulmonary hygiene with chest physiotherapy (CPT) (breathing exercises to strengthen thoracic muscles) a minimum of twice a day (in the morning and at bedtime).

    ▪ Have the child use a mucus clearance device to assist with mucus removal.

    ▪ Administer bronchodilators through a metered dose inhaler (MDI) or hand-held nebulizer to promote expectoration of excretions.

    ▪ Administer dornase alfa (Pulmozyme) through a nebulizer to decrease viscosity of mucus.

    ▪ Promote physical activity that the child enjoys to improve mental well-being, self-esteem, and mucus secretion.

  o Client Education

    ▪ Provide instructions regarding the medication regimen, dietary considerations, and infection control precautions.

- Gastrointestinal complications

  o Children who have cystic fibrosis are at increased risk for hospitalization related to gastrointestinal complications (meconium ileus, pancreatic fibrosis, distal intestinal obstruction syndrome).

  o Nursing Actions

    ▪ Administer pancreatic enzymes with meals and snacks.

      □ The amount of enzyme replacement will vary among children based on each child's deficiency and response to the replacement.

    ▪ Encourage the child to select meals and snacks if appropriate.

    ▪ Facilitate high-caloric, high-protein intake through meals and snacks.

    ▪ Multiple vitamins and water-soluble forms of vitamins A, D, E, and K are often prescribed.

  o Client Education

    ▪ Encourage the use of stool softeners or laxatives.

    ▪ Instruct the child and family that the capsules may be swallowed whole or opened to sprinkle the contents on a small amount of food.

CHAPTER 19: CYSTIC FIBROSIS

 Application Exercises

1. Cystic fibrosis is hereditary and transmitted as an _____ trait. Thus, both parents must be carriers of the gene.

2. A nurse is caring for a child who is suspected of having cystic fibrosis. Which of the following tests should the nurse prepare to administer to confirm this diagnosis?

    A. Sweat chloride

    B. Blood glucose

    C. Arterial blood gases

    D. Ultrasound

3. A nurse should expect the stools of a child who has cystic fibrosis to be

    A. hard and dry with difficult evacuation.

    B. dark colored and tarry.

    C. blood streaked with mucus strands.

    D. fatty and foul smelling.

4. Which of the following are assessment findings seen in a child who has cystic fibrosis? (Select all that apply.)

    _____ Shortness of breath

    _____ Clubbing of fingers and toes

    _____ Barrel-shaped chest

    _____ Thin, watery mucus drainage

    _____ Rapid growth spurts

5. Which of the following is an appropriate nursing intervention for a child with cystic fibrosis?

    A. Administer fat-soluble forms of vitamins A, D, E, and K.

    B. Give pancreatic enzymes with food and snacks.

    C. Place the child on a low-calorie, low-protein diet.

    D. Limit fluids throughout the day.

CHAPTER 19: CYSTIC FIBROSIS

 Application Exercises Answer Key

1. Cystic fibrosis is hereditary and transmitted as an _____ trait. Thus, both parents must be carriers of the gene.

 Autosomal recessive

 Autosomal recessive traits are inherited when both parents carry the defective gene.

 NCLEX® Connection: Physiological Adaptation, Pathophysiology

2. A nurse is caring for a child who is suspected of having cystic fibrosis. Which of the following tests should the nurse prepare to administer to confirm this diagnosis?

 A. Sweat chloride

 B. Blood glucose

 C. Arterial blood gases

 D. Ultrasound

 A sweat chloride test is used to diagnose cystic fibrosis. This test measures the amount of chloride in skin sweat. Abnormally high concentrations of sodium and chloride are unique to cystic fibrosis. A normal chloride concentration of sweat is less than 40 mEq/L. Cystic fibrosis is very likely to be present in infants who have chloride values greater than 40 mEq/L. Children who have values greater than 60 mEq/L are diagnosed with cystic fibrosis. The other tests may be used to determine the condition of a child who has cystic fibrosis, but they are not diagnostic of the disorder.

 NCLEX® Connection: Reduction of Risk Potential, Diagnostic Tests

3. A nurse should expect the stools of a child who has cystic fibrosis to be

 A. hard and dry with difficult evacuation.

 B. dark colored and tarry.

 C. blood streaked with mucus strands.

 D. fatty and foul smelling.

 Stool analysis of a child with cystic fibrosis indicates the presence of steatorrhea (undigested fat) and azotorrhea (foul-smelling from protein). The stools are large, loose, fatty, sticky, and foul-smelling.

 NCLEX® Connection: Reduction of Risk Potential, System Specific Assessment

4. Which of the following are assessment findings seen in a child who has cystic fibrosis? (Select all that apply.)

__X__	**Shortness of breath**
__X__	**Clubbing of fingers and toes**
__X__	**Barrel-shaped chest**
_____	Thin, watery mucus drainage
_____	Rapid growth spurts

Shortness of breath may be seen early in the disease. As the disease progresses, clubbing of fingers and toes and a barrel-shaped chest may develop. Cystic fibrosis results in thick, viscous mucus and delayed growth and development.

Ⓝ NCLEX® Connection: Reduction of Risk Potential, System Specific Assessment

5. Which of the following is an appropriate nursing intervention for a child with cystic fibrosis?

A. Administer fat-soluble forms of vitamins A, D, E, and K.

B. Give pancreatic enzymes with food and snacks.

C. Place the child on a low-calorie, low-protein diet.

D. Limit fluids throughout the day.

The child with cystic fibrosis must be administered pancreatic enzymes for digestion. This is because the increased viscosity of mucus gland secretions causes obstruction of the pancreatic ducts and prevents the necessary enzymes from reaching the duodenum. There is a decreased absorption of fat-soluble vitamins, so the child must be administered water-soluble forms of these vitamins. The child should be on a high-calorie, high-protein diet to promote adequate growth and development. The child should be encouraged to drink adequate fluids to prevent dehydration and decrease viscosity of secretions.

Ⓝ NCLEX® Connection: Physiological Adaptation, Illness Management

UNIT 2: NURSING CARE OF CHILDREN WITH SYSTEM DISORDERS

Section: Cardiovascular and Hematologic Disorders

- Cardiovascular Disorders
- Hematologic Disorders

NCLEX® CONNECTIONS

When reviewing the chapters in this section, keep in mind the relevant sections of the NCLEX® outline, in particular:

CLIENT NEEDS: PHARMACOLOGICAL AND PARENTERAL THERAPIES

Relevant topics/tasks include:
- Adverse Effects/ Contraindications/Side Effects/Interactions
  - Monitor for anticipated interactions among the client's prescribed medications and fluids.
- Dosage Calculation
  - Use clinical decision making/critical thinking when calculating dosages.
- Medication Administration
  - Review pertinent data prior to medication administration.

CLIENT NEEDS: REDUCTION OF RISK POTENTIAL

Relevant topics/tasks include:
- Changes/Abnormalities in Vital Signs
  - Apply knowledge of client pathophysiology when measuring vital signs.
- Potential for Complications of Diagnostic Tests/ Treatments/Procedures
  - Monitor the client for signs of bleeding.
- System Specific Assessment
  - Assess the client for abnormal peripheral pulses after a procedure or treatment.

CLIENT NEEDS: PHYSIOLOGICAL ADAPTATION

Relevant topics/tasks include:
- Alterations in Body Systems
  - Evaluate achievement of the client's treatment goals.
- Hemodynamics
  - Provide the client with strategies to manage decreased cardiac output.
- Illness Management
  - Apply knowledge of client pathophysiology to illness management.

UNIT 2	NURSING CARE OF CHILDREN WITH SYSTEM DISORDERS
Section	Cardiovascular and Hematologic Disorders
Chapter 20	Cardiovascular Disorders

@ Overview

- Heart disease may be congenital or it may be acquired, as is the case with rheumatic heart disease.

- Anatomic abnormalities present at birth can lead to congenital heart disease (CHD). These abnormalities result primarily in heart failure and hypoxemia.

- Rheumatic fever is a self-limiting inflammatory disease of the connective tissue. System involvement includes the connective tissue of the heart, joints, central nervous system, skin, and subcutaneous tissue.

    o Rheumatic heart disease is the major complication of rheumatic fever, and it results in cardiac valve damage.

CONGENITAL HEART DISEASE (CHD)

@ Overview

- Anatomic defects of the heart prevent normal blood flow to the pulmonary and/or systemic system.

- Many defects will spontaneously close, but some will require surgical repair.

- Most children with CHD will be diagnosed in the first year of life, but certain children may not exhibit manifestations until later.

- Children with CHD have an increased incidence of other anatomic defects, which may impact their care.

Assessment

- Risk Factors

    o Cardiac development occurs very early in fetal life, making it difficult to identify the cause of defects.

    o Maternal factors

      ▪ Rubella in early pregnancy

      ▪ Alcohol and/or other substance abuse during pregnancy

      ▪ Diabetes mellitus

    o Genetic factors

      ▪ History of congenital heart disease in other family members

      ▪ Trisomy 21 (Down syndrome)

      ▪ Presence of other congenital anomalies or syndromes

- Subjective and Objective Data

 View Media Supplement:

- Ventricular Septal Defect (Image)
- Pulmonary Stenosis (Image)
- Coarctation of the Aorta (Image)
- Tetralogy of Fallot (Image)

CONGENITAL HEART DEFECT	MANIFESTATIONS
Ventricular septal defect (VSD) – A hole in the septum between the right and left ventricle that results in increased pulmonary blood flow (left-to-right shunt)	<ul><li>Loud, harsh murmur that is not usually audible until pulmonary pressures drop at about 4 to 8 weeks of age</li><li>Heart failure</li><li>Failure to thrive</li><li>Small, possibly asymptomatic defects</li></ul>
Atrial septal defect (ASD) – A hole in the septum between the right and left atria that results in increased pulmonary blood flow (left-to-right shunt)	<ul><li>Loud, harsh murmur</li><li>Mild heart failure</li><li>Possible enlarged right atrium</li><li>Increased oxygen saturations in the right atrium</li><li>Asymptomatic (possibly)</li></ul>
Patent ductus arteriosus (PDA) – A condition in which the normal fetal circulation conduit between the pulmonary artery and the aorta fails to close and results in increased pulmonary blood flow (left-to-right shunt)	<ul><li>Murmur (machine-hum)</li><li>Wide pulse pressure</li><li>Bounding pulses</li><li>Asymptomatic (possibly)</li></ul>

CONGENITAL HEART DEFECT	MANIFESTATIONS
Pulmonary stenosis – A narrowing of the pulmonary valve or pulmonary artery that results in obstruction of blood flow from the ventricles	• Systolic ejection murmur • Right ventricular enlargement • Exercise intolerance • Cyanosis with severe narrowing
Aortic stenosis – A narrowing at, above, or below the aortic valve	• Murmur • Left ventricular enlargement • Chest pain; exercise intolerance; weak, thready pulses; hypotension; dizziness; and syncope
Coarctation of the aorta – A narrowing of the lumen of the aorta, usually at or near the ductus arteriosus, that results in obstruction of blood flow from the ventricles	• Increased blood pressure and oxygen saturation in the upper extremities compared to the lower extremities • Nosebleeds • Headaches, vertigo, leg pain, weak or absent lower extremity pulses (indicate decreased cardiac output)
Transposition of the great arteries – A condition in which the aorta is connected to the right ventricle instead of the left, and the pulmonary artery is connected to the left ventricle instead of the right	• Murmur • Severe cyanosis appearing hours to days after birth (as the PDA closes) • Cardiomegaly • Heart failure
Tricuspid atresia – A complete closure of the tricuspid valve that results in mixed blood flow	• No blood flow from the right atrium to the right ventricle • Severe cyanosis within hours of birth (increased as the PDA closes) • Heart failure • Chronic hypoxemia • Failure to thrive and growth retardation
Tetralogy of Fallot – Four defects that result in mixed blood flow • Pulmonary stenosis • Ventricular septal defect • Overriding aorta • Right ventricular hypertrophy	• Murmur • Cyanosis, severe dyspnea, clubbing of the fingers, hypercyanotic spells, and acidosis • Polycythemia, clot formation • Child frequently assuming a squatting position (decreases venous return) • Failure to thrive and growth retardation

- o   Manifestations of heart failure (HF)
  - ▪   Impaired myocardial function
    - □   Tachycardia, murmurs, extra sounds (S_3 and S_4) diaphoresis, decreased urinary output, fatigue, generalized pallor or mottling, cool extremities, weak peripheral pulses, slow capillary refill, cardiomegaly, anorexia, and failure to thrive

- ■ Pulmonary congestion
    - □ Tachypnea, dyspnea, crackles heard in lungs, retractions, nasal flaring, use of accessory muscle, stridor, grunting, recurrent respiratory infections, and exercise intolerance
- ■ Systemic venous congestion
    - □ Hepatomegaly, enlarged spleen, peripheral edema, ascites, and neck vein distention (not seen in infants)
- ○ Manifestations of hypoxemia
    - ■ Cyanosis, poor weight gain, tachypnea, dyspnea, clubbing, and polycythemia

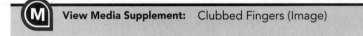
View Media Supplement: Clubbed Fingers (Image)

- ■ Hypercyanotic spells (blue, or "Tet," spells) are manifested as acute cyanosis and hyperpnea to detect anemia, polycythemia, and electrolyte imbalances.
- ○ Laboratory Tests
    - ■ Hemoglobin (Hgb), hematocrit (Hct), and serum electrolytes
- ○ Diagnostic Procedures
    - ■ ECG monitoring
        - □ Identifies cardiac dysrhythmias
        - □ Nursing Actions
            - ▸ Assist with the application of electrodes.
            - ▸ Assist with maintaining the child in a quiet position.
        - □ Client Education
            - ▸ Tell the child that the test will not be painful.
    - ■ Radiography (chest x-ray)
        - □ Demonstrates cardiomegaly and increased or decreased pulmonary vascularity associated with congenital anomalies
        - □ Nursing Actions
            - ▸ Assist with positioning the client.
    - ■ Echocardiography
        - □ Confirms cardiac dysfunction in children without resorting to cardiac catheterization
        - □ Nursing Actions
            - ▸ Assist with positioning the child.

- Cardiac catheterization

  □ Cardiac catheterization is an invasive test used for diagnosing, repairing some defects, and evaluating dysrhythmias. A radiopaque catheter is peripherally inserted and threaded into the heart with the use of fluoroscopy. A contrast medium (may be iodine-based) is injected, and images of the blood vessels and heart are taken as the medium is diluted and circulated throughout the body.

  □ Nursing Actions

    ▸ Preprocedure

      ▷ Perform a nursing history and physical exam. Signs and symptoms of infections, such as a severe diaper rash, may necessitate canceling the procedure if femoral access is required.

      ▷ Check for allergies to iodine and shellfish.

      ▷ Provide age-appropriate teaching.

      ▷ Describe how long the procedure will take, how the child will feel, and what care will be required after the procedure.

      ▷ Provide for NPO status 4 to 6 hr prior to the procedure. (If the procedure is performed as outpatient, be sure the child and family are given instructions in advance.)

      ▷ Obtain baseline vital signs including oxygen saturation.

      ▷ Locate and mark the dorsalis pedis and posterior tibial pulses on both extremities.

      ▷ Administer presedation as prescribed based on the child's age, height, weight, condition, and type of procedure being performed.

    ▸ Postprocedure

      ▷ Provide for continuous cardiac monitoring and oxygen saturation to assess for bradycardia, dysrhythmias, hypotension, and hypoxemia.

      ▷ Assess pulses for equality and symmetry.

      ▷ Assess temperature and color. A cool extremity with skin that blanches may indicate arterial obstruction.

      ▷ Assess insertion site (femoral or antecubital area) for bleeding and/or hematoma.

      ▷ Maintain clean dressing.

      ▷ Monitor I&O to assess for adequate urine output, hypovolemia, or dehydration.

      ▷ Monitor for hypoglycemia. Intravenous fluids with dextrose may be necessary.

  ▷ Prevent bleeding by maintaining the affected extremity in a straight position for 4 to 8 hr.

  ▷ Encourage oral intake, starting with clear liquids.

  ▷ Encourage the child to void to promote excretion of the contrast medium.

□ Client Education

  ▸ Encourage fluid intake to help with the removal of the dye from the body.

  ▸ Advise the parents and child to monitor the site for infection.

Collaborative Care

- Nursing Care

  ○ General Interventions

    ▪ Remain calm when providing care.

    ▪ Keep the child well-hydrated.

    ▪ Conserve the child's energy by providing frequent rest periods; clustering care; providing small, frequent meals; bathing PRN; and keeping crying to a minimum in cyanotic children.

    ▪ Perform daily weight and I&O to monitor fluid status and nutritional status.

    ▪ Monitor heart rate, blood pressure, serum electrolytes, and renal function to assess for complications.

    ▪ Provide support and resources for parents to promote developmental growth in the child.

    ▪ Monitor family coping and provide support.

    ▪ Improve cardiac function by administering prescribed medications.

    ▪ Maintain fluid and electrolyte balance.

      □ Administer potassium supplements if prescribed. These may not be indicated if the child is concurrently taking an ACE inhibitor.

      □ Maintain sodium and fluid restrictions if prescribed.

    ▪ Decrease workload of the heart.

      □ Maintain bedrest

      □ Position the infant in a car seat or hold him at a 45° angle. Keep safety restraints low and loose on the abdomen.

      □ Allow the child to sleep with several pillows and instruct her to maintain a semi-Fowler's or Fowler's position while awake.

    ▪ Provide for adequate nutrition.

      □ Plan to feed the infant using a feeding schedule of every 3 hr. The infant should be rested, which occurs soon after awakening.

- Use a soft preemie nipple or a regular nipple with a slit to provide an enlarged opening.

- Hold the infant in a semi-upright position.

- Allow the infant to rest during feedings, taking approximately 30 min to complete the feeding.

- Gavage feed the infant if he is unable to consume enough formula or breast milk.

- Increase caloric density of formula gradually from 20 kcal/oz to 30 kcal/oz.

- Encourage mothers who are breastfeeding to alternate feedings with high-density formula or fortified breast milk.

- Increase tissue oxygenation.

  - Provide cool, humidified oxygen via an oxygen hood (or tent), mask, or nasal cannula.

  - Suction the airway as indicated.

  - Monitor oxygen saturation every 2 to 4 hr.

- Medications

  - Digoxin (Lanoxin)

    - Improves myocardial contractility

    - Nursing Actions

      - Monitor the pulse and withhold the medication as ordered. Generally if an infant's pulse is less than 90/min, the medication should be withheld. In children, the medication should be withheld if the pulse is less than 70/min.

      - Monitor for toxicity as evidenced by bradycardia, dysrhythmias, nausea, vomiting, or anorexia.

      - Monitor serum digoxin levels.

  - Captopril (Capoten) or enalapril (Vasotec)

    - Angiotensin-converting enzyme (ACE) inhibitors reduce afterload by causing vasodilation, resulting in decreased pulmonary and systemic vascular resistance.

    - Nursing Considerations

      - Monitor blood pressure before and after the medication is administered.

      - Monitor for signs of hyperkalemia.

    - Client Education

      - Parents should be instructed to monitor blood pressure frequently.

  - Furosemide (Lasix) or chlorothiazide (Diuril)

    - Potassium-wasting diuretics rid the body of excess fluid and sodium.

- Nursing Considerations
  - Monitor intake and output.
  - Monitor for signs of hypokalemia.
  - Monitor weight daily.

- Interdisciplinary Care

  - Dieticians should be consulted to assist the family with appropriate food choices.

- Care After Discharge

  - Client Education
    - Cardiac catheterization
      - Teach the family how to monitor for possible complications (bleeding, infection, thrombosis).
      - Limit activity for 24 hr.
      - Encourage fluids.
    - Digoxin administration
      - Take pulse prior to medication administration. Notify provider if pulse is lower than specified rate.
      - Administer digoxin every 12 hr.
      - Direct oral elixir toward the side and back of mouth when administering.
      - Give water following administration to prevent tooth decay if the child has teeth.
      - If a dose is missed, do not give an extra dose or increase the next dose.
      - If the child vomits, do not re-administer the dose.
      - Observe for signs of digoxin toxicity (decreased heart rate, decreased appetite, nausea, and/or vomiting). Notify the provider if these occur.
      - Keep the medication in a locked cabinet.
    - Diuretic administration
      - Mix the oral elixir in a small amount of juice to disguise the bitter taste and prevent intestinal irritation.
      - Observe for side effects of diuretics, which may include nausea, vomiting, and diarrhea.
      - Observe for signs and symptoms of serum potassium level imbalances (muscle weakness, irritability, excessive drowsiness, increased or decreased heart rate).
    - Encourage the child to eat foods high in potassium, such as bran cereals, potatoes, tomatoes, bananas, melons, oranges, and orange juice.
    - Teach the family to monitor weight daily.

- Instruct the family to report signs and symptoms of worsening heart failure, such as increased sweating and decreased urinary output (fewer wet diapers or less frequent toileting).

- Client Outcomes

  - The child will maintain an adequate cardiac output to maintain activities of daily living.

  - The child will maintain appropriate weight.

Complications

- Potential cardiac catheterization complications and interventions

  - Nausea, vomiting

  - Low-grade fever

  - Loss of pulse in the catheterized extremity

  - Transient dysrhythmias

  - Acute hemorrhage from entry site

  - Nursing Actions

    - Apply direct continuous pressure at 2.5 cm (1 in) above the catheter entry site to localize pressure over the location of the vessel puncture.

    - Position the child flat to reduce the gravitational effect on the rate of bleeding.

    - Notify the provider immediately.

    - Prepare for the possible administration of replacement fluids and/or medication to control emesis.

  - Client Education

    - Monitor for signs of infection.

    - Monitor for bleeding.

- Hypoxemia

  - A hypercyanotic spell can result in severe hypoxemia, which leads to cerebral hypoxemia, and should be treated as an emergency.

  - Nursing Actions

    - Immediately place the child in the knee-chest position, attempt to calm the child, and call for help.

- Bacterial endocarditis or subacute bacterial endocarditis

  - Children with congenital or acquired heart disease are at increased risk for infection of the valves or lining of the heart.

- o The child should follow the American Heart Association's recommendations for bacterial endocarditis prophylaxis. These include receiving prophylactic antibiotic therapy prior to dental and surgical procedures (dental extractions, endodontic surgery, surgical procedures that involve the respiratory or gastrointestinal mucosa).

- o Causative organisms include *Streptococcus viridians* and *Staphylococcus aureus*.

- o Nursing Actions

  - Administer antibiotics parenterally for approximately 8 weeks.

- o Client Education

  - Counsel the family about the need for prophylactic antibiotics prior to dental extractions (endodontic surgery, surgical procedures that involve the respiratory or gastrointestinal mucosa).

- Heart failure requiring transplant

  - o Cardiomyopathy and congenital heart disease are causes of heart failure.

  - o Nursing Actions

    - Maintain pharmacological support as ordered (oxygen, diuretics, digoxin, afterload reducers such as ACE inhibitors).

    - Provide family and child support.

  - o Client Education

    - Teach the importance of adhering to the medication regimen.

    - Inform the child and family about infection control precautions.

RHEUMATIC FEVER

Overview

- Rheumatic fever is an inflammatory disease that occurs as a reaction to Group A β-hemolytic streptococcus (GABHS) infection of the throat.

Assessment

- Risk Factors

  - o Rheumatic fever usually occurs within 2 to 6 weeks following an untreated or partially treated upper respiratory infection (strep throat) with GABHS.

- Subjective and Objective Data

  - o History of recent upper respiratory infection

  - o Fever

  - o Fatigue

  - o Sore throat

- ○ Activity intolerance

- ○ Poor appetite

- ○ Tachycardia, cardiomegaly, prolonged PR interval, new or changed heart murmur, muffled heart sounds, pericardial friction rub, and reports of chest pain, which may indicate carditis

- ○ Nontender, subcutaneous nodules over bony prominence

- ○ Large joints (knees, elbows, ankles, wrists, shoulders) that have painful swelling indicating polyarthritis
  - ■ Symptoms last a few days and then disappear without treatment, frequently returning in another joint.

- ○ Pink, nonpruritic macular rash on the trunk and inner surfaces of extremities that appears and disappears rapidly, indicating erythema marginatum.

- ○ CNS involvement (chorea) including involuntary, purposeless muscle movements; muscle weakness; involuntary facial movements; difficulty performing fine motor activities; labile emotions; and random, uncoordinated movements of the extremities

- ○ Irritability, poor concentration, and behavioral problems

- ○ Laboratory Tests
  - ■ Throat culture for GABHS
  - ■ Blood samples
    - □ Elevated or rising serum antistreptolysin-O (ASO) titer – Most reliable
    - □ Elevated C-reactive protein (CRP) or sedimentation rate – In response to an inflammatory reaction

- ○ Diagnostic Procedures
  - ■ Cardiac function
    - □ ECG to reveal the presence of conduction disturbances and to evaluate the function of the heart and valves
    - □ Nursing Actions
      - ▸ Position the child correctly for the procedure.
    - □ Client Education
      - ▸ Explain the need for decreased movement during the procedure.
  - ■ The diagnosis of rheumatic fever is made on the basis of modified Jones criteria. The child should demonstrate the presence of two major criteria or the presence of one major and two minor criteria following an acute infection with GABHS infection.
    - □ Major criteria
      - ▸ Carditis
      - ▸ Subcutaneous nodules

- ▸ Polyarthritis
- ▸ Rash (erythema marginatum)
- ▸ Chorea
- ▫ Minor criteria
  - ▸ Fever
  - ▸ Arthralgia

Collaborative Care

- Medications
  - ○ Penicillin (Pen V) or erythromycin (EryPed)
    - Administer antibiotics as prescribed to eliminate the streptococcal infection.
    - Nursing Considerations
      - ▫ Assess the child for an allergic response (anaphylaxis, hives, rashes). Assess for nausea, vomiting, or diarrhea.
    - Client Education
      - ▫ Stress the importance of finishing the entire course of the medication.
- Care After Discharge
  - ○ Client Education
    - Reinforce with the child and family the importance of completing the entire 10- to 14-day course of antibiotics as prescribed, even if the child starts to feel better after a few doses.
    - Promote rest and adequate nutrition.
    - Provide information and reassurance related to the development of chorea and its self-limiting nature.
    - Follow the provider's prescribed prophylactic treatment regimen, which may include one of the following: two daily oral doses of 200,000 units of penicillin, a monthly intramuscular injection of 1.2 million units of penicillin G, or a daily oral dose of 1 g of sulfadiazine (Microsulfon). The length of prophylaxis treatment may vary but may be a minimum of 5 years or until 18 years of age.
  - ○ Follow-up
    - Seek medical care if infection recurrence is suspected.
    - Obtain antibiotic prophylaxis therapy for all dental work and invasive procedures.
    - Arrange for medical follow-up every 5 years.

Complications

- Rheumatic heart disease
  - Nursing Actions
    - Monitor for cardiac rate, rhythm, and presence of murmurs.
    - Prepare the child for valve replacement.
  - Client Education
    - Encourage the child to adhere to medical follow-up care.

CHAPTER 20: CARDIOVASCULAR DISORDERS

(A) Application Exercises

1. Match the description of the structural defect to the correct specific cardiac defect nomenclature.

_____ Ventricular septal defect	A. A narrowing at, above, or below the aortic valve
_____ Atrial septal defect	B. A hole in the septum between the right and left ventricles
_____ Patent ductus arteriosus	C. Complete closure of the tricuspid valve
_____ Pulmonary stenosis	D. A hole in the septum between the right and left atria
_____ Aortic stenosis	E. Consists of four anomalies: pulmonary stenosis, ventricular septal defect, overriding aorta, and right ventricular hypertrophy
_____ Coarctation of the aorta	F. The failure to close of the normal fetal circulation conduit between the pulmonary artery and the aorta
_____ Transposition of the great arteries	G. A narrowing of the pulmonary valve or pulmonary artery
_____ Tricuspid atresia	H. A condition in which the aorta is connected to the right ventricle instead of the left, and the pulmonary artery is connected to the left ventricle instead of the right
_____ Tetralogy of Fallot	I. A narrowing of the lumen of the aorta, usually at or near the ductus arteriosus

2. A nurse is assessing an infant who has congenital heart disease. Which of the following should the nurse recognize as manifestations of heart failure? (Select all that apply.)

_____ Bradycardia

_____ Cool extremities

_____ Peripheral edema

_____ Increased urinary output

_____ Nasal flaring

3. A nurse is providing teaching to the mother of an infant who is to start taking digoxin (Lanoxin). Which of the following instructions should the nurse include?

A. "Do not allow your baby to drink anything after the digoxin is administered."

B. "Digoxin speeds the heart rate up to allow the heart to pump out more fluid."

C. "It is important to administer the correct amount at regularly scheduled times."

D. "If your baby vomits a dose, you should repeat the dose to ensure that he gets the correct amount."

4. A nurse is caring for a 2-year-old child who is cyanotic and is in the hospital for a cardiac catheterization to repair cardiac defects. The child will be transferred to the pediatric ICU following the procedure. Which of the following is an appropriate nursing action when providing care to this child?

    A. Place on NPO status for 12 hr prior to the procedure.

    B. Check for iodine or shellfish allergies prior to the procedure.

    C. Elevate the affected extremity following the procedure.

    D. Restrict fluids following the procedure until the gag reflex is intact.

5. Match the medication with the intended effect.

_____	Digoxin (Lanoxin)	A. Rids body of excess fluid and sodium
_____	Furosemide (Lasix)	B. Increases tissue oxygenation
_____	Captopril (Capoten)	C. Improves myocardial contractility
_____	Oxygen	D. Reduces afterload

6. A nurse is caring for a child who is suspected of having rheumatic fever. Which of the following manifestations support this diagnosis? (Select all that apply.)

    _____ Erythema marginatum (rash)

    _____ Continuous joint pain of the digits

    _____ Tender, subcutaneous nodules

    _____ Decreased erythrocyte sedimentation rate

    _____ Elevated C-reactive protein

    _____ Uncoordinated movements of the extremities

7. Rheumatic fever can be avoided by identification of _____ infections and treatment with _____.

CHAPTER 20: CARDIOVASCULAR DISORDERS

(A) Application Exercises Answer Key

1. Match the description of the structural defect to the correct specific cardiac defect nomenclature.

B	Ventricular septal defect	A. A narrowing at, above, or below the aortic valve
D	Atrial septal defect	B. A hole in the septum between the right and left ventricles
F	Patent ductus arteriosus	C. Complete closure of the tricuspid valve
G	Pulmonary stenosis	D. A hole in the septum between the right and left atria
A	Aortic stenosis	E. Consists of four anomalies: pulmonary stenosis, ventricular septal defect, overriding aorta, and right ventricular hypertrophy
I	Coarctation of the aorta	F. The failure to close of the normal fetal circulation conduit between the pulmonary artery and the aorta
H	Transposition of the great arteries	G. A narrowing of the pulmonary valve or pulmonary artery
C	Tricuspid atresia	H. A condition in which the aorta is connected to the right ventricle instead of the left, and the pulmonary artery is connected to the left ventricle instead of the right
E	Tetralogy of Fallot	I. A narrowing of the lumen of the aorta, usually at or near the ductus arteriosus

(N) **NCLEX® Connection: Physiological Adaptation, Pathophysiology**

2. A nurse is assessing an infant who has congenital heart disease. Which of the following should the nurse recognize as manifestations of heart failure? (Select all that apply.)

_____ Bradycardia
__**X**__ **Cool extremities**
__**X**__ **Peripheral edema**
_____ Increased urinary output
__**X**__ **Nasal flaring**

Impaired cardiac function may manifest as cool extremities, tachycardia, and decreased urinary output; systemic venous congestion may manifest as pulmonary edema; and pulmonary congestion may manifest as nasal flaring.

 NCLEX® Connection: Reduction of Risk Potential, System Specific Assessment

3. A nurse is providing teaching to the mother of an infant who is to start taking digoxin (Lanoxin). Which of the following instructions should the nurse include?

    A. "Do not allow your baby to drink anything after the digoxin is administered."

    B. "Digoxin speeds the heart rate up to allow the heart to pump out more fluid."

    C. "It is important to administer the correct amount at regularly scheduled times."

    D. "If your baby vomits a dose, you should repeat the dose to ensure that he gets the correct amount."

The correct amount of digoxin should be administered at regularly scheduled times to maintain therapeutic blood levels. If the infant has teeth, the dose should be followed by water to prevent tooth decay. Digoxin slows the heart rate. If the infant vomits after the dose, it should not be re-administered because there is no way to know if the infant received any of the medication.

 NCLEX® Connection: Pharmacological and Parenteral Therapies, Expected Effects/Outcomes

4. A nurse is caring for a 2-year-old child who is cyanotic and is in the hospital for a cardiac catheterization to repair cardiac defects. The child will be transferred to the pediatric ICU following the procedure. Which of the following is an appropriate nursing action when providing care to this child?

    A. Place on NPO status for 12 hr prior to the procedure.

    B. Check for iodine or shellfish allergies prior to the procedure.

    C. Elevate the affected extremity following the procedure.

    D. Restrict fluids following the procedure until the gag reflex is intact.

Iodine-based dyes may be used in this procedure. If the child is allergic to iodine or shellfish, use of such a dye could lead to anaphylaxis. The child only needs to be NPO 4 to 6 hr prior to the procedure. The affected extremity should be maintained in a straight position. Fluids should be encouraged after the procedure to maintain adequate urine output and promote excretion of the dye.

 NCLEX® Connection: Reduction of Risk Potential, Potential for Complications of Diagnostic Tests/Treatments/Procedures

5. Match the medication with the intended effect.

__C__	Digoxin (Lanoxin)	A. Rids body of excess fluid and sodium
__A__	Furosemide (Lasix)	B. Increases tissue oxygenation
__D__	Captopril (Capoten)	C. Improves myocardial contractility
__B__	Oxygen	D. Reduces afterload

 NCLEX® Connection: Pharmacological and Parenteral Therapies, Expected Effects/Outcomes

6. A nurse is caring for a child who is suspected of having rheumatic fever. Which of the following manifestations support this diagnosis? (Select all that apply.)

__X__	**Erythema marginatum (rash)**
_____	Continuous joint pain of the digits
_____	Tender, subcutaneous nodules
_____	Decreased erythrocyte sedimentation rate
__X__	**Elevated C-reactive protein**
__X__	**Uncoordinated movements of the extremities**

Erythema marginatum, elevated C-reactive protein, and uncoordinated movements of the extremities are all manifestations of rheumatic fever. Migratory joint pain of the large joints, nontender subcutaneous nodules beneath the skin, and increased erythrocyte sedimentation rate are also manifestations.

Ⓝ **NCLEX® Connection: Reduction of Risk Potential, System Specific Assessment**

7. Rheumatic fever can be avoided by identification of _____ infections and treatment with _____.

GABHS, antibiotics (penicillin, or erythromycin if the child is allergic to penicillin)

Early identification of GABHS and subsequent appropriate antimicrobial treatment can help prevent the development of rheumatic fever.

Ⓝ **NCLEX® Connection: Physiological Adaptation, Infectious Disease**

UNIT 2	NURSING CARE OF CHILDREN WITH SYSTEM DISORDERS
Section	Cardiovascular and Hematologic Disorders
Chapter 21	Hematologic Disorders

Overview

- Blood disorders that may affect children include:

  ○ Epistaxis

  ○ Iron deficiency anemia

  ○ Sickle cell anemia

  ○ Hemophilia

EPISTAXIS

Overview

- Epistaxis is common in childhood.

- Epistaxis may be spontaneous or induced by trauma to the nose.

- Epistaxis may produce anxiety for the child and parents.

- Epistaxis is rarely an emergency.

Assessment

- Risk Factors

  ○ Trauma, such as picking or rubbing the nose, may cause mucous membranes in the nose, which are vascular and fragile, to tear and bleed.

  ○ Low humidity, allergic rhinitis, an upper respiratory virus, blunt injury, or a foreign body in the nose may all precipitate a nosebleed.

  ○ Medications, such as antihistamines that dry mucous membranes, may increase the number of nosebleeds.

  ○ Medications that affect clotting factors, such as warfarin (Coumadin), may increase bleeding.

  ○ Epistaxis may be the result of underlying diseases (Willebrand's disease, hemophilia, idiopathic thrombocytopenia purpura [ITP], leukemia).

- Subjective Data

    o History of bleeding gums or blood in body fluids and/or stool

    o History of trauma, illness, allergies, or placing foreign bodies in the nose

- Objective Data

    o Physical Assessment Findings

        - Active bleeding from nose

        - Restlessness and agitation

Collaborative Care

- Nursing Care

    o Maintain a calm demeanor with the child and family.

    o Have the child sit up with the head tilted slightly forward to promote draining of blood out of the nose instead of down the back of the throat. Swallowing blood can promote coughing and lead to nausea, vomiting, and diarrhea.

    o Apply pressure to the lower nose, or instruct the child to use her thumb and forefinger to press the nares together for 5 to 10 min.

    o If needed, cotton or tissue can be packed into the side of the nose that is bleeding.

    o Encourage the child to breathe through her mouth while her nose is bleeding.

    o Apply ice across the bridge of the nose if possible.

    o Keep the child from rubbing or picking her nose after bleeding is stopped.

- Care After Discharge

    o Client Education

        - Keep fingernails short.

        - Use a humidifier during the dry winter months.

        - Have the child open her mouth when sneezing.

        - For recurrences, remind the child to sit up and slightly forward so blood does not flow down the throat and cause coughing.

        - Inform the family that bleeding may last 20 to 30 min.

- Client Outcomes

    o The child will have decreased episodes of epistaxis.

Complications

- Excessive Bleeding

    ○ Nursing Actions

        ■ Provide support to the child during cauterization or packing.

    ○ Client Education

        ■ Instruct the child and family to seek medical care if bleeding lasts longer than 30 min or is caused by an injury/trauma.

IRON DEFICIENCY ANEMIA

Overview

- Iron deficiency anemia is the most common anemia in children ages 6 months to 2 years. It is also commonly diagnosed in adolescents 12 to 20 years of age.

- RBCs with decreased Hgb levels will have a decreased capacity to carry oxygen to tissue.

- The production of Hgb requires iron. Iron deficiency will result in decreased Hgb levels in RBCs.

- Iron deficiency anemia usually results from an inadequate dietary supply of iron.

- Manifestations are related to the degree of anemia and the result of decreased oxygen to the tissues.

- Prolonged anemia can lead to:

    ○ Growth retardation

    ○ Developmental delays

Assessment

- Risk Factors

    ○ Premature birth resulting in decreased iron stores

    ○ Excessive intake of cows' milk in toddlers.

        ■ Milk is not a good source of iron.

        ■ Milk takes the place of iron-rich solid foods.

    ○ Malabsorption disorders due to prolonged diarrhea

    ○ Poor dietary intake of iron

    ○ Periods of rapid growth, such as adolescence

- ○ Increased iron requirements (blood loss)

- ○ Infection

- ○ Chronic disorders (folate deficiency, sickle cell anemia, hemophilia).

- • Subjective and Objective Data

    - ○ Shortness of breath

    - ○ Tachycardia

    - ○ Dizziness or fainting with exertion

    - ○ Pallor

    - ○ Nail bed deformities

    - ○ Fatigue, irritability, and muscle weakness

    - ○ Impaired healing, loss of skin elasticity, and thinning of hair

    - ○ Abdominal pain, nausea, vomiting, and loss of appetite

    - ○ Low-grade fever

    - ○ Systolic heart murmur and/or heart failure

    - ○ Laboratory Tests

NORMAL VALUES		
AGE	HGB	HCT
2 months	9.0 to 14.0 g/dL	28% to 42%
6 to 12 years	11.5 to 15.5 g/dL	35% to 45%
12 to 18 years	13.0 to 16.0 g/dL (male) 12.0 to 16.0 g/dL (female)	37% to 49% (male) 36% to 46% (female)

- ■ CBC – Decreased RBC count, decreased Hgb, and decreased Hct

- ■ RBC indices – Decreased, indicating microcytic/hypochromic RBCs

    - □ Mean corpuscular volume (MVC) – Average size of RBC

    - □ Mean corpuscular Hgb (MCH) – Average weight of RBC

    - □ Mean corpuscular hemoglobin concentration (MCHC) – Amount of Hgb relative to size of cell

- ■ Reticulocyte count – May be decreased (indicates bone marrow production of RBCs)

Collaborative Care

- • Nursing Care

    - ○ Provide iron supplements for preterm or low birth weight infants.

    - ○ Encourage breastfeeding for infants younger than 4 to 6 months of age.

- o   Recommend iron-fortified formula for infants who are not being breastfed.

- o   Modify the infant's diet to include high iron, vitamin C, and protein content.

- o   Restrict milk intake in toddlers.

    - ▪   Limit milk intake to 32 oz (950 mL) per day.

    - ▪   Avoid giving milk until after a meal.

    - ▪   Do not allow toddlers to carry bottles or cups of milk.

- o   Allow for frequent rest periods.

- o   If packed RBCs are required, follow protocols for administration.

- •   Medications

    - o   Iron Supplements

        - ▪   Nursing Considerations

            - □   Give 1 hr before or 2 hr after milk or antacid to prevent decreased absorption.

            - □   Gastrointestinal side effects (diarrhea, constipation, nausea) are common at the start of therapy. These will decrease over time.

            - □   Administer iron supplements on an empty stomach. However, administration may not be tolerated during initial treatment and may be given after meals.

            - □   Give vitamin C to help increase absorption.

            - □   Use a straw with liquid preparation to prevent staining of teeth. After administration, the child should rinse his mouth with water.

            - □   Evenly distribute doses throughout the day to maximize RBC production by providing bone marrow with a continuous supply of iron.

            - □   Use a Z-track into deep muscle for parenteral injections. Do not massage after injection.

        - ▪   Client Education

            - □   Educate the child and family to expect stools to be black.

- •   Care After Discharge

    - o   Client Education

        - ▪   Advise the family that diarrhea, constipation, or nausea may occur at the start of therapy, but these side effects are usually self-limiting.

        - ▪   Provide information regarding appropriate iron administration

        - ▪   Increase fiber and fluids to prevent constipation.

- Dietary sources of iron
  - Infants – Cereal and iron-fortified formula
  - Older children – Dried legumes; dried fruits; nuts; green, leafy vegetables; iron-fortified breads; iron-fortified flour; poultry; and red meat
- Store iron in a child-proof bottle out of the reach of children to help prevent accidental overdose.
- Encourage parents to allow the child to rest.
- Inform parents that the length of treatment will be determined by the child's response to the treatment. Hgb levels can take up to 3 months to increase.
- Instruct parents to return for follow-up laboratory tests to determine the effectiveness of treatment.
- Client Outcomes
  - The child's RBC count will be within the expected reference range.
  - The child will have increased energy and demonstrate the ability to perform ADLs.

Complications

- Heart failure
  - Heart failure can develop due to the increased demand on the heart to increase oxygen to tissues.
  - Nursing Actions
    - Treat anemia.
    - Monitor cardiac rhythm.
    - Give cardiac medications as prescribed.
  - Client Education
    - Educate the child and family on the signs and symptoms of heart failure.
    - Teach the family how to monitor pulse rates.
- Developmental delay
  - Nursing Actions
    - Accurately assess level of functioning.
    - Improve nutritional intake.
    - Refer to appropriate developmental services.
  - Client Education
    - Provide support to the family.

SICKLE CELL ANEMIA

Overview

- Sickle cell disease (SCD) is a group of diseases in which there is abnormal sickle hemoglobin S (HbS).

- Manifestations and complications of sickle cell anemia are the result of RBC sickling, which leads to increased blood viscosity, obstruction of blood flow, and tissue hypoxia.

  - Manifestations of sickle cell anemia are not usually apparent before 4 to 6 months of age, due to the presence of fetal Hgb in infants.

    - The RBCs have the ability to develop a sickled shape. This is usually precipitated by increased oxygen demands (infection, emotional stress, pain) or decreased levels of oxygen (pulmonary infections, high altitude).

- Tissue hypoxia causes tissue ischemia, which results in pain.

- Increased destruction of RBCs also occurs.

- Sickle cell crisis is the exacerbation of sickle cell anemia.

- Sickle cell anemia is usually diagnosed soon after birth. If not, toddlers or preschoolers will present in crisis following an infection of the respiratory or GI tract.

Assessment

- Risk Factors

  - Sickle cell anemia (SCA) is the most common type of this group and is found primarily in African-Americans. Other forms of SCD may affect individuals of Mediterranean, Indian, or Middle Eastern descent.

  - SCA is an autosomal recessive genetic disorder in which normal hemoglobin A (HbA) is partially or completely replaced with HbS.

  - Children with sickle cell trait do not manifest the disease but can pass the trait to their offspring.

- Subjective and Objective Data

  - Family history of sickle cell anemia or sickle cell trait

  - Reports of pain, crisis, and management

  - Shortness of breath/fatigue

  - Tachycardia

  - Pallor or jaundice

  - Nail bed deformities

  - Lethargy, irritability, and muscle weakness

- o Impaired healing, loss of skin elasticity, and thinning of hair
- o Abdominal pain, nausea, vomiting, and loss of appetite
- o Low-grade fever
- o Systolic heart murmur and heart failure

CRISIS	MANIFESTATIONS
Vaso-occlusive (painful episode) • Usually lasts 4 to 6 days	• Acute 　o Severe pain, usually in bones, joints, and abdomen 　o Swollen joints, hands, and feet 　o Anorexia, vomiting, and fever 　o Hematuria 　o Obstructive jaundice 　o Visual disturbances • Chronic 　o Increased risk of respiratory infections and/or osteomyelitis 　o Retinal detachment and blindness 　o Systolic murmurs 　o Renal failure and enuresis 　o Liver failure 　o Seizures 　o Deformities of the skeleton
Sequestration	• Excessive pooling of blood in the liver (hepatomegaly) and spleen (splenomegaly) • Tachycardia, dyspnea, weakness, pallor, and shock
Aplastic	• Extreme anemia as a result of decreased RBC production
Hyperhemolytic	• Increased rate of RBC destruction leading to anemia, jaundice, and/or reticulocytosis

- o Laboratory Tests
  - ▪ CBC to detect anemia
  - ▪ Sickledex (sickle solubility test) – A screening tool that will detect the presence of HbS but will not differentiate the trait from the disease
  - ▪ Hgb electrophoresis – Separates the various forms of Hgb and is the definitive diagnosis of sickle cell anemia
- o Diagnostic Procedures
  - ▪ Transcranial Doppler (TCD) test
    - ▫ Used to assess intracranial vascular flow and detect the risk for cerebrovascular accident (CVA).
    - ▫ Children ages 2 to 16 who have SCA should have this test performed annually.

Collaborative Care

- Nursing Care

  - Promote rest to decrease oxygen consumption of the tissue.

  - Administer oxygen as prescribed if hypoxia is present.

  - Maintain fluid and electrolyte balance.

    - Monitor I&O.

    - Give oral fluids.

    - Administer IV fluids with electrolyte replacement.

  - Pain Management

    - Use an interdisciplinary approach.

    - Treat mild to moderate pain with acetaminophen (Tylenol) or ibuprofen (Advil). Manage severe pain with opioid analgesics.

    - Apply comfort measures, such as warm packs to painful joints.

  - Administer blood products, usually packed RBCs, and exchange transfusions per facility protocol. Observe for signs of hypervolemia and transfusion reaction.

  - Treat and prevent infection.

    - Administer antibiotics.

    - Perform frequent hand hygiene.

    - Give oral prophylactic penicillin.

    - Administer immunizations to include pneumococcal vaccine (PVC), meningococcal vaccine (MCV4), and yearly seasonal influenza vaccine.

  - Monitor and report laboratory results – RBCs, Hgb, Hct, and liver function

  - Encourage passive range-of-motion exercises to prevent venous stasis.

- Medications

  - Opioids – Codeine, morphine sulfate, oxycodone, hydrocodone (Dilaudid), and methadone (Dolophine)

    - Opioids provide analgesia for pain management.

    - Nursing Considerations

      - Administer orally (immediate or sustained release) or by IV route.

      - Administer on a regular schedule to maintain good pain control.

      - Use patient-controlled analgesia if appropriate.

    - Client Education

      - Educate the child and family about the need to avoid activities that require mental alertness.

- Care After Discharge

  - Client Education

    - Provide emotional support, and refer to social services if appropriate.

    - Instruct in signs and symptoms of crisis and infection.

    - Advise the family of the importance of promoting rest and adequate nutrition for the child.

    - Encourage the child and family to maintain good hand hygiene and avoid individuals with colds/infection/viruses.

    - Give specific directions regarding fluid intake requirements, such as how many bottles or glasses of fluid should be consumed daily.

    - Provide information about genetic counseling.

    - Encourage maintenance of up-to-date immunizations.

    - Advise the child to wear a medical identification wristband or medical identification tags.

- Client Outcomes

  - The child will have a decrease in the number of crisis occurrences.

  - The child will have good pain control.

Complications

- CVA

  - Nursing Actions

    - Assess and report signs and symptoms, which include:

      - Seizures

      - Abnormal behavior

      - Weak extremity and/or inability to move an extremity

      - Slurred speech

      - Changes in vision

      - Vomiting

      - Severe headache

  - Client Education

    - Blood transfusions should be performed every 3 to 4 weeks following a CVA.

- Acute chest syndrome
  - May be life threatening
  - Nursing Actions
    - Assess and report signs and symptoms, which include:
      - Chest pain
      - Fever of 38.9° C (102° F) or higher
      - Congested cough
      - Tachycardia
      - Dyspnea
      - Retractions
      - Decreased oxygen saturations

HEMOPHILIA

Overview

- Hemophilia is a disorder that results in an impaired ability to control bleeding.

- Bleeding time is extended due to lack of clotting factors. Bleeding may be internal or external.

- Manifestations may be present early in infancy but may not be evident until infants begins teething, sitting up, or crawling.

- Parents may observe excessive bruising with minor falls or contact.

- Hemophilia has different levels of severity depending on the percentage of clotting factor a child's body contains. For example, a child with mild hemophilia may have up to 49% of the normal factor VIII in his body, while a person with severe hemophilia has very little factor VIII.

- Both hemophilia A and B are X-linked recessive disorders.

TYPES OF HEMOPHILIA	
HEMOPHILIA A	HEMOPHILIA B
• Deficiency of factor VIII • Also referred to as classic hemophilia • Accounts for 80% of cases	• Deficiency of factor IX • Also referred to as Christmas disease

Assessment

- Subjective Data

    o Episodes of bleeding, excessive bleeding, reports of joint pain and stiffness, impaired mobility, and activity intolerance

- Objective Data

    o Physical Assessment Findings

        ■ Active bleeding, which includes bleeding gums, epistaxis, hematuria, and/or tarry stools

        ■ Hematomas and/or bruising

        ■ Hemarthrosis as evidenced by joint pain, stiffness, warmth, swelling, redness, loss of range of motion, and deformities

        ■ Headache, slurred speech, and a decreased level of consciousness

    o Laboratory Tests

        ■ Prolonged partial thromboplastin time (PTT)

        ■ Factor-specific assays to determine deficiency

    o Diagnostic Procedures

        ■ DNA testing

            □ Detects classic hemophilia trait in females

Collaborative Care

- Nursing Care

    o Management of bleeding in the hospital

        ■ Avoid taking temperature rectally.

        ■ Avoid unnecessary skin punctures and use surgical aseptic technique.

        ■ Apply pressure for 5 min after injections, venipuncture, or needle sticks.

        ■ Monitor urine, stool, and nasogastric fluid for occult blood.

        ■ Control localized bleeding.

            □ Administer factor replacement.

            □ Observe for side effects, which include headache, flushing, low sodium, and alterations in heart rate and blood pressure.

            □ Encourage the child to rest and immobilize the affected joints.

            □ Elevate and apply ice to the affected joints.

- Medications
  - 1-deamino-8-D-arginine vasopressin (DDAVP) is a synthetic form of vasopressin that increases plasma factor VIII (antihemophilic factor [AHF])
    - Effective for mild, but not severe, hemophilia
    - Nursing Considerations
      - May be given prior to dental or surgical procedures
  - Factor VIII, products that contain factor VIII, pooled plasma, and recombinant products
    - Used to prevent and treat hemorrhage
    - Nursing Considerations
      - Administer by IV infusion.
    - Client Education
      - Instruct the child and family that treatment may require numerous doses.
  - Corticosteroids
    - Used to treat hematuria, acute episodes of hemarthrosis, and chronic synovitis
    - Nursing Considerations
      - Monitor for infection and bleeding.
    - Client Education
      - Encourage the child and family to maintain good hand hygiene and avoid individuals with colds/infection/viruses.
  - Nonsteroidal anti-inflammatory agents
    - Used to treat chronic synovitis
    - Nursing considerations
      - Monitor for infection.
    - Client Education
      - Encourage the child to take the medication with food.
- Interdisciplinary Care
  - An interdisciplinary approach includes the primary care provider, nurse, physical therapist, and social worker.

- Care After Discharge

  ○ Client Education

  - Teach parents to prevent bleeding at home.

    □ Place the infant or child in a padded crib.

    □ Provide a safe home and a play environment that is free of clutter. Place padding on corners of furniture.

    □ Dress toddlers in extra layers of clothing to provide additional padding.

    □ Set activity restrictions to avoid injury. Acceptable activities include low-contact sports (tennis, swimming, golf). While participating in these activities, children should wear protective equipment.

    □ Encourage the use of soft-bristled toothbrushes

  - Encourage regular exercise and physical therapy after active bleeding is controlled.

  - Encourage the family to maintain up-to-date immunizations.

  - Teach the importance of wearing a medical identification wristband or medical identification tags.

  - Teach signs and symptoms of internal bleeding and hemarthrosis.

  - Encourage the family to participate in a support group.

- Client Outcomes

  ○ The child will have decreased bleeding episodes.

  ○ The child will be free from injury.

Complications

- Uncontrolled bleeding (intracranial hemorrhage, airway obstruction from bleeding in mouth, neck, or chest)

  ○ Nursing Actions

  - Monitor vital signs for evidence of impending shock.

  - Take measures to control bleeding.

  - Administer recombinant factor VIII concentrate during bleeding episodes to treat excessive bleeding or hemarthrosis.

  - Administer a blood transfusion as prescribed.

- ■ Conduct a neurologic assessment for evidence of intracranial bleed.
- ■ Provide prophylaxis treatment. Regimens include infusion of factor VIII concentrate:
  - □ Prior to joint bleed
  - □ Three times a week after the first joint bleed
  - □ After joint bleed, in a high dose, followed for 2 days with a lower dose and then continued every other day for 1 week
- ○ Client Education
  - ■ Tell the client to report signs of bleeding.
- • Joint deformity (most often elbows, knees, and ankles)
  - ○ Repeated episodes of hemarthrosis (bleeding into joint spaces) lead to impaired range of motion, pain, tenderness, and swelling, which can develop into joint deformities.
  - ○ Nursing Actions
    - ■ Take appropriate measures to rest, immobilize, elevate, and apply ice to the affected joints during active bleeding.
    - ■ Encourage active range of motion after active bleeding is controlled.
    - ■ Encourage maintenance of ideal weight to minimize stress on joints.
    - ■ Encourage maintenance of regular exercise and physical therapy.

CHAPTER 21: HEMATOLOGIC DISORDERS

 Application Exercises

1. A nurse is providing teaching about the management of epistaxis to a child and his family. Which of the following positions should the nurse instruct the child to take when experiencing a nosebleed?

    A. Sit up and lean forward.

    B. Sit up and tilt the head back.

    C. Lie down supine.

    D. Lie in a prone position.

2. A nurse is providing education regarding management of epistaxis. Which of the following are appropriate interventions for a child to take during an episode of epistaxis? (Select all that apply.)

    _____ Press nares together for 5 to 10 min.

    _____ Breathe through the nose until bleeding stops.

    _____ Pack cotton or tissue into the naris that is bleeding.

    _____ Use a humidifier.

    _____ Apply ice across the bridge of the nose.

3. A nurse is providing teaching about epistaxis. Which of the following statements by a child's parent indicates the need for further teaching regarding epistaxis?

    A. "If my child has a nosebleed, I should bring him to the emergency department to prevent excessive blood loss."

    B. "It is common for children to develop nosebleeds because the skin inside the nose is fragile."

    C. "If my child's nosebleed lasts longer than 30 min, he may need to have nasal packing placed inside his nose."

    D. "I know that my child may develop a nosebleed from allergies or injuries."

4. A nurse is providing teaching to the parent of a child who is receiving a new prescription for liquid oral iron supplements. Which of the following statements indicates the parent understands the teaching?

    A. "I should call the doctor if my child has tarry stools."

    B. "My child may develop diarrhea while he is taking iron supplements."

    C. "I will give the iron with milk to help prevent an upset stomach."

    D. "My child should rinse his mouth after taking the iron supplement."

5. A nurse is administering parenteral iron dextran by IM injection to a school-age child. Which of the following is an appropriate intervention?

    A. Administer the medication into a deep muscle using the Z-track method.

    B. Use the deltoid muscle for administration.

    C. Massage the injection site for comfort after administration.

    D. Give no more than 3 mL of iron during a single administration.

6. A nurse is providing dietary teaching to a group of parents. Which of the following foods should the nurse include when discussing foods that are good sources of iron? (Select all that apply)

   _____   Dried fruit

   _____   Low-fat yogurt

   _____   Chicken

   _____   Grapes

   _____   Ground beef

7. A nurse is caring for an infant whose screening test reveals that he may have sickle cell disease. Which of the following tests is a definitive diagnosis for sickle cell anemia?

A. Sickle solubility test (Sickledex)

B. Hgb electrophoresis

C. CBC

D. Transcranial Doppler

8. A nurse is caring for a child who has sickle cell crisis and is hospitalized. Nursing interventions to prevent infection in the child include administering

A. IV fluids with electrolyte replacement.

B. opioid pain medication.

C. a pneumococcal vaccine.

D. exchange transfusions.

9. A nurse is planning teaching regarding intervention techniques for the family of a toddler who has recently been diagnosed with hemophilia. Identify the rationale for each of the suggested interventions.

INTERVENTION	RATIONALE
Pad corners of furniture and dress the child in extra clothing.	
Use child safety gates.	
Decrease clutter in the home.	
Use soft toothbrushes and/or water irrigating devices for oral care.	
Obtain a medical identification wristband or medical identification tags for the child.	

CHAPTER 21: HEMATOLOGIC DISORDERS

 Application Exercises Answer Key

1. A nurse is providing teaching about the management of epistaxis to a child and his family. Which of the following positions should the nurse instruct the child to take when experiencing a nosebleed?

   A. Sit up and lean forward.

   B. Sit up and tilt the head back.

   C. Lie down supine.

   D. Lie in a prone position.

   Sitting up with the head tilted slightly forward promotes draining of blood out of the nose instead of down the back of the throat. Swallowing of blood can promote coughing and lead to nausea, vomiting, and diarrhea. The other positions are not effective.

    NCLEX® Connection: Physiological Adaptation, Illness Management

2. A nurse is providing education regarding management of epistaxis. Which of the following are appropriate interventions for a child to take during an episode of epistaxis? (Select all that apply.)

__X__	**Press nares together for 5 to 10 min.**
_____	Breathe through the nose until bleeding stops.
__X__	**Pack cotton or tissue into the naris that is bleeding.**
_____	Use a humidifier.
__X__	**Apply ice across the bridge of the nose.**

   Pressing the nares together, packing the nose with cotton or tissue, and applying ice across the bridge of the nose are all appropriate interventions during an episode of epistaxis. The child should be instructed to breathe through her mouth while her nose is bleeding. Use of a humidifier in the winter may help decrease the incidence of epistaxis, but it will not treat an acute nosebleed.

    NCLEX® Connection: Physiological Adaptation, Illness Management

3. A nurse is providing teaching about epistaxis. Which of the following statements by a child's parent indicates the need for further teaching regarding epistaxis?

   A. "If my child has a nosebleed, I should bring him to the emergency department to prevent excessive blood loss."

   B. "It is common for children to develop nosebleeds because the skin inside the nose is fragile."

   C. "If my child's nosebleed lasts longer than 30 min, he may need to have nasal packing placed inside his nose."

   D. "I know that my child may develop a nosebleed from allergies or injuries."

   A nosebleed is not an emergency, and it usually can be managed at home with proper instruction to the child and family.

    NCLEX® Connection: Physiological Adaptation, Illness Management

4. A nurse is providing teaching to the parent of a child who is receiving a new prescription for liquid oral iron supplements. Which of the following statements indicates the parent understands the teaching?

> A. "I should call the doctor if my child has tarry stools."
>
> B. "My child may develop diarrhea while he is taking iron supplements."
>
> C. "I will give the iron with milk to help prevent an upset stomach."
>
> **D. "My child should rinse his mouth after taking the iron supplement."**

> Liquid iron supplements can stain teeth and should be taken with a straw or dropper. The child should rinse his mouth after swallowing the medication. Development of constipation and tar-colored stools are expected when taking iron supplements. Taking iron with milk decreases absorption and should be discouraged.

 NCLEX® Connection: Pharmacological and Parenteral Therapies, Adverse Effects/ Contraindications/Side Effects/Interactions

5. A nurse is administering parenteral iron dextran by IM injection to a school-age child. Which of the following is an appropriate intervention?

> **A. Administer the medication into a deep muscle using the Z-track method.**
>
> B. Use the deltoid muscle for administration.
>
> C. Massage the injection site for comfort after administration.
>
> D. Give no more than 3 mL of iron during a single administration.

> If iron dextran is to be administered by IM injection, the nurse should use the Z-track method into a deep, large muscle to prevent staining and injuring tissue. The deltoid muscle is not a large enough muscle mass for administration of an irritating medication. Massaging the injection site should be avoided to prevent permanent skin staining with the dark-colored iron product. No more than 2 mL (1 mL when injecting into the deltoid) should be injected when administering an IM injection into a large muscle.

 NCLEX® Connection: Pharmacological and Parenteral Therapies, Adverse Effects/ Contraindications/Side Effects/Interactions

6. A nurse is providing dietary teaching to a group of parents. Which of the following foods should the nurse include when discussing foods that are good sources of iron? (Select all that apply)

> | __X__ | **Dried fruit** |
> | _____ | Low-fat yogurt |
> | __X__ | **Chicken** |
> | _____ | Grapes |
> | __X__ | **Ground beef** |

> Dried fruit, chicken, and ground beef are good sources of iron. Low-fat yogurt and grapes are not good sources of iron.

NCLEX® Connection: Basic Care and Comfort, Nutrition and Oral Hydration

7. A nurse is caring for an infant whose screening test reveals that he may have sickle cell disease. Which of the following tests is a definitive diagnosis for sickle cell anemia?

    A. Sickle solubility test (Sickledex)

    B. Hgb electrophoresis

    C. CBC

    D. Transcranial Doppler

    Hgb electrophoresis diagnosis sickle cell anemia and differentiates it from sickle cell trait. The Sickledex test is a screening test for sickle cell anemia and trait. The CBC tests for a variety of general problems, such as anemia and infection. Transcranial Doppler is used to diagnose the presence of a CVA.

 NCLEX® Connection: Reduction of Risk Potential, Diagnostic Tests

8. A nurse is caring for a child who has sickle cell crisis and is hospitalized. Nursing interventions to prevent infection in the child include administering

    A. IV fluids with electrolyte replacement.

    B. opioid pain medication.

    C. a pneumococcal vaccine.

    D. exchange transfusions.

    Administration of vaccines for pneumococcal pneumonia, meningococcal disease, and influenza can help prevent infection. The other interventions are used for fluid volume deficits (IV fluid administration), extreme pain (opioid pain medication), and decreasing the number of circulating sickled cells (exchange transfusions).

 NCLEX® Connection: Safety and Infection Control, Standard/Transmission-Based/Other Precautions

9. A nurse is planning teaching regarding intervention techniques for the family of a toddler who has recently been diagnosed with hemophilia. Identify the rationale for each of the suggested interventions.

INTERVENTION	RATIONALE
Pad corners of furniture and dress the child in extra clothing.	The toddler is acquiring new motor skills and is more likely to fall into furniture. Padding will decrease the possibility of injury and subsequent bleeding.
Use child safety gates.	Safety gates will prevent the toddler from accessing stairs and other dangerous areas.
Decrease clutter in the home.	The toddler is more likely to fall and experience bleeding if there is additional clutter in the home.
Use soft toothbrushes and/or water irrigating devices for oral care.	Soft toothbrushes, tooth cleaning appliances, and/or water irrigating devices will help prevent bleeding gums in the toddler.
Obtain a medical identification wristband or medical identification tags for the child.	A medical identification wristband or medical identification tags informs others of the child's condition if parents are not present.

Ⓝ NCLEX® Connection: Physiological Adaptation, Illness Management

UNIT 2: NURSING CARE OF CHILDREN WITH SYSTEM DISORDERS

Section: Gastrointestinal Disorders

- Acute Infectious Gastrointestinal Disorders
- Gastrointestinal Structural and Inflammatory Disorders

NCLEX® CONNECTIONS

When reviewing the chapters in this section, keep in mind the relevant sections of the NCLEX® outline, in particular:

CLIENT NEEDS: BASIC CARE AND COMFORT	CLIENT NEEDS: REDUCTION OF RISK POTENTIAL	CLIENT NEEDS: PHYSIOLOGICAL ADAPTATION
Relevant topics/tasks include:	Relevant topics/tasks include:	Relevant topics/tasks include:
• Elimination	• Potential for Alterations in Body Systems	• Alterations in Body Systems
○ Assess and manage the client with an alteration in elimination.	○ Monitor the client's output for changes from baseline.	○ Identify signs, symptoms, and incubation periods of infectious diseases.
• Nutrition and Oral Hydration	• System Specific Assessment	• Illness Management
○ Monitor the client's hydration status.	○ Perform focused assessment and reassessment.	○ Implement interventions to manage the client recovering from an illness.
	• Therapeutic Procedures	• Pathophysiology
	○ Provide pre and/or postoperative education.	○ Understand general principles of pathophysiology.

UNIT 2	NURSING CARE OF CHILDREN WITH SYSTEM DISORDERS
Section	Gastrointestinal Disorders
Chapter 22	Acute Infectious Gastrointestinal Disorders

Overview

- Diarrhea may be mild to severe and it may be acute or chronic. It may result in mild to severe dehydration.

    - Acute diarrhea may follow secondary to an upper respiratory or urinary tract infection or antibiotic use.

    - Acute infectious diarrhea (infectious gastroenteritis) is a result of various bacterial, viral, and/or parasitic infections. The onset of gastroenteritis is often abrupt with rapid loss of fluids and electrolytes from persistent vomiting and diarrhea.

    - Chronic diarrhea is related to chronic conditions (malabsorption syndrome, lactose intolerance, food allergies, inflammatory bowel disease).

Assessment

- Risk Factors

    - Exposure to causative agent, recent travel

    - Risk factors for *Enterobius vermicularis* (pinworm) include crowded places (school, day care) or crowded living spaces (such as more than one family living together).

- Subjective and Objective Data

    - Reports of fatigue, malaise, change in behavior, change in stool pattern, poor appetite, weight loss, and pain

    - Assess for signs and symptoms of dehydration.

        - Dry, pale skin

        - Cool lips

        - Dry mucous membranes

        - Decreased skin turgor

        - Diminished urinary output

        - Concentrated urine

        - Thirst

        - Rapid pulse

- Sunken fontanels
- Decreased blood pressure

SIGNS AND SYMPTOMS OF SPECIFIC PATHOGENS		
PATHOGEN	MANIFESTATIONS	TRANSMISSION/INCUBATION
Rotavirus	• Commonly causes diarrhea in young children • Induces fever and vomiting for 2 days • Produces watery diarrhea for 5 to 7 days	• Transmission is fecal-oral. • The incubation period is 48 hr.
Escherichia coli (E. coli)	• Causes watery diarrhea for 1 to 2 days, followed by abdominal cramping and bloody diarrhea • Could lead to hemolytic uremic syndrome (HUS)	• Transmission depends on the strain of E. coli. • The incubation period is 3 to 4 days.
Salmonella nontyphoidal groups	• Causes nausea, vomiting, abdominal cramping, bloody diarrhea, and fever (may be afebrile in infants) • Causes headache, confusion, drowsiness, and seizures • May lead to meningitis or septicemia	• Transmission occurs from person to person, but also from undercooked meats and poultry. • The incubation period is 6 to 72 hr.
Clostridium difficile (C. difficile)	• Causes mild, watery diarrhea for a few days • May cause less severe symptoms in children than adults • May cause leukocytosis, hypoalbuminemia, and high fever in certain children • May lead to pseudomembranous colitis	• Transmission occurs through contact with colonized spores, and it is commonly transmitted in health care settings. • There is a nonspecified incubation period.
Clostridium botulinum (C. botulinum)	• Causes abdominal pain, cramping, and diarrhea • May cause respiratory compromise or CNS symptoms	• Transmission occurs through contaminated food products. • The incubation period is 12 to 26 hr.

SIGNS AND SYMPTOMS OF SPECIFIC PATHOGENS		
PATHOGEN	MANIFESTATIONS	TRANSMISSION/INCUBATION
Staphylococcus	• Causes food poisoning resulting in severe diarrhea, nausea, and vomiting	• Transmission occurs through food that is inadequately cooked or refrigerated. • The incubation period is 1 to 8 hr.
Enterobius vermicularis (pinworm) is a parasitic worm that is white, threadlike, and approximately ⅓ to ½ inch long.	• Causes perianal itching, enuresis, sleeplessness, restlessness, and irritability due to itching	• Transmission is fecal-oral with infestation beginning when eggs are inhaled or swallowed.
Giardia lamblia	• Causes the following in children 5 years of age or younger: ○ Diarrhea ○ Vomiting ○ Anorexia • Causes the following in older children: ○ Abdominal cramps ○ Intermittent loose, malodorous, pale, greasy stools	• Transmission occurs from person to person. • The nonmotile stage of protozoa may survive in the environment for months.

   ○ Laboratory Tests

      ▪ Perform a CBC with differential to determine anemia and/or infection.

      ▪ Hct, Hgb, BUN, creatinine, and urine-specific gravity levels are usually elevated with dehydration.

      ▪ Stool test for occult blood.

      ▪ Perform a urinalysis.

   ○ Diagnostic Procedures

      ▪ Tape test

         □ A tape test should be performed to check for *Enterobius vermicularis*.

         □ Nursing Actions

            ▸ Provide instructions to the parents.

- □ Client Education
  - ▸ Tell the parents to place transparent tape over the child's anus at night. The tape should be removed the following morning prior to the child toileting or bathing. If possible, have the parent apply the tape after the child has gone to sleep and remove it before the child awakens.
  - ▸ Inform the parents that the specimen should be brought to the laboratory for microscopic evaluation.
  - ▸ Teach the parents to use good hand hygiene during this procedure.
- ■ Infectious gastroenteritis
  - □ Rotavirus – Enzyme immunoassay (stool sample)
  - □ *E. coli* – Sorbitol-MacConkey agar (stool sample)
  - □ Salmonella – Gram-stained stool culture
  - □ *C. difficile* – Stool culture
  - □ *C. botulinum* – Blood and stool culture
  - □ Staphylococcus – Identification of organism in stool, blood, food, or aspirate
  - □ *G. lamblia* – Enzyme immunoassay (stool sample)

Collaborative Care

- Nursing Care
  - ○ Obtain baseline height and weight.
  - ○ Obtain daily weights at the same time each day.
  - ○ Avoid taking a rectal temperature.
  - ○ Assess and monitor I&O (urine and stool).
  - ○ Initiate IV fluids as ordered.
  - ○ Administer antibiotic as prescribed.
  - ○ Administer oral rehydration therapy (ORT).
    - ■ Start replacement with an oral replacement solution (ORS) of 75 to 90 mEq of Na^+/L at 40 to 50 mL/kg over 4 hr.
    - ■ Determine the need for further rehydration after initial replacement.
      - □ Initiate maintenance therapy with ORS of 40 to 60 mEq of Na^+/L and limit to 150 mL/kg/day.
        - ▸ Give ORS alternately with appropriate intake.
          - ▷ Give infants water, breast milk, or lactose-free formula if supplementary fluid is needed.
          - ▷ Older children may resume their regular diets for additional intake.
        - ▸ Replace each diarrheal stool with 10 mL/kg of ORS for ongoing diarrhea.

- Medications

  - Metronidazole (Flagyl) and tinidazole (Tindamax)

    - Indicated for *C. difficile* and *G. lamblia*

    - Nursing Considerations

      - Monitor for allergies.

      - Monitor for GI upset.

    - Client Education

      - Instruct the client to take the medication as prescribed and to report any GI disturbances.

  - Mebendazole (Vermox), albendazole (Albenza), and pyrantel pamoate (Pin-Rid, Antiminth) – Indicated for *Enterobius vermicularis*

    - Nursing Considerations

      - Administer in a single dose that may need to be repeated in 2 weeks.

      - Administer mebendazole for children older than 2 years of age.

    - Client Education

      - Instruct the family that the medication may need to be repeated within 3 weeks.

- Care After Discharge

  - Client Education

    - Have the parents inform the child's school or day care center of the infection/infestation. The child should stay home during the incubation period.

    - Teach the family to use commercially prepared ORS when the child experiences diarrhea. Foods and fluids to avoid include:

      - Fruit juices, carbonated sodas, and gelatin, which all have high carbohydrate content, low electrolyte content, and a high osmolality

      - Caffeine, due to its mild diuretic effect

      - Chicken or beef broth, which has too much sodium and not enough carbohydrates

      - Bananas, rice, applesauce, and toast (BRAT diet)

        - This diet has low nutritional value, high carbohydrate content, and low electrolytes.

    - Provide frequent skin care to prevent skin breakdown.

    - Teach the family how to avoid the spread of infectious diseases.

      - Change bed linens and underwear daily for several days.

      - Cleanse toys and child care areas thoroughly to prevent further spread or reinfestation.

□ Keep toys separate and avoid shaking linens to prevent the spread of disease.

□ Shower frequently.

□ Avoid undercooked or under-refrigerated food.

□ Perform proper hand hygiene after toileting and after changing diapers.

□ Do not share dishes and utensils. Wash them in hot, soapy water or in the dishwasher.

□ Clip nails and discourage nail biting and thumb sucking.

□ Clean toilet areas.

- Client Outcomes

  o The child will remain free of infection.

  o The child will maintain adequate hydration

Complications

- Dehydration

TYPE OF DEHYDRATION	MANIFESTATIONS
Isotonic	• Water and sodium are lost in nearly equal amounts. • Major loss of fluid from extracellular fluid leads to a reduced volume of circulating fluid. • Hypovolemic shock may result. • Serum sodium is within normal limits (130 to 150 mEq/L).
Hypotonic	• Electrolyte loss is greater than water loss. • Water changes from extracellular fluid to intracellular fluid. • Physical manifestations are more severe with smaller fluid loss. • Serum sodium is less than 130 mEq/L.
Hypertonic	• Water loss is greater than electrolyte loss. • Fluid shifts from intracellular to extracellular. • Shock is less likely. • Neurologic changes (change in level of consciousness, irritability, hyperreflexia) may occur. • Serum sodium concentration is greater than 150 mEq/L.

LEVEL OF DEHYDRATION	WEIGHT LOSS	MANIFESTATIONS
Mild	5% in infants 3% to 4% in children	• Behavior, mucous membranes, anterior fontanel, pulse, and blood pressure are all within normal limits. • Capillary refill is greater than 2 seconds. • Slight thirst may be experienced. • Urine-specific gravity is greater than 1.020.
Moderate	10% in infants 6 to 8% in children	• Capillary refill is between 2 and 4 seconds. • Thirst and irritability may be experienced. • Pulse is slightly increased with normal to orthostatic blood pressure. • Mucous membranes are dry and tears and skin turgor are decreased. • Urine-specific gravity is greater than 1.020 (oliguria).
Severe	15% in infants 10% in children	• Capillary refill is greater than 4 seconds. • Tachycardia is present and orthostatic blood pressure may progress to shock. • Extreme thirst is present. • Mucous membranes are very dry and skin is tented. • The anterior fontanel is sunken. • Oliguria or anuria is present.

○ Nursing Actions

■ Administer IV fluids as prescribed (usually dextrose 5% in a saline solution).

■ Provide fluid replacement rapidly for isotonic and hypotonic dehydration, but provide fluid replacement for 24 to 48 hr for hypertonic dehydration to prevent cerebral edema.

■ Avoid antiemetics because vomiting usually resolves with treatment of dehydration.

■ Determine the cause of diarrhea. Antibiotics are usually reserved for children who are immunocompromised.

○ Client Education

■ Teach the client to monitor weight daily.

■ Teach the client to consume small amounts of liquids several times a day to prevent vomiting.

CHAPTER 22: ACUTE INFECTIOUS GASTROINTESTINAL DISORDERS

(A) Application Exercises

Scenario: A 5-month-old infant who is lethargic is brought to the emergency department by his parents. The parents tell the nurse that the infant has experienced fever, vomiting, and diarrhea for the past 2 days. They also state that the child is unable to tolerate clear liquids. The nurse suspects gastroenteritis.

1. Indicate the findings the nurse should anticipate when completing the infant's head-to-toe admission assessment?

ASSESSMENT	FINDINGS
Level of consciousness	
Head	
Lung fields	
Cardiovascular system	
Abdomen	
Urinary status	
Bowel status	
Activity level	
Nutrition/fluid intake	
Skin turgor	

2. The infant weighed 9.1 kg (20 lb) before the onset of symptoms. During the assessment, his weight is recorded as 8.2 kg (18 lb). His capillary refill takes about 3 seconds, and his skin turgor is decreased. Based on this information, the nurse should assess his level of dehydration as

    A. none.

    B. mild.

    C. moderate.

    D. severe.

3. The infant's stool cultures are returned with a diagnosis of rotavirus. The parents state that they also have a 2-year-old child at home and are afraid of spreading the disease. What suggestions should the nurse give to the parents that will be most beneficial to them?

4. A child has lost electrolytes and some water through vomiting. The child's serum sodium is 115 mEq/L. The nurse determines that the child is _____.

5. Which of the following fluids is an appropriate choice for rehydrating a child who has experienced diarrhea due to *E. coli* for the past 3 days?

   A. Oral rehydration therapy

   B. IV isotonic saline with glucose

   C. Gelatin

   D. Chicken broth

6. Which of the following findings demonstrated by a child should cause the nurse to suspect the presence of *Enterobius vermicularis* (pinworm)?

   A. Bloody diarrhea

   B. Perianal itching

   C. Moderate dehydration

   D. Abdominal pain

CHAPTER 22: ACUTE INFECTIOUS GASTROINTESTINAL DISORDERS

(A) Application Exercises Answer Key

Scenario: A 5-month-old infant who is lethargic is brought to the emergency department by his parents. The parents tell the nurse that the infant has experienced fever, vomiting, and diarrhea for the past 2 days. They also state that the child is unable to tolerate clear liquids. The nurse suspects gastroenteritis.

1. Indicate the findings the nurse should anticipate when completing the infant's head-to-toe admission assessment?

ASSESSMENT	FINDINGS
Level of consciousness	Irritable and lethargic
Head	Sunken fontanel and pale, sunken eyes
Lung fields	Clear with no retractions or nasal flaring; good air exchange
Cardiovascular system	Low blood pressure; increased pulse that is thready in nature
Abdomen	Distended; hyperactive bowel sounds; infant cries upon palpation; infant verbalizes cramping or displays discomfort by crying and hunching over
Urinary status	Diminished urine output; concentrated urine when wet; elevated specific gravity
Bowel status	Frequent stools; watery stool consistency with a greenish appearance; possible blood-tinged stool that is foul smelling
Activity level	Lethargic; infant wants to be held by parents and is not interested in surroundings
Nutrition/fluid intake	Disinterested and unable to tolerate formula/ breast milk and/or clear liquids
Skin turgor	Tented; poor turgor; excoriated in diaper area

 NCLEX® Connection: Physiological Adaptation, Infectious Disease

2. The infant weighed 9.1 kg (20 lb) before the onset of symptoms. During the assessment, his weight is recorded as 8.2 kg (18 lb). His capillary refill takes about 3 seconds, and his skin turgor is decreased. Based on this information, the nurse should assess his level of dehydration as

    A. none.

    B. mild.

    C. moderate.

    D. severe.

    The infant has moderate dehydration because he has lost about 10% of his body weight, his capillary refill takes 3 seconds or slightly longer, and decreased skin turgor is present. With mild dehydration, weight loss is around 5%, and other parameters may be slightly higher than what is expected for the infant, but they will still be within normal limits. In severe dehydration, 15% of body weight is lost, capillary refill takes more than 4 seconds, and tenting of the skin is seen when turgor is assessed.

 NCLEX® Connection: Physiological Adaptation, Fluid and Electrolyte Imbalances

3. The infant's stool cultures are returned with a diagnosis of rotavirus. The parents state that they also have a 2-year-old child at home and are afraid of spreading the disease. What suggestions should the nurse give to the parents that will be most beneficial to them?

    Perform frequent hand hygiene. Wash hands after each diaper change and when coming into close contact with other children.

    Disinfect the area around the child and/or keep the sick child in one area when sleeping and/or playing.

    Place dirty diapers in a closed receptacle.

    Wash any soiled sheets immediately.

    Do not share cups or utensils among family members. Wash utensils in hot, soapy water or place in dishwasher.

 NCLEX® Connection: Physiological Adaptation, Infectious Disease

4. A child has lost electrolytes and some water through vomiting. The child's serum sodium is 115 mEq/L. The nurse determines that the child is _____.

    Hypotonic

    The child has hypotonic dehydration with net loss of more electrolytes than water (hyponatremia). In hypertonic dehydration, water loss is much more than electrolyte loss, and hypernatremia results. In isotonic dehydration, electrolytes and sodium are lost in equal amounts and serum sodium levels are normal.

 NCLEX® Connection: Physiological Adaptation, Fluid and Electrolyte Imbalances

5. Which of the following fluids is an appropriate choice for rehydrating a child who has experienced diarrhea due to *E. coli* for the past 3 days?

   A. Oral rehydration therapy

   B. IV isotonic saline with glucose

   C. Gelatin

   D. Chicken broth

   Oral rehydration solution is made specifically for replacing water and electrolytes lost during diarrhea. It is less expensive and will be less painful than IV therapy. Gelatin is high in carbohydrates, is low in electrolytes, and has a high osmolality; therefore, it is ineffective for rehydration. Broth is high in sodium and has no carbohydrates.

    NCLEX® Connection: Physiological Adaptation, Illness Management

6. Which of the following findings demonstrated by a child should cause the nurse to suspect the presence of *Enterobius vermicularis* (pinworm)?

   A. Bloody diarrhea

   B. Perianal itching

   C. Moderate dehydration

   D. Abdominal pain

   Severe perianal itching is a common symptom of pinworm infestation. Other symptoms include enuresis, irritability, restlessness, and difficulty sleeping. None of the other findings indicate pinworm infestation.

    NCLEX® Connection: Physiological Adaptation, Infectious Disease

UNIT 2	NURSING CARE OF CHILDREN WITH SYSTEM DISORDERS
Section	Gastrointestinal Disorders
Chapter 23	Gastrointestinal Structural and Inflammatory Disorders

Overview

- Gastrointestinal structural disorders include:

    o Gastroesophageal reflux disease (GERD)

    o Hypertropic pyloric stenosis

    o Hirschsprung's disease

    o Intussusception

    o Appendicitis and Meckel's diverticulum

        ▪ These affect structures in the gastrointestinal tract, but they are inflammatory discords.

    o Cleft lip and palate

        ▪ These are considered structural disorders, but they have different assessment findings and management.

GASTROINTESTINAL STRUCTURAL AND INFLAMMATORY DISORDERS

Overview

- Gastroesophageal reflux (GER) occurs when the gastric contents reflux back up into the esophagus, making esophageal mucosa vulnerable to injury from gastric acid and resulting in gastroesophageal reflux disease (GERD). GER in infants is usually self-limiting and resolves by the end of the first year of life.

    o GER(D) may result in failure to thrive, bleeding, and difficulty with swallowing.

- Hypertropic pyloric stenosis is the thickening of the pyloric sphincter, which creates an obstruction.

- Hirschsprung's disease, or congenital aganglionic megacolon, is a structural anomaly of the gastrointestinal (GI) tract that is caused by lack of ganglionic cells in segments of the colon and results in mechanical obstruction.

  o Stool accumulates due to lack of peristalsis in the noninnervated area of the bowel (usually rectosigmoid), causing the bowel to dilate.

  o Hirschsprung's disease is usually diagnosed in infants, but chronic milder symptoms may occur in late childhood.

- Meckel's diverticulum is a complication resulting from failure of the omphalomesenteric duct to fuse during embryonic development.

  o The diverticulum may be up to 4 inches in length and is found in the small intestine.

- Intussusception is the telescoping of the intestine over itself. This usually occurs in infants and young children up to 5 years of age, but it is most common between 5 and 9 months of age.

- Appendicitis is inflammation of the appendix caused by an obstruction of the opening of the appendix, possibly due to fecal matter, swollen lymphoid tissue, or (in rare cases) a parasite.

- Consequences from peritonitis can lead to electrolyte imbalances and shock.

Assessment

- Risk Factors

  o GER(D) is more likely to occur in premature infants and infants born with congenital defects (neurologic disorders, esophageal disorders, hiatal hernia, cystic fibrosis, cerebral palsy).

  o Hypertrophic pyloric stenosis has a genetic component.

  o Hirschsprung's disease may be either an acute or chronic disorder.

  o Intussusception with cystic fibrosis

- Subjective and Objective Data

STRUCTURAL DISORDER	FINDINGS

GER(D)	• Infant
	  o Excessive spitting up or forceful vomiting, irritability, excessive crying, blood in stool or vomitus, arching of back and stiffening
	  o Apnea or apparent life-threatening event
	• Older child
	  o Reports of heartburn, abdominal pain, difficulty swallowing, chronic cough, and Sandifer syndrome (in which there is repetitive stretching and arching of head and neck that may mimic seizure activity)

STRUCTURAL DISORDER	FINDINGS
Hypertrophic pyloric stenosis	• Vomiting that often occurs 30 to 60 min after a meal and becomes projectile as obstruction worsens • Constant hunger • Olive-shaped mass in the right upper quadrant of the abdomen and possible peristaltic wave that moves from left to right when lying supine • Failure to gain weight and signs of dehydration, such as skin that is dry and/or pale, cool lips, dry mucous membranes, decreased skin turgor, diminished urinary output, concentrated urine, thirst, rapid pulse, sunken eyes, and decreased blood pressure

Hirschsprung's disease	• Newborn
	  ○ Failure to pass meconium within 24 to 48 hr, refusal to eat, episodes of vomiting bile, and abdominal distention
	• Infant
	  ○ Failure to thrive, constipation, abdominal distention, episodes of vomiting and diarrhea
	• Older child
	  ○ Constipation, abdominal distention, visible peristalsis, ribbon-like stool, palpable fecal mass, and a malnourished appearance

Intussusception	• Normal comfort interrupted by periods of sudden and acute pain • Palpable, sausage-shaped mass in the right upper quadrant of the abdomen and/or a tender, distended abdomen • Stools that are mixed with blood and mucus that resemble the consistency of red currant jelly
Appendicitis	• Abdominal pain; generalized pain that typically begins at the peri-umbilical area and localizes to the right lower quadrant (pain may be most intense at McBurney's point, located about halfway between the anterior superior iliac crest and the umbilicus.); pain that increases with movement; rigid abdomen • Fever, tachycardia, possible vomiting, constipation and/or diarrhea, anorexia, pallor, lethargy, and/or irritability
Meckel's diverticulum	• Abdominal pain, bloody stools without pain, bright red mucus in infant stools

  ○ Laboratory Tests

  ▪ Serum electrolyte levels will be consistent, with changes occurring due to vomiting and resulting in:

    □ Decreased sodium and potassium levels

    □ Increased pH and bicarbonate caused by metabolic alkalosis

- An elevated BUN indicates dehydration.
- A CBC may show an elevated WBC count greater than 10,000/mm³ with a shift to left (increased immature neutrophils, referred to as bands), as well as an elevated C-reactive protein, but this may not be specific to the diagnosis.

○ Diagnostic Procedures

- Hypertrophic pyloric stenosis
  - □ Ultrasound of the abdomen
    - ▸ An ultrasound will reveal an elongated, sausage-shaped mass and an elongated pyloric area.

- GERD
  - □ Upper GI series to detect GI structural abnormalities
  - □ 24-hr intraesophageal pH monitoring study
    - ▸ Measures the amount of gastric acid reflux into the esophagus
  - □ Endoscopy with biopsy to detect esophagitis and strictures
  - □ Scintigraphy
    - ▸ Identifies cause of gastric content aspiration

- Hirschsprung's disease
  - □ Rectal biopsy
    - ▸ Full-thickness biopsies are done and will reveal the absence of ganglion cells.

- Intussusception
  - □ Ultrasound, barium enema

- Appendicitis
  - □ CT scan of the abdomen
    - ▸ The CT scan will show an enlarged diameter of appendix, as well as thickening of the appendiceal wall.

- Meckel's diverticulum
  - □ Radionucleotide scan
    - ▸ This scan will show the presence of gastric mucosa.
    - ▸ Nursing Actions
      - ▹ Assist with positioning.
      - ▹ Administer contrast medium if prescribed.
      - ▹ Monitor for signs of bleeding following biopsies.
    - ▸ Client Education
      - ▹ Instruct client about the need to remain still.

Collaborative Care

- Nursing Care
  - Vomiting
    - Position the child on her side or with her head elevated to prevent aspiration.
    - Document the amount and characteristics of vomitus, and describe vomiting behavior to aid in diagnosis of etiology.
    - Monitor fluid and electrolyte balance to assess for deficits.
    - Provide oral care after the child vomits to prevent damage to teeth from hydrochloric acid contact.
  - GER –Treatment for infants/children is based on the severity of symptoms:
    - Offer small, frequent feedings of thickened formula.
    - Position the child with her head elevated at 30° after she has eaten.
    - Place infants in a prone position for sleep, which can prevent aspiration of stomach contents. This is only recommended for infants with severe GERD.
    - Administer a proton pump inhibitor, such as omeprazole (Prilosec), or an H_2-receptor antagonist, such as ranitidine (Zantac).
- Therapeutic Procedures

STRUCTURAL DISORDER	PROCEDURE
GER(D)	Surgical manipulation or Nissen fundoplication (wraps the fundus of the stomach around the distal esophagus to decrease the chance of reflux)
Hypertrophic pyloric stenosis	Surgical incision into the pyloric sphincter (pylorotomy)
Hirschsprung's disease	Surgical removal of the aganglionic section (may require temporary colostomy)
Intussusception	Surgical reduction if inflating the bowel with air or administering a barium enema is not successful
Appendicitis	Surgical removal of appendix via laparoscopic or open method
Meckel's diverticulum	Surgical removal of diverticulum

- Nursing Actions
  - Preoperative
    - Prepare the child and family for the surgical or therapeutic procedure.
    - Maintain good hydration by administering electrolytes and fluid replacement.

- □ Postoperative

  - ▸ Institute incremental feedings beginning with a solution of clear liquid/glucose/electrolytes and assessing for readiness to progress back to breast milk or formula. The infant may continue to vomit for 24 to 48 hr after surgery.

  - ▸ Position infants with their heads slightly elevated to prevent reflux. Infants usually progress well and are discharged on the second or third postoperative day.

- ■ Client Education

  - □ Teach the parents signs and symptoms of dehydration.

  - □ Teach the parents to assess the incision and monitor for signs of infection.

  - □ Demonstrate proper hand hygiene techniques.

  - □ Encourage the parents to be active in the care of the child.

  - □ Teach the parents of a child who has a temporary colostomy for Hirschsprung's disease how to perform colostomy care before discharge.

- ● Client Outcomes

  - ○ The child will remain free from infection.

  - ○ The child will remain hydrated.

  - ○ The child will maintain adequate nutrition.

  - ○ The child will maintain adequate elimination.

Complications

- ● GERD

  - ○ Recurrent pneumonia, weight loss, and failure to thrive

    - ■ Repeated reflux of stomach contents can lead to erosion of the esophagus or pneumonia if stomach contents are aspirated. Esophageal damage can lead to the inability to eat.

    - ■ Nursing Actions

      - □ Monitor for signs and symptoms of pneumonia and failure to thrive.

      - □ Thicken feedings as prescribed.

      - □ Sit the child upright and feed small, frequent meals.

    - ■ Client Education

      - □ Teach the parents about feeding techniques to promote gastric emptying, proper positioning, and use of medication.

- ● Appendicitis

  - ○ Peritonitis

- Occurs when the intestinal lining and/or peritoneum is perforated, allowing intestinal contents to enter the peritoneal cavity. Peritonitis may result from a ruptured appendix. Peritonitis often occurs within 48 hr of onset of appendicitis.

- Nursing Actions
  - Assess for peritonitis.
    - Rigid, board-like abdomen
    - Absent bowel sounds
    - Severe pain
    - Fever
    - Increased WBCs
    - Possible shock and death
  - Pain management
    - Assess for pain using a developmentally appropriate tool.
    - Administer analgesics as prescribed.
  - Manage IV fluid therapy.
  - Administer IV antibiotics for infection.
  - Manage nasogastric tube suction.
  - Provide preoperative and postoperative nursing care.
  - Provide surgical wound care with wound irrigation and/or dressings if delayed wound closure is necessary.
  - Provide psychosocial support for the child and family.

- Client Education
  - Educate the child and parents about preoperative care, such as the need to maintain NPO status and the need for pain medication.
  - Educate the child and parent about postoperative care, such as early ambulation, advancement of diet, wound care, and monitoring for infection.

- Hirschsprung's disease
  - Enterocolitis
    - Enterocolitis is inflammation of the bowel resulting in fever and explosive diarrhea with the child appearing very ill.
    - Treatment is aimed at resolving enterocolitis, preventing bowel perforation, maintaining hydration, initiating antibiotic therapy, and performing surgery for colostomy or ileostomy if there is extensive bowel involvement.
    - Nursing Actions
      - Monitor abdominal girth.

- ▸ Measure abdominal girth with a paper tape measure at the level of the umbilicus or at the widest point of the abdomen.

- ▸ Mark the area with a pen to assure continuity of future measurements.

- ☐ Monitor for signs of sepsis, peritonitis, or shock caused by enterocolitis.

- ☐ Monitor and manage fluid, electrolyte, and blood product replacement.

- ☐ Administer antibiotics as prescribed.

- Meckel's diverticulum

  - ○ GI hemorrhage and bowel obstruction

    - ■ Hemorrhage may occur with ruptured Meckel's diverticulum.

    - ■ Nursing Actions

      - ☐ Monitor for signs of gastric distention and/or vomiting.

      - ☐ Monitor for signs of bleeding.

      - ☐ Test stools for occult blood.

      - ☐ Monitor complete blood counts for signs of anemia

      - ☐ Provide general preoperative care.

      - ☐ Encourage bed rest.

    - ■ Client Education

      - ☐ Teach signs and symptoms of obstruction.

      - ☐ Teach signs and symptoms of hemorrhage.

CLEFT LIP AND PALATE

 Overview

- Cleft lip (CL) results from the incomplete fusion of the oral cavity during intrauterine life. Cleft palate (CP) results from the incomplete fusion of the palatine plates during intrauterine life.

  > **(M) View Media Supplement:** Cleft Palate (Image)

- Although a cleft lip and palate may occur together, either defect may also appear alone. The defects can be unilateral (one sided) or bilateral (two sided)

- Cleft palate repair (palatoplasty) traditionally takes place after the palate has developed, but new surgical techniques may allow repair to take place earlier.

- Surgery may be done in stages throughout several years.

- Nursing interventions include preoperative teaching, postoperative care, and family support.

Assessment

- Risk Factors

  - May be multifactorial, including:

    - Heredity (as the incidence of cleft palate is higher in relatives of people with the defect)

    - Teratogens (especially maternal intake of phenytoin [Dilantin]), maternal smoking, and family tendency)

- Objective Data

  - Physical Assessment Findings

    - CL defect is visible, but CP alone may only be visible when examining the mouth.

Collaborative Care

- Nursing Care

  - Support and encourage parents in the general care of their child preoperatively and postoperatively.

  - Promote parent-infant bonding.

  - Promote healthy self-esteem throughout the child's development.

- Interdisciplinary Care

  - Care of the child with CL and CP requires care from members of various disciplines (plastic surgeon, orthodontist, ENT specialist, speech and language therapist, occupational therapist, dietary consult, social services worker).

- Surgical Interventions

  - Cheiloplasty (repair of cleft lip early in infancy) and palatoplasty (repair of cleft palate)

    - If both defects are present, cleft lip repair is generally performed first, followed by cleft palate repair at a later date. New techniques in anesthesia and newborn surgery are allowing closure at an earlier time. Closure of the palate should be done early enough to prevent speech defects.

    - Nursing Actions

      - Preoperative

        - Cleft lip and cleft palate repair

          - Inspect the infant's lip and palate using a gloved finger to palpate the infant's palate.

          - Assess the infant's ability to suck.

          - Obtain the infant's baseline weight.

          - Observe interaction between the family and infant.

▷ Determine family coping and support.

▷ Refer parents to appropriate support groups.

▷ Consult with social services to provide needed services (financial, insurance) for the family and infant.

□ Postoperative

▸ Cleft lip and cleft palate repair

▷ Perform standard postoperative care, including assessment of vital signs and pain management using an age-appropriate tool.

▷ Keep the infant pain free postoperatively to decrease crying and stress on repair.

▷ Administer analgesics as prescribed.

▷ Assess the operative sites for signs of crusting and infection. Use saline on a sterile swab to clean the incision site. Apply antibiotic ointment if prescribed.

▷ Assess the infant's ability to eat. Monitor I&O and weigh daily.

▷ Observe the family's interaction with the infant.

▷ Assess family coping and support.

▸ Cleft lip repair

▷ Monitor the integrity of the postoperative protective device to ensure proper positioning.

▷ Position the infant upright (infant car seat position), on her back, or on her side in the immediate postoperative period to maintain the integrity of the repair.

▷ Apply elbow restraints to keep the infant from pulling at the repair site. The cuff of the restraints may be pinned to the infant's clothing. A jacket restraint may be necessary to prevent an older infant from rolling over.

▷ Restraints should be removed periodically to assess skin, allow limb movement, and provide for comfort.

▷ Use saline on a sterile swab to clean the incision site. Apply antibiotic ointment if prescribed.

▷ Gently aspirate secretions of mouth and nasopharynx to prevent respiratory complications.

▸ Cleft palate repair

▷ Change the infant's position frequently to facilitate breathing. The infant may be placed on the abdomen in the immediate postoperative period.

▷ Maintain intravenous fluids until the infant is able to eat and drink.

▷ Monitor packing, which is usually removed in 2 to 3 days.

▷ Avoid placing objects (tongue depressor, pacifier) in the infant's mouth after cleft palate repair.

▷ Avoid using objects for feeding (forks, spoons, pacifiers, straws) that could harm the cleft palate repair.

▷ Avoid foods that could damage the palate repair.

▷ The infant may be discharged on a soft diet.

- Client Education

  □ Preoperative

  ▸ Encourage and support parents as they bond with the infant and provide care.

  ▸ Support the mother's decision to continue breastfeeding her infant. Instruct her to place the breast fully into the newborn's mouth, making a seal. Assist her to be open to alternatives, such as using breast milk placed in special feeding devices, if necessary.

  ▸ Provide instruction to promote feeding. Teach the parents to use an enlarged nipple, stimulate the infant's suck reflex, and ensure that the infant swallows appropriately. To prevent choking and coughing, steady gentle pressure should be held on the bottom of the bottle.

  ▸ Teach parents to limit feedings to 20 to 30 min to prevent fatigue. Also teach parents to allow the infant to rest frequently after each feeding.

  ▸ Identify alternate feeding devices (special nipples for bottles).

  ▸ Teach parents to feed the infant in an upright position.

  ▸ Teach parents to burp the infant more frequently due to the amount of air swallowed. This will help prevent aspiration and abdominal distention.

  ▸ Teach parents how to use bulb suction as needed.

  ▸ Prepare parents for impending surgery.

  □ Postoperative

  ▸ Inform the parents that the infant may require elbow restraints for 4 to 6 weeks. Instruct the parents in the proper use of the restraints and to periodically remove them one at a time to allow for exercise.

  ▸ Assist parents with proper feeding techniques.

  ▸ Instruct parents in proper care of operative site.

- Client Outcomes

  ○ The child will remain free from infection.

  ○ The child's suture line will remain intact.

  ○ The child will maintain nutrition.

Complications

- Aspiration
  - Aspiration is the result of fluids entering the structural defect.
  - Nursing Actions
    - Feed the infant in an upright position.
    - Burp the infant often.
    - Use a bulb syringe to suction oral and nasopharyngeal secretions.
  - Client Education
    - Teach the parents the proper position for feeding.
    - Instruct the parents to learn CPR.
- Ear infections and hearing loss
  - Related to altered structure and recurrent infections
  - Nursing Actions
    - Feed the infant in an upright position. Monitor temperature.
  - Client Education
    - Teach parents signs/symptoms of ear infections.
    - Encourage early intervention.
- Speech and language delay
  - More common with cleft palate
  - Client Education
    - Refer to early intervention.
    - Refer parents to a speech therapist for care.
- Dental problems
  - Teeth may not erupt normally and orthodontia is usually necessary later in life.
  - Client Education
    - Instruct the parents and child (if age appropriate) to promote healthy dental hygiene.
    - Encourage parents to seek early dental care.

CHAPTER 23: GASTROINTESTINAL STRUCTURAL AND INFLAMMATORY DISORDERS

 Application Exercises

1. Match the following structural defects with the correct assessment data.

_____	Hirschsprung's disease	A. Olive-shaped mass in the right upper quadrant
_____	Intussusception	B. Painless, bloody stools
_____	Hypertrophic pyloric stenosis	C. Failure to pass meconium in newborns
_____	GER(D)	D. Stool of red currant jelly consistency
_____	Meckel's diverticulum	E. Excess spitting up or forceful vomiting

Scenario: A 6-year-old child is brought to an outpatient facility by his mother. The mother tells the nurse that her child has been experiencing abdominal pain that has lasted almost 2 days without relief. The child is nauseous, has slight constipation, a low-grade fever, and no appetite. He is admitted to an acute pediatric care facility. Soon after admission his pain begins to worsen.

2. When assessing the child for possible appendicitis, where should the nurse expect his abdominal pain to be located?

3. Which of the following diagnostic or laboratory test results should cause the nurse to suspect that the child has appendicitis? (Select all that apply.)

    _____ Increased BUN levels

    _____ Increased WBCs

    _____ Increased band (immature neutrophil) count

    _____ Urinalysis containing a large numbers of bacteria

    _____ Barium enema testing positive for structural defect

    _____ Rectal biopsy showing aganglionic cells

4. The child is diagnosed with acute appendicitis and is sent to surgery. During surgery, a ruptured appendix is found, which has resulted in peritonitis. List the nursing interventions the nurse should plan to initiate when the child returns to the pediatric unit.

Scenario: A nurse is caring for a newborn who has a cleft lip. The newborn's mother plans to breastfeed.

5. What discharge instructions should the nurse give to the parents?

6. The infant returns to the hospital for surgical repair of the cleft lip. List several teaching points the nurse should advise the family to watch for when observing the newborn for possible signs of infection.

7. An infant has undergone surgical repair of a cleft palate. Which of the following instructions should the nurse provide for the infant's family regarding prevention of damage to the surgical site? (Select all that apply.)

_____ Maintain pain management.

_____ Remove any packing from inside the infant's mouth when it becomes soiled.

_____ Use a cotton-tipped swab to clean the inside of the infant's mouth.

_____ Use elbow restraints.

_____ Give the infant soft finger foods.

CHAPTER 23: GASTROINTESTINAL STRUCTURAL AND INFLAMMATORY DISORDERS

(A) Application Exercises Answer Key

1. Match the following structural defects with the correct assessment data.

__C__	Hirschsprung's disease	A. Olive-shaped mass in the right upper quadrant
__D__	Intussusception	B. Painless, bloody stools
__A__	Hypertrophic pyloric stenosis	C. Failure to pass meconium in newborns
__E__	GER(D)	D. Stool of red currant jelly consistency
__B__	Meckel's diverticulum	E. Excess spitting up or forceful vomiting

(N) **NCLEX® Connection: Reduction of Risk Potential, System Specific Assessment**

Scenario: A 6-year-old child is brought to an outpatient facility by his mother. The mother tells the nurse that her child has been experiencing abdominal pain that has lasted almost 2 days without relief. The child is nauseous, has slight constipation, a low-grade fever, and no appetite. He is admitted to an acute pediatric care facility. Soon after admission his pain begins to worsen.

---

2. When assessing the child for possible appendicitis, where should the nurse expect his abdominal pain to be located?

Pain is usually most intense in the right lower quadrant, over McBurney point, which is halfway between the anterior superior iliac crest and the umbilicus.

(N) **NCLEX® Connection: Reduction of Risk Potential, System Specific Assessment**

3. Which of the following diagnostic or laboratory test results should cause the nurse to suspect that the child has appendicitis? (Select all that apply.)

_____	Increased BUN levels
__X__	**Increased WBCs**
__X__	**Increased band (immature neutrophil) count**
_____	Urinalysis containing a large numbers of bacteria
_____	Barium enema testing positive for structural defect
_____	Rectal biopsy showing aganglionic cells

Increased WBCs with an increased neutrophil count may indicate appendicitis. An increased BUN level may indicate dehydration with hypertrophic pyloric stenosis. Large numbers of bacteria in urinalysis may indicate a urinary tract infection. A barium enema indicating structural defect may be diagnostic of intussusception. Rectal biopsy demonstrating aganglionic cells indicates Hirschsprung's disease.

(N) **NCLEX® Connection: Reduction of Risk Potential, Laboratory Values**

4. The child is diagnosed with acute appendicitis and is sent to surgery. During surgery, a ruptured appendix is found, which has resulted in peritonitis. List the nursing interventions the nurse should plan to initiate when the child returns to the pediatric unit.

> **Administer IV pain medications and antibiotics.**
>
> **Monitor vital signs per facility protocol.**
>
> **Provide nasogastric tube maintenance until bowel motility returns.**
>
> **Provide postoperative activity (turning, initiating deep breathing, moving extremities, ambulating) as ordered.**
>
> **Support coping mechanisms of the child and family.**
>
> **Provide teaching for the child and family.**
>
> **Provide surgical wound care.**

Ⓝ NCLEX® Connection: Reduction of Risk Potential, Potential for Complications From Surgical Procedures and Health Alterations

---

Scenario: A nurse is caring for a newborn who has a cleft lip. The newborn's mother plans to breastfeed.

5. What discharge instructions should the nurse give to the parents?

> **Provide a quiet, calm environment for feeding. Hold the newborn upright while feeding to prevent choking. Burp the newborn frequently because the newborn swallows a lot of air while eating. If breastfeeding, place the breast fully into the newborn's mouth, making a seal. If bottle feeding, use a specialized nipple or a large syringe attached to rubber tubing. Instill the formula slowly, observing that the newborn is swallowing. Do not be afraid if milk comes through the newborn's nose. This is okay because the cleft palate opens directly into the nasal cavity. Don't tire the newborn. Eating can be difficult and stressful. Limit feeding times to 20 to 30 min. Also, teach parents to observe for ear infections and encourage speech attempts and any activities that will increase bonding, such as cuddling or talking to the newborn.**

Ⓝ NCLEX® Connection: Physiological Adaptation, Alterations in Body Systems

6. The infant returns to the hospital for surgical repair of the cleft lip. List several teaching points the nurse should advise the family to watch for when observing the newborn for possible signs of infection.

> **Redness, swelling, purulent drainage at the surgical site**
>
> **Increased irritability**
>
> **Loss of appetite**
>
> **Fever**

Ⓝ NCLEX® Connection: Physiological Adaptation, Alterations in Body Systems

7. An infant has undergone surgical repair of a cleft palate. Which of the following instructions should the nurse provide for the infant's family regarding prevention of damage to the surgical site? (Select all that apply.)

<u> X </u>   **Maintain pain management.**

<u>   </u>   Remove any packing from inside the infant's mouth when it becomes soiled.

<u>   </u>   Use a cotton-tipped swab to clean the inside of the infant's mouth.

<u> X </u>   **Use elbow restraints.**

<u> X </u>   **Give the infant soft finger foods.**

Pain management is important to prevent the infant from attempting to pick at the incision site. It is also effective in preventing crying and fussing, which could also damage the site. Elbow restraints prevent the infant from sticking objects inside the mouth. Giving finger foods avoids the possibility of using forks or other hard objects that might disturb the surgical site. If packing is in place, parents should not pull it out unless specifically told to do so. Using a swab in the infant's mouth could damage the surgical site.

Ⓝ NCLEX® Connection: Physiological Adaptation, Alterations in Body Systems

UNIT 2: NURSING CARE OF CHILDREN WITH SYSTEM DISORDERS

Section: Genitourinary and Reproductive Disorders

- Enuresis and Urinary Tract Infections
- Structural Disorders of the Genitourinary Tract and Reproductive System
- Renal Disorders

NCLEX® CONNECTIONS

When reviewing the chapters in this section, keep in mind the relevant sections of the NCLEX® outline, in particular:

CLIENT NEEDS: BASIC CARE AND COMFORT

Relevant topics/tasks include:

- Elimination
  - Assess and manage the client with an alteration in elimination (e.g., bowel, urinary).
- Nutrition and Oral Hydration
  - Monitor the client's hydration status.

CLIENT NEEDS: REDUCTION OF RISK POTENTIAL

Relevant topics/tasks include:

- Changes/Abnormalities in Vital Signs
  - Assess and respond to changes in the client's vital signs.
- Laboratory Values
  - Notify the provider about laboratory test results.
- Potential for Complications of Diagnostic Tests/Treatments/Procedures
  - Use precautions to prevent injury and/or complications associated with a procedure or diagnosis.

CLIENT NEEDS: PHYSIOLOGICAL ADAPTATION

Relevant topics/tasks include:

- Alterations in Body Systems
  - Monitor and maintain devices and equipment used for drainage.
- Fluid and Electrolyte Imbalances
  - Manage the care of the client with a fluid and electrolyte imbalance.
- Illness Management
  - Identify client data that need to be reported immediately.

UNIT 2	NURSING CARE OF CHILDREN WITH SYSTEM DISORDERS
Section	Genitourinary and Reproductive Disorders
Chapter 24	Enuresis and Urinary Tract Infections

Overview

- Enuresis is defined as uncontrolled or unintentional urination that occurs after a child is beyond an age at which bladder control is achieved.

- A urinary tract infection (UTI) is an infection in any portion of the urinary tract (cystitis, urethritis, pyelonephritis).

ENURESIS

Overview

- Inappropriate urination must occur at least twice a week for at least 3 months and the child must be at least 5 years of age before a diagnosis of enuresis is considered.

- Enuresis is more commonly seen in males.

- Organic causes related to genitourinary dysfunction must be ruled out prior to diagnosis of enuresis.

Assessment

- Risk Factors

  o Enuresis has no clear etiology, but it may be related to:

    ▪ Family history of enuresis

    ▪ Disorders associated with bladder dysfunction

    ▪ Emotional factors

- Subjective Data

  o History of toilet training, voiding behaviors, and bowel movement patterns

  o History of chronic or acute illness (urinary tract infection, diabetes mellitus, sickle cell disease, neurologic deficits)

  o History of family disruptions or other emotional stressors

  o Family history of enuresis

  o Fluid intake, especially in the evening

Collaborative Care

- Nursing Care

  - Evaluate the child's and family's understanding of enuresis.

  - Educate the child and family regarding the management of enuresis (fluid restriction prior to bedtime, bladder training, medications).

  - Evaluate the child's self-esteem.

  - Evaluate the child's coping strategies and available support systems.

  - Evaluate the family's coping.

  - Evaluate peer and family support groups.

- Medications

  - Antidiuretics – Desmopressin acetate (DDAVP)

    - Used to reduce the volume of urine in the bladder

    - Nursing Considerations

      - Inform the family of possible side effects (headache, nausea, flushing, mild abdominal cramps, fluid retention)

    - Client Education

      - Encourage the family to restrict the child's fluid intake after dinner.

      - Instruct the family to administer the medication at bedtime.

      - Instruct the family to keep nasal medications in the refrigerator.

  - Tricyclic antidepressants – Imipramine hydrochloride (Tofranil)

    - Nursing Considerations

      - Inform the family of possible side effects (dry mouth, constipation, insomnia, anxiety).

    - Client Education

      - Instruct the family to administer the mediation 1 hr before bedtime.

  - Anticholinergics – Oxybutynin chloride (Ditropan)

    - Reduces bladder contractions

    - Nursing Considerations

      - Monitor for effectiveness of therapy.

    - Client Education

      - Instruct the child and family to watch for side effects (dry mouth, drowsiness, nausea, allergic reaction).

- Therapeutic Procedures
  - Bladder stretching exercises
    - The child should drink fluid and hold the urine as long as possible, which may increase the functional size of the bladder. Pelvic muscle exercises should be practiced throughout the day to help with bladder control.
    - Client Education
      - Teach the child how to hold urine for as long as possible.
      - Teach the child how to perform pelvic muscle exercises to improve bladder control.
- Care After Discharge
  - Client Education
    - Explain to the family that enuresis is not a behavioral problem and should not be punished.
    - Help the parents identify ways to improve the child's self-image related to enuresis.
    - Advise the child and parents that therapies for enuresis may be helpful for a short time, but they may not provide a cure. Support the child and parents in their decisions.
- Client Outcomes
  - The child will eliminate nighttime wetness.
  - The child will maintain positive self-esteem.

Complications

- Emotional problems (poor self-esteem, altered body image, social isolation, fears)
  - Nursing Actions
    - Support the child and family by listening to concerns and correcting misperceptions.
    - Make referrals to appropriate resources (support groups, counseling) as needed.
  - Client Education
    - Assist the child and family to understand the emotional aspects of the disorder. Early interventions can alleviate long-term emotional issues.
    - Suggest that the child and family participate in a support group.

URINARY TRACT INFECTIONS

Overview

- An upper urinary tract infection (UTI) is a conditions such as pyelonephritis. Urinary reflux from the bladder into the ureters may contribute to pyelonephritis.

- Untreated UTIs may lead to renal damage/failure or urosepsis.

- Organisms that cause UTIs include *Escherichia coli* (most common), *Proteus*, *Pseudomonas*, *Klebsiella*, and *Staphylococcus aureus*.

- Diagnosis is made by detection of bacteria in the urine.

Assessment

- Risk Factors

    o Urinary stasis

    o Urinary tract anomalies

    o Reflux within the urinary tract system

    o Constipation

    o Onset of toilet training

    o Female gender (due to short urethra in close proximity to the rectum)

    o Synthetic, tight underwear and wet bathing suits

    o Sexual activity

- Subjective Data

    o Presenting symptoms vary depending on age.

    - Urinary frequency with voiding of small amounts, urgency, and nocturia

    - Dysuria, bladder cramping, or spasms

    - Discomfort or pain in back or abdomen

    - Urinary incontinence in a child already toilet trained

    - Infants

        □ Irritability/fussiness

        □ Crying upon urination

        □ Poor feeding

        □ Nausea, vomiting, and diarrhea

- Objective Data

  o Physical Assessment Findings

    ■ Fever

    ■ Diaper rash, perineal itching, and a reddened perineal area

  o Laboratory Tests

    ■ Urinalysis and urine culture and sensitivity

      □ Sterile catheterization and/or suprapubic aspiration is the most accurate method for obtaining urine for urinalysis and culture in children less than 2 years of age.

      □ Obtain a clean-catch urine sample from children who are able to cooperate.

      □ Nursing Actions

        ▸ If a suprapubic aspiration is to be performed, confirm that consent has been obtained.

        ▸ To prevent a falsely low bacterial count, avoid having the child drink a large amount of oral fluids prior to obtaining a urine specimen.

        ▸ Take the specimen for culture to the laboratory without delay.

        ▸ Expected findings

          ▹ Urine culture – Positive for infecting organisms

          ▹ Urinalysis – Positive for bacteria and protein, cloudy, foul-smelling, bright red, and tea- or cola-colored with a pH greater than 7

          ▹ Microscopic exam of urine – RBC and WBC reveal greater than 100,000 organisms/mL

      □ Client Education

        ▸ Educate the child and family about the procedure for collecting a suprapubic aspiration, invasive urine catheterization, or clean-voided specimen.

  o Diagnostic Procedures

    ■ Cystoscopy, voiding cystoureterography, intravenous pyelograms (IVP), and urodynamic tests

      □ These tests may be used after the resolution of a UTI to assess for anatomic or physical defects.

        ▸ Nursing Actions

          ▹ Educate the child and family about the procedure for the diagnostic test prescribed.

          ▹ Assess the child for allergy to iodine/shellfish if a contrast medium is used.

▷ Sedate infants and young children if required. Assist the older child to remain quiet during the examinations.

▷ Maintain the child on NPO status after midnight in preparation for a cystoscopy and IVP. IVP requires bowel preparation.

▷ Prepare the child if catheterization is necessary.

▷ Monitor the child after the procedure, according to facility protocol.

Collaborative Care

- Nursing Care

  o Encourage frequent voiding and complete emptying of the bladder.

  o Encourage fluids.

  o Monitor urine output.

  o Prepare the child for diagnostic tests.

  o Administer a mild analgesic (acetaminophen [Tylenol]) for pain management.

  o Encourage sitz baths PRN.

- Medications

  o Antibiotics – Sulfamethoxazole and trimethoprim (Septra)

    ■ Penicillins, cephalosporins, and nitrofurantoin (Macrobid)

    ■ Nursing Considerations

      □ Monitor for potential allergic response.

    ■ Client Education

      □ Instruct parents to have the child complete all prescribed antibiotics, even if symptoms are no longer present.

- Care After Discharge

  o Client Education

    ■ Instruct the family to watch for signs and symptoms of recurrence of UTIs (dysuria, frequency, urgency).

    ■ Provide instruction to prevent recurrence.

      □ Teach females to wipe the perineal area from front to back.

      □ Teach parents to retract and clean the foreskin of male infants.

      □ Instruct the child and parents to keep underwear dry.

      □ Suggest the use of cotton underwear.

      □ Tell the child to maintain adequate hydration.

      □ Instruct avoidance of bubble baths.

- □ Encourage frequent voiding.

- □ Encourage complete emptying of bladder using double voiding.

- □ Advise the child to avoid constipation and straining with bowel movements.

- □ Encourage adolescents who are sexually active to void immediately after intercourse.

- Client Outcomes

  - ○ The child will be free from urinary tract infection.

  - ○ The child will have preserved renal function.

Complications

- Progressive kidney injury

- Urosepsis

  - ○ Nursing Actions

    - ▪ Monitor for signs and symptoms of UTIs.

  - ○ Client Education

    - ▪ Reinforce teaching about prevention, early identification, and treatment of UTIs.

CHAPTER 24: ENURESIS AND URINARY TRACT INFECTIONS

Ⓐ Application Exercises

Scenario: A nurse is caring for a 4-year-old child who is being seen for the second time with a UTI.

1. Which of the following findings should the nurse expect during an initial assessment? (Select all that apply.)

_____ Light-colored urine

_____ Dysuria

_____ Foul-smelling urine

_____ Epigastric pain

_____ Oliguria

2. The child is to return to the office in 1 week for follow-up and is scheduled for a voiding cystourethrogram (VCUG) in 2 weeks. The mother asks what the purpose of the VCUG is. How should the nurse respond?

3. The nurse is providing teaching to the mother to help prevent another UTI. Which of the following instructions should the nurse include in the teaching? (Select all that apply.)

_____ Avoid giving the child bubble baths.

_____ Change the child's bathing suit immediately after swimming.

_____ Encourage the child to go to the bathroom every 6 hr.

_____ Have the child wear cotton, rather than nylon, underpants.

_____ Instruct the child to wipe from front to back after voiding.

CHAPTER 24: ENURESIS AND URINARY TRACT INFECTIONS

 Application Exercises Answer Key

Scenario: A nurse is caring for a 4-year-old child who is being seen for the second time with a UTI.

1. Which of the following findings should the nurse expect during an initial assessment? (Select all that apply.)

    _____ Light-colored urine

    __X__ **Dysuria**

    __X__ **Foul-smelling urine**

    _____ Epigastric pain

    _____ Oliguria

    Dysuria, foul-smelling urine, left flank pain, and dark-colored urine are findings consistent with a UTI. Epigastric pain and oliguria are consistent with renal failure.

    Ⓝ **NCLEX® Connection: Physiological Adaptation, Infectious Disease**

2. The child is to return to the office in 1 week for follow-up and is scheduled for a voiding cystourethrogram (VCUG) in 2 weeks. The mother asks what the purpose of the VCUG is. How should the nurse respond?

    The VCUG checks for problems of the urethra and bladder, specifically problems with bladder emptying. Having two UTIs in such a short time is unusual for an infant; therefore, it is important to find out the cause of the infection. The VCUG will be scheduled after eradication of the UTI.

    Ⓝ **NCLEX® Connection: Reduction of Risk Potential, Diagnostic Tests**

3. The nurse is providing teaching to the mother to help prevent another UTI. Which of the following instructions should the nurse include in the teaching? (Select all that apply.)

    __X__ **Avoid giving the child bubble baths.**

    __X__ **Change the child's bathing suit immediately after swimming.**

    _____ Encourage the child to go to the bathroom every 6 hr.

    __X__ **Have the child wear cotton, rather than nylon, underpants.**

    __X__ **Instruct the child to wipe from front to back after voiding.**

    Bubble baths should not be used for a child who is prone to UTIs. The wet lining of a bathing suit can foster bacterial growth; therefore, wet clothing should be changed as soon as possible. Cotton underwear will keep the perineal area drier than nylon, preventing bacterial growth. Parents should encourage the child to go to the bathroom every 2 to 4 hr to prevent urine stasis. The perineal area should be wiped from front to back; otherwise, bacteria is being introduced into the urinary meatus.

    Ⓝ **NCLEX® Connection: Physiological Adaptation, Infectious Disease**

UNIT 2	NURSING CARE OF CHILDREN WITH SYSTEM DISORDERS
Section	Genitourinary and Reproductive Disorders
Chapter 25	Structural Disorders of the Genitourinary Tract and Reproductive System

Overview

- Various structural disorders may be evident at birth and may affect normal genitourinary and reproductive function. These disorders include bladder exstrophy, hypospadias, epispadias, phimosis, cryptorchidism, and hydrocele.

- Children become aware of and are very interested in the genital area, normality of genital function, and gender differences between the ages of 3 and 6 years of age. Due to this, repair of structural defects should be done ideally between 6 to 15 months of age, but before age 3, to minimize impact on body image and to promote healthy development.

Assessment

- Risk Factors

  o Hypospadias and epispadias may have a genetic link.

  o Ambiguous genitalia may be associated with congenital adrenal hyperplasia.

- Objective Data

  o Physical Assessment Findings

    ▪ Defect may or may not be visible.

    ▪ Bladder exstrophy is the protrusion of the bladder through an abdominal opening resulting from failure of the abdominal wall and other underlying structures to fuse in utero.

    ▪ Hypospadias occurs when the location of the urethral meatus is below the glans penis or on the ventral surface of the penis. Hypospadias may be accompanied by a chordee, which is a fibrous band on the ventral side of the penis resulting in a ventral curvature of the penis.

    ▪ Epispadias occurs when the location of the urethral meatus is on the dorsal side of the penis.

    ▪ Phimosis is the narrowing of the preputial opening of the foreskin that prevents the foreskin from retracting over the glans penis.

    ▪ Cryptorchidism is the failure of one or both testicles to descend through the inguinal canal.

- Hydrocele is an abnormal collection of fluid in the scrotum.
- Ambiguous genitalia are congenital malformations that prevent visual identification of a child's sex.

○ Diagnostic Procedures

- Ambiguous genitalia – Chromosome analysis is used to determine genetic karyotype.

  □ Ultrasonography is useful in assessing the presence or absence of genital and urinary structures.

  □ Biochemical tests may detect adrenal cortical syndromes.

  □ Nursing Actions

  ▸ Provide support for parents during the diagnosis.

  ▸ Administer sedation and assist with the procedure as needed.

  □ Client Education

  ▸ Advise the family and/or child about the procedure and what to expect.

  ▸ If NPO status is necessary, explain the parameters to the family and/or child.

Collaborative Care

- Nursing Care

  ○ Nursing care should focus on education and support of the family and child.

  - Evaluate the family's perception of the child's defect, family support, and coping.
  - Assist parents to identify ways to help the child maintain a good self-image.

- Surgical Interventions

  - Structural defects will be treated with surgical intervention. The goal of most structural defect repairs is to preserve or create normal urinary and sexual function. Early intervention will minimize emotional trauma.

  - Nursing Actions

    □ Preoperative

    ▸ Provide education to the child and family related to the procedure and expectations for postoperative care.

    ▸ Provide emotional support to the child and family.

    ▸ Encourage parent to express concerns and fears related to the surgical procedure and outcomes.

- □ Postoperative
  - ‣ Assess pain using an appropriate pain assessment tool.
  - ‣ Administer pain medication as prescribed. An antispasmodic, such as oxybutynin (Ditropan), may be prescribed to treat painful bladder spasms.
  - ‣ Monitor intake and output.
  - ‣ Monitor urinary catheters, drains, or stints.
  - ‣ Provide wound and/or dressing care.
  - ‣ Monitor for signs of infection, such as redness, warmth, drainage, or edema at surgical site. Monitor for fever, lethargy, and foul-smelling urine.
  - ‣ Do not provide tub baths for at least 1 week.
  - ‣ Limit activity as prescribed.
- ■ Client Education
  - □ Explain procedures at the appropriate level for child and/or parents.
  - □ Use age-appropriate interventions to allay fears and anxiety.
  - □ Help the child understand that surgery is not a punishment, and it will not mutilate the body.
- ● Client Outcomes
  - ○ The child will be free from infection.
  - ○ The child will recover from surgical procedure without complications.

Complications

- ● Infection
  - ○ Nursing Action
    - ■ Observe for signs of infection including fever, skin inflammation, foul urine odor, cloudy urine, and/or urinary frequency.
  - ○ Client Education
    - ■ Teach the family to observe for signs of infection.
    - ■ Teach the family to report any signs of infection immediately.
- ● Emotional problems (poor self-esteem, altered body image, social isolation, fears)
  - ○ Nursing Actions
    - ■ Support the child and family by listening to concerns and correcting misperceptions.
    - ■ Use play therapy for toddlers and preschoolers.
  - ○ Client Education
    - ■ Educate the child and family regarding support groups.

CHAPTER 25: STRUCTURAL DISORDERS OF THE GENITOURINARY TRACT AND REPRODUCTIVE SYSTEM

(A) Application Exercises

1. Match the structural genitourinary disorders with their definitions.

_____	Hypospadias	A. A fibrous band on the ventral side of the penis resulting in a ventral curvature of the penis
_____	Epispadias	B. Narrowing of the preputial opening of the foreskin that prevents retraction of the foreskin over the glans penis
_____	Phimosis	C. Failure of one or both testicles to descend into the scrotum
_____	Bladder exstrophy	D. Collection of fluid in the scrotal sac
_____	Cryptorchidism	E. Urethral meatus located on the ventral side of the glans penis
_____	Chordee	F. Protrusion of bladder through lower abdominal wall
_____	Hydrocele	G. Urethral meatus located on the dorsal side of the glans penis

2. Identify emotional problems that a young child may develop related to structural disorders and interventions the nurse may use with the family and child.

CHAPTER 25: STRUCTURAL DISORDERS OF THE GENITOURINARY TRACT AND REPRODUCTIVE SYSTEM

 Application Exercises Answer Key

1. Match the structural genitourinary disorders with their definitions.

__E__	Hypospadias	A. A fibrous band on the ventral side of the penis resulting in a ventral curvature of the penis
__G__	Epispadias	B. Narrowing of the preputial opening of the foreskin that prevents retraction of the foreskin over the glans penis
__B__	Phimosis	C. Failure of one or both testicles to descend into the scrotum
__F__	Bladder exstrophy	D. Collection of fluid in the scrotal sac
__C__	Cryptorchidism	E. Urethral meatus located on the ventral side of the glans penis
__A__	Chordee	F. Protrusion of bladder through lower abdominal wall
__D__	Hydrocele	G. Urethral meatus located on the dorsal side of the glans penis

 NCLEX® Connection: Reduction of Risk Potential, Therapeutic Procedures

2. Identify emotional problems that a young child may develop related to structural disorders and interventions the nurse may use with the family and child.

A young child who has a genitourinary or reproductive structural disorder may develop poor self-esteem, altered body image, social isolation, or fears. The nurse should provide support to the child and family by listening to concerns and correcting misperceptions. Play therapy should be used to allow young children to express their feelings.

 NCLEX® Connection: Reduction of Risk Potential, Complications From Surgical Procedures and Health Alterations

UNIT 2	NURSING CARE OF CHILDREN WITH SYSTEM DISORDERS
Section	Genitourinary and Reproductive Disorders

Chapter 26	Renal Disorders

Overview

- Acute glomerulonephritis (AGN)

  - Acute glomerulonephritis may occur as a single episode or may be the result of a disease, usually following an infectious process. The most common types are pneumococcal, streptococcal, and viral infections.

  - Oliguria, edema, hypertension, circulatory congestion, hematuria, and proteinuria are common findings associated with AGN.

- Nephrotic syndrome is a group of symptoms, not a disease. It is the most common presentation of glomerular injury in children. Three forms of the syndrome include primary, congenital, and secondary nephrotic syndrome. The most common form of disease in children is minimal change nephrotic syndrome and accounts for 80% of all cases.

ACUTE GLOMERULONEPHRITIS (AGN)

Overview

- Acute poststreptococcal glomerulonephritis (APSGN) is the most common of the postinfectious renal diseases.

  - APSGN is an antibody-antigen disease that occurs as a result of certain strains of the Group A ß-hemolytic streptococcal infection and is most commonly seen in children between the ages of 6 and 7.

  - The exact mechanism of the pathophysiology for APSGN is not certain. It is believed that immune complexes develop and become trapped in the glomerular capillary loop at the basement membrane. This produces swelling and occlusion of the capillary lumen and results in alterations in the glomerular filtration rate.

  - Renal manifestations usually occur 10 to 21 days post infection.

  - Prognosis varies depending upon the specific cause, but spontaneous recovery generally occurs after the acute illness. Recurrence is not common.

Assessment

- Risk Factors

  o Infection with pneumococcal, streptococcal, or viral agent

- Subjective Data

  o Recent upper respiratory infection or streptococcal infection

  o Lack of specific reports (Older children may report abdominal discomfort, headaches, painful urination, and anorexia/nausea.)

- Objective Data

  o Physical Assessment Findings

    ■ Decreased glomerular filtration rate leading to decreased urine output

    ■ Anorexia

    ■ Pallor

    ■ Vague reports of discomfort (headache, abdominal pain, dysuria)

    ■ Dyspnea

    ■ Orthopnea

    ■ Moist crackles on auscultation

    ■ Distended neck veins

    ■ Periorbital edema

    ■ Facial edema that is worse in the morning but then spreads to extremities and abdomen with progression of the day

    ■ Mild to severe hypertension

    ■ Pale appearance, irritability, and lethargy (The child seems ill.)

  o Laboratory Tests

    ■ Throat culture to identify possible streptococcus infection (usually negative by the time of diagnosis)

    ■ Urinalysis – Proteinuria, smoky or tea-colored urine, hematuria, cell debris (red cells and casts), elevated specific gravity

    ■ Renal function – Elevated BUN and creatinine

    ■ Antistreptolysin-O (ASO) titer – Positive indicator for the presence of streptococcal antibodies

    ■ Antihyaluronidase (AHase), antideoxyribonuclease B (ADNase-B), and streptozyme antibodies may be present.

    ■ Serum complement (C3) – Decreased initially; increases as recovery takes place; returns to normal at 8 to 10 weeks post glomerulonephritis

- ○ Diagnostic Procedures
  - ■ Chest x-ray
    - □ Used to identify pulmonary complications, especially during the edematous phase
      - ▸ Pulmonary edema
      - ▸ Cardiac enlargement
      - ▸ Pleural effusions
    - □ Nursing Actions
      - ▸ Ensure that adolescents are not pregnant.
      - ▸ Assist with proper positioning.
    - □ Client Education
      - ▸ Explain the procedure to the child and family.

Collaborative Care

- • Nursing Care
  - ○ Monitor I&O.
  - ○ Monitor daily weights; weigh the child on the same scale with the same amount of clothing daily.
  - ○ Monitor vital signs.
  - ○ Monitor neurologic status and observe for behavior changes, especially in children who have edema, hypertension, and gross hematuria. Implement seizure precautions if condition indicates.
  - ○ Encourage adequate nutritional intake within restriction guidelines. A regular diet with elimination of high sodium foods will be appropriate for most.
    - ■ Restrict foods high in potassium during periods of oliguria.
    - ■ Provide small, frequent meals of favorite foods due to a decrease in appetite.
    - ■ Refer the child for dietary consultation if indicated.
  - ○ Manage fluid restrictions as prescribed. Fluids may be restricted during periods of edema and hypertension.
  - ○ Monitor skin for breakdown areas and prevent pressure sores.
    - ■ Encourage frequent turning and repositioning.
    - ■ Keep skin dry.
    - ■ Pad bony prominences and use a specialty mattress.
    - ■ Elevate edematous body parts.
  - ○ Assess tolerance for activity. Provide for frequent rest periods.

- ○ Provide for age-appropriate diversional activities.

- ○ Cluster care to facilitate rest and tolerance of activity.

- ○ Monitor and prevent infection.

  - ■ Advise the child to turn, cough, and deep breathe to prevent pulmonary involvement.

  - ■ Monitor vital signs, especially temperature, for changes secondary to infection.

  - ■ Maintain good hand hygiene.

  - ■ Administer antibiotic therapy as prescribed.

- ○ Provide emotional support.

- ● Medications

  - ○ Diuretics and antihypertensives

    - ■ Used to removal accumulated fluid and manage hypertension

    - ■ Nursing Considerations

      - □ Monitor blood pressure.

      - □ Monitor intake and output.

      - □ Monitor for electrolyte imbalances, such as hypokalemia.

      - □ Observe for side effects of medications.

    - ■ Client Education

      - □ Encourage the child to eat food high in potassium if potassium-sparing diuretics are not used.

      - □ Inform the child and family that dizziness can occur with the use of antihypertensives.

      - □ Instruct the child and family to take the medication as prescribed and notify the provider if side effects occur. Give instructions to continue the medication unless instructed otherwise.

- ● Interdisciplinary Care

  - ○ Obtain a dietary consult.

- ● Care After Discharge

  - ○ Client Education

    - ■ Encourage the child to verbalize feelings related to body image.

    - ■ Educate the child regarding appropriate dietary management.

    - ■ Encourage adequate rest.

    - ■ Educate the family about the need for follow-up care. The child should be seen by the provider weekly for several weeks and then monthly until the disease is fully resolved.

- Teach the family how to monitor blood pressure and daily weight.
- Teach the family about administration and side effects of diuretics and antihypertensive medications.
- Encourage the child and family to avoid contact with others who may be ill.

- Client Outcomes

  ○ The child will maintain optimal renal function.

  ○ The child will maintain blood pressure within the normal reference range.

  ○ The child and family will have adequate support.

NEPHROTIC SYNDROME

Overview

- Nephrotic syndrome

  ○ In nephrotic syndrome, alterations in the glomerular membrane allow proteins (especially albumin) to pass into the urine, resulting in decreased serum osmotic pressure. The exact cause of glomerular alteration is not well understood and is thought to be due to metabolic, biochemical, physiochemical, or immune-mediated causes.

  ○ Nephrotic syndrome is characterized by hyperlipidemia, proteinuria, hypoalbuminemia, and edema.

  ○ Management of nephrotic syndrome is aimed at reducing the excretion of protein, reducing fluid retention, preventing infection, and preventing complications.

Assessment

- Risk Factors

  ○ Minimal change nephrotic syndrome (MCNS)

    - Peak incidence is between 2 and 7 years of age.
    - Cause is unknown, but it may have a multifactorial etiology (immune-mediated, biochemical).

  ○ Secondary nephrotic syndrome (occurs after or is associated with glomerular damage due to a known cause).

  ○ Congenital nephrotic syndrome (an inherited disorder).

- Subjective Data

  ○ Weight gain over a short period of days or weeks

  ○ Poor appetite, possibly anorexia, nausea and vomiting, and diarrhea

  ○ Decreased activity levels

  ○ Irritability

- Objective Data
  - Physical Assessment Findings
    - Weight gain
    - Edema (facial/periorbital) is worse in morning and decreases as the day progresses
    - Ascites and dependent edema (especially in the labia, scrotum, legs, and ankles)
    - Dark, frothy urine, decreased urine output, and oliguria
    - Normal or slightly elevated blood pressure
  - Laboratory Tests
    - Urinalysis/24-hr urine collection
      - Proteinuria – Protein greater than 3+ or 4+ (greater than 3.5 g in 24 hr)
      - Hyaline casts
      - Increased specific gravity
      - Color change
    - Serum chemistry
      - Hypoalbuminemia – Reduced serum protein and albumin
      - Hyperlipidemia– Elevated serum lipid levels
      - Hemoconcentration– Elevated Hgb, Hct, and platelets
  - Diagnostic Procedures
    - Kidney biopsy is indicated only if nephrotic syndrome is unresponsive to steroid therapy.
      - Biopsy will show damage to the epithelial cells lining the basement membrane of the kidney.

Collaborative Care

- Nursing Care
  - Provide rest.
  - Monitor I&O. Monitor urine for specific gravity and protein.
  - Monitor daily weights; weigh the child on the same scale with the same amount of clothing.
  - Monitor edema and measure abdominal girth daily. Measure at the widest area, usually at or above the umbilicus. Assess degree of pitting, color, and texture of skin.
  - Monitor and prevent infection.
    - Assist the child to turn, cough, and deep breathe to prevent pulmonary involvement.
    - Monitor vital signs, especially temperature, for changes secondary to infection.

- ■ Maintain good hand hygiene.
- ■ Administer antibiotic therapy as prescribed.
- ○ Encourage nutritional intake within restriction guidelines. Salt and fluids may be restricted during the edematous phase. Increase protein in diet to replace protein losses.
- ○ Cluster care to provide for rest periods.
- ○ Assess skin for breakdown areas. Prevent pressure sores.
  - ■ Avoid use of urinary collection bags in very young children.
  - ■ Pad bony prominences or use a specialty mattress to reduce breakdown of skin.
  - ■ Encourage frequent turning and repositioning of the child.
  - ■ Keep the child's skin dry.
  - ■ Elevate edematous body parts.
- Medications
  - ○ Corticosteroid – Prednisone (Deltasone)
  - ○ Nursing Considerations
    - ■ Administer for 7 to 21 days (based on response) and then taper over several months with decreasing doses until discontinued.
    - ■ Monitor for infection.
  - ○ Client Education
    - ■ Educate the child and family to avoid large crowds (to decrease the risk of infection).
    - ■ Instruct the family to administer the medication on alternate days after the first 4 weeks of therapy.
    - ■ Inform the child and family that using corticosteroids can increase appetite, cause weight gain (especially in the face), and cause mood swings.
  - ○ Diuretic – Furosemide (Lasix)
    - ■ Eliminates excess fluid from the body
    - ■ Nursing Considerations
      - □ Encourage the child to eat foods that are high in potassium.
      - □ Monitor serum electrolyte levels periodically.

- o 25% albumin
  - ■ Increases plasma volume and decreases edema
  - ■ Nursing Considerations
    - □ Administer per protocol.
    - □ Monitor I&O.
    - □ Watch for anaphylaxis.
- o Cyclophosphamide (Cytoxan)
  - ■ Administer for children who cannot tolerate prednisone or who have repeated relapses of MCNS.
- Interdisciplinary Care
  - o Obtain a dietary consult.
- Care After Discharge
  - o Client Education
    - ■ Encourage the child to verbalize feelings related to body image.
    - ■ Educate the child regarding appropriate dietary management.
    - ■ Encourage adequate rest.
    - ■ Educate the family about the need for follow-up care. The child should be seen by the health care provider weekly for several weeks and then monthly until the disease is fully resolved.
    - ■ Inform the family of strategies to decrease the risk of infection (good hand hygiene, up-to-date immunizations, avoidance of infected people).
    - ■ Teach the family how to monitor blood pressure, daily weight, and protein in urine. Instruct the family to notify the provider if symptoms worsen, which indicates relapse.
    - ■ Teach the family about administration and side effects of medication.
    - ■ Provide support to families and make appropriate referrals as needed. Relapses can cause physical, emotional, and financial stress for the child and family.
  - o Client Outcomes
    - ■ The child will be free of infection.
    - ■ The child will maintain optimal renal function.
    - ■ The child will maintain a blood pressure that is within a normal reference range.
    - ■ The child and family will have adequate support.

Complications

- Sepsis/Infection

    o Steroid therapy increases the risk for infection.

        ▪ Common infections seen in children with nephrotic syndrome include pneumonia, peritonitis, and cellulitis.

    o Nursing Actions

        ▪ Keep the child away from potential infection sources.

        ▪ Monitor for signs of infection.

    o Client Education

        ▪ Educate about the importance of completing the full dose of antibiotic.

        ▪ Educate about the need for performing frequent hand hygiene.

        ▪ Educate about signs and symptoms of infection and when to contact the provider.

        ▪ Educate about potential infection sources (live plants, sick family members).

CHAPTER 26: RENAL DISORDERS

 Application Exercises

Scenario: A child with acute poststreptococcal glomerulonephritis (APSGN) is admitted to the pediatric ICU for overnight observation.

1. When obtaining a nursing history from the child's mother, the nurse should expect a recent _____ infection.

2. Which of the following physical assessment findings should the nurse expect? (Select all that apply.)

   _____ Flattened neck veins

   _____ Decreased blood pressure

   _____ Pallor

   _____ Reports of anorexia

   _____ Lethargy

3. What interventions should the nurse include in the child's plan of care?

4. A child who has nephrotic syndrome is admitted. Which of the following should the nurse expect to find? (Select all that apply.)

   _____ Decreased specific gravity

   _____ Proteinuria

   _____ Hypoalbuminemia

   _____ Hyperlipidemia

   _____ Hematuria

CHAPTER 26: RENAL DISORDERS

 Application Exercises Answer Key

Scenario: A child with acute poststreptococcal glomerulonephritis (APSGN) is admitted to the pediatric ICU for overnight observation.

1. When obtaining a nursing history from the child's mother, the nurse should expect a recent _____ infection.

    Streptococcal

    Typically, a streptococcal infection precedes the majority of cases of acute glomerulonephritis. Other infections that can cause glomerulonephritis include pneumococcal infections and viral infections.

 NCLEX® Connection: Physiological Adaptation, Infectious Disease

2. Which of the following physical assessment findings should the nurse expect? (Select all that apply.)

    _____ Flattened neck veins

    _____ Decreased blood pressure

    __X__ **Pallor**

    __X__ **Reports of anorexia**

    __X__ **Lethargy**

    A child with APSGN will likely present with pallor, reports of anorexia, and lethargy. Distended neck veins and increased blood pressure are expected findings.

 NCLEX® Connection: Reduction of Risk Potential, System Specific Assessment

3. What interventions should the nurse include in the child's plan of care?

    Monitor daily weights. Monitor vital signs. Administer antihypertensives as prescribed. Administer diuretics as prescribed. Monitor I&O. Monitor urine output for:

        a. Color

        b. Specific gravity as ordered

        c. Protein dipsticks as ordered

    Implement fluid restrictions as ordered. Limit sodium intake with diet as ordered.

 NCLEX® Connection: Physiological Adaptation, Illness Management

4. A child who has nephrotic syndrome is admitted. Which of the following should the nurse expect to find? (Select all that apply.)

           Decreased specific gravity

  X   **Proteinuria**

  X   **Hypoalbuminemia**

  X   **Hyperlipidemia**

           Hematuria

The child's specific gravity will most likely be elevated due to the presence of protein and casts in urine. The child who has nephrotic syndrome is experiencing increased permeability at the basement membrane. This child will experience hypoalbuminemia and hyperlipidemia. There is rarely hematuria.

Ⓝ **NCLEX® Connection: Reduction of Risk Potential, System Specific Assessment**

UNIT 2: NURSING CARE OF CHILDREN WITH SYSTEM DISORDERS

Section: Musculoskeletal Disorders

- Fractures
- Musculoskeletal Congenital Disorders
- Chronic Neuromusculoskeletal Disorders

NCLEX® CONNECTIONS

When reviewing the chapters in this section, keep in mind the relevant sections of the NCLEX® outline, in particular:

CLIENT NEEDS: BASIC CARE AND COMFORT	CLIENT NEEDS: PHARMACOLOGICAL AND PARENTERAL THERAPIES	CLIENT NEEDS: REDUCTION OF RISK POTENTIAL

Relevant topics/tasks include:
- Mobility/Immobility
  - Apply, maintain, or remove orthopedic devices.
- Nonpharmacological Comfort Interventions
  - Assess the client's need for pain management and intervene as needed using non-pharmacological comfort measures.
	Relevant topics/tasks include:
	- Adverse Effects/Contraindications/Side Effects/Interactions
	  - Identify a contraindication to the administration of a medication to the client.
	- Medication Administration
	  - Administer and document medications given by common routes.
	- Pharmacological Pain Management
	  - Use pharmacological measures for pain management, as needed.
		Relevant topics/tasks include:
		- Potential for Complications of Diagnostic Tests/Treatments/Procedures
		  - Use precautions to prevent injury and/or complications associated with a procedure or diagnosis.
		- System Specific Assessment
		  - Assess the client for abnormal peripheral pulses after a procedure or treatment.
		- Therapeutic Procedures
		  - Use precautions to prevent further injury when moving a client with a musculoskeletal condition.

UNIT 2	NURSING CARE OF CHILDREN WITH SYSTEM DISORDERS
Section	Musculoskeletal Disorders
Chapter 27	Fractures

Overview

- A fractures occurs when the resistance between a bone and an applied stress yields to the applied stress, resulting in a disruption to the integrity of the bone.

- Bone healing and remodeling is faster in children than in adults, due to a thicker periosteum and good blood supply.

- Epiphyseal plate injuries may result in altered bone growth.

- Radiographic evidence of previous fractures in various stages of healing or in infants may be the result of physical abuse or osteogenies imperfecta.

Assessment

- Risk Factors

  o Children and older adults are more likely to experience fractures.

  o Developmental characteristics, ordinary play activities, and recreation place children at risk for injury (falls from climbing or running; trauma to bones from skateboarding, skiing, playing soccer, or playing basketball).

- Subjective Data

  o Pain

  o Muscle spasms (occur from the pulling forces of the bone when not aligned)

  o Loss of function

  o Report of the child refusing to ambulate or crawl

- Objective Data

  o Physical Assessment Findings

    ▪ Common types of fractures in children

      □ Plastic deformation (bend) – The bone is bent no more than 45°.

      □ Buckle (torus) – A bulge or raised area is present at the fracture site.

- □ Greenstick – A fracture occurs in only one cortex of the bone.

- □ Spiral fracture – occurs from twisting motion (may be due to physical abuse)

View Media Supplement: Fractures (Image)

- □ Complete – Fragments remain attached.

- □ Incomplete – Bone fragments are still attached.

  ▸ The fracture line can be transverse, oblique, or spiral.

- □ Simple or closed – The fracture occurs without a break in the skin

- □ Open or compound – The fracture occurs with an open wound and bone protruding.

- □ Complicated fracture – The fracture results in injury to other organs and tissues.

- ▪ Crepitus – A grating sound created by the rubbing together of bone fragments

- ▪ Deformity – May observe internal rotation of extremity, shortened extremity, and visible bone with open fracture

- ▪ Visible muscle spasms – Occur from the pulling forces of the bone when not aligned

- ▪ Edema – Swelling from trauma

- ▪ Ecchymosis – Bleeding into underlying soft tissues from trauma

- ▪ Neurovascular Assessment

  - □ Pain– Assess the child's pain level, location, and frequency. Assess pain using an age-appropriate rating scale and have the child describe the pain.

  - □ Sensation – Assess the child for numbness or a tingling sensation of the extremity. Loss of sensation may indicate nerve damage.

  - □ Skin temperature – Assess the extremity for temperature. The extremity should be warm, not cool, to touch.

  - □ Skin color – Assess the color of the affected extremity. Check distal to the injury and look for changes in pigmentation.

  - □ Capillary refill – Press the nail beds of the affected extremity until blanching occurs. Blood return should be within 3 seconds.

  - □ Pulses – Pulses should be palpable and strong. Pulses should also be equal to the pulses of the unaffected extremity.

  - □ Movement – The child should be able to move the affected extremity in passive motion.

- o Diagnostic Procedures
  - Radiographic assessment
    - Radiographic films are the most common diagnostic tool used for fractures.
    - Nursing Actions
      - ‣ Instruct and assist the child to remain still during the procedure.
      - ‣ Sedate the child if prescribed.
    - Client Education
      - ‣ Educate the child and parents about what to expect during the procedure.
      - ‣ Provide emotional support.

Collaborative Care

- Nursing Care
  - o Provide emergency care at the time of injury.
    - Maintain ABCs.
    - Monitor vital signs, pain, and neurologic status.
    - Assess the neurovascular status of the injured extremity.
    - Position the child in a supine position.
    - Stabilize the injured area, avoiding unnecessary movement.
    - Elevate the affected limb and apply ice packs.
    - Administer analgesics as prescribed.
    - Keep the child warm.
  - o General nursing interventions
    - Assess pain frequently using an age-appropriate pain tool and use appropriate pain management, both pharmacological and nonpharmacological.
    - Monitor neurovascular status on a regular schedule. Report any change in status.
    - Maintain proper alignment.
    - Promote range of motion of fingers, toes, and unaffected extremities.
    - Instruct the child and family regarding activity restrictions.
- Medications
  - o Analgesics
    - Administer analgesics for pain.
    - Nursing Considerations (for use of opioid analgesia)
      - When using opioid analgesia, monitor for respiratory depression.
      - When using opioid analgesia, monitor for constipation.

- Client Education
  - Educate the child and parents about the need for adequate pain relief.
  - Educate about the need for proper nutrition and hydration.
- Interdisciplinary Care
  - Orthopedic specialists are generally consulted for fracture care in children.
  - Notify social services in situations in which abuse is suspected.
- Therapeutic Procedures
  - Casting
    - Plaster of paris casts are heavy, are not water resistant, and can take 10 to 72 hr to dry. Synthetic fiberglass casts are light, are water resistant, and dry very quickly (in 5 to 30 min).
    - Prior to casting, the skin area should be observed for integrity, cleaned, and dried. Bony prominences should be padded to prevent skin breakdown. The casting material is then applied by the provider.
    - Nursing Actions
      - Position the child on a firm mattress. Use an over-bed trapeze for older children.
      - Elevate the cast above the level of the heart during the first 24 to 48 hr to prevent swelling.
      - Apply ice for the first 24 hr to decrease swelling.
      - Turn and position the child every 2 hr so that dry air circulates around and under the cast for faster drying. This will also prevent pressure from changing the shape of the cast.
        - Do not use heat lamps or warm hair dryers.
      - Turn the child frequently while supporting all extremities and joints.
      - Instruct the child to keep the affected extremity supported (with a sling) or elevated when sitting.
      - Assess for increased warmth or hot spots on the cast surface, which could indicate infection.
      - If a wound is present, monitor the skin through the window that has been placed in an area of the cast to allow for skin inspection.
      - Monitor for drainage on the cast. Outline any drainage on the outside of the cast with a marker (and note date and time) so it can be monitored for any additional drainage.
      - Assess the general skin condition and the area around the cast edges.
      - Provide routine skin care and thorough perineal care to maintain skin integrity.

- Use moleskin over any rough area of the cast that may rub against the child's skin.

- Cover areas of the cast with plastic to avoid soiling from urine or feces.

- Assist with proper crutch fitting and reinforce proper use.

- Client Education

  - Teach the child and parents that when the cast is applied it will feel warm, but it will not burn the child.

  - Teach the parents and child to report pain that is extremely severe or is not relieved 1 hr after the administration of pain medication.

  - Teach the parents and child how to perform neurovascular checks and when to contact the provider.

  - Give instructions for the proper use of crutches for lower extremity casts.

  - Reinforce skin and perineal care with a spica cast.

  - Instruct the child not to place any foreign objects under the cast to avoid trauma to the skin.

  - Reinforce use of proper restraints when transporting the child in any vehicle.

  - Teach the child and parents about cast removal and cast cutter.

  - Instruct the child to soak the extremity in warm water and then apply lotion after the cast has been removed

- Traction care – Traction, countertraction, and friction are the three components used to align, immobilize, and reduce muscle spasms associated with certain fractures. Through the use of a forward-pulling force and a backward force, adding or removing weight controls the degree of force applied to maintain traction and alignment. The type of traction used will vary depending on the fracture, age of the child, and associated injuries.

  - Skin traction uses a pulling force that is applied by weights (may be used intermittently). Using tape and straps applied to the skin along with boots and/or cuffs, weights are attached by a rope to the extremity (Buck's traction, Russell's traction).

  - Skeletal traction uses a continuous pulling force that is applied directly to the skeletal structure and/or specific bone. A pin or rod is inserted through or into the bone. Force is applied through the use of weights attached by rope. Skeletal traction (90°/90° traction) allows the child to change positions without interfering with the pull of the traction and decreases complications associated with immobility and traction.

  - Halo traction is another type of skeletal traction that uses a halo-type bar that encircles the head. Screws are inserted into the outer table of the skull. The halo is attached to either bed traction or rods that are secured to a vest worn by the child.

View Media Supplement:
- Balanced Suspension Traction (Image)   • Halo (Image)

- Nursing Actions
  - Maintain body alignment and realign if the child seems uncomfortable or reports pain.
  - Provide pharmacological and nonpharmacological interventions for the management of pain and muscle spasms.
  - Notify the health care provider if the child experiences severe pain from muscle spasms that is unrelieved with medications and/or repositioning.
  - Assess and monitor neurovascular status
  - Routinely monitor the child's skin integrity and document findings.
  - Assess pin sites for pain, redness, swelling, drainage, or odor. Provide pin care per facility protocol.
  - Assess for changes in elimination and maintain usual patterns of elimination.
  - Assess that all the hardware is tight and that the bed is in the correct position.
  - Assess and maintain weights so that they hang freely and the ropes are free of knots. Do not lift or remove weights unless prescribed and supervised by the provider or physical therapist.
  - Assure that the wrench to release the rods is attached to the vest when using halo traction in the event that CPR is necessary.
  - Move the child in halo traction as a unit without applying pressure to the rods. This will prevent loosening of the pins and pain.
  - Consult with the provider for an over-bed trapeze to assist the child to move in bed.
  - Provide range of motion and encourage activity of non-immobilized extremities to maintain mobility and prevent contractures.
  - Promote frequent position changing within restrictions of traction.
  - Remove sheets from the head of the bed to the foot of the bed, and remake the bed in the same manner.
- Client Education
  - Educate about the need to provide adequate hydration and nutrition while in traction.
  - Educate and reinforce about the use and need for stool softeners.
  - Teach the child and parents signs of infection.
  - Teach the child to report any signs of compartment syndrome immediately.

- Surgical Interventions

  - Depending on the type of fracture, surgical intervention may be required. The most common fractures requiring surgery include supracondylar fractures and fractures of the humerus and femur.

  - Surgical reduction is achieved by either a closed (no incision) or open (with incision) reduction with or without pinning.

    - Nursing Actions

      - Monitor for signs of infection at the incision site.

      - Encourage mobilization as soon as prescribed.

      - Medicate for pain as needed.

    - Client Education

      - Teach and reinforce to the child and parents what to expect before and after the procedure, including NPO status.

      - Educate about the need for pain medication.

  - Care After Discharge

    - Teach and reinforce proper cast care, as well as pin care if indicated.

    - Teach and reinforce how to perform neurovascular checks and when to call or return to the provider.

    - Instruct the child and parents about the need for and use of antipruritic medications if prescribed by the provider.

    - Instruct the parents to maintain physical restrictions as prescribed.

    - Instruct the parents in appropriate pain management.

    - Instruct the parents to report signs and symptoms of increasing pain, redness, inflammation and/or fever to the health care provider.

    - Instruct the parents regarding the importance of follow-up care as instructed by the provider.

- Client Outcomes

  - The child will heal without complications.

  - The child will maintain normal bowel function.

  - The child will remain free of infection.

Complications

- Compartment syndrome

  - Compartment syndrome occurs when pressure within one or more of the muscle compartments of the extremity compromises circulation resulting in an ischemia-edema cycle with compromised neurovascular status.

  - Pressure can result from external sources, such as a tight cast or a constrictive, bulky dressing. Internal sources, such as an accumulation of blood or fluid within the muscle compartment, can also cause pressure.

  - If untreated, tissue necrosis can result. Neuromuscular damage occurs within 4 to 6 hr.

  - Findings

    - Increased pain that is unrelieved with elevation

    - Intense pain when passively moved

    - Paresthesia or numbness

    - Pallor

  - Nursing Actions

    - Assess the extremity at frequent intervals. Notify the provider if compartment syndrome is suspected so that the cast may be cut.

    - Prevention

      - Loosen the constrictive dressing or cut the bandage or tape.

      - Elevate the extremity and apply ice. If compartment syndrome is suspected, to ensure adequate perfusion the arm should not be elevated above the level of the heart.

    - Prepare the child for fasciotomy.

  - Client Education

    - Instruct the child to report pain that is not relieved by analgesics, pain that continues to increase in intensity, numbness or tingling, or a change in color of the extremity.

- Osteomyelitis

  - Infection within the bone secondary to a bacterial infection from an outside source, such as with an open fracture (endogenous) or from a bloodborne bacterial source (hematogenous)

  - Signs and symptoms

    - The child will appear ill.

    - The child will not want to use the affected extremity.

    - The site of infection will be tender, and bone pain will worsen with movement.

    - Warmth, erythema, edema, and fever may occur.

- o Nursing Actions
  - Assist in diagnostic procedures, such as obtaining skin, blood, and bone cultures.
  - Assist with joint or bone biopsy.
  - Administer IV and oral antibiotic therapy.
  - Assist with proper positioning to promote comfort.
  - Administer pain medication as prescribed.
  - Consult with the parents and health care provider regarding home care needs.
- o Client Education
  - Educate the child and parents about the length of treatment that may be needed.
  - Remind the child and parents to avoid bearing any weight until cleared by the provider.
  - Advise the parents to provide for diversional activities consistent with the child's level of development.
  - Educate the child about the need for proper nutrition.

CHAPTER 27: FRACTURES

 Application Exercises

Scenario: An 8-year-old child is admitted to the hospital with a fractured right femur after falling off of his skateboard. He is placed in balanced suspension traction with a pin in the distal portion of the femur. The nurse notes that the skin around the site is red with a small amount of serosanguineous drainage. The right lower leg is pale and warm, pedal pulses are present, and capillary refill is 2 seconds. His vital signs are within normal limits, he denies having numbness or tingling, and his pain is relieved with morphine sulfate.

1. Describe the proper body alignment to be used for this child.

2. Describe what the nurse should do if she is unable to detect a dorsalis pedis pulse in the child's right leg.

3. Describe how the nurse should explain the care of the pin site to the child's parent.

4. A nurse is caring for a child who has an arm cast. Which of the following is an early sign of altered neurovascular function?

   A. Increased capillary refill

   B. Pain

   C. Inability to detect a pulse distal to the cast

   D. Inability to move distal extremity

5. Match the following fractures to the accurate descriptions.

   _____ Buckle

   _____ Green stick

   _____ Plastic deformation

   _____ Spiral

   A. Only one cortex of the bone has a fracture.

   B. A twisting motion causes the fracture.

   C. The fracture site contains a bulge or raised area.

   D. The bone is bent no more than 45°.

CHAPTER 27: FRACTURES

 Application Exercises Answer Key

Scenario: An 8-year-old child is admitted to the hospital with a fractured right femur after falling off of his skateboard. He is placed in balanced suspension traction with a pin in the distal portion of the femur. The nurse notes that the skin around the site is red with a small amount of serosanguineous drainage. The right lower leg is pale and warm, pedal pulses are present, and capillary refill is 2 seconds. His vital signs are within normal limits, he denies having numbness or tingling, and his pain is relieved with morphine sulfate.

1. Describe the proper body alignment to be used for this child.

The child should be lying in a supine position, a flat pillow should be used to support his head, and his hips should be aligned with his shoulders.

 NCLEX® Connection: Basic Care and Comfort, Mobility/Immobility

2. Describe what the nurse should do if she is unable to detect a dorsalis pedis pulse in the child's right leg.

If a dorsalis pedis pulse is not detected, the nurse should feel for a posterior tibial pulse. If the posterior tibial pulse is unable to be located, she should continue moving up the child's body until a pulse is detected. The rest of the neurovascular assessment should be performed on both of the child's legs. In addition, the nurse should obtain a Doppler to assess for a pulse. Then, the nurse should contact the health care provider regarding the assessment, including pulses not detected. Physical therapy can also be contacted to assess the traction.

 NCLEX® Connection: Basic Care and Comfort, Mobility/Immobility

3. Describe how the nurse should explain the care of the pin site to the child's parent.

The nurse should explain that the area will be inspected daily. Pin care may include cleaning around the pin site with sterile water, 0.9% sodium chloride, or another ordered solution, and applying an ointment and sterile gauze around the site. The health care provider may prefer to let a scab form over the pin site and not order pin care.

 NCLEX® Connection: Reduction of Risk Potential, Complications of Diagnostic Tests/Treatments/Procedures

4. A nurse is caring for a child who has an arm cast. Which of the following is an early sign of altered neurovascular function?

    A. Increased capillary refill

    B. Pain

    C. Inability to detect a pulse distal to the cast

    D. Inability to move distal extremity

    Pain, or an increase in pain, is an early sign of neurovascular function. Numbness/tingling (paresthesias) pale skin, and slowed capillary refill are other early signs. Cool or cold extremities and an inability to move the distal extremity are all late signs of impaired neurovascular function.

 NCLEX® Connection: Basic Care and Comfort, Mobility/Immobility

5. Match the following fractures to the accurate descriptions.

    C   Buckle   A. Only one cortex of the bone has a fracture.

    A   Green stick   B. A twisting motion causes the fracture.

    D   Plastic deformation   C. The fracture site contains a bulge or raised area.

    B   Spiral   D. The bone is bent no more than 45°.

 NCLEX® Connection: Physiological Adaptation, Pathophysiology

UNIT 2	NURSING CARE OF CHILDREN WITH SYSTEM DISORDERS
Section	Musculoskeletal Disorders
Chapter 28	Musculoskeletal Congenital Disorders

Overview

- Congenital clubfoot is a complex deformity of the ankle and foot. Description of the deformity will be dependent upon the position of the ankle and foot. The most common deformity is talipes equinovarus (inward and downward position), and it may be bilateral.

  o Congenital clubfoot occurs as an isolated defect or is diagnosed in association with other disorders, including cerebral palsy and spina bifida.

- Developmental dysplasia of the hip (DDH) is a broad term that is used to describe a variety of disorders resulting in abnormal development of the hip structures.

  o DDH may be identified during prenatal or postnatal periods or early in childhood.

- Scoliosis is a complex deformity of the spine that also affects the ribs.

  o Scoliosis is characterized by a lateral curvature of the spine and spinal rotation that causes rib asymmetry.

  o Not all curvatures of the spine are scoliosis. A curve of less than 10° may be a postural variation.

  o Idiopathic or structural scoliosis is the most common form of scoliosis and can be seen in isolation or associated with other conditions.

View Media Supplement:

- Club Foot (Image)   • Developmental Dysplasia of the Hip (DDH) (Image)

Assessment

- Risk Factors

  o Clubfoot

    ▪ The etiology is not known, but it may be related to abnormal embryonic development.

    ▪ Clubfoot is classified as positional (intrauterine crowding), syndromic (associated with other deformities), or congenital (idiopathic).

    ▪ Variations of the deformity and manifestations may be present in one or both feet.

- ○ DDH may be affected by family history, gender, birth order, intrauterine position, and/or laxity of a joint.

  - Predisposing factors include intrauterine placement, mechanical situations (size of infant, multiple births, breech presentation), and genetic factors.

- ○ Idiopathic scoliosis can be congenital, idiopathic, or acquired (result of neuromuscular disorders).

  - Idiopathic scoliosis may be present at birth or occur in early childhood. Onset usually occurs during the preadolescent growth spurt.

  - Idiopathic scoliosis may have a genetic link.

- Subjective and Objective Data

  - ○ The defect may be visible or the child and/or family may report findings such as a clicking sound with diaper changes (with DDH) or clothing that does not hang correctly (with scoliosis).

  - ○ Clubfoot

DEFORMITY NAME	MANIFESTATION
Talipes equinovarus (most common)	Plantar flexion with feet bending inward
Talipes calcaneus	Dorsiflexion of feet with toes higher than heels
Talipes equinus	Plantar flexion of feet with toes lower than heels
Talipes varus	Inversion of feet (toes pointing toward midline)
Talipes valgus	Eversion of feet (toes pointing laterally)

  - ○ DDH

    - Asymmetrical gluteal and thigh folds

    - Limited abduction of hips

    - One knee that appears shorter when the infant is supine with thighs flexed at 90° towards the abdomen (Allis sign)

    - For infants from birth to 3 months of age, the provider performs the Barlow and Ortolani tests. The hips are taken through adduction (the thighs are brought towards the midline) and abduction, and an audible click or clunk is heard as the head of the femur on the affected hip can be moved from the socket (Barlow test) and then reduced back into the socket (Ortolani test) by manipulation of the joint.

    - For children able to walk, observe postural gait.

      - □ Abnormal downward tilting of pelvis on the unaffected side when bearing weight on the affected side (Trendelenburg sign)

      - □ Waddling gait or abnormal lordosis of spine if bilateral dislocation

- ○ Scoliosis
  - Asymmetry in scapula, ribs, flanks, shoulders, and hips
  - Improperly fitting clothing (one leg shorter than the other)
- ○ Diagnostic Procedures
  - Clubfoot
    - □ Prenatal ultrasound
      - ▸ Used to identify the deformity
    - □ Radiograph
      - ▸ Used to determine bone placement and tissue involvement for clubfoot
  - DDH
    - □ Ultrasound
      - ▸ An ultrasound should be performed at 2 weeks of age to determine the cartilaginous head of the femur.
    - □ X-ray
      - ▸ An x-ray can diagnose DDH in infants older than 4 months of age.
  - Scoliosis
    - □ Screen during preadolescence for boys and girls.
      - ▸ Observe the child, who should be wearing only underwear, from the back.
      - ▸ Have the child bend over at the waist with arms hanging down and observe for asymmetry of ribs and flank.
    - □ Diagnosis is made using x-rays of the child in a standing position from the neck to the groin and determining the angle of curvature using the Cobb technique with a scoliometer.
    - □ Nursing Actions
      - ▸ Assist with positioning as needed.
      - ▸ Sedate the child if prescribed.
    - □ Client Education
      - ▸ Explain and reinforce diagnostic procedures.
      - ▸ Provide emotional support.

Collaborative Care

- Nursing Care
- ○ Interventions for the child with clubfoot or DDH
  - Encourage parents to hold and cuddle the child.
  - Encourage parents to meet the developmental needs of the child.

- ■ Assess and maintain the cast or harness used to treat clubfoot or DDH.

- ■ Perform neurovascular and skin integrity checks after cast or harness placement.

- • Therapeutic Procedures

  - ○ Clubfoot – Management of clubfoot will depend upon the severity of the deformity.

    - ■ Passive exercise should be performed for a minor deformity

    - ■ Serial casting is begun after birth before the newborn is discharged home. Weekly casting to stretch the skin and other structures of the foot is done until maximum correction is accomplished.

    - ■ Surgical intervention should occur if maximum correction is not achieved by 3 months of age.

    - ■ Nursing Actions

      - □ If casted, assess neurovascular status.

    - ■ Client Education

      - □ Educate the family about how to perform gentle stretching of the foot as prescribed.

      - □ Educate the family about the importance of serial casting, cast care, and follow-up appointments.

  - ○ DDH – Pavlik harness

    - ■ A Pavlik harness can be used from birth up to 5 or 6 months of age. It is a noninvasive device for keeping hips in a continually abducted position, which allows for the femoral head to remain in contact with the acetabulum.

    - ■ The infant will wear the harness continuously for 3 to 5 months, until the hip is determined, by radiograph, to be stable. Frequent follow-up will be needed for strap adjustment.

    - ■ Nursing Actions

      - □ Perform frequent assessment of skin integrity.

      - □ Ensure proper positioning at all times.

      - □ Assess the family's ability to adjust the harness.

    - ■ Client Education

      - □ Instruct the family to keep the harness on continuously, except during bathing, if prescribed.

      - □ Instruct the family to return for follow-up visits weekly at the start of therapy and then as needed.

      - □ Teach and reinforce skin care. Encourage application of a cotton shirt and cotton socks under the harness to prevent irritation and the avoidance of powders and lotions.

- ○ DDH – Hip spica cast

  - ■ A hip spica cast can be used for infants older than 6 months of age. It can also be used in children whose hips were not stabilized by use of the Pavlik harness. A short course of traction is sometimes used prior to the application of a hip spica cast.

  - ■ Nursing Actions

    - □ Assess and maintain the hip spica cast.

    - □ Perform frequent neurovascular checks.

    - □ Perform range of motion with the unaffected extremities.

    - □ Perform frequent assessment of skin integrity, especially in the diaper area.

    - □ Assess for pain control using an age-appropriate pain tool. Intervene as indicated.

    - □ Evaluate hydration status frequently.

    - □ Assess elimination status daily.

  - ■ Client Education

    - □ Reinforce teaching regarding positioning, turning, neurovascular assessments, and care of the cast.

      - ▸ Position casts on pillows.

      - ▸ Keep the casts elevated until dry.

      - ▸ Encourage frequent position changes to allow for drying.

      - ▸ Handle the casts with the palm of the hand until dry.

    - □ Note color and temperature of toes on casted extremity.

    - □ Give sponge baths to avoid wetting the cast.

    - □ Use a waterproof barrier around the genital opening of spica cast to prevent soiling with urine or feces.

    - □ Educate regarding care after discharge with emphasis on using appropriate equipment (stroller, wagon, car seat) for maintaining mobility.

- ○ Scoliosis – Bracing and exercise

 View Media Supplement: Brace for Scoliosis (Image)

  - ■ Mild scoliosis (curvature of 10 to 20°) is treated with bracing and exercise to maintain strength and to maintain muscles of the abdomen and spine.

  - ■ Nursing Actions

    - □ Monitor for signs of skin breakdown in the child wearing a brace.

    - □ Monitor adherence to therapy.

- Client Education
  - Reinforce that the brace will not correct the curve but will help to stabilize it until growth is completed.
  - Suggest decorating the brace to encourage acceptance by adolescents.
  - Instruct the child and family about the importance of adherence. Instruct the child to wear the brace 23 out of 24 hr a day.
  - Reinforce teaching done by a physical therapist.
  - Reinforce the need to exercise along with the use of the brace.
  - Reinforce the need to assess skin for breakdown. Educate the child and/or family to have the child wear a cotton t-shirt under the brace and to avoid the use of powders and lotions.

- Surgical Interventions
  - Surgery is generally needed for curves greater than 40°. A type of internal fixation system (Harrington, Dwyer, Zielke) may be used to straighten and realign the spine along with a bony fusion to stabilize the correction.
  - Repair is performed from either an anterior and/or posterior approach. The type of instrumentation selected is based on surgeon preference and client needs.
  - The goal of repair is to achieve maximal correction and maximal mobility with minimal complications.
  - Nursing Actions
    - Preoperative
      - Inform the adolescent to obtain autologous (self-donated) blood donations and assist them.
      - Obtain routine laboratory studies, including a type and cross match for blood as prescribed.
      - Orient the adolescent and family to the ICU.
      - Inform the adolescent and/or family about what can be expected during the postoperative period, such as monitoring equipment, NG tube, chest tubes, indwelling catheters, and self-administering analgesic pumps.
    - Postoperative
      - Monitor the adolescent initially in the intensive care unit.
      - Perform standard postoperative care to prevent complications.
      - Monitor pain using an age-appropriate pain tool.
      - Administer analgesia using a patient-controlled analgesic pump as prescribed.
      - Turn the adolescent frequently by log rolling to prevent damage to the spinal fusion.
      - Assess skin for pressure areas, especially if a brace has been prescribed.

- □ Prevent rubbing and pressure from brace.

- □ Provide skin care by keeping skin clean and dry.

- □ Monitor surgical and drain sites for signs of infection. Provide wound care as prescribed.

- □ Assess bowel sounds and monitor, observing for paralytic ileus.

- □ Monitor for decreases in hemoglobin and hematocrit. Observe for signs of bleeding.

- □ Administer blood transfusion as prescribed. The adolescent may have self-donated blood available for transfusion.

- □ Encourage mobility as soon as tolerated.

- □ Perform range of motion on unaffected extremities.

- □ Provide age-appropriate activities and opportunities to visit with friends and family during the hospital stay.

- ○ Client Education

  - ■ Preoperative

    - □ Reinforce teaching (use of incentive spirometer, turning, coughing, deep breathing) to prevent complications.

    - □ Perform extensive preoperative teaching to educate the adolescent and/or family and to promote cooperation and participation in recovery.

    - □ Demonstrate the use of a patient-controlled analgesic pump if age appropriate.

    - □ Demonstrate log rolling that will be used after surgery.

    - □ Demonstrate the respiratory therapy techniques that will be used postoperatively to reduce complications of anesthesia.

    - □ Discuss medical terms that are unfamiliar to the adolescent and/or family.

  - ■ Postoperative

    - □ Emphasize the importance of physical therapy and proper positioning of the spine.

    - □ Encourage independence following surgery for the adolescent who has a brace.

    - □ Encourage the adolescent to contact friends when able.

    - □ Emphasize the necessity of follow-up care.

- • Care After Discharge

  - ○ Client Education

    - ■ Reinforce the expected course of treatment and recovery.

    - ■ Suggest that the family arrange the environment to facilitate the adolescent's ability to be as independent as possible (keep favorite items within reach).

    - ■ Emphasize the necessity of follow-up care.

- Client Outcomes

  o The child will maintain a functional foot with minimal complications with clubfoot.

  o The child will remain free from complications of immobility.

  o The child will increase and maintain optimal mobilization.

Complications

- Complications for clubfoot, DDH, and scoliosis will be related to:

  o Postoperative complications (atelectasis, ileus, wound infection)

  o Effects of immobilization (decreased muscle strength, bone demineralization, decreased metabolic rate, altered bowel motility).

  o Effects of casting or bracing (skin breakdown, neurovascular alterations).

- Infection

  o Infection may be caused by bacteria, such as *Staphylococcus aureus*.

  o Nursing Actions

    ▪ Monitor vital signs. Observe changes in temperature that could be associated with complications of infection.

    ▪ Keep the cast dry and intact.

    ▪ Monitor for changes in neurovascular status (numbness; tingling; decreased mobility, sensation, or capillary refill).

    ▪ Reposition the child frequently.

    ▪ Maintain a high-fiber diet and promote adequate hydration.

    ▪ Monitor bowel and bladder elimination. Report any changes, especially the decrease or absence of bowel sounds or distention.

    ▪ Report any foul odor from cast or urine.

    ▪ Observe changes in behavior, especially increasing irritability in infants.

  o Client Education

    ▪ Reinforce expected complications of specific treatment or procedure with the child and/or family.

    ▪ Reinforce the need to notify the provider with any concerns or signs of complications.

    ▪ Educate the child and/or family about follow-up.

CHAPTER 28: MUSCULOSKELETAL CONGENITAL DISORDERS

 Application Exercises

1. A nurse is caring for a preschooler who walks but has difficulty keeping up with peers. The nurse is assessing the preschooler for possible right developmental dysplasia of the hip (DDH). Which of the following assessments should the nurse use to assess for DDH?

    A. Barlow test

    B. Trendelenburg sign

    C. Manipulation of right foot and ankle

    D. Ortolani test

2. A nurse is caring for a toddler who is diagnosed with hip dysplasia and has been placed in a hip spica cast. The child's mother asks the nurse why a Pavlik harness is not being used. Which of the following responses by the nurse appropriately addresses the mother's question?

    A. "The Pavlik harness is used for children with scoliosis, not hip dysplasia."

    B. "The Pavlik harness is used for school-age children."

    C. "The Pavlik harness cannot be used for your child because her condition is too severe."

    D. "The Pavlik harness is used for infants less than 6 months of age."

3. A nurse is completing preoperative teaching with an adolescent client who is going to receive spinal instrumentation for scoliosis. Which of the following information should the nurse include in the teaching?

    A. "You will go home the same day of surgery."

    B. "You will have minimal pain."

    C. "You will need to receive blood."

    D. "You will not be able to eat until the day after surgery."

CHAPTER 28: MUSCULOSKELETAL CONGENITAL DISORDERS

 Application Exercises Answer Key

1. A nurse is caring for a preschooler who walks but has difficulty keeping up with peers. The nurse is assessing the preschooler for possible right developmental dysplasia of the hip (DDH). Which of the following assessments should the nurse use to assess for DDH?

   A. Barlow test

   B. Trendelenburg sign

   C. Manipulation of right foot and ankle

   D. Ortolani test

   > The Trendelenburg sign should be used to assess for possible hip dysplasia in a preschooler who is walking. In Trendelenburg sign, the preschooler bears weight on the affected leg while holding on to something for balance. The examiner observes from behind for abnormal downward tilting of the pelvis on the unaffected side. The Barlow and Ortolani tests for DDH are most useful for infants 2 to 3 months of age. It involves manipulating the hips to feel for instability. Manipulation of the foot and ankle is an assessment for clubfoot.

 NCLEX® Connection: Reduction of Risk Potential, System Specific Assessment

2. A nurse is caring for a toddler who is diagnosed with hip dysplasia and has been placed in a hip spica cast. The child's mother asks the nurse why a Pavlik harness is not being used. Which of the following responses by the nurse appropriately addresses the mother's question?

   A. "The Pavlik harness is used for children with scoliosis, not hip dysplasia."

   B. "The Pavlik harness is used for school-age children."

   C. "The Pavlik harness cannot be used for your child because her condition is too severe."

   D. "The Pavlik harness is used for infants less than 6 months of age."

   > The Pavlik harness is only used for infants less than 6 months of age.

 NCLEX® Connection: Reduction of Risk Potential, Therapeutic Procedures

3. A nurse is completing preoperative teaching with an adolescent client who is going to receive spinal instrumentation for scoliosis. Which of the following information should the nurse include in the teaching?

    A. "You will go home the same day of surgery."

    B. "You will have minimal pain."

    C. "You will need to receive blood."

    D. "You will not be able to eat until the day after surgery."

The adolescent will need to receive blood as indicated for this procedure. None of the other statements are correct. The adolescent will need to stay in the hospital overnight after the surgery, and the surgery involves pain that is commonly controlled using a PCA pump. The client will start with a clear liquid diet that will be advanced as tolerated. If able to tolerate food, there is no reason the adolescent must be NPO.

Ⓝ **NCLEX® Connection: Reduction of Risk Potential, Complications From Surgical Procedures and Health Alterations**

UNIT 2	NURSING CARE OF CHILDREN WITH SYSTEM DISORDERS
Section	Musculoskeletal Disorders

Chapter 29	Chronic Neuromusculoskeletal Disorders

Overview

- Chronic neuromusculoskeletal disorders affect the brain, muscles, joints, and skeletal structures of the body.

- Cerebral palsy (CP) is a nonprogressive impairment of motor function, especially that of muscle control, coordination, and posture.

- Spina bifida refers to defects in intrauterine closure of the boney spine. Spina bifida is further classified as spina bifida occulta and spina bifida cystica (meningocele or myelomeningocele, which are visible defects in the spine with a saclike protrusion at any level of the spinal column at the midline of the back).

  ○ In meningocele, the sac contains meninges and spinal fluid. Myelomeningocele contains meninges, spinal fluid, and nerves

- Down syndrome is a chromosomal abnormality.

- Juvenile idiopathic arthritis (JIA) is a group of chronic autoimmune inflammatory diseases affecting joints and other tissues. There is chronic inflammation of the synovium of the joints with effusion that leads to wearing down and damage to the articular cartilage.

- Muscular dystrophy (MD) is a group of inherited disorders with progressive degeneration of symmetric skeletal muscle groups.

CEREBRAL PALSY (CP)

Overview

- CP is the most common permanent physical disability in children.

- CP may cause abnormal perception and sensation; visual, hearing, and speech impairments; seizures; and cognitive disabilities.

- CP manifests differently in each child. Developmental outcomes vary and are dependent on the severity of the injury. Many children with CP are able to perform most, if not all, developmental tasks, and more than half will be able to work outside the home as adults. Others will require complete care for their entire lives.

Assessment

- Risk Factors

    o The exact cause of CP is not known. Prenatal, perinatal, and postnatal risk factors known to be associated with CP include:

        ▪ Existing brain anomalies, cerebral infections, head trauma (shaken baby syndrome), and /or anoxia to the brain

        ▪ Premature birth

        ▪ Multiple births

        ▪ Extremely low or very low birth weights in newborns

        ▪ Inability of the placenta to provide the developing fetus with oxygen and nutrients

        ▪ Interruption of oxygen delivery to the fetus during birth

        ▪ Kernicterus as a result of high levels of bilirubin in the neonatal period

- Subjective Data

    o Parents may describe concerns with development.

    o Developmental early warning signs about which parents may be concerned

        ▪ Poor head control or absence of smiling in a 3-month-old infant

        ▪ Difficulty with dressing and diaper changes due to stiff arms or legs during infancy and early childhood. The child may push away or arch his back.

        ▪ A floppy or limp body in infants.

        ▪ An inability to sit up without support in an 8-month-old infant

        ▪ Use of only one side of the body to play or move about

        ▪ Feeding difficulties (moving food from side to side with tongue, inability to swallow safely).

    o Painful muscle spasms

- Objective Data

    o Physical Assessment Findings

        ▪ Persistent primitive reflexes (Moro or tonic neck)

        ▪ Motor function showing muscle tightness or spasticity, involuntary movements, and disturbance in gait or mobility

- Assessment findings associated with specific types of CP
  - Spastic
    - Spastic CP is characterized by hypertonicity (muscle tightness or spasticity); increased deep tendon reflexes; clonus; and poor control of motion, balance, and posture.
    - Spastic CP may cause Impairments of fine and gross motor skills.
    - Spastic CP may present in all extremities (quadriplegia), similar parts of the body (diplegia), three limbs (triplegia), one limb (monoplegia), or one side of the body (hemiplegia). It often causes affected limbs to be shorter and thinner.
    - Associated scoliosis may be present.
    - Gait may appear crouched with a scissoring motion of the legs with intoeing and use of primarily the balls of the feet in a tip-toe fashion.
    - Spastic CP may present with contractures, especially the heel cord, hips, or knees. Wrists and elbow are in a flexed position with clenching of the hand.
    - Flexor, adductor, and internal rotator muscles are more affected than the extensor and external adductor or rotator muscles.
  - Dyskinetic
    - Movements increase with stress but are absent with sleep. Normal deep tendon reflexes are present with absence of clonus.
    - Speech may be impaired.
  - Athetoid
    - Findings include involuntary jerking movements that appear slow, writhing, and wormlike. These movements involve the trunk, neck, face, and tongue.
  - Dystonic
    - Slow, twisting movements occur that affect the trunk and extremities.
  - Ataxic
    - Evidence of wide-based gait and difficulty with coordination
    - Poor ability to do repetitive movements is a result
    - Difficulty with quick or precise movements (writing or buttoning a shirt)
    - Jerky speech pattern is present

- ○ Diagnostic Procedures

  - ■ Complete neurological assessment

  - ■ MRI

    - □ Used to evaluate structures or abnormal areas located near bone (Sedation may be necessary.)

    - □ Nursing Actions

      - ▸ Tell the child to remain still during the procedure.

      - ▸ Sedate the child if prescribed.

    - □ Client Education

      - ▸ Provide emotional support.

Collaborative Care

- Nursing Care

  - ○ Monitor developmental milestones.

  - ○ Evaluate the need for hearing and speech evaluations.

  - ○ Promote independence with self-care activities as much as possible. Assist the child to maintain a positive self-image and a high level of self-esteem.

  - ○ Determine the extent of family coping and support.

  - ○ Assess the family's awareness of available resources.

  - ○ Assess the child's developmental level and approach the child in a way that is appropriate for the child's developmental level, rather than chronological age.

  - ○ Communicate with the child directly, but include parents as needed.

  - ○ Help the child to use augmented communication, such as electronic devices for speech and other types of communication tools.

  - ○ Include the family in physical care of the hospitalized child with cerebral palsy.

    - ■ Ask the family about routine care and encourage them to provide it if appropriate.

    - ■ Encourage the family to help verify the child's needs if communication is impaired.

  - ○ Maintain an open airway by elevating the head of the child's bed (this is especially important if the child has increased oral secretions).

  - ○ Ensure suction equipment is available if required. Suction oral secretions as needed.

  - ○ Monitor for pain (especially with muscle spasms) using a developmentally appropriate pain tool.

- ○ Administer medication for pain and/or spasms as prescribed.
- ○ Ensure adequate nutrition.
  - ■ Assess for the possibility of aspiration for children who are severely disabled.
  - ■ Determine the child's ability to take oral nutrition.
  - ■ Ascertain the correct positioning for feeding the child. Use head positioning and manual jaw control methods as needed.
  - ■ Provide foods that are similar to foods eaten at home when possible. Administer supplements as prescribed.
  - ■ Administer feedings by gastric tube as prescribed.
  - ■ Maintain weight/height chart.
- ○ Provide skin care.
  - ■ Assess skin under splints and braces if applicable.
  - ■ Maintain skin integrity by turning the child to keep pressure off bony prominences.
  - ■ Keep skin clean and dry.
- ○ Provide rest periods as needed.
- ● Medications
  - ○ Baclofen (Lioresal)
    - ■ Used as a centrally acting skeletal muscle relaxant that decreases muscle spasm and severe spasticity
    - ■ Nursing Considerations
      - □ Administer orally or intrathecally via a specialized, surgically implanted pump.
      - □ Monitor effectiveness of the medication.
      - □ Monitor for muscle weakness, increased fatigue, or less-common side effects (diaphoresis, constipation).
    - ■ Client Education
      - □ Educate the family about expected responses of medications.
      - □ Reinforce with the family the side effects of medications, such as drowsiness, and when to call the provider.
      - □ Instruct the family to bring the child to see the provider every 4 to 6 weeks to monitor effectiveness of therapy and to receive refills.
  - ○ Diazepam (Valium)
    - ■ Skeletal muscle relaxant used to decrease muscle spasms and severe spasticity
    - ■ Nursing Considerations
      - □ Use in older children and adolescents.
      - □ Monitor for drowsiness and fatigue.

- Client Education
  - Educate the family about expected responses to medications.
  - Reinforce with the family the side effects of the medication and when to call the provider.

- Interdisciplinary Care

  - Coordinate care with other professionals, such as speech therapists, physical and recreational therapists, education specialists, and/or medical specialists.

  - Initiate referral for technical aids that can assist with coordination, speaking, mobility, and an increased level of independence, such as that which may be achieved with the use of a voice activated wheelchair.

  - Surgical intervention may be needed for tendon release to correct contractures or other spastic deformities.

- Care After Discharge

  - Client Education

    - Reinforce the therapeutic plan of care.

    - Reinforce the need for rest periods.

    - Reinforce feeding schedule and feeding techniques if changes were made during hospitalization.

    - Reinforce adherence to medication regimen.

    - Encourage regular dental care.

    - Encourage parents to provide developmental stimulation.

    - Teach wound care if needed.

    - Help the family identify resources needed (respite care).

    - Suggest participation in a support group for CP.

- Client Outcomes

  - The child will develop and maintain optimal functioning.

  - The child will maintain adequate nutrition and growth.

Complications

- Aspiration of oral secretions

  - Nursing Actions

    - Keep the child's head elevated.

    - Keep suction available if copious oral secretions are present or the child has difficulty with swallowing foods and/or fluids.

- Client Education
  - Educate the family about feeding techniques to decrease the risk of aspiration.
  - Encourage the family to take CPR classes.
- Potential for injury
  - Nursing Actions
    - Make sure the child's bed rails are raised to prevent falls from the bed.
    - Pad side rails and wheelchair arms to prevent injury.
    - Secure the child in mobility devices, such as wheelchairs.
    - Encourage the child to receive adequate rest to prevent injury at times of fatigue.
    - Encourage the use of helmets, seat belts, and other safety equipment.
  - Client Education
    - Educate the child and family about safety precautions.

SPINA BIFIDA

Overview

- Neural tube defects (NTDs) are present at birth and affect the CNS and osseous spine.
- The degree of neurologic dysfunction is determined by the level of sac protrusion and tissue involvement.
  - Spina bifida occulta – A defect in the bony spine that is invisible to the eye and has no manifestations or problems
  - Spina bifida cystica
    - Meningocele – A spinal defect and sac-like protrusion are present, but only spinal fluid and meninges are present in the sac. After the sac is repaired, no further symptoms are usually seen because spinal nerves are not damaged.
    - Myelomeningocele – The sac includes meninges, spinal fluid, and nerves.
      - Impairments will present depending on the level of spinal injury, from complete paralysis to a slightly decreased sensation in the lower extremities. Other findings may include joint deformities, bowel and bladder incontinence, developmental delays, hydrocephalus, and a high risk for latex allergy.

View Media Supplement: Spina Bifida (Image)

Assessment

- Risk Factors

  - Neural tube defects are caused by the failure of the neural tube to close in the first 3 to 5 weeks of gestation.

  - Neural tube defects have been linked to insufficient folic acid in the maternal diet.

  - An elevated alpha-fetoprotein (AFP) may indicate the presence of a neural tube defect.

- Subjective Data

  - Assess prenatal history, especially exposure to and intake of folic acid.

  - Assess family history for neural tube defects.

- Objective Data

  - Physical Assessment Findings

    - Inspect the sac at birth to determine whether it is intact.

    - Inspect the lumbosacral area for dimpling. This may indicate spina bifida occulta.

    - Ongoing assessments

      - Assess for an increase in head circumference, which may occur rapidly with hydrocephalus until normal cranial growth is reached.

      - Assess skin integrity for pressure sores caused by decreased sensation in the affected trunk and extremities.

      - Identify allergies. Specifically assess for latex allergy.

      - Assess cognitive development. This may be permanently delayed in some children.

      - Assess bladder/bowel functioning. Functioning is permanently affected in all children with spina bifida.

      - Monitor for manifestations of infection, including elevation of body temperature, nausea, vomiting, and fatigue.

  - Laboratory Tests

    - Laboratory studies may be used to determine causative pathogens for meningitis or UTI.

  - Diagnostic Procedures

    - Maternal serum analysis

      - Maternal serum should be tested for serum alpha-fetoprotein levels between 15 and 20 weeks of gestation (it is best to test between 16 and 18 weeks). Elevated levels will require further testing, such as an amniocentesis.

- Amniocentesis
  - □ An amniocentesis should be performed to test amniotic fluid for levels of alpha-fetoprotein. Elevated levels may indicate neural tube defects.
- MRI, ultrasound, CT, and myelography
  - □ These tests may be used to determine brain and spinal cord involvement.
- Radioallergosorbent test (RAST)
  - □ A RAST detects the presence of latex allergy.

Collaborative Care

- Nursing Care
  - ○ Assess for infant-parent attachment.
  - ○ Provide care of the sac.
    - Assess the integrity of the sac at least every 2 hr.
    - Avoid activities that may damage or break the sac.
    - Apply moist, nonadhering dressing to cover the sac.
  - ○ Place the child in the prone position until the sac is repaired.
    - Promote skin integrity.
    - Keep skin clean and dry.
    - Keep pressure off bony prominences.
    - Reposition the child hourly.
    - Assess skin under splints or braces.
  - ○ Provide range of motion to legs. This may be passive or active, depending on the disability.
  - ○ Position the extremities to maintain alignment and prevent contractures or deformities, especially in children who have paralysis.
  - ○ Use an appropriate pain assessment tool.
  - ○ Assess for self-esteem and body image disturbances, which arise due to bowel and bladder incontinence, use of mobility aids, inability to keep up with peers, and other physical and social problems.
  - ○ Assess the family's knowledge of available resources.
  - ○ Assess the family's coping and support.
  - ○ Monitor head circumference for signs of increasing intracranial pressure or shunt failure.
  - ○ Monitor for elevations in body temperature and other signs and symptoms of infection.

- o Use nonlatex gloves, catheters, and other equipment to decrease the risk of latex allergy.

- o Work with the child and parents on bladder control measures.

  - ■ Teach clean, intermittent self-catheterization (CIC) to the parents and to the child if the child is developmentally capable of performing the skills.

  - ■ Work with the family on other strategies for acceptable bladder care (incontinence supplies, condom catheters).

  - ■ Note color, clarity, odor, and amount of urine. Monitor for UTIs. Administer antibiotics as prescribed.

- o Monitor bowel function for constipation and incontinence.

  - ■ Avoid taking temperatures rectally to prevent irritation of rectal sphincter.

  - ■ Administer laxatives or enemas as ordered to assist bowel function.

- o Teach principles of nutrition and work with the family to prevent obesity.

- Medications

  - o Oxybutynin chloride (Ditropan) and tolterodine (Detrol)

    - ■ These are antispasmodics that are used to improve bladder capacity and continence.

    - ■ Client Education

      - □ Educate the family about the need for proper and timely administration of medications.

      - □ Educate the family about the need for periodic monitoring of medication levels.

- Interdisciplinary Care

  - o Occupational therapy, physical therapy, and social services may all be involved in the care of a child who has spina bifida.

- Therapeutic Procedures

  - o The insertion of feeding tubes may be necessary.

    - ■ Nursing Actions

      - □ Prepare the child and parents for the procedure.

    - ■ Client Education

      - □ Explain the procedure and anticipated postoperative care.

- Surgical Interventions
  - Closure of a myelomeningocele sac is done as soon as possible to prevent complications of injury and infection.
    - Nursing Actions
      - Preoperative
        - Reinforce the information that was provided by the health care provider.
        - Cover the exposed sac with a sterile, moist (with 0.9% sodium chloride), nonadherent dressing until surgery.
        - Place the newborn in a prone position until surgery to protect the sac.
    - Client Education
      - Teach the parents about what to expect postoperatively.
      - Teach the parents proper positioning techniques.
      - Teach the parents to avoid touching the sac.
  - Surgical shunt
    - Will be inserted if hydrocephalus develops
    - Nursing Actions
      - Postoperatively
        - Measure the head circumference and abdominal girth of infants.
        - Observe for signs of increased intracranial pressure (high-pitched cry, bulging fontanels, vomiting, irritability).
        - Avoid positioning the child on the shunt site.
    - Client Education
      - Teach the family the signs and symptoms of shunt malfunction.
      - Reinforce the need to seek care with any sign of shunt malfunction.
  - Bladder surgery
    - May be performed to manage bladder dysfunction (either spasms or flaccidity)
    - Nursing Actions
      - Monitor for signs of bladder dysfunction.
      - Monitor for signs of bladder infection.
      - Monitor for bleeding.
      - Teach the child and family care of stoma (vesicostomy) if applicable.

- ○ Orthopedic surgeries
  - Corrections of associated potential problems, such as clubfoot, scoliosis, and other malformations of the feet and legs
  - Nursing Actions
    - □ Monitor for signs of infection.
    - □ Administer pain medications.
    - □ Provide cast care if cast is present.
    - □ Monitor for neurosensory deficits.
  - Client Education
    - □ Educate the family about signs and symptoms of infection.
    - □ Educate the family about cast and splint care if indicated.
- Client Outcomes
  - ○ The child will reach and maintain optimal levels of functioning.
  - ○ The child will be free from injury.

Complications

- Skin ulceration
  - ○ Caused by prolonged pressure in one area
  - ○ Nursing Actions
    - Monitor skin for breakdown.
    - Reposition frequently to prevent pressure on bony prominences.
    - Monitor skin under splints and braces.
  - ○ Client Education
    - Teach the child and parents to monitor skin integrity.
- Latex allergy
  - ○ The child has a high risk of allergy to latex. Allergy responses range from urticaria to wheezing, which may progress to anaphylaxis. There may also be an allergy to certain foods (bananas, avocados, kiwi, chestnuts).
  - ○ Nursing Actions
    - Test for allergy.
    - Reduce exposure.
  - ○ Client Education
    - Educate the parents to avoid exposing the child to latex.
    - Provide the family with a list of household items that may contain latex (disposable diapers, cleaning or kitchen gloves, elastic found in clothing)

- Educate the family about how to identify signs and symptoms of allergic reaction and report them to the provider.

- Provide instruction in the use of epinephrine (EpiPen).

- Increased intracranial pressure

    ○ Signs and symptoms

        - Infants – High-pitched cry, lethargy, vomiting, bulging fontanels, and/or widening cranial suture lines

        - Children – Headache, lethargy, nausea, vomiting, double vision, decreased school performance of learned tasks, decreased level of consciousness, and seizures

    ○ Caused by shunt malfunction

    ○ Nursing Actions

        - Use gentle movements when performing range-of-motion exercises.

        - Minimize environmental stressors (noise, frequent visitors).

        - Assess and manage pain.

    ○ Client Education

        - Teach the signs and symptoms of shunt malfunction and teach the child and family to report any signs and symptoms to the health care provider immediately.

DOWN SYNDROME

Overview

- Clinical manifestations of Down syndrome

    ○ Hypotonicity, congenital heart defects, thyroid dysfunction, congenital hypothyroidism, dysfunctional immune system, and high risk for leukemia

    ○ The presence of cognitive defects with an IQ that will vary in range with an average of 50

Assessment

- Risk Factors

    ○ The exact etiology of Down syndrome is probably multifactorial. There is a higher incidence in infants born to mothers who are older than 35 years of age.

- Objective Data

    ○ Physical Assessment Findings

        - Small head

        - Flattened forehead

        - Low-set ears

- Upward slant to eyes

- Protruding tongue and narrow, high-arched palate

- Underdeveloped nasal bone (results in a flattened appearance to the nasal bridge)

- Hypotonia (decreased muscle tone)

- Transverse palmar crease

- Plantar space and wide space between the great toe and second toe

- Congenital heart defects (may be present)

  o Diagnostic Procedures

- Prenatal testing for alpha-fetoprotein in maternal serum – Low in the presence of Down syndrome

- Chromosome analysis

  □ Prenatal testing, such as an amniocentesis, should be conducted for chromosome analysis to confirm the genetic abnormality.

  □ Nursing Actions

  ▸ Assist in the positioning of the child.

  ▸ Provide support to the parents and child.

  □ Client Education

  ▸ Teach the child what to expect with the procedure.

Collaborative Care

- Nursing Care

  o Swaddle infants to maintain warmth and security.

  o Support the parents and child at the time of diagnosis.

  o Reinforce physical care of the child.

- Feeding

- Management of secretions and prevention of upper respiratory infections

- Skin care

- Positioning

  o Emphasize the child's strengths while being aware of limitations to ensure safety.

- Interdisciplinary Care

  o Refer the family and child to early intervention. The child should receive speech, physical, and occupational therapy.

  o Identify and refer the child and parents to a support group.

- Surgical Interventions

  ○ Interventions for surgical repair will depend on the associated congenital anomalies. These may include cardiac defects or strabismus.

    ■ Nursing Actions

      □ Listen to concerns of the parents and discuss ethical dilemmas regarding treatment for physical defects.

      □ Provide standard postoperative care with emphasis on wound care, respiratory care, and pain management.

    ■ Client Education

      □ Teach postoperative and home care management.

      □ Reinforce the therapeutic plan of care.

- Care After Discharge

  ○ Client Education

    ■ Reinforce with the parents that the child needs holding and cuddling but may not be able to cling or hold the parent due to associated hypotonia, not a lack of attachment.

    ■ Teach parents how to position the child to prevent injury or complications due to hypotonicity and laxity of joints.

    ■ Encourage parents to change infants' positions frequently to help promote aeration of the lungs and prevent pooling of secretions.

    ■ Reinforce the follow-up of associated physical conditions.

      □ Hearing and vision

      □ Thyroid function

      □ Ear, nose, and throat (highly prone to otitis)

    ■ When it is age appropriate, a radiological exam should be used to rule out atlantoaxial instability before the child is allowed to participate in certain sports.

    ■ Teach the parents the importance of providing food and fluids to maintain adequate nutrition and prevent issues with constipation.

    ■ Emphasize the need to provide a well-balanced diet for adequate nutrition. Poor eating habits may result in obesity later in life.

    ■ Reinforce feeding techniques with parents.

    ■ Plot the child's height and weight on Down syndrome growth charts.

    ■ Reinforce care of the skin. Use mild soaps to prevent drying and apply moisturizing creams daily or as needed (highly prone to dry and cracking of skin and lips).

- Teach the parents how to prevent physical complications.
  - Avoid infection by engaging in good hand hygiene.
  - Increase fiber in diet to avoid constipation.
  - Encourage physical activity.
  - Follow-up
    - Advise parents to seek regular checkups for the child.

Complications

- Respiratory infections

  - Respiratory infections are common due to decreased muscle tone and poor drainage of mucus because of hypotonicity and associated under-developed nasal bone.

  - Nursing Actions

    - Rinse the child's mouth with water after feeding and at other times of the day when it is dry. Mucous membranes are dry due to constant mouth breathing, which also increases the risk for respiratory infection.

    - Provide cool mist humidification and clearing of the nasal passages with a bulb syringe as needed.

    - Encourage exercise in older children.

  - Client Education

    - Teach the parents and child good hand hygiene. Encourage frequent repositioning of the child to promote respiratory function.

    - Teach parents to perform postural drainage and percussion if needed.

    - Reinforce the need for routine immunizations.

    - Teach parents to seek health care at the earliest sign of infection.

    - Reinforce the need to follow the antibiotic schedule if prescribed.

JUVENILE IDIOPATHIC ARTHRITIS (JIA)

Overview

- Classifications of JIA include systemic arthritis, oligoarthritis, and polyarthritis with or without rheumatoid factor.

- No definitive diagnosis is available, but the onset of the disorder starts prior to 16 years of age, and symptoms occur in one or more joints and last for 6 weeks or longer with no other cause identified.

- Peak incidence is between 1 and 3 years of age.

- JIA is rarely life-threatening, and it may subside over time, but it can result in residual joint deformities and altered joint function.

Assessment

- Risk Factors

    o Susceptible individuals who have an autoimmune response to internal or external triggers

- Subjective and Objective Data

    o Joint swelling, stiffness, redness, and warmth

    o Mobility limitations

    o Fever

    o Rash

    o Nodules under the skin

    o Delayed growth and development

    o Enlarged lymph nodes

    o Visual changes and uveitis (inflammation in the anterior chamber of the eye)

    o Laboratory Tests

        ▪ Erythrocyte sedimentation rate (ESR) – May or may not be elevated

        ▪ CBC with differential may demonstrate elevated WBCs, especially during exacerbations.

        ▪ Antinuclear antibodies (ANA) indicate an increased risk for uveitis.

        ▪ Rheumatoid factor may or may not be present.

    o Diagnostic Procedures

        ▪ Radiographic studies

            □ Radiographic studies may be used for baseline comparison. X-rays may demonstrate increased synovial fluid in the joint, which causes soft tissue swelling or widening of the joint. Later findings may include osteoporosis and narrowed joint spaces.

            □ Nursing Actions

                ‣ Assist with positioning.

                ‣ Ensure that adolescent females are not pregnant.

Collaborative Care

- Nursing Care

    o Care of the child who has JIA is primarily outpatient.

    o Include the family in the child's care so they are prepared for home care.

    o Regularly evaluate the child's pain and response to prescribed analgesics.

- o Encourage the child to participate in a physical therapy program to increase mobility and prevent deformities.

- o Encourage activity as tolerated.

- o Teach parents to apply splints for nighttime sleep. Splints should be applied to knees, wrists, and hands to decrease pain and prevent flexion deformities.

- o Encourage proper positioning with sleep. Encourage the use of electric blankets or sleeping bags for extra warmth.

- o Provide firm mattress and discourage use of pillows under knees. Use no pillow or flat pillow for head.

- o Encourage full range-of-motion exercises when pain and inflammation have subsided.

- o Apply heat or warm moist packs to the child's affected joints prior to exercise.

- o Encourage warm baths.

- o Identify alternate ways for the child to meet developmental needs, especially during periods of exacerbation.

- o Encourage self-care by allowing adequate time for completion.

- o Encourage a well-balanced diet that is high in fiber and contains adequate fluids to prevent constipation from immobility.

- o Encourage participation in school and contact with peers.

- o Collaborate with the school nurse and teachers to arrange for care during the school day (medication administration, rest periods, extra time to get to classes, extra sets of books, split days).

- Medications

  - o NSAIDs – Naproxen (Naprelan), ibuprofen (Motrin), and tolmetin sodium (Tolectin)

    - ■ NSAIDs control pain and inflammation.

    - ■ Nursing Considerations

      - □ Instruct the child and family to administer NSAIDs as prescribed.

      - □ Instruct the child and family that NSAIDs should be taken with food to minimize gastric irritation.

    - ■ Client Education

      - □ Teach the child and family to report changes in stool and GI discomfort or increase in bruising immediately.

  - o Methotrexate (Rheumatrex)

    - ■ A cytotoxic disease modifying antirheumatic drug (DMARD) that slows joint degeneration and progression of rheumatoid arthritis when NSAIDs do not work alone

    - ■ Nursing Considerations

      - □ Monitor liver function tests and CBC regularly.

- ■ Client Education
  - □ Teach adolescents to avoid alcohol.
  - □ Discuss the use of effective birth control to avoid birth defects while taking this medication.
- ○ Corticosteroids
  - ■ Glucocorticoids provide symptomatic relief of inflammation and pain. They are reserved for life-threatening complications, severe arthritis, and uveitis.
  - ■ Nursing Considerations
    - □ Administer as eye solution, orally, or intravenously.
    - □ Administer at the lowest effective dose for short-term therapy and then discontinue by tapering the dose. An injection into the intraarticular space may provide effective pain relief.
  - ■ Client Education
    - □ Advise the child and family that weight gain, especially in the face, is a common side effect.
    - □ Monitor height and weight.
    - □ Advise the family that an alteration in growth is a possible long-term complication of corticosteroids.
    - □ Advise the child to avoid exposure to potentially infectious agents.
    - □ Advise the child and family to practice healthy eating habits.
- ○ Etanercept (Enbrel)
  - ■ Etanercept is a tumor necrosis factor alpha-receptor blocker, another DMARD, that is used when methotrexate is not effective for immunosuppressive action.
  - ■ Nursing Considerations
    - □ Administer etanercept once or twice each week by subcutaneous injection.
  - ■ Client Education
    - □ Educate about the potential for allergic reactions.
    - □ Teach the child and family to avoid exposure to infectious agents.
- • Interdisciplinary Care
  - ○ Occupational therapy, and physical therapy may be consulted when caring for the child who has JIA.
- • Care After Discharge
  - ○ Client Education
    - ■ Assist parents in obtaining accommodations in school.
    - ■ Reinforce exercises prescribed by physical and occupational therapy. These may include exercise in a warm water pool.

- Caution parents against using aspirin during viral illnesses due to the risk of Reye syndrome.

- Teach the child and parents nonpharmacological pain management techniques (e.g., distraction, relaxation).

- Encourage regular eye exams.

- Client Outcomes

    ○ The child will remain free from deformities and impaired joint mobility.

    ○ The child will reach and maintain optimal levels of functioning.

Complications

- Joint deformity and functional disability

    ○ Nursing Actions

        - Reinforce the individualized therapeutic plan of care.

        - Advocate for the child when treatments are not producing expected results.

    ○ Client Education

        - Encourage the child and family to adhere to the treatment regimen.

        - Encourage self-care and active participation in an exercise program.

MUSCULAR DYSTROPHY (MD)

Overview

- Muscular dystrophy (MD) is the largest group of diseases that affects muscle function in children.

- Loss of muscular strength is insidious.

- Developmental milestones are likely to be met until the onset of the disease.

- Onset of disease, pace of progression, and muscle group affected depend on the type of MD.

- Duchenne (pseudohypertrophic) muscular dystrophy (DMD) is the most common form of MD. Inherited as an X-linked recessive trait, DMD has an onset between 3 and 7 years of age. Life expectancy with current technology for DMD reaches into early adulthood.

- Management of DMD is symptomatic to assist with maintaining the highest level of mobility and preventing complications as the disease progresses.

Assessment

- Risk Factors

    ○ DMD – Family history of MD

- Subjective Data

    o Family reports of delay in walking; changes in gait; and difficulties with running, climbing stairs, and riding a bike.

- Objective Data

    o Physical Assessment Findings

        ▪ Muscular weakness in lower extremities

        ▪ Muscular hypertrophy, especially in calves

        ▪ Mild delay in motor skill development

        ▪ Mobility with general muscle strength declining over time

        ▪ Unsteady, wide-based or waddling gait and loss of walking ability (usually by age 12)

        ▪ Difficulty riding a tricycle, running, and rising from a seated position

        ▪ Mild cognitive delay with learning disabilities

        ▪ Cardiovascular complications (associated with the progression of DMD) – Weight loss, increased fatigue during usual ADLs, and orthopnea

    o Laboratory Tests

        ▪ DNA analysis using peripheral blood, serum polymerase chain reaction (PCR) for the dystrophin gene mutation, or muscle tissue biopsy

        ▪ Serum creatine kinase (CK) – Elevated

        ▪ Electromyography (EMG) may also be used

Collaborative Care

- Nursing Care

    o Assess and monitor

        ▪ The child's ability to perform ADLs

        ▪ The child's respiratory function, including depth, rhythm, and rate of respirations during sleep and daytime hours

        ▪ The child's cardiac function

        ▪ The child and parent's understanding of long-term effects

        ▪ The child and parent's coping and support

    o Maintain optimal physical function for as long possible.

        ▪ Encourage the child to be independent for as long as possible and to perform ADLs.

        ▪ Perform range of motion exercises and provide appropriate physical activity. Include stretching exercises, strength and muscle training, and breathing exercises.

- ■ Maintain proper body alignment and encourage the child to reposition self frequently to avoid skin breakdown.

- ■ Apply splints and braces as prescribed.

- ○ Maintain respiratory functioning.

  - ■ Encourage the use of incentive spirometry.

  - ■ Position the child to enhance expansion of lungs.

  - ■ Provide oxygen as prescribed.

  - ■ Provide noninvasive ventilation as prescribed.

- ○ Encourage adequate fluid intake.

- ○ Monitor and encourage adequate nutritional intake.

- ● Medications

  - ○ Prednisone (Deltasone)

    - ■ Prednisone is a corticosteroid that increases muscle strength.

    - ■ Nursing Considerations

      - □ Monitor for infection.

    - ■ Client Education

      - □ Instruct the child and parents to avoid potentially infectious agents.

      - □ Teach the child and family to practice healthy eating habits.

- ● Interdisciplinary Care

  - ○ Encourage the parents to consider assistance with care as disease progresses (respite care, long-term care, home health care).

  - ○ Refer the child and parents to support groups for MD.

- ● Surgical Interventions

  - ○ Surgery may be indicated for release or repair of contractures or for insertion of a gastrostomy tube or tracheostomy.

  - ○ Surgical release of contractures

    - ■ Nursing Actions

      - □ Provide standard postoperative care with emphasis on monitoring respiratory status, cast care (if applicable), skin and wound care, and elimination.

    - ■ Client Education

      - □ Provide preoperative teaching for the child and parents.

      - □ Educate the family about signs and symptoms of infection.

- ● Care After Discharge

- o Client Education
  - Provide information regarding social supports and programs available to the child and parents.
  - Provide information regarding respite care and home care services available to the child and parents.
  - Encourage routine physical exams and immunizations.
  - Facilitate discussion of end-of-life decisions when appropriate, including the use of mechanical ventilation and feeding tubes.
  - Encourage and provide for genetic counseling for parents.
- Client Outcomes
  - o The child will maintain optimal levels of functioning.

Complications

- Respiratory compromise
  - o Respiratory muscles unable the child to maintain adequate respirations.
  - o Nursing Actions
    - Help the child turn hourly or more frequently.
    - Have the child use deep breathing and coughing.
    - Suction as needed.
    - Administer oxygen as prescribed.
    - Use intermittent positive pressure ventilation and mechanically-assisted cough devices if indicated.
    - Administer antibiotics as prescribed.
  - o Client Education
    - Discuss mechanical ventilation options with the child and parents.

CHAPTER 29: CHRONIC NEUROMUSCULOSKELETAL DISORDERS

 Application Exercises

1. A nurse is caring for a child who has cerebral palsy. Which of the following medications should the nurse expect to administer to treat painful muscle spasms? (Select all that apply.)

_____ Baclofen (Lioresal)

_____ Diazepam (Valium)

_____ Oxybutynin chloride (Ditropan)

_____ Methotrexate (Rheumatrex)

_____ Prednisone (Deltasone)

2. A nurse is caring for a school-age child who has juvenile idiopathic arthritis. Which of the following are appropriate home care instructions? (Select all that apply.)

_____ Sleep on a firm mattress.

_____ Use cold compresses for joint pain.

_____ Take ibuprofen (Motrin) on an empty stomach.

_____ Take frequent rest periods throughout the day.

_____ Perform range-of-motion exercises when inflammation has subsided.

3. A nurse is completing discharge teaching with the parents of an infant who has Down syndrome. Which of the following interventions should the nurse discuss with the parents to prevent recurrent respiratory infections? (Select all that apply.)

_____ Perform frequent hand hygiene.

_____ Keep the infant in Fowler's position most of the time to prevent choking.

_____ Use a bulb syringe to remove nasal mucus.

_____ Keep the infant's mouth moist by rinsing frequently with water.

_____ Administer antibiotics prophylactically to prevent infection.

4. A nurse is caring for a child who has muscular dystrophy. For which of the following findings should the nurse assess? (Select all that apply.)

_____ Purposeless, involuntary, abnormal movements

_____ Spinal defect and sac-like protrusion

_____ Muscular weakness in lower extremities

_____ Unsteady, wide-based or waddling gait

_____ Upward slant to the eyes

CHAPTER 29: CHRONIC NEUROMUSCULOSKELETAL DISORDERS

 Application Exercises Answer Key

1. A nurse is caring for a child who has cerebral palsy. Which of the following medications should the nurse expect to administer to treat painful muscle spasms? (Select all that apply.)

   __X__   **Baclofen (Lioresal)**

   __X__   **Diazepam (Valium)**

   _____   Oxybutynin chloride (Ditropan)

   _____   Methotrexate (Rheumatrex)

   _____   Prednisone (Deltasone)

Baclofen and diazepam are both muscle relaxants that are used to treat painful muscle spasms. Oxybutynin chloride is an anti-spasmodic, anticholinergic medication used to decrease bladder spasms. Methotrexate is a cytotoxic disease modifying anti-rheumatic drug (DMARD) that slows joint degeneration and progression of rheumatoid arthritis and is used for children with juvenile idiopathic arthritis (JIA). Prednisone is a corticosteroid that increases muscle strength for children who have muscular dystrophy and decreases inflammation in children with JIA.

 NCLEX® Connection: Pharmacological and Parenteral Therapies, Expected Actions/Outcomes

2. A nurse is caring for a school-age child who has juvenile idiopathic arthritis. Which of the following are appropriate home care instructions? (Select all that apply.)

   __X__   **Sleep on a firm mattress.**

   _____   Use cold compresses for joint pain.

   _____   Take ibuprofen (Motrin) on an empty stomach.

   __X__   **Take frequent rest periods throughout the day.**

   __X__   **Perform range-of-motion exercises when inflammation has subsided.**

The child should sleep on a firm mattress to help prevent joint deformities and maintain body alignment, take frequent rest periods throughout the day to conserve energy, and perform rang-of-motion exercises when inflammation has subsided so as to minimize pain. Heat (or warm, moist packs), rather than cold compresses, will provide comfort and relieve stiffness. Ibuprofen should be taken with food to prevent GI distress.

NCLEX® Connection: Physiological Adaptation, Illness Management

3. A nurse is completing discharge teaching with the parents of an infant who has Down syndrome. Which of the following interventions should the nurse discuss with the parents to prevent recurrent respiratory infections? (Select all that apply.)

__X__	**Perform frequent hand hygiene.**
_____	Keep the infant in Fowler's position most of the time to prevent choking.
__X__	**Use a bulb syringe to remove nasal mucus.**
__X__	**Keep the infant's mouth moist by rinsing frequently with water.**
_____	Administer antibiotics prophylactically to prevent infection.

Prevention methods should include performing proper hand hygiene, using a bulb syringe to remove nasal mucus, and keeping mucous membranes moist. It is also important to change the infant's position frequently to promote proper respiratory function. Therefore, placing the infant in Fowler's position most of the time is not advised. Antibiotics should not be used prophylactically to prevent infection.

 NCLEX® Connection: Reduction of Risk Potential, Complications From Surgical Procedures and Health Alterations

4. A nurse is caring for a child who has muscular dystrophy. For which of the following findings should the nurse assess? (Select all that apply.)

_____	Purposeless, involuntary, abnormal movements
_____	Spinal defect and sac-like protrusion
__X__	**Muscular weakness in lower extremities**
__X__	**Unsteady, wide-based or waddling gait**
_____	Upward slant to the eyes

Muscular weakness in the lower extremities and an unsteady, wide-based or waddling gait are assessment findings consistent with muscular dystrophy. A child with cerebral palsy may show purposeless, involuntary, abnormal movements; a child with spina bifida may show a spinal defect and sac-like protrusion; and a child with Down syndrome may have an upward slant to the eyes.

NCLEX® Connection: Reduction of Risk Potential, System Specific Assessment

UNIT 2: NURSING CARE OF CHILDREN WITH SYSTEM DISORDERS

Section: Integumentary Disorders

- Skin Infections and Infestations
- Dermatitis and Acne
- Burns

NCLEX® CONNECTIONS

When reviewing the chapters in this section, keep in mind the relevant sections of the NCLEX® outline, in particular:

CLIENT NEEDS: PHARMACOLOGICAL AND PARENTERAL THERAPIES

Relevant topics/tasks include:

- Dosage Calculation
  - Perform calculations needed for medication administration.
- Parenteral/Intravenous Therapy
  - Apply knowledge and concepts of mathematics/ nursing procedures/ psychomotor skills when caring for a client receiving intravenous and parenteral therapy.
- Pharmacological Pain Management
  - Assess the client's need for administration of a PRN pain medication.

CLIENT NEEDS: REDUCTION OF RISK POTENTIAL

Relevant topics/tasks include:

- Changes/Abnormalities in Vital Signs
  - Apply knowledge of client pathophysiology when measuring vital signs.
- Laboratory Values
  - Recognize deviations from normal for values of albumin, ALT, AST, ammonia, bilirubin, bleeding time, calcium, cholesterol, digoxin, ESR, lithium, magnesium, phosphorous/phosphate, protein, urine.
- Potential for Complications of Diagnostic Tests/Treatments/ Procedures
  - Evaluate responses to procedures and treatments.

CLIENT NEEDS: PHYSIOLOGICAL ADAPTATION

Relevant topics/tasks include:

- Alterations in Body Systems
  - Provide care for the client with an infectious disease.
- Fluid and Electrolyte Imbalances
  - Apply knowledge of pathophysiology when caring for the client with fluid and electrolyte imbalances.
- Medical Emergencies
  - Apply knowledge of nursing procedures and psychomotor skills when caring for a client experiencing a medical emergency.

UNIT2	NURSING CARE OF CHILDREN WITH SYSTEM DISORDERS
Section	Integumentary Disorders

Chapter 30   Skin Infections and Infestations

Overview

- More than 50% of skin disorders in children are a form of dermatitis. The inflammatory response appears similar, but the causative agent and course of the dermatitis have wide variations.

- Most changes caused by dermatitis are reversible, unless complicated by ulceration, infection, and/or scratching.

- Viruses cause epidermal inflammation and formation of vesicles or warts.

- Dermatophytoses cause fungal infections, which affect the stratum corneum, hair, and nails. The lesions are superficial and not in the skin.

- Pediculosis (head lice) is a contagious parasitic infestation.

  o Pediculosis is transmitted through the sharing of personal items (hair brushes, combs, hats) or when personal items are kept close together.

  o Female lice lays eggs (nits) that attach to the hair follicles and hatch within 7 to 10 days.

  o Lice can live up to 1 month on the host, but only 48 hr without the host.

  o Movement and saliva of the lice cause pruritus.

- Scabies is a contagious skin infestation caused by a microscopic mite.

- Lyme disease is caused by a spirochete, which is contained within the saliva and feces of ticks (mainly deer ticks). The spirochete is transferred to an individual's bloodstream when the tick attaches to the person's skin.

Assessment

- Risk Factors

  o Causes of skin lesions in children include genetic factors and systemic illnesses (rheumatic fever, cancer).

  o Causative agents include bacteria, viruses, fungi, mites, and infected insects.

  o Risks for developing bacterial skin infections include:

    - Immunodeficiency disorders (AIDS, leukemia, solid tumors [lymphoma])

- Long-term immunosuppressive therapy (corticosteroids)
  - Lice infestation can occur during periods of time when children are in close contact (e.g., day care, school, summer camp) and sharing personal care items (comb/hair brush, hats).
  - Scabies spreads quickly under crowded conditions. Infestation may also occur with the sharing of infested clothing, towels, and bedding. Individuals with weakened immune systems are at the greatest risk for infestation.
- Subjective Data
  - Nursing history information should include:
    - Recent exposure to a causative agent, such as a virus, food, medication, animal, or plant.
    - Reports of itching and/or pain in areas such as the head, genitals, joints, and back.
- Objective Data
  - Physical Assessment Findings

INFECTION/CAUSATIVE AGENTS	MANIFESTATIONS
Impetigo contagiosa bacteria • Staphylococcus	• Appears as a red macule that becomes a vesicle and ruptures • Has thick, crusted, amber-colored exudate (honey-colored crust) • Spreads easily
Verruca (warts) • Human papillomavirus	• Appears as a well-circumscribed grey or brown papule with rough papillomatous texture
Cold sores and fever blisters • Herpes simplex virus type1 Genital herpes • Herpes simplex virus type 2	• Appears as a group of vesicles on inflamed skin, usually around the lips or genitalia • Is accompanied by a painful burning sensation • Dries, exfoliates, and heals within 8 to 10 days
Tinea capitis (ringworm, head) – Fungus • Trichophyton tonsurans • Microsporum canis	• Appears as circular, scaly patches with or without areas of alopecia • Begins in the scalp and possibly progresses to the neck or hairline
Tinea corporis (ringworm, body) – Fungus • Trichophyton rubrum • Trichophyton mentagrophytes • Microsporum canis	• Appears as circular, scaly, red patches • Has a clear center that spreads peripherally to the edges of the lesion

INFECTION/CAUSATIVE AGENTS	MANIFESTATIONS
Candidiasis (thrush) – Fungus • *Candida albicans*	• Appears as inflamed areas with white exudate that peel and bleed easily
Pediculosis (lice) – Parasite • *Pediculus humanus capitis* (head lice) • *Pediculus corporis* (body lice) • *Pediculus pubis* (pubic lice)	• Begins with generalized itching on head or genital area • Progresses to visible lesions from scratching, which can become infected with bacteria or fungi • Involves nits in hair that are visible, behind ears, at base of scalp, and occasionally in eyelashes and brows (With heavy infestations, live lice may also be seen.)
Scabies mite • *Sarcoptes scabiei*	• Appears as grayish-brown, threadlike burrows with a black dot at the end (mite) • Involves eczematous eruption in infants • Is accompanied by intense itching that can cause sores to become infected • Appears as lesions in interdigital, antecubital, popliteal, and inguinal areas

Lyme disease
• Borrelia burgdorferi
	• Has symptoms of viral-like illness
	• Has three stages
	  ○ Stage 1 – Rash of red ring about 3 to 31 days after possible tick bite
	  ○ Stage 2 – Neurologic, cardiac, and musculoskeletal involvement
	  ○ Stage 3 – Musculoskeletal pain in joints and supporting structures, as well as neurological problems

- ○ Laboratory Tests
    - ■ Wound culture (for bacterial infections)
    - ■ Serologic testing (for Lyme disease)
- ○ Diagnostic Procedures
    - ■ Identify the parasite.
        - □ *Pediculus humanus capitis* (head lice) are small (but visible), wingless, free-moving, and grayish tan in color.
        - □ Nits (small, white oval eggs) attach to hair follicles about 6 mm (0.25 in) from the scalp and are difficult to remove from hair shafts. They may resemble dandruff.
        - □ Translucent (empty) nits may be found farther down the hair shaft.

□ Nursing Actions

▸ Conduct a microscopic exam of tissue or lesions.

□ Client Education

▸ Teach the child and parents how to eliminate the infestation. Treatment will depend on which parasite is identified.

▸ Reinforce the need to follow the therapeutic plan to prevent reinfestation and spread.

Collaborative Care

- Nursing Care

  ○ Assess the general condition of the skin, hair, and nails, including color (redness, pallor, cyanosis), cleanliness, warmth, swelling, and bleeding of mucous membranes.

  ○ Assess for presence, pattern, and location of vesicles, warts, rash, hives, or open wounds.

  ○ Assess for signs of a wound infection.

    ■ Swelling

    ■ Purulent drainage

    ■ Pain

    ■ Increased temperature

    ■ Redness extending beyond the wound margin

  ○ Gently clean affected areas.

  ○ Apply topical antibiotics or antifungal creams as prescribed.

  ○ Trim and clean the child's fingernails.

  ○ Encourage the child to wear gloves at night to prevent scratching.

INFECTION/CAUSATIVE AGENTS	MANAGEMENT
Impetigo contagiosa • Staphylococcus	• Use compresses of 1:20 aluminum acetate in water (Burow's solution) to remove crusted exudate. • Use topical antibacterial or oral antibiotics.
Verruca (warts) • Human papillomavirus	• Use destructive therapy (may leave scarring). The condition may resolve without treatment. • Avoid irritation (rubbing, scratching) to prevent spread.
Cold sores and fever blisters • Herpes simplex virus type 1 Genital herpes • Herpes simplex virus type 2	• Use aluminum acetate in water during the weeping stage. A topical or oral antiviral medication may be used to lessen the duration and decrease the severity. Lesions usually heal without scarring. • Prevent secondary infection.

INFECTION/CAUSATIVE AGENTS	MANAGEMENT
Tinea capitis (ringworm, head) • *Trichophyton tonsurans* • *Microsporum canis*	• Administer oral griseofulvin (Grifulvin) for 6 to 8 weeks or oral terbinafine (Lamisil) for 2 to 4 weeks. • Apply topical antifungal medications that are appropriate for the affected areas (clotrimazole [Lotrimin], miconazole [Monistat 7]). • Use a selenium sulfide shampoo.
Tinea corporis (ringworm, body) • *Trichophyton rubrum* • *Trichophyton mentagrophytes* • *Microsporum canis*	• Administer oral griseofulvin for several months. • Use topical antifungal medications that are appropriate for the affected areas (clotrimazole, miconazole). Apply 2.5 cm (1 in) past the edge of the lesion and continue treatment for 1 to 2 weeks after resolution of the lesion.
Candidiasis (thrush) • *Candida albicans*	• Apply nystatin (Mycostatin) ointment or solution to affected areas.
Pediculosis • *Pediculus humanus capitis* (head lice) • *Pediculus corporis* (body lice) • *Pediculus pubis* (pubic lice)	• Apply an over-the-counter or prescribed pediculicide shampoo to the infected child and family according to product instructions. • Do not use hair products with conditioner prior to treatment. Hair should not be rewashed for 1 to 2 days following treatment. • Use a comb designed to remove nits. Inspect hair every 2 to 3 days for 2 to 3 weeks. • Treat the child again at specific intervals based on inspection results and the pediculicide product used. • Wear clean clothing after treatment. • Wash clothing, linens, combs, and hairbrushes worn or used 2 days prior to treatment in hot water (54° C [130° F]). Place clothing and linens in a dryer on high heat until dry. • Dry clean clothes that are nonwashable. • Nonwashable items should be sealed in a plastic bag for 2 weeks. • Vacuum areas occupied by the infected child.
Scabies • *Sarcoptes scabiei*	• Apply topical medication from the child's neck to his toes. • Give the child clean clothes, towels, and bedding. • Leave on the child's skin for 8 to 12 hr. • Bathe the child to remove the medication.

INFECTION/CAUSATIVE AGENTS	MANAGEMENT
Lyme disease • *Borrelia burgdorferi*	• Administer oral antibiotics. Use amoxicillin (Amoxil) for children younger than 8 years of age and doxycycline (Vibramycin) for children older than 8 years of age. • Use erythromycin (E-Mycin) or cefuroxime (Zinacef) for children who are allergic to penicillin. • Treat for a period of 14 to 21 days. • Monitor the child for up to 30 days following a tick bite. Instruct parents to seek medical care immediately if skin lesion or viral-type illness develops.

- Care After Discharge
  - Client Education
    - Teach the family how to avoid the spread of infections.
      - Use good hand hygiene.
      - Avoid sharing clothing, hats, combs, brushes, and/or towels.
      - Keep the child from touching the affected area by using distraction.
      - Do not squeeze vesicles.
      - Apply topical medications as prescribed.
      - Administer oral medications as prescribed.
        - ▸ Remind parents to bring children taking griseofulvin for periodic laboratory tests to monitor renal and liver function.
      - Clean surfaces that might be harboring causative agents, including bed linens, clothing, and furniture.
    - Discourage the use of home remedies for lice.
    - Teach the family how to prevent arthropod bites.
      - Avoid tick-infested areas. If bitten, carefully remove ticks and observe skin for development of any reactions.
      - Wear light-colored clothing when going into areas that may have ticks so that ticks can be identified and removed.
      - Apply insect repellants cautiously to avoid neurologic complications.
- Client Outcomes
  - The child will be free of infection.

Complications

- Secondary infection (staphylococcus, streptococcus, *Haemophilus influenzae*)
  - Clinical manifestations may include:
    - Red inflammation of skin with swelling

Complications

- Secondary infection (staphylococcus, streptococcus, *Haemophilus influenzae*)
  - Clinical manifestations may include:
    - Red inflammation of skin with swelling
    - Lymphangitis (red streaking)
    - Enlargement of lymph nodes
    - Development of abscess
    - Fever and malaise
  - Nursing Actions
    - Administer antibiotics, antipyretics, and antipruritics as prescribed.
    - Monitor effects of prescribed medications.
    - Keep lesions clean and dry.
    - Apply dressings as prescribed.
  - Client Education
    - Reinforce the therapeutic management plan with emphasis on maintaining health and hygiene.
    - Reinforce hand hygiene as a good way to prevent infections.
    - Encourage the child and parents to trim nails short and discourage scratching.

CHAPTER 30: SKIN INFECTIONS AND INFESTATIONS

 Application Exercises

1. Which of the following are the manifestations of scabies? (Select all that apply.)

_____ Nits present

_____ Thread-like rash between fingers and other moist areas

_____ Circular rash on extremities

_____ Pruritus

_____ Eczematous eruptions in infants

2. A phone triage nurse receives a call from a father who reports possible head lice on his child. Which of the following information should the nurse tell the father?

    A. Wash the child's hair immediately after treatment.

    B. Treat the head lice with an over-the-counter preparation.

    C. Throw the child's stuffed animals away.

    D. Treat household pets for this condition.

3. Match the following skin disorders with their causative agents.

_____	Impetigo contagiosa	A. *Trichophyton tonsurans*
_____	Head lice	B. Staphylococcus
_____	Lyme disease	C. Herpes simplex virus type 1
_____	Cold sore and fever blister	D. *Borrelia burgdorferi*
_____	Ringworm	E. *Pediculosis humanus capitis*

CHAPTER 30: SKIN INFECTIONS AND INFESTATIONS

 Application Exercises Answer Key

1. Which of the following are the manifestations of scabies? (Select all that apply.)

_____	Nits present
__X__	**Thread-like rash between fingers and other moist areas**
_____	Circular rash on extremities
__X__	**Pruritus**
__X__	**Eczematous eruptions in infants**

Scabies is caused by the scabies mite, which burrows into the skin. The mite is often found between the fingers or in other moist areas, such as antecubital, popliteal, or inguinal areas. The burrows seen on the skin often appear grayish-brown and thread-like with a black dot at the end (the mite). Skin lesions are pruritic in nature. In infants, the skin lesions may look like eczema. The presence of nits indicates pediculosis, and a circular rash on extremities may indicate Lyme disease or ringworm.

 NCLEX® Connection: Physiological Adaptation, Infectious Disease

2. A phone triage nurse receives a call from a father who reports possible head lice on his child. Which of the following information should the nurse tell the father?

A. Wash the child's hair immediately after treatment.

B. Treat the head lice with an over-the-counter preparation.

C. Throw the child's stuffed animals away.

D. Treat household pets for this condition.

The father should be instructed that over-the-counter products may be purchased to treat lice. The child's hair should not be washed for 1 to 2 days after the treatment. Lice only live for a short period of time, so it is not appropriate to inform the parent that they live for a long time. Throwing away the child's stuffed animals is not necessary, because laundering them will be sufficient. Lice are not transmitted from human to animal, so household pets do not require treatment.

 NCLEX® Connection: Physiological Adaptation, Infectious Disease

3. Match the following skin disorders with their causative agents.

__B__	Impetigo contagiosa	A. *Trichophyton tonsurans*
__E__	Head lice	B. Staphylococcus
__D__	Lyme disease	C. Herpes simplex virus type 1
__C__	Cold sore and fever blister	D. *Borrelia burgdorferi*
__A__	Ringworm	E. *Pediculosis humanus capitis*

 NCLEX® Connection: Physiological Adaptation, Infectious Disease

UNIT 2	NURSING CARE OF CHILDREN WITH SYSTEM DISORDERS
Section	Integumentary Disorders
Chapter 31	Dermatitis and Acne

Overview

- Common skin conditions of the pediatric population include:

    o   Contact dermatitis

    o   Atopic dermatitis

    o   Acne

CONTACT DERMATITIS

Overview

- Contact dermatitis is an inflammatory reaction of the skin. It is caused when the skin comes into contact with chemicals or other irritants (feces, urine, soaps, poison ivy, animals, metals, dyes, medications).

    o   Diaper dermatitis may be caused by detergents, soaps, and/or chemicals that come in contact with the genital area. It may also be a result of *Candida albicans*.

    o.   Contact dermatitis is a result of exposure to urushiol, an oil found in poisonous plants.

    o   Seborrheic dermatitis (cradle cap) has an unknown etiology but is most common in infancy and then again at puberty.

Assessment

- Risk Factors

    o   Use of diapers

    o   Exposure to wild plants

- Subjective Data

    o   Constant pruritus

- Objective Data

    o Physical Assessment Findings

        ■ Diaper dermatitis

            □ Red, inflamed skin on areas in most contact with urine, feces, and/or chemical irritants. Note whether the irritation is within or across the inguinal folds.

            □ Lesions manifested are varied in type and pattern. Satellite lesions are characteristic of *Candida albicans*.

            □ Involved areas usually include folds of the buttocks, inner thighs, and scrotum.

        ■ Contact dermatitis

            □ The area of reaction will vary depending on exposure. The reaction may be mild to severe and include redness, swelling, blisters, and pruritus

        ■ Medication reactions

            □ Reactions may occur immediately after administration of the medication, if previously taken, or they may be delayed. It may take up to 7 days for a child who has never been exposed to a particular medication to have an adverse response.

            □ Reactions may range from a simple rash to a full body response, and they may be mild to severe. These reactions may look similar to other skin disorders.

            □ A sudden onset of a generalized inflammatory response with itching and gastrointestinal (GI) discomfort may occur. However, this response can progress to anemia and kidney and/or liver dysfunction.

        ■ Seborrheic dermatitis

            □ Thick, yellowish, scaly adhesions occur on the scalp, eyelids, and external ear canals.

Collaborative Care

- Nursing Care

    o Diaper dermatitis

        ■ Promptly remove the wet diaper.

        ■ Clean urine off the perineal area with a nonirritating cleanser. Cleanse the perineal area of feces with warm water and mild soap.

        ■ Wash skin folds and the genital area frequently with water.

        ■ Expose the affected area to air.

        ■ Use superabsorbent disposable diapers to reduce skin exposure.

        ■ Apply a skin barrier, such as zinc oxide. Do not wash it off with each diaper change.

- Use cornstarch to reduce friction between the diaper and the skin.
  - ○ Contact dermatitis
    - Rinse areas that have been exposed to poisonous plants with cold running water.
    - Remove all clothing that has come into contact with the plant and wash with alcohol followed by water.
    - Use calamine lotion or compresses of ammonium acetate in water (Burow solution) on affected skin.
    - Encourage baths with commercial colloidal oatmeal.
    - Apply a topical corticosteroid gel.
    - Encourage the child not to scratch skin to prevent a secondary infection from developing.
  - ○ Medication reactions
    - Discontinue the medication.
    - Initiate emergency response for anaphylaxis.
  - ○ Seborrheic dermatitis
    - Treat by gently scrubbing the scalp with mild pressure and shampoo daily with mild soap or antiseborrheic shampoo.
- Medications
  - ○ Antihistamines – Hydroxyzine (Atarax) or diphenhydramine (Benadryl)
    - Administer in cases of allergic/medication reactions.
    - Nursing Considerations
      - □ Administer the medication as prescribed.
    - Client Education
      - □ Educate the family on the importance of the medication and administering on schedule.
      - □ Reinforce the sedating effect of some antihistamines and the need for parents to monitor the child and provide for safety during use.
  - ○ Antibiotics
    - Use to treat secondary infections.
    - Nursing Considerations
      - □ Administer medications as prescribed.
    - Client Education
      - □ Educate the family about the importance of continuing the medication as prescribed.

- Care After Discharge
  - Client Education
    - Encourage frequent diaper changes.
    - Advise parents that their child should avoid bubble baths and harsh soaps.
    - Encourage children to wear long sleeves and pants.
    - Educate parents to remove an offending agent as soon as exposure takes place.
- Client Outcomes
  - The child's skin will heal without complications and/or will remain intact.
  - The child will be free of infections.

Complications

- Infection
  - Caused by breaks in the skin from scratching
  - Nursing Actions
    - Monitor the area for signs of infection.
    - Keep fingernails trimmed short.
    - Cleanse the area with mild soap and water.
    - Administer antipruritics as prescribed.
  - Client Education
    - Educate the family and child about avoiding offending agents.

ATOPIC DERMATITIS (AD)

Overview

- Atopic dermatitis (AD) is a type of eczema (eczema describes a category of integumentary disorders, not a specific disorder with a determined etiology) that is characterized by pruritus and associated with a history of allergies that are of an inherited tendency (atopy).

- New lesions develop with continued scratching and increase the risk of secondary infection.

- Classifications of atopic dermatitis are based on the child's age, how the lesions are distributed, and the appearance of the lesions.

- AD cannot be cured but can be well controlled.

Assessment

- Risk Factors
  - Presence of allergic condition and family history of atopy
  - Previous skin disorder and exacerbation of present skin disorder
  - Exposure to irritating and/or causative agents
- Subjective Data
  - Recent exposure to any irritant (medication, food, soap, contact with animals)
  - Intense pruritus
- Objective Data
  - Physical Assessment Findings

CLASSIFICATION	DISTRIBUTION	LESIONS
Infants – Onset at 2 to 6 months of age with spontaneous remission by 3 years of age	• Generalized distribution of lesions on cheeks, scalp, trunk, hands and feet, as well as extensor surfaces of extremities	• Usually symmetric • Weeping and oozing or crusty and scaly • Erythematous vesicles and papules
Children 1 to 12 years of age – Progression of infant form or starts at 2 years of age with full symptoms evident by 5 years of age	• Redness or irritation in the flexor spaces (the antecubital and popliteal fossae, on wrists, ankles, and feet)	• Red or tan-colored patches or clusters of papules • Hyperpigmented • Dry • Thickened skin • Keratosis pilaris
Adolescents – Onset at age 12 and may continue into adulthood	• Similar distribution to children	• Same as for children • Papules that appear blended together • Larger, dry, thickened patches

- Unaffected skin may appear dry and rough.
- Hypopigmentation of skin may occur in small, diffuse areas.
- Pallor surrounds the nose, mouth, and ears.
- A bluish discoloration is present underneath the eyes.
- Numerous infections of the nails are present.
- Lymphadenopathy occurs, especially around affected areas.
- Signs of a wound infection are present (swelling, purulent drainage, pain, increased temperature, redness extending beyond the wound margin).

Collaborative Care

- Nursing Care

    ○ Keep skin hydrated with tepid baths (with/without soap or emulsifying oil), then apply an emollient within 3 min of bathing. Two or three baths may be given daily with one prior to bedtime.

    ○ Dress the child in cotton clothing. Avoid wools or synthetic fabrics.

    ○ Avoid excessive heat and perspiration, which increases itching.

    ○ Avoid irritants (bubble baths, soaps, perfumes, fabric softeners).

    ○ Provide support to the child and family.

    ○ Wash skin folds and genital area frequently with water.

        ■ Assist in identifying causative agent.

- Medications

    ○ Antihistamines – Hydroxyzine (Atarax) or diphenhydramine (Benadryl)

        ■ Should be administered in cases of medication reactions

        ■ Client Education

            □ Reinforce the sedating effect of some antihistamines and the need for parents to monitor the child during use.

            □ Reinforce safety of the child when using sedating antihistamines.

    ○ Antihistamines – Loratadine (Claritin) or fexofenadine (Allegra)

        ■ Oral antihistamine for antipruritic effect

        ■ Nursing Considerations

            □ Administer the medication as prescribed.

        ■ Client Education

            □ Inform the parents that it is preferred for use during the daytime.

    ○ Antibiotics

        ■ Antibiotics should be used to treat secondary infections.

    ○ Topical corticosteroids

        ■ Topical corticosteroids may be used intermittently to reduce or control flare-ups. They may be low, moderate, or high potency and are prescribed based on the degree of skin involvement (extremity versus eyelids), age of the child, and consequences from side effects.

- ○ Nonsteroidal agents
  - ■ Used to decrease inflammation during flare-ups
  - ■ Nursing Considerations
    - □ Use for children older than 2 years of age.
    - □ Use at the start of an exacerbation of AD when skin turns red and starts to itch.
- ○ Client Education
  - ■ Reinforce the signs of infection.
  - ■ Instruct the family to:
    - □ Change diapers when wet or soiled.
    - □ Keep nails short and trimmed.
    - □ Place gloves or cotton socks over hands for sleeping.
    - □ Dress young children in soft, cotton, one-piece, long-sleeve, long-pant outfits.
    - □ Remove items that may promote itching (woolen blankets, scratchy fabrics). Use cotton whenever possible.
    - □ Use mild detergents to wash clothing and linens. The wash cycle may be repeated without soap.
    - □ Avoid latex products, second-hand smoke, furry pets, dust, and molds.
    - □ Encourage tepid baths without the use of soap. Avoid oils and powders.
    - □ Follow specific directions regarding topical medications, soaks, and baths. Emphasize the importance of understanding the sequence of treatments to maximize the benefit of therapy and prevent complications.
    - □ Avoid overheating the bedroom during winter months. Use a room humidifier.
    - □ Maintain treatment to prevent flare-up.
    - □ Follow up with the health care provider as directed.
    - □ Participate in support groups.
- ● Client Outcomes
  - ○ The child will be free from exacerbations.
  - ○ The child will remain free from itching.
  - ○ The child's skin will remain intact.
  - ○ The child will remain free from infection.
  - ○ The child will maintain a positive self-image.

Complications

- Infection
    - Caused by breaks in the skin from scratching
  - Nursing Actions
    - Keep nails trimmed.
    - Administer antipruritics as prescribed.
    - Monitor the area for signs of infection.
    - Cleanse the area with mild soap and water.
  - Client Education
    - Educate the family and child to avoid offending agents.

ACNE

Overview

- Acne is the most common skin condition during adolescence.
- Acne is self-limiting and non life-threatening. However, it poses a threat to self-image for adolescents.
- Acne involves the pilosebaceous follicles (hair follicle and sebaceous gland complex) of the face, neck, chest, and upper back.
- *Propionibacterium acnes* (*P. acnes*) is the bacteria associated with inflammation in acne.

Assessment

- Risk Factors
  - Acne may be genetic.
  - Acne is more common in males than in females.
  - Hormonal fluctuations may result in acne flares in females.
  - The use of cosmetic products containing ingredients such as petrolatum and lanolin may increase acne outbreaks.
  - Although there is no dietary intake link with acne, adolescents working at fast food restaurants may have an increased incidence of acne due to exposure to cooking grease.

- Subjective and Objective Data

    ○ Report of exacerbations and remissions

    ○ Physical Assessment Findings

        ▪ Lesions (comedones) are either open (blackheads) or closed (whiteheads). Both are most often found on the face, neck, back, and chest.

        ▪ *P. acnes* may lead to inflammation manifesting as papules, pustules, nodules, or cysts.

Collaborative Care

- Nursing Care

    ○ Discuss the process of acne with the child and family.

    ○ Discuss the importance of adherence with the prescribed plan of care.

    ○ Provide written instructions to accompany verbal instructions.

    ○ Teach the child to gently wash the face and other affected areas, avoiding scrubbing and abrasive cleaners.

    ○ Teach the child and family about medications prescribed, especially side effects.

    ○ Monitor for signs of mood changes or suicidal ideation in adolescents who are taking Isotretinoin 13-cis-retinoic acid (Accutane)

    ○ Provide support and encouragement to the child and family.

MEDICATION	ACTION	NURSING CONSIDERATIONS
Tretinoin (Retin-A)	• Interrupts abnormal keratinization that causes microcomedones	• Inform the child that tretinoin may irritate the skin. Instruct the child to apply within 20 to 30 min after washing the face. • Tell the child to: 　○ Use a pea-size amount of medication and apply at night. 　○ Avoid sun exposure. 　○ Use sunscreen (SPF 15 or greater) to avoid sunburn.
Benzoyl peroxide	• Antibacterial agent • Inhibits growth of *P. acnes*	• Benzoyl peroxide may bleach bed linens, towels, and clothing, but not skin.

MEDICATION	ACTION	NURSING CONSIDERATIONS
Topical antibacterial agents	• Inhibits growth of *P. acnes*	• Various topical or oral antibacterial agents may be used. However, be alert to allergic reactions. • Avoid overexposure to the sun. • Use sunscreen with an SPF of 15 or greater when exposure to sun is unavoidable.
Isotretinoin 13-cis-retinoic acid (Accutane)	• Affects factors involved in the development of acne	• Isotretinoin 13-cis-retinoic acid is only prescribed by dermatologists. • Side effects include dry skin and mucous membranes, dry eyes, decreased night vision, headaches, photosensitivity, elevated cholesterol and triglycerides, depression, suicidal ideation, and/or violent behaviors. • Monitor for behavioral changes. • Isotretinoin 13-cis-retinoic acid is teratogenic. Therefore, it is contraindicated in women of childbearing age who are not taking oral contraceptives.

- Care After Discharge

    o Client Education

        ▪ Reinforce that adherence to the therapeutic plan is essential to preventing acne flares.

        ▪ Encourage the child to eat a balanced, healthy diet.

        ▪ Encourage sleep, rest, and daily exercise.

        ▪ Teach the child to wash the affected area gently with a mild cleanser once or twice daily, and not to pick or squeeze comedones.

        ▪ Encourage frequent shampooing.

        ▪ Encourage family support of the child and family members to assist the child in coping with body-image changes.

        ▪ Instruct the child to wear protective clothing and sunscreen when outside.

        ▪ Teach the child to avoid the use of tanning beds.

        ▪ Reinforce the need for follow-up and monitoring of cholesterol and triglycerides, especially in adolescents who are taking isotretinoin 13-cis-retinoic acid.

        ▪ Reinforce the importance of using oral contraceptives while taking isotretinoin 13-cis-retinoic acid

- Client Outcomes

  - The child's skin will heal without complications.

  - The child will experience relief from pruritus.

  - The child will maintain a positive self-image.

  - The child will remain free from infection.

Complications

- Infection and cellulitis

  - Caused by lesions of dermatitis and/or acne or breaks in the skin from scratching

  - Nursing Actions

    - Monitor the area for signs of infection.

    - Cleanse the area with mild soap and water.

    - Assess for signs of redness, swelling, and pain, which may indicate cellulitis.

    - Assess for fever.

  - Client Education

    - Educate the family and child on avoidance of offending agents.

    - Instruct the child and family to keep fingernails trimmed and short.

    - Use antipruritics as prescribed.

    - Teach the family signs and symptoms of cellulitis and to notify the health care provider if they occur.

CHAPTER 31: DERMATITIS AND ACNE

 Application Exercises

1. An infant is brought to the public health clinic by his mother for immunizations. The mother shows the nurse the infant's scalp, which is half-covered by thick, crusty, yellowish, solid patches. The mother asks the nurse, "Is this something he caught from other children at day care?" Which of the following responses by the nurse is appropriate?

    A. "The patches are from not washing the infant's head regularly."

    B. "The cause is unknown and not contagious."

    C. "The patches are due to an infection the infant has."

    D. "The cause is due to the infant acquiring it from another child at daycare."

2. Match each type of dermatitis with its description.

_____	Diaper dermatitis	A. Weeping, red vesicles and papules
_____	Atopic dermatitis	B. Comedones or pustules
_____	Acne	C. Red, inflamed skin
_____	Seborrheic dermatitis	D. Thick, yellow, scaly areas

3. A nurse is caring for an adolescent client who has acne and is prescribed isotretinoin 13-cis-retinoic acid (Accutane). Which of the following laboratory values should be monitored?

    A. Cholesterol and triglycerides

    B. BUN and creatinine

    C. Serum potassium

    D. Serum sodium

CHAPTER 31: DERMATITIS AND ACNE

 Application Exercises Answer Key

1. An infant is brought to the public health clinic by his mother for immunizations. The mother shows the nurse the infant's scalp, which is half-covered by thick, crusty, yellowish, solid patches. The mother asks the nurse, "Is this something he caught from other children at day care?" Which of the following responses by the nurse is appropriate?

    A. "The patches are from not washing the infant's head regularly."

    B. "The cause is unknown and not contagious."

    C. "The patches are due to an infection the infant has."

    D. "The cause is due to the infant acquiring it from another child at daycare."

The nurse should inform the infant's mother that the cause is unknown and that it is not contagious. The other responses are not appropriate regarding this condition.

 NCLEX® Connection: Reduction of Risk Potential, Alterations in Body Systems

2. Match each type of dermatitis with its description.

C	Diaper dermatitis	A. Weeping, red vesicles and papules
A	Atopic dermatitis	B. Comedones or pustules
B	Acne	C. Red, inflamed skin
D	Seborrheic dermatitis	D. Thick, yellow, scaly areas

NCLEX® Connection: Reduction of Risk Potential, System Specific Assessment

3. A nurse is caring for an adolescent client who has acne and is prescribed isotretinoin 13-cis-retinoic acid (Accutane). Which of the following laboratory values should be monitored?

    A. Cholesterol and triglycerides

    B. BUN and creatinine

    C. Serum potassium

    D. Serum sodium

Isotretinoin 13-cis-retinoic acid can raise cholesterol and triglyceride levels. There is no indication to monitor BUN, creatine, or serum potassium and sodium levels.

NCLEX® Connection: Pharmacological and Parenteral Therapies, Adverse Effects/ Contraindications/Side Effects/Interactions

UNIT 2   NURSING CARE OF CHILDREN WITH SYSTEM DISORDERS

Section   Integumentary Disorders

Chapter 32   Burns

 Overview

- Thermal, chemical, electrical, and radioactive agents can cause burns, which result in cellular destruction of the skin layers and underlying tissue. The type of burn and the severity of the burn impact the treatment plan.

    o   Thermal burns occur when there is exposure to flames, steam, or hot liquids.

    o   Chemical burns occur when there is exposure to a caustic agent. Cleaning agents used in the home (drain cleaner, bleach) and agents used in the industrial setting (caustic soda, sulfuric acid) cause chemical burns.

    o   Electrical burns occur when an electrical current passes through the body. This type of burn may result in severe damage, including loss of organ function, tissue destruction with the subsequent need for amputation of a limb, and cardiac and/or respiratory arrest.

    o   Radiation burns most frequently occur as a result of therapeutic treatment for cancer or from sunburn.

- In addition to destruction of body tissue, a burn injury results in loss of:

    o   Temperature regulation

    o   Sweat and sebaceous gland function

    o   Sensory function

- Metabolism increases to maintain body heat.

- Burns are initially considered clean due to a lack of pathogens. However, they may become contaminated by dirt or unclean water.

 View Media Supplement: Percentage of Burns (Image)

- The severity of the burn is based on the percentage of total body surface area (TBSA). Standardized charts for age groups are used to identify the extent of the injury.

    o   Depth of the burn

    o   Body location of the burn

- o Age of the child

- o Causative agent

- o Presence of other injuries

- o Involvement of the respiratory system

- o Overall health of the child

- Burn management occurs in three phases.

  - o Emergent (resuscitative phase)

    - ■ Occurs the first 24 to 48 hr after the burn occurs

  - o Acute

    - ■ Begins when resuscitation is finished

    - ■ Ends when the wound is covered by tissue

  - o Rehabilitative

    - ■ Begins when most of the burn area is healed

    - ■ Ends when reconstructive and corrective procedures are complete (may last for years)

Assessment

- Risk Factors

  - o Lack of supervision

  - o Developmental growth of the child

- Subjective Data

  - o To evaluate the extent of damage when assessing burns, it is important to know:

    - ■ The type of burning agent (dry heat, moist heat, chemical, electrical, ionizing radiation)

    - ■ The duration of contact

    - ■ The area of the body in which the burn occurred

- Objective Data

  - o Physical Assessment Findings

DEPTH	APPEARANCE	SENSATION/HEALING	EXAMPLE
Superficial • Damage to epidermis	• Pink to red in color with no blisters, mild edema, and no eschar	• Painful • Heals within 5 to 10 days • No scarring	• Sunburn

DEPTH	APPEARANCE	SENSATION/HEALING	EXAMPLE
Superficial partial thickness • Damage to the entire epidermis and some parts of the dermis	• Pink to red in color with blisters, mild to moderate edema, and no eschar	• Pain is present. • It heals within 14 days. • No scarring is present.	• Flame or burn scalds
Deep partial thickness • Damage to the entire epidermis and some parts of the dermis	• Red to white in color with no blisters, moderate edema, and soft and dry eschar	• Pain is present and the burn is sensitive to touch. • It heals within 14 to 36 days. • Scarring is likely. • Possible grafting is involved	• Flame and burn scalds • Grease, tar, or chemical burns • Exposure to hot objects for prolonged time
Full thickness • Damage to the entire epidermis and dermis and possible damage to the subcutaneous tissue • Nerve damage	• Red to tan, black, brown, or white in color with no blisters, severe edema, and hard and inelastic eschar	• As burn heals, painful sensations return and severity of pain increases. • It heals within weeks to months • Scarring is present. • Grafting is required.	• Burn scalds • Grease, tar, chemical or electrical burns
Deep full thickness • Damage to all layers of the skin that extends to muscle, tendons and bones	• Black in color with no edema and hard and inelastic eschar	• No pain is present. • It heals within weeks to months. • Scarring is present.	• Flame, electrical, grease, tar, and chemical burns

 View Media Supplement: Stages of Burns (Image)

- Inhalation damage findings may include burn injury on lips and face, singed hairs, and edema of the larynx. Clinical manifestations may not be evident for 24 to 48 hr and are seen as wheezing, hoarseness, and increased respiratory secretions.

- Carbon monoxide inhalation (suspected if the injury took place in an enclosed area) findings include erythema and edema, followed by sloughing of the respiratory tract mucosa.

- Altered level of consciousness, spiking fever, and hypoactive bowel signs may be signs of impending sepsis.

- Observe for irritability, crying, and restlessness.

- Hypovolemia or shock may result when injury to at least 20 to 30% TBSA occurs. Fluid shifts from the intercellular and intravascular space to the interstitial space.

- Hypotension, tachycardia, and decreased cardiac output may occur.

○ Laboratory Tests

- Laboratory values that should be evaluated – CBC, serum electrolytes, BUN, ABGs, fasting blood glucose, random blood glucose, liver enzymes, urinalysis, and clotting studies.

  □ Initial fluid shift (first 24 hr after injury)

  ▸ Hgb and Hct – Elevated due to loss of fluid volume and fluid shifts into interstitial (third spacing) fluid (hemoconcentration)

  ▸ Sodium – Decreased due to third spacing (hyponatremia)

  ▸ Potassium – Increased due to cell destruction (hyperkalemia)

  □ Fluid mobilization (48 to 72 hr after injury)

  ▸ Hgb and Hct – Decreased due to fluid shift from interstitial back into vascular fluid

  ▸ Sodium – Remains decreased due to renal and wound loss

  ▸ Potassium – Decreased due to renal loss and movement back into cells (hypokalemia)

  ▸ WBC – Initially increased and then decreased with left shift

  ▸ Blood glucose – Elevated due to stress response

  ▸ ABGs – Slight hypoxemia, metabolic acidosis

  ▸ Total protein and albumin – Low due to fluid loss

Collaborative Care

- Nursing Care
  - ○ Minor burns
    - ▪ Stop the burning process.
      - □ Remove clothing or jewelry that may conduct heat.
      - □ Apply cool water soaks or run cool water over the injury. Do not use ice.
      - □ Flush chemical burns with large amounts of water.
      - □ Cover the burn with a clean cloth to prevent contamination and hypothermia.
      - □ Provide warmth.
      - □ If necessary, bring the child to a health care facility for medical care.
      - □ Provide analgesia.
      - □ Cleanse with mild soap and tepid water (avoid excess friction).
      - □ Use antimicrobial ointment.
      - □ Apply dressing (nonadherent, hydrocolloid) if the burn area is irritated by clothing.
      - □ Educate the family to avoid using greasy lotions or butter on burns.
      - □ Educate the family to monitor for signs of infection.
      - □ Check immunization status for tetanus and determine the need for immunization.
  - ○ Moderate and major burns
    - ▪ Maintain airway and ventilation.
    - ▪ Provide humidified supplemental oxygen as prescribed.
    - ▪ Monitor vital signs.
    - ▪ Maintain cardiac output.
      - □ Initiate intravenous access.
      - □ Fluid replacement is important during the first 24 hr.
        - ▸ Isotonic crystalloid solutions, such as 0.9% sodium chloride or lactated Ringer's solution, are used during the early stage of burn recovery.
        - ▸ Colloid solutions, such as albumin or synthetic plasma expanders (Hespan), may be used after the first 24 hr of burn recovery.
        - ▸ Maintain urine output of 1 to 2 mL/kg/hr if the child weighs less than 30 kg (66 lb).
        - ▸ Maintain urine output of 30 mL/hr if the child weighs more than 30 kg (66 lb).
        - ▸ Be prepared to administer blood products as prescribed.

    ☐   Monitor for manifestations of septic shock.

        ▸   Alterations in sensorium (confusion)

        ▸   Increased capillary refill time

        ▸   Spiking fever

        ▸   Decreased bowel sounds

        ▸   Decreased urine output

    ☐   Notify the health care provider of findings.

- Pain Management

    ☐   Establish ongoing monitoring of pain and effectiveness of pain treatment.

    ☐   Avoid IM or subcutaneous injections.

    ☐   Use intravenous opioid analgesics, such as morphine sulfate, hydromorphone (Dilaudid), and fentanyl (Sublimaze).

    ☐   Monitor for respiratory depression when using opioid analgesics.

    ☐   Administer pain medications prior to dressing changes or procedures.

    ☐   Use nonpharmacologic methods for pain control (guided imagery, music therapy, therapeutic touch) to enhance the effects of analgesic medications and lead to more effective pain management.

- Prevent infection.

    ☐   Follow standard precautions when performing wound care.

    ☐   Restrict plants and flowers due to the risk of contact with pseudomonas.

    ☐   Restrict consumption of fresh fruits and vegetables.

    ☐   Limit visitors.

    ☐   Use reverse isolation if prescribed.

    ☐   Monitor for signs and symptoms of infection and report them to the provider.

    ☐   Use client-designated equipment, such as blood pressure cuffs and thermometers.

    ☐   Administer tetanus toxoid if indicated.

    ☐   Administer antibiotics if infection is present.

- Nutritional support

    ☐   Increase caloric intake to meet increased metabolic demands and prevent hypoglycemia.

    ☐   Increase protein intake to prevent tissue breakdown and promote healing.

    ☐   Provide enteral therapy or total parenteral nutrition (TPN) if necessary due to decreased gastrointestinal motility and increased caloric needs.

- Restoration of mobility
  - □ Maintain correct body alignment, splint extremities, and facilitate position changes to prevent contractures.
  - □ Maintain active and passive range of motion.
  - □ Assist with ambulation as soon as the child is stable.
  - □ Apply pressure dressings to prevent contractures and scarring.
  - □ Closely monitor areas at high risk for pressure sores (heels, sacrum, back of head).
- Psychological support
  - □ Provide developmentally appropriate support for the child.
  - □ Assist with coping.

- Medications
  - Topical agents

ANTIMICROBIAL CREAM	USES AND ADVANTAGES	DISADVANTAGES
Silver nitrate 0.5%	• Used on wounds that are exposed to air or with modified or occlusive dressings • May affect joint movement • Reduces fluid evaporation • Bacteriostatic against pseudomonas and staphylococcus • Inexpensive	• Does not penetrate eschar • Stains clothing and linen • Discolors the wound, making assessment difficult • Painful upon application
Silver sulfadiazine 1% (Silvadene)	• Used with occlusive dressings • Maintains joint mobility • Effective against gram-negative and gram-positive bacteria	• May cause transient neutropenia • Does not penetrate eschar • Painful to remove from the wound • Decreases granulocyte formation • Contraindicated for children who have allergies to sulfa

ANTIMICROBIAL CREAM	USES AND ADVANTAGES	DISADVANTAGES
Mafenide acetate (Sulfamylon)	• Used on wounds that are exposed to air • Used as a solution for occlusive dressings to keep the dressing moist • Penetrates eschar and goes into underlying tissues • Effective with electrical and infected wounds • Biostatic against gram-positive and gram-negative organisms	• Painful to apply and remove (cream) • May cause metabolic acidosis or hypercapnia • Inhibits wound healing • May cause hypersensitivity
Bacitracin	• Used on wounds that are exposed to air or with modified dressings • Maintains joint mobility • Bacteriostatic against gram-positive organisms • Painless and easy to apply	• Limited effectiveness on gram-negative organisms

- Morphine sulfate
  - Analgesia
  - Nursing Considerations
    - Administer IV just prior to the start of a procedure.
    - Monitor for respiratory depression.
    - Monitor pain relief.
  - Client Education
    - Educate the child and family on the safety precautions needed with opioid administration.
- Midazolam (Versed), fentanyl (Sublimaze), propofol (Diprivan), and nitrous oxide
  - Sedation and analgesia
  - Nursing Considerations
    - Administer IV just prior to the start of a procedure.
    - Monitor the need for sedation.
    - Monitor pain relief.
  - Client Education
    - Educate the child and the family about the safety precautions needed with opioid administration.

- Interdisciplinary Care

  ○ Initiate referral to a dietician, social worker, psychological counselor, or occupational/physical therapist if indicated.

  ○ Respiratory therapy to improve pulmonary function may also be needed.

- Therapeutic Procedures

  ○ Wound care

    ■ Nursing Actions

      □ Premedicate with an analgesic as prescribed prior to all wound care.

      □ Remove all previous dressings.

      □ Assess for odors, drainage, and discharge.

      □ Cleanse the wound as prescribed, removing all previous ointments (it is important to cleanse the wound thoroughly).

      □ Assist with debridement.

        ▸ Administer hydroxyzine (Vistaril) or diphenhydramine (Benadryl) for pruritus.

          ▷ Provide hydrotherapy (place the client in a warm tub of water or use warm running water, as if to shower) to cleanse the wound. Use once or twice a day for up to 20 min.

            ♦ Use mild soap or detergent to gently wash burns and then rinse with room-temperature water.

            ♦ Encourage the child to exercise his joints during the hydrotherapy treatment.

            ♦ Ensure that the child does not become hypothermic during the treatment.

        ▸ Enzymatic

          ▷ Apply a topical enzyme to break down and remove dead tissue.

          ▷ Apply a thin layer of topical antibiotic ointment as prescribed and cover with a dressing using surgical aseptic technique.

  ○ Skin coverings

    ■ Biologic skin coverings may be used to promote healing of large burns.

      □ Allograft (homograft) – Skin donated by human cadavers that is used for partial and full thickness burn wounds

      □ Xenograft – Obtained from animals, such as pigs, for partial thickness burn wounds

      □ Synthetic skin coverings – Used for partial thickness burn wounds

- Permanent skin coverings may be the treatment of choice for burns covering large areas of the body.
  - Autografts
    - Sheet graft – Sheet of skin used to cover the wound
    - Mesh graft – Sheet of skin placed in a mesher so skin graft has small slits in it; allows graft to cover larger areas of burn wound
    - Artificial skin – Synthetic product that is used for partial and full-thickness burn wounds (healing is faster)
    - Cultured epithelium – Epithelia cells cultured for use when grafting sites are limited
- Nursing Actions
  - Maintain immobilization of the graft site.
  - Elevate the extremity.
  - Provide wound care to the donor site.
  - Administer pain medication.
  - Monitor for signs of infection before and after skin coverings or grafts are applied.
    - Discoloration of unburned skin surrounding burn wound
    - Green color to subcutaneous fat
    - Degeneration of granulation tissue
    - Development of subeschar hemorrhage
    - Hyperventilation indicating systemic involvement of infection
    - Unstable body temperature
- Client Education
  - Instruct the child to keep the extremity elevated.
  - Instruct the family to report signs and symptoms of infection.

- Care After Discharge
  - Initiate a referral for home health nursing care.
  - Initiate a referral to occupational therapy for evaluation of the home environment and assistance to relearn how to perform ADLs.
  - Initiate a referral to social services for community support services.
  - Client Education
    - Instruct the child to continue to perform range-of-motion exercises and to work with a physical therapist to prevent contractures.
    - Provide instructions about how to assess the wound for infection and how to perform wound care.

(S)

- Teach age-appropriate safety measure for the home (covering electrical outlets, supervising children when in the bath, keeping irons out of reach of children, teaching the dangers of playing with matches).

- Teach the family to avoid sun exposure between 10 a.m. and 4 p.m, wear protective clothing, and apply sunscreen to prevent sunburn.

- Client Outcomes

    o The child will remain free of complications.

    o The child will be able to perform ADLs.

    o The child will verbalize an understanding of self care.

Complications

- Airway injury

    o Thermal injuries to the airway may result from steam or chemical inhalation, aspiration of scalding liquid, and explosion while breathing. If the injury took place in an enclosed space, carbon monoxide poisoning should be suspected.

    o Clinical manifestations may be delayed for 24 to 48 hr.

    o Signs and symptoms include progressive hoarseness, brassy cough, difficulty swallowing, drooling, increased secretions, adventitious breath sounds, and expiratory sounds that include audible wheezes, crowing, and stridor.

    o Nursing Actions

    - Maintain airway and ventilation, and provide oxygen as prescribed.

    o Client Education

    - Educate the child and family about airway management (deep breathing, coughing, elevating the head of the bed).

- Fluid and Electrolyte Imbalances

    o Nursing Actions

    - Assess fluid volume status.

        □ Daily weights

        □ Meticulous intake and output.

    - Monitor laboratory results and compare to previous data.

    - Administer IV fluids and electrolytes.

    o Client Education

    - Educate the child and family about signs and symptoms of electrolyte imbalances and the need to alert the provider immediately.

- Wound infections
  - Nursing Actions
    - Assess for discoloration, edema, odor, and drainage.
    - Assess for fluctuations in temperature and heart rate.
    - Obtain a wound culture.
    - Administer antibiotics as prescribed.
    - Monitor laboratory results, observing for anemia and infection.
    - Maintain surgical aseptic technique with dressing changes.
  - Client Education
    - Educate the child and family about the importance of infection control.

CHAPTER 32: BURNS

 Application Exercises

Scenario: A nurse in an emergency department is preparing to admit two children who were burned in a house fire. The first child is a 9-month-old infant with burns to her feet and legs. The second child is 3 years old with burns to his hands, arms, and anterior thorax. The cause of the house fire was due to the 3-year-old child playing with matches.

1. Why should the nurse be concerned about respiratory complications in the children?

2. What will be the focus of discharge teaching for the parents of these children?

3. A child is brought by his parent to the health clinic. The child has superficial partial thickness burns to his shoulders from sun exposure. Which of the following interventions is indicated for this type of burn?

    A. Start an IV infusion of dextrose 5% in lactated Ringer's solution.

    B. Apply cool, wet compresses.

    C. Wash the area using a soft-bristle brush.

    D. Administer morphine sulfate for pain relief.

4. A nurse is caring for a child admitted 48 hr ago with full thickness burns to 40% of her body. Which of the following are expected findings for this client? (Select all that apply.)

    _____   Hypotension

    _____   Tachycardia

    _____   Hypokalemia

    _____   Hypernatremia

    _____   Decreased hematocrit

CHAPTER 32: BURNS

 Application Exercises Answer Key

Scenario: A nurse in an emergency department is preparing to admit two children who were burned in a house fire. The first child is a 9-month-old infant with burns to her feet and legs. The second child is 3 years old with burns to his hands, arms, and anterior thorax. The cause of the house fire was due to the 3-year-old child playing with matches.

1. Why should the nurse be concerned about respiratory complications in the children?

> **Carbon monoxide poisoning is a risk for both children because the fire was contained in an enclosed room where carbon monoxide can easily build up. In addition, due to the 3-year-old child's burns, both immediate and ongoing assessment for thermal burns to the upper airway should be carried out. Findings of respiratory tract involvement, such as wheezing, increasing secretions, and adventitious breath sounds, may not be present during the initial assessment, but may be delayed for up to 48 hr after the burn injury.**

 NCLEX® Connection: Reduction of Risk Potential, Alterations in Body Systems

2. What will be the focus of discharge teaching for the parents of these children?

> **Discharge teaching will be focused on preventing further injuries and safeguarding the home. In addition, teaching related to wound care, identifying signs and symptoms of infection, and nutrition support (with a high-protein, high-calorie diet) should be carried out.**

 NCLEX® Connection: Health Promotion and Maintenance, Developmental Stages and Transitions

3. A child is brought by his parent to the health clinic. The child has superficial partial thickness burns to his shoulders from sun exposure. Which of the following interventions is indicated for this type of burn?

A. Start an IV infusion of dextrose 5% in lactated Ringer's solution.

B. Apply cool, wet compresses.

C. Wash the area using a soft-bristle brush.

D. Administer morphine sulfate for pain relief.

> **The child has sustained superficial partial thickness burns, which require the application of cool compresses to minimize the burning sensation. IV fluid is not necessary in a superficial burn injury. Scrubbing a superficial partial thickness burn is unnecessary unless debris is imbedded; however, gentle cleansing with tepid water may be indicated. Morphine sulfate is indicated for major burns; in this case, cool compresses should ease the initial pain.**

 NCLEX® Connection: Physiological Adaptation, Illness Management

4. A nurse is caring for a child admitted 48 hr ago with full thickness burns to 40% of her body. Which of the following are expected findings for this client? (Select all that apply.)

    __X__   **Hypotension**

    __X__   **Tachycardia**

    _____   Hypokalemia

    _____   Hypernatremia

    _____   Decreased hematocrit

A child who has full thickness burns to 40% of her body may experience burn hypovolemia and shock. Immediately after the burn injury, fluids shift from the intracellular space into the interstitial space. Fluid leaks from the capillaries at the site of the burn and throughout the body. Due to the loss of fluids in the intracellular space and the intravascular space, the client experiences hypovolemia, resulting in hypotension and tachycardia. Leakage of fluid from the intracellular space causes hyperkalemia. Sodium is retained in the interstitial space, leading to hyponatremia. Due to hypovolemia, hematocrit is elevated.

Ⓝ NCLEX® Connection: Physiological Adaptation, Fluid and Electrolyte Imbalances

UNIT 2: NURSING CARE OF CHILDREN WITH SYSTEM DISORDERS

Section: Endocrine Disorders

- Diabetes Mellitus
- Growth Hormone Deficiency

NCLEX® CONNECTIONS

When reviewing the chapters in this section, keep in mind the relevant sections of the NCLEX® outline, in particular:

CLIENT NEEDS: PHARMACOLOGICAL AND PARENTERAL THERAPIES

Relevant topics/tasks include:
- Adverse Effects/ Contraindications/Side Effects/Interactions
  - Notify the provider of side effects, adverse effects, and contraindications of medications and parenteral therapy.
- Expected Actions/Outcomes
  - Evaluate therapeutic effect of medications.
- Medication Administration
  - Titrate dosage of medication based on assessment and ordered parameters.

CLIENT NEEDS: REDUCTION OF RISK POTENTIAL

Relevant topics/tasks include:
- Diagnostic Tests
  - Evaluate the results of diagnostic testing and intervene as needed.
- System Specific Assessment
  - Assess the client for signs of hypoglycemia or hyperglycemia.
- Therapeutic Procedures
  - Educate the client about treatments and procedures.

CLIENT NEEDS: PHYSIOLOGICAL ADAPTATION

Relevant topics/tasks include:
- Alterations in Body Systems
  - Educate the client about managing health problems.
- Fluid and Electrolyte Imbalances
  - Evaluate the client's response to interventions to correct fluid or electrolyte imbalance.
- Illness Management
  - Apply knowledge of client pathophysiology to illness management.

UNIT 2	NURSING CARE OF CHILDREN WITH SYSTEM DISORDERS
Section	Endocrine Disorders
Chapter 33	Diabetes Mellitus

 Overview

- Diabetes mellitus is characterized by chronic hyperglycemia due to problems with insulin secretion and/or the effectiveness of endogenous insulin (insulin resistance).

- Diabetes mellitus is a contributing factor for the development of cardiovascular disease, hypertension, renal failure, blindness, and stroke as individuals age.

Assessment

- Risk Factors

   ○ Genetics can predispose a person to the occurrence of type 1 and type 2 diabetes mellitus.

   ○ Toxins and viruses can predispose an individual to diabetes by destroying the beta cells, leading to type 1 diabetes mellitus.

   ○ Obesity, physical inactivity, high triglycerides (greater than 250 mg/dL), and hypertension may lead to the development of insulin resistance and type 2 diabetes mellitus.

- Subjective and Objective Data

   ○ Blood glucose alterations

      ▪ Hypoglycemia – Blood glucose level less than 70 mg/dL

AUTONOMIC NERVOUS SYSTEM RESPONSES RAPID ONSET	IMPAIRED CEREBRAL FUNCTION GRADUAL ONSET
• Hunger, lightheadedness, and shakiness • Nausea • Anxiety and irritability • Pale, cool skin • Diaphoresis • Irritability • Normal or shallow respirations • Tachycardia and palpitations	• Strange or unusual feelings • Decreasing level of consciousness • Difficulty in thinking and inability to concentrate • Change in emotional behavior • Slurred speech • Headache and blurred vision • Seizures leading to coma

- Hyperglycemia – Blood glucose levels usually greater than 250 mg/dL
  - Thirst
  - Frequent urination
  - Hunger
  - Skin that is warm, dry, and flushed with poor turgor
  - Dry mucous membranes
  - Soft eyeballs
  - Weakness
  - Malaise
  - Rapid, weak pulse; hypotension
  - Rapid, deep respirations with acetone/fruity odor due to ketones (Kussmaul respirations)

- Laboratory Tests
  - Diagnostic criteria for diabetes includes two findings (on separate days) of one of the following:
    - Symptoms of diabetes plus a casual plasma glucose concentration of greater than 200 mg/dL (without regard to time since last meal)
    - A fasting blood glucose greater than 126 mg/dL
    - A 2-hour glucose of greater than 200 mg/dL with an oral glucose tolerance test
  - Fasting blood glucose
    - Client Education
      - Ensure that the child has fasted (no food or drink other than water) for 8 hr prior to the blood draw. Antidiabetic medications should be postponed until after the level is drawn.
  - Oral glucose tolerance test
    - Client Education
      - Instruct the client to consume a balanced diet for the 3 days prior to the test. Then instruct the client to fast for the 10 to 12 hr prior to the test. A fasting blood glucose level is drawn at the start of the test. The client is then instructed to consume a specified amount of glucose. Blood glucose levels are drawn every 30 min for 2 hr. The child must be assessed for hypoglycemia throughout the procedure.
  - Glycosylated hemoglobin (HbA1c)
    - The expected reference range is 4% to 6%, but an acceptable target for children who have diabetes may be 6.5% to 8% with a total target goal of less than 7%.

- o Diagnostic Procedures
  - Self-monitored blood glucose (SMBG)
    - □ Follow or ensure that the child follows the proper procedure for blood sample collection and use of a glucose meter. Supplemental short-acting insulin may be prescribed for elevated pre-meal glucose levels.
    - □ Client Education
      - ▸ Instruct the child to check the accuracy of the strips with the control solution provided.
      - ▸ Advise the child to keep a record of the SMBG that includes time, date, serum glucose level, insulin dose, food intake, and other events that may alter glucose metabolism, such as activity level or illness.

Collaborative Care

- Nursing Care
  - o Monitor the following:
    - Blood glucose levels and factors affecting levels (other medications)
    - Intake and output and weight
    - Skin integrity and healing status of any wounds, paying close attention to the feet and folds of the skin
    - Sensory alterations (tingling, numbness)
    - Visual alterations
    - Presence of recurrent infections
    - Dietary practices
    - Exercise patterns
    - The child's proficiency at self-monitoring blood glucose
    - The child's proficiency at self-administering medication
  - o Follow agency policy for nail care. Some protocols allow for trimming toenails straight across with clippers and filing edges with a nail file. If clippers or scissors are contraindicated, the child should file the nails straight across.
  - o Teach proper foot care.
    - Inspect feet daily. Wash feet daily with mild soap and warm water.
    - Pat feet dry gently, especially between the toes.
    - Use mild foot powder (powder with cornstarch) on sweaty feet.
    - Do not use commercial remedies for the removal of calluses or corns.
    - Perform nail care after a bath/shower if possible.
    - Separate overlapping toes with cotton or lambs' wool.

- Avoid open-toe, open-heel shoes. Leather shoes are preferred to plastic ones. Wear slippers with soles. Do not go barefoot. Shake out shoes before putting them on.

- Wear clean, absorbent socks or stockings that are made of cotton or wool and have not been mended.

- Do not use hot water bottles or heating pads to warm feet. Wear socks for warmth.

- Avoid prolonged sitting, standing, and crossing of legs.

○ Teach the child to cleanse cuts with warm water and mild soap, gently dry, and apply a dry dressing. Instruct the child and parents to monitor healing and to seek intervention promptly.

○ Provide nutritional guidelines.

- Plan meals to achieve appropriate timing of food intake, activity, onset, and peak of insulin. Calories and food composition should be similar each day.

- Eat at regular intervals and do not skip meals.

- Count grams of carbohydrates consumed.

- Recognize that 15 g of carbohydrates are equal to 1 carbohydrate exchange.

- Restrict calories and increase physical activity as appropriate to facilitate weight loss (for children who are obese or to prevent obesity).

- Include fiber in the diet to increase carbohydrate metabolism and to help control cholesterol levels.

- Avoid concentrated sweets.

- Use artificial sweeteners.

- Keep fat content below 30% of the total caloric intake.

○ Teach the child appropriate techniques for SMBG, including obtaining blood samples, recording and responding to results, and correctly handling supplies and equipment.

○ Teach the child guidelines to follow when sick.

- Monitor blood glucose levels every 3 to 4 hr.

- Continue to take insulin or oral antidiabetic agents.

- Consume 4 oz of sugar-free, non-caffeinated liquid every 0.5 hr to prevent dehydration.

- Meet carbohydrate needs by eating soft foods if possible. If not, consume liquids that are equal to the usual carbohydrate content.

- Test urine for ketones and report if abnormal (should be negative to small).

- Rest.

- Call the health care provider if:

  □ Blood glucose is higher than 240 mg/dL.

  □ Fever higher than 38.9° C (102° F), fever does not respond to acetaminophen (Tylenol), or fever lasts more than 12 hr.

- □ Disorientation or confusion occurs.
- □ Rapid breathing is experienced.
- □ Vomiting occurs more than once.
- □ Diarrhea occurs more than five times or for longer than 24 hr.
- □ Liquids cannot be tolerated.
- □ Illness lasts longer than 2 days.

○ Teach the child measures to take in response to signs and symptoms of hypoglycemia, (shakiness, diaphoresis, anxiety, nervousness, chills, nausea, headache, weakness, confusion).

- ■ Check blood glucose levels.

- ■ Follow guidelines outlined by the health care provider/diabetes educator. Guidelines may include:
  - □ Treat with 15 to 20 g carbohydrates.
  - □ Recheck blood glucose in 15 min.
  - □ If still low (less than 70 mg/dL), give 15 to 20 g more of carbohydrates.
    - ▸ Examples – 4 oz orange juice, 2 oz grape juice, 8 oz milk, glucose tablets per manufacturer's suggestion to equal 15 g
  - □ Recheck blood glucose in 15 min.
  - □ If blood glucose is within normal limits, take 7 g protein (if the next meal is more than an hour away).
    - ▸ Examples – 1 oz of cheese (1 string cheese), 2 tablespoons of peanut butter, or 8 oz of milk

- ■ If the child is unconscious or unable to swallow, administer glucagon SC or IM and notify the health care provider. Administer liquid with glucose as soon as tolerated. Watch for vomiting and take precaution against aspiration.

○ Teach the child and parents signs and symptoms of hyperglycemia (hot, dry skin and fruity breath) and measures to take in response to hyperglycemia.

- ■ Encourage oral fluid intake.
- ■ Administer insulin as prescribed.
- ■ Restrict exercise when blood glucose levels are greater than 250 mg/dL.
- ■ Test urine for ketones and report if findings are abnormal.
- ■ Consult the health care provider if symptoms progress.

○ Encourage the child to wear a medical identification wristband.

- Medications

  - Most children are on an insulin regimen that frequently consists of more than one type of insulin (rapid, short, intermediate, and/or long acting). Insulin given in this manner is administered one or more times per day and based on a child's blood glucose level.

  - Some children are given an insulin pump, which is a small pump that is worn externally, contains insulin, and delivers insulin as programmed via a needle inserted into the subcutaneous tissue. The catheter should be changed at least every 3 days.

  - The rate of onset, peak, and duration of action varies for each different type of insulin.

TYPE	TRADE NAME	ONSET	PEAK	DURATION
Rapid acting	Insulin lispro (Humalog)	Less than 15 min	0.5 to 1 hr	3 to 4 hr
Short acting	Regular insulin (Humulin R)	0.5 to 1 hr	2 to 3 hr	5 to 7 hr
Intermediate acting	NPH insulin (Humulin N)	1 to 2 hr	4 to 12 hr	18 to 24 hr
Long acting	Insulin glargine (Lantus)	1 hr	none	10.4 to 24 hr

- Nursing Considerations

  - Observe the child perform self-administration of insulin and offer additional instruction as indicated.

  - Do not mix insulin glargine (Lantus) with other insulins due to incompatibility.

- Client Education

  - Provide information regarding self-administration of insulin.

    - Rotate injection sites (prevent lipohypertrophy) within one anatomic site (prevent day-to-day changes in absorption rates).

    - Inject at a 90° angle (45° angle if thin). Aspiration for blood is not necessary.

    - When mixing a rapid- or short-acting insulin with a longer-acting insulin, draw up the shorter-acting insulin into the syringe first and then the longer-acting insulin (this reduces the risk of introducing the longer-acting insulin into the vial of the shorter-acting insulin).

- Interdisciplinary Care

  - Refer the child to a diabetes educator for comprehensive education in diabetes management.

- Client Outcomes

  o The child will have blood glucose levels within an acceptable range.

  o The child will be able to self-administer insulin

  o The child will be able to monitor for complications and intervene as necessary.

  o The child will maintain adequate dietary intake to support growth and development.

Complications

- Diabetic ketoacidosis (DKA)

  o DKA is an acute, life-threatening condition characterized by hyperglycemia (greater than 300 mg/dL), resulting in the breakdown of body fat for energy and an accumulation of ketones in the blood and urine. The onset is rapid, and the mortality rate is high.

  o Causes of DKA include insufficient insulin (usually failure to take the appropriate dose), acute stress (as from trauma or surgery), and poor management of acute illness.

  o Nursing Actions

    ▪ Assess subjective and objective data for a blood glucose level greater than 300 mg/dL.

      □ Reports of nausea, vomiting, and/or abdominal pain (DKA/metabolic acidosis)

      □ Reports of frequent urination, thirst, and hunger

      □ Reports of confusion

      □ Change in mental status

      □ Signs of dehydration (e.g., dry mucous membranes, weight loss, sunken eyeballs resulting from fluid loss such as polyuria)

      □ Kussmaul respiration pattern, rapid and deep respirations, fruity scent to the breath (DKA/metabolic acidosis)

    ▪ Provide rapid isotonic fluid (0.9% sodium chloride) replacement to maintain perfusion to vital organs. Often large quantities are required to replace losses. Monitor the child for evidence of fluid volume excess.

    ▪ Follow with a hypotonic fluid (0.45% sodium chloride) to continue replacing losses to total body fluid.

    ▪ When serum glucose levels approach 250 mg/dL, add glucose to IV fluids to minimize the risk of cerebral edema associated with drastic changes in serum osmolality.

      □ Administer Regular insulin 0.1 unit/kg as an IV bolus dose and then follow with a continuous intravenous infusion of regular insulin at 0.1 unit/kg/hr.

    ▪ Monitor glucose levels hourly.

- Monitor serum potassium levels. Potassium levels will initially be elevated. With insulin therapy, potassium will shift into cells and the child will need to be monitored for hypokalemia. Provide potassium replacement therapy in all replacement IV fluids as indicated by lab values. Make sure urinary output is adequate before administering potassium.

- Administer sodium bicarbonate by slow IV infusion for severe acidosis (pH of less than 7.0). Monitor potassium levels because a correction of acidosis that occurs too quickly may lead to hypokalemia.

  o Client Education

  - Reinforce instructions to manage blood glucose levels.

- Hypoglycemia

  o Decreased level of consciousness

  o Nursing Actions

  - Follow facility protocol for hypoglycemia.

  - Administer 50% glucose IV bolus for unresponsive clients.

  - Follow with a snack of 15 to 20 g of carbohydrates as tolerated.

  - Monitor blood glucose levels every hour.

CHAPTER 33: DIABETES MELLITUS

 Application Exercises

1. A nurse is reviewing sick day management with a parent of a child who has type 1 diabetes mellitus. Which of the following should the nurse include in the teaching? (Select all that apply.)

_____ Monitor blood glucose levels every 3 hr.

_____ Discontinue taking insulin until feeling better.

_____ Drink 8 oz of fruit juice every hour.

_____ Test urine for ketones.

_____ Call the health care provider if blood glucose is greater than 240 mg/dL.

2. Place the following steps used to treat hypoglycemia detected by low blood glucose levels in the correct order.

_____ Recheck blood glucose in 15 min.

_____ Eat 15 g of carbohydrates.

_____ If still low, eat 15 g more of carbohydrates.

_____ Stop activity and sit down.

_____ Recheck blood glucose in 15 min.

3. A child who has type 1 diabetes mellitus is taking twice-daily insulin injections consisting of a combination of insulin lispro (Humalog) and NPH insulin. The child eats breakfast at 8 a.m. daily. At what time should the child inject the morning insulin? Provide a rationale.

Scenario: A nurse is conducting a health promotion class for a group of adolescents who have type 1 diabetes mellitus.

4. Which of the following should the nurse include when identifying causes of a hypoglycemic reaction? (Select all that apply.)

_____ Urinary tract infection

_____ Skipping breakfast

_____ Exercising strenuously

_____ Taking an extra dose of insulin

_____ Stress

5. Which of the following should the nurse include when instructing the adolescents about signs and symptoms related to hypoglycemia? (Select all that apply.)

_____ Frequent urination

_____ Increased energy level

_____ Nausea

_____ Irritability

_____ Sweating and pallor

_____ Deep, rapid, and labored respirations

CHAPTER 33: DIABETES MELLITUS

 Application Exercises Answer Key

1. A nurse is reviewing sick day management with a parent of a child who has type 1 diabetes mellitus. Which of the following should the nurse include in the teaching? (Select all that apply.)

   X   **Monitor blood glucose levels every 3 hr.**

   _____   Discontinue taking insulin until feeling better.

   _____   Drink 8 oz of fruit juice every hour.

   X   **Test urine for ketones.**

   X   **Call the health care provider if blood glucose is greater than 240 mg/dL.**

   During acute illness, it is very important to check blood glucose levels frequently to identify hyperglycemia. Urine should be checked for ketones because the presence of ketones is an indication that proteins and fats are being broken down for energy and this can result in diabetic ketoacidosis. The health care provider should be notified if the blood glucose level exceeds 240 mg/dL and if ketones are present in the urine, as this may require a change in insulin dosage. Insulin should not be discontinued because acute illness results in hyperglycemia, even if intake has decreased. Eight ounces of sugar-free, noncaffeinated liquid should be consumed to prevent dehydration. Fruit juice is high in carbohydrates and can contribute to hyperglycemia.

    NCLEX® Connection: Physiological Adaptation, Illness Management

2. Place the following steps used to treat hypoglycemia detected by low blood glucose levels in the correct order.

   3   Recheck blood glucose in 15 min.

   2   Eat 15 g of carbohydrates.

   4   If still low, eat 15 g more of carbohydrates.

   1   Stop activity and sit down.

   5   Recheck blood glucose in 15 min.

    NCLEX® Connection: Reduction of Risk Potential, System Specific Assessment

3. A child who has type 1 diabetes mellitus is taking twice-daily insulin injections consisting of a combination of insulin lispro (Humalog) and NPH insulin. The child eats breakfast at 8 a.m. daily. At what time should the child inject the morning insulin? Provide a rationale.

   The child should inject the insulin between 7:45 and 7:50 a.m. because the onset of action of insulin lispro is within 10 to 15 min after the injection.

    NCLEX® Connection: Pharmacological and Parenteral Therapies, Expected Actions/Outcomes

Scenario: A nurse is conducting a health promotion class for a group of adolescents who have type 1 diabetes mellitus.

4. Which of the following should the nurse include when identifying causes of a hypoglycemic reaction? (Select all that apply.)

_____ Urinary tract infection

__X__ **Skipping breakfast**

__X__ **Exercising strenuously**

__X__ **Taking an extra dose of insulin**

_____ Stress

Skipping a meal (especially if the usual insulin dose is taken), exercising strenuously, and taking an extra dose of insulin may cause hypoglycemia. Infections and stress may cause hyperglycemia.

 NCLEX® Connection: Physiological Adaptation, Pathophysiology

5. Which of the following should the nurse include when instructing the adolescents about signs and symptoms related to hypoglycemia? (Select all that apply.)

_____ Frequent urination

_____ Increased energy level

__X__ **Nausea**

__X__ **Irritability**

__X__ **Sweating and pallor**

_____ Deep, rapid, and labored respirations

Signs and symptoms of hypoglycemia include nausea, nervousness and irritability, and sweatiness with pale skin. Frequent urination and deep, rapid, labored respirations (Kussmaul respirations) are signs of hyperglycemia. Increased energy level is not seen in either hypoglycemia or hyperglycemia.

 NCLEX® Connection: Reduction of Risk Potential, System Specific Assessment

UNIT 2	NURSING CARE OF CHILDREN WITH SYSTEM DISORDERS
Section	Endocrine Disorders
Chapter 34	Growth Hormone Deficiency

Overview

- Human growth hormone (GH), somatotropin, is a naturally occurring substance that is secreted by the pituitary gland.

- GH is important for normal growth, development, and cellular metabolism.

- A deficiency in GH prevents somatic growth throughout the body.

- Other hormones that work with GH to control metabolic processes include adrenocorticotropic hormone (ACTH), thyroid stimulating hormone (TSH), and the gonadotropins (follicle-stimulating hormone [FSH] and luteinizing hormone [LH]).

- Hypopituitarism is the diminished or deficient secretion of pituitary hormones (primarily GH). Consequences of the condition depend on the degree of the deficiency.

- Achondroplasia is a genetic disorder that causes nonproportional (short-limbed) dwarfism.

  - Besides short stature, achondroplasia causes a relatively long trunk with shortened upper parts of arms and legs, large head with prominent forehead, flattened bridge of the nose, shortened hands and fingers, and decreased muscle tone.

  - Children who have achondroplasia tend to have physical disabilities, such as scoliosis, breathing difficulties (due to small chests), and lower back pain.

  - Achondroplasia is not successfully treated with GH.

Assessment

- Risk Factors

  - Structural factors (tumors, trauma, structural defects, surgery)

  - Heredity disorders

  - Other pituitary hormone deficiencies (deficiencies of TSH or ACTH)

  - Most often, GH deficiencies are idiopathic.

- Subjective Data

  - Reports of lack of activity

- Objective Data
  - Physical Assessment Findings
    - Short stature with growth during the first year within expected percentile ranges
      - A decrease in percentiles usually starts by the second year and may be as low as the fifth percentile.
      - Height is usually more delayed than weight, which appears appropriate.
    - Normal skeletal proportions
    - Delayed eruption of permanent teeth
    - Underdeveloped jaw, resulting in overcrowding of teeth
  - Laboratory Tests
    - Plasma insulin-like growth factor-1 (IGF-1) and IGF binding protein-3 (IGFBP-3) levels
      - Further evaluation is indicated if the values are 1 standard deviation below the mean for age and gender.
    - Blood studies to determine hypothyroidism, hypoadrenalism, and hypoaldosteronism
    - Radioimmunoassays to determine GH levels
  - Nursing Actions
    - Collect the appropriate amount of blood for the test.
    - Explain the laboratory procedure to the family and child.
  - Client Education
    - The child should fast the night before the test.
  - Diagnostic Procedures
    - GH stimulation
      - GH stimulation testing is generally done for children who have a low level of IGF-1 and IGFBP3 and a poor growth.
      - GH secretion is stimulated by administering glucose or having the child exercise. Blood samples are then taken at set time intervals to measure the release of GH.
    - Radiologic assessments
      - Assess the child's skeletal maturity by comparing epiphyseal centers on an x-ray to age-appropriate published standards.
      - Perform a general skeletal survey in children under 3 years of age, or survey the hands and wrists in older children. This will provide information about growth as well as epiphyseal function.
      - Nursing Actions
        - Assist in positioning the child.

- Computed tomographic (CT) scanning, magnetic resonance imaging (MRI), and skull x-rays
  - Used to identify tumors or other structural defects
  - Nursing Actions
    - Monitor the child during the procedure.
    - Sedate the child, if prescribed.
  - Client Education
    - Provide emotional support.
- Evaluation of the growth curve
  - Nursing Actions
    - Accurately obtain and plot height and weight measurements.
    - Assess height velocity or height over time.
    - Determine height-to-weight relationship.
    - Project target height in context of genetic potential.

Collaborative Care

- Nursing Care
  - The child's height and weight are measured and marked on a growth chart as part of every visit to the primary care provider.
    - The height of a child is more affected than weight. Bone age usually matches height age.
    - Measure children who are fewer than 3 years of age at least every 6 months and children older than 3 years of age every year.
  - Assess and monitor effectiveness of GH replacement. GH is supplied by recombinant DNA technology.
  - Administer other hormone replacements (thyroid hormone) if prescribed.
  - Provide support to the child and family regarding psychosocial concerns (altered body image, depression). Reassure the child and family that there are no cognitive delays or deficits.
  - Stress the importance of maintaining realistic expectations based on the child's age and abilities.

- Medications

    o Somatropin

        - Used as a human growth hormone that is a replacement for deficiency in growth hormones

        - Nursing Considerations

            □ Administer the medication via subcutaneous injections.

            □ Use cautiously in children who are receiving insulin.

- Interdisciplinary Care

    o Consult with an endocrinologist.

    o Psychological counseling may be indicated to help the child and family cope during this period of time.

- Care After Discharge

    o Nursing Actions

        - Inform the child and parents that there should not be any significant side effects when GH replacement therapy is used in appropriate doses for GH deficiency.

        - Inform the child and parents that GH will assist with muscle growth and help improve self-esteem.

    o Client Education

        - Teach the child and parents how to administer medication by subcutaneous injection for home use.

        - Instruct the child and parents that GH should be administered 6 to 7 days a week.

        - Inform the child and parents that GH is usually continued until bone maturation takes place. This may be 16 years of age or older for boys and 14 years of age or older for girls.

        - Encourage the child and family to seek evaluation during early adulthood. Children with GH deficiency in childhood should be evaluated in early adulthood to determine the need for continued replacement therapy.

- Client Outcomes

    o The child will show improvement in growth patterns.

    o The child will show improvement in self-esteem.

Complications

- GH deficiency without hormone replacement may result in disruption of vertical growth, delayed epiphyseal closure, retarded bone age, delayed sexual development, and premature aging later in life.

CHAPTER 34: GROWTH HORMONE DEFICIENCY

 Application Exercises

1. Match the diagnostic tests below with their findings related to growth disorders.

_____	X-rays of wrist and hand	A. Determines GH level
_____	IGF-1	B. Identifies pituitary gland tumor
_____	MRI	C. Determines bone age
_____	GH stimulation	D. Measures effect of glucose on GH

2. A parent of a school-age child with GH deficiency asks the nurse how long his son will need to take injections for his growth delay. Which of the following responses by the nurse is appropriate?

A. "Injections are usually continued until age 10 for girls and age 12 for boys."

B. "Injections need to continue until your child reaches the fifth percentile on the growth chart."

C. "Injections should be continued until bone maturation is complete, usually between 14 and 16 years of age."

D. "The injections will need to be administered throughout your child's entire life."

CHAPTER 34: GROWTH HORMONE DEFICIENCY

(A) Application Exercises Answer Key

1. Match the diagnostic tests below with their findings related to growth disorders.

   C   X-rays of wrist and hand   A. Determines GH level

   A   IGF-1   B. Identifies pituitary gland tumor

   B   MRI   C. Determines bone age

   D   GH stimulation   D. Measures effect of glucose on GH

(N) **NCLEX® Connection: Reduction of Risk Potential, Diagnostic Tests**

2. A parent of a school-age child with GH deficiency asks the nurse how long his son will need to take injections for his growth delay. Which of the following responses by the nurse is appropriate?

A. "Injections are usually continued until age 10 for girls and age 12 for boys."

B. "Injections need to continue until your child reaches the fifth percentile on the growth chart."

C. "Injections should be continued until bone maturation is complete, usually between 14 and 16 years of age."

D. "The injections will need to be administered throughout your child's entire life."

GH replacement continues until the endocrinologist determines that the child's bone maturation is complete. This usually occurs around age 14 for girls and age 16 for boys. However, all children should be assessed on an individual basis to determine adequate growth. Percentiles of growth on the growth chart are not used to determine when therapy is complete. GH treatments should not continue after the child's bone growth is complete. Nonetheless, the child with GH deficiency should be re-evaluated in young adulthood to determine the need for GH replacement.

(N) **NCLEX® Connection: Pharmacological and Parenteral Therapies, Expected Actions/ Outcomes**

UNIT 2: NURSING CARE OF CHILDREN WITH SYSTEM DISORDERS

Section: Immune and Infectious Disorders

- Immunizations
- Communicable Diseases
- Acute Otitis Media
- HIV/AIDS

NCLEX® CONNECTIONS
When reviewing the chapters in this section, keep in mind the relevant sections of the NCLEX® outline, in particular:

CLIENT NEEDS: SAFETY AND INFECTION CONTROL	CLIENT NEEDS: HEALTH PROMOTION AND MAINTENANCE	CLIENT NEEDS: PHYSIOLOGICAL ADAPTATION

Relevant topics/tasks include:
- Standard Precautions/Transmission-Based Precautions/Surgical Asepsis
  ○ Understand communicable diseases and the modes of organism transmission.
  ○ Apply principles of infection control standard precautions.
  ○ Utilize appropriate precautions for immunocompromised clients.
	Relevant topics/tasks include:
	- Health and Wellness
	  ○ Assess the client's knowledge of immunization schedules and educate as needed.
	- Health Promotion/Disease Prevention
	  ○ Provide information about healthy behaviors and health promotion/maintenance recommendations.
		Relevant topics/tasks include:
		- Alterations in Body Systems
		  ○ Identify signs, symptoms and incubation periods of infectious diseases.
		- Pathophysiology
		  ○ Identify pathophysiology related to an acute or chronic condition.
		- Unexpected Response to Therapies
		  ○ Recognize signs and symptoms of complications and intervene appropriately when providing client care.

UNIT 2	NURSING CARE OF CHILDREN WITH SYSTEM DISORDERS
Section	Immune and Infectious Disorders

Chapter 35	Immunizations

Overview

- Administration of a vaccine causes production of antibodies that prevent illness from a specific microbe.

- Active immunity is long-term and occurs over time as the body produces antibodies in response to an infection or to an immunization and becomes immune as a result of the primary immune response.

- Passive immunity is temporary and occurs after immunization with antibodies in the form of immune globulins for individuals who require immediate protection against a disease to which exposure has already occurred, when passed between a mother and her fetus, and when transmitted to an infant through breast milk.

- Most immunizations consist of killed vaccines or live, attenuated, or weakened viruses.

MEDICATION CLASSIFICATION: VACCINATIONS

- Childhood Vaccinations (To see a listing of vaccinations by age, go to the Web site of the Centers for Disease Control [http://www.cdc.gov] for updates.)

    o Diphtheria and tetanus toxoids and acellular pertussis vaccine (DTaP) – Doses at 2, 4, 6, and 15 to 18 months and again at 4 to 6 years of age

    o Tetanus and diphtheria toxoids and pertussis vaccine (DTaP) – One dose at 11 to 12 years of age

    o Tetanus and diphtheria (Td) booster – One dose every 10 years following DTaP

    o *Haemophilus influenza* type b (Hib) – Doses at 2, 4, 6, and at 12 to 15 months

    o Rotavirus (RV) oral vaccine – Available in two formulations

        ■ RotaTeq requires three doses beginning at 6 weeks of age, with subsequent doses 4 to 10 weeks apart. RotaTeq vaccination should be completed before 32 weeks of age. Vaccination should not be initiated for infants 15 weeks of age or older.

        ■ Rotarix requires 2 doses beginning at 6 weeks of age with the next dose 4 weeks later. All doses should be completed by 8 months of age.

    o Inactivated poliovirus vaccine (IPV) – Doses at 2, 4, and 6 to 18 months and again at 4 to 6 years

- o Measles, mumps, and rubella vaccine (MMR) – Doses at 12 to 15 months and at 4 to 6 years

- o Varicella vaccine – One dose at 12 to 15 months and again at 4 to 6 years or 2 doses administered 4 weeks apart if administered after age 13

- o Pneumococcal conjugate vaccine (PCV) – Doses at 2, 4, 6, and 12 to 15 months

- o Hepatitis A (Hep A) – Two doses 6 months apart after 12 months of age

- o Hepatitis B (Hep B) – Within 12 hr after birth with additional doses at 1 to 2 months and 6 to 18 months of age

- o Seasonal influenza vaccine – Annually beginning at 6 months, the trivalent inactivated influenza vaccine (TIV) should be given. Starting at 2 years of age, the live attenuated influenza vaccine (LAIV) (nasal spray) should be used. October through November is the ideal time, but December is acceptable.

- o Meningococcal vaccine (MCV4) – One dose at 11 to 12 years of age (earlier if specific risk factors are present)

- o Human Papilloma Virus (HPV2, HPV4) – Three doses should be given over a 6-month interval for females at 11 to 12 years of age (minimum age is 9 years). The second dose should be administered 2 months after the first dose, and the third dose should be administered 6 months after the first dose. HPV4 may be given to males starting at age 9 years of age.

Purpose

- • Expected Pharmacological Action

  - o Immunizations produce antibodies that provide active immunity. Immunizations may take months to have an effect, but they confer long-lasting protection against infectious diseases.

- • Therapeutic Uses

  - o Eradication of infectious diseases (polio, smallpox)

  - o Prevention of childhood and adult infectious diseases and their complications (measles, diphtheria, mumps, rubella, tetanus, *H. influenza*)

(S) Complications/Contraindications/Precautions

- • An anaphylactic reaction to a vaccine is a contraindication for receiving further doses of that vaccine.

- • An anaphylactic reaction to a vaccine is a contraindication for using other vaccines containing that substance.

- • Contraindications to all immunizations include severe allergies to any component of a vaccine.

- • Moderate or severe illnesses with or without fever are contraindications to receiving immunizations. With acute febrile illness, vaccination is deferred until symptoms resolve. The common cold and other minor illnesses are not contraindications.

- Contraindications to vaccinations require health care providers to analyze data and weigh the risks that come with vaccinating or not vaccinating.

- Immunocompromised individuals are defined by the Centers for Disease Control (CDC) as those with hematologic or solid tumors, congenital immunodeficiency, or long-term immunosuppressive therapy, including corticosteroids.

IMMUNIZATION	SIDE EFFECTS	CONTRAINDICATIONS
DTaP	• Local reaction at the injection site • Fever and irritability • Crying that cannot be consoled and lasts up to 3 hr • Seizures • Rare – Acute encephalopathy	• An occurrence of encephalopathy 7 days after the administration of the immunization • An occurrence of seizures within 3 days of the immunization • A history of uncontrollable, inconsolable crying after receiving a prior vaccination (may have lasted more than 3 hr and occurred within 48 hr of vaccination)
Hib	• Mild local reactions and a low grade fever • Rare – Fever (temperature greater than 38.5° C [101.3° F]), vomiting, and crying	
RV		• Diarrhea and vomiting (in infants) • Use caution with children who are immunocompromised (with HIV infection or from medication administration).
IPV	• Local reaction at injection site • Possible allergic reaction in children allergic to streptomycin, neomycin, or bacitracin (These medications are contained in the vaccine in small amounts.) • Rare – Vaccine-associated paralytic poliomyelitis	• Allergy to neomycin (Mycifradin) and/or streptomycin and polymyxin B • Pregnancy

IMMUNIZATION	SIDE EFFECTS	CONTRAINDICATIONS
MMR	• Local reactions (rash; fever; swollen glands in cheeks, in the neck, and under the jaw) • Possibility of joint pain lasting for days to weeks • Risk for anaphylaxis and thrombocytopenia	• Pregnancy • Allergy to gelatin and neomycin • History of thrombocytopenia or thrombocytopenic purpura • Immunosuppression (with HIV infection or from medication administration) • Recent transfusion with blood products or immunoglobulins
Varicella vaccine	• Varicella-like rash that is local or generalized (vesicles on the body)	• Pregnancy • Cancers of blood and lymphatic system • Allergy to gelatin neomycin • Immunosuppression (with HIV or from medication administration)
PCV	• Mild local reactions, fever, and no serious adverse effects	• Pregnancy

Hep A and Hep B	• Local reaction at the injection site	• Hep A
		  ○ Pregnancy (may be a contraindication)
		• Hep B
		  ○ Allergy to baker's yeast

Seasonal influenza vaccine	• TIV – Mild local reaction, and fever
	• LAIV – Headache, cough, and fever
	• Rare – Risk for Guillain-Barré syndrome (ascending paralysis, weakness of lower extremities, difficulty breathing)
		• Hypersensitivity to eggs
		• LAIV
		  ○ Fewer than 2 years
		  ○ Immunosuppression
		  ○ Chronic disease

Meningococcal Conjugate vaccine (MCV4)	• Mild local reaction • Rare – Risk for allergic response	• History of Guillain-Barré syndrome
HPV2 and HPV4	• Mild local reaction and fever • Fainting (shortly after receiving the vaccination) • Rare – Risk for Guillain-Barré syndrome	• Pregnancy • Hypersensitivity to yeast

Nursing Administration

- Infants and Children

    o Obtain parental consent for children.

    o Note the date, route, and site of vaccination on the child's immunization record at the time of immunization.

    o Give intramuscular vaccinations in the vastus lateralis or ventrogluteal muscle in infants and young children, and into the deltoid muscle for older children and , adolescents.

    o Give subcutaneous injections in the outer aspect of the upper arm or anterolateral thigh.

    o Use an appropriately sized needle for the route, site, age, and amount of medication.

    o Use strategies to minimize discomfort.

    o Provide for distraction.

    o Do not allow the child to delay the procedure.

    o Encourage the parents to use comforting measures during the procedure (cuddling, pacifiers) and after the procedure (application of cool compresses to injection site, gentle movement of the involved extremity).

    o Provide praise afterward.

    o Apply a colorful bandage, if appropriate.

    o Have emergency medications and equipment on standby in case the child experiences an allergic response, such as anaphylaxis (rare).

    o Follow storage and reconstitution directions. If reconstituted, use within 30 min.

    o Provide written vaccine information sheets and review the content with parents or clients.

    o Instruct the parents and child to observe for complications and to notify the provider if side effects occur.

    o Encourage the parents to maintain up-to-date immunizations for the child.

    o Document the administration of the vaccine, including the date, route, and site of vaccination; type, manufacturer, lot number, and expiration date of the vaccine; and name, address and signature of the child and/or parent.

    o Instruct the parents to avoid administering aspirin to the child to treat fever or local reaction, due to the risk of the development of Reye syndrome

    o Instruct the parents to premedicate infants and children with nonopioid analgesics/ antipyretics prior to immunizations and for the following 24 hr. Use acetaminophen for infants 2 to 6 months of age. Ibuprofen may be administered starting at 6 months of age.

    o Instruct the parents to apply a topical anesthetic prior to the injection.

Nursing Evaluation of Medication Effectiveness

- Depending on therapeutic intent, effectiveness may be evidenced by:

  ○ Improvement of local reaction to vaccination with absence of pain, fever, and swelling at the site of injection

  ○ Development of immunity

CHAPTER 35: IMMUNIZATIONS

(A) Application Exercises

Scenario: A nurse in a well-infant clinic is examining a 2-month-old infant who has not been examined since he was 2 days old. The infant weighs 5 kg (11 lb) and his birth weight was 8 lb 2 oz. The mother states that he has yellow discharge from his nose and a cough. They live in a rural area and usually have no transportation.

1. What data should the nurse gather at this point concerning the infant's immunization status?

2. The infant's axillary temperature is 38° C (100.4° F). What should the nurse do?

3. What immunizations (if any) should the nurse prepare to administer to the infant at this visit?

4. What support should the nurse offer to the infant's mother to ensure future immunizations for her infant?

5. What teaching should the nurse provide to the mother about the immunizations the infant receives today?

6. Which of the following sets of injections is typically given at the 4-month checkup?

    A. DTaP, Hib, RV, IPV, PCV, and Hep B

    B. DTaP, RV, IPV, PCV, and Hep B

    C. DTaP, Hib, RV, IPV, and PCV

    D. DTaP, MMR, PVC, varicella, and Hep A

7. A nurse is instructing the father of a toddler about strategies to promote comfort after the toddler receives an immunization. Which of the following strategies are recommended? (Select all that apply.)

    _____ Administer aspirin.

    _____ Apply cool compresses to the site.

    _____ Administer a safe dose of children's acetaminophen (Tylenol) or ibuprofen (Advil).

    _____ Encourage the toddler to use the affected extremity gently.

    _____ Apply a heating pad to the site.

CHAPTER 35: IMMUNIZATIONS

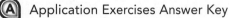 Application Exercises Answer Key

Scenario: A nurse in a well-infant clinic is examining a 2-month-old infant who has not been examined since he was 2 days old. The infant weighs 5 kg (11 lb) and his birth weight was 8 lb 2 oz. The mother states that he has yellow discharge from his nose and a cough. They live in a rural area and usually have no transportation.

1. What data should the nurse gather at this point concerning the infant's immunization status?

   Determine if the infant had a Hep B injection at the hospital prior to discharge.

   Verify that the infant had no other immunizations prior to this point in his life.

   Ask the mother about any allergies.

   NCLEX® Connection: Health Promotion and Maintenance, Immunizations

2. The infant's axillary temperature is 38° C (100.4° F). What should the nurse do?

   The nurse may take a rectal temperature to verify that the infant has a low-grade temperature elevation. The nurse should auscultate the lungs and examine the infant to confirm that the infant is not seriously ill. If the infant has only mild to moderate illness, the nurse should proceed with the scheduled immunizations. Because of the infant's infrequent contact with health care, it is important not to miss an opportunity to immunize if possible.

   NCLEX® Connection: Health Promotion and Maintenance, Immunizations

3. What immunizations (if any) should the nurse prepare to administer to the infant at this visit?

   The infant should receive Hep B, DTaP, Hib, RV, IPV, and PCV.

   NCLEX® Connection: Health Promotion and Maintenance, Immunizations

4. What support should the nurse offer to the infant's mother to ensure future immunizations for her infant?

   Provide information regarding implications for the infant if immunizations are not received.

   Provide a list of clinics in the area that will provide free or reduced-rate immunizations. Assist the mother to call and set up appointments.

   Discuss transportation options and assist the mother to develop a plan to implement.

   Assist the mother to identify support people who will be able to assist her.

   NCLEX® Connection: Health Promotion and Maintenance, Immunizations

5. What teaching should the nurse provide to the mother about the immunizations the infant receives today?

The mother should be given vaccine information sheets from the Centers for Disease Control.

The nurse should inform the mother of possible side effects to expect (fever, discomfort at the injection site) and ways to manage these side effects (administration of acetaminophen [Tylenol]).

The nurse should listen to any concerns the mother has about immunizing her infant and answer any questions.

(N) NCLEX® Connection: Health Promotion and Maintenance, Immunizations

6. Which of the following sets of injections is typically given at the 4-month checkup?

A. DTaP, Hib, RV, IPV, PCV, and Hep B

B. DTaP, RV, IPV, PCV, and Hep B

C. DTaP, Hib, RV, IPV, and PCV

D. DTaP, MMR, PVC, varicella, and Hep A

The DTaP, Hib, RV, IPV, and PCV immunizations should be given at 3 months of age. At 6 months of age, the infant should receive the DTaP, RV, IPV, PCV, and Hep B immunizations. In addition to these immunizations, infants 6 to 12 months of age should receive yearly seasonal influenza vaccinations. DTaP, MMR, PVC, varicella, and Hep A immunizations should be given to toddlers 12 months to 3 years of age. In addition, toddlers should receive the Hep A vaccine in two doses, at least 6 months apart, and a yearly seasonal influenza vaccine.

(N) NCLEX® Connection: Health Promotion and Maintenance, Immunizations

7. A nurse is instructing the father of a toddler about strategies to promote comfort after the toddler receives an immunization. Which of the following strategies are recommended? (Select all that apply.)

_____ Administer aspirin.

__X__ **Apply cool compresses to the site.**

__X__ **Administer a safe dose of children's acetaminophen (Tylenol) or ibuprofen (Advil).**

__X__ **Encourage the toddler to use the affected extremity gently.**

_____ Apply a heating pad to the site.

Application of cool compresses, administration of safe doses of acetaminophen or ibuprofen, and gentle use of the extremity are all comfort strategies useful for discomfort in an injection site. Aspirin should not be used because of the risk for Reye syndrome. Use of heat will not provide comfort for a sore injection site.

(N) NCLEX® Connection: Health Promotion and Maintenance, Immunizations

UNIT 2	NURSING CARE OF CHILDREN WITH SYSTEM DISORDERS		
Section	Immune and Infectious Disorders		
Chapter 36	Communicable Diseases		

Overview

- Communicable diseases are easily spread through airborne, droplet, or direct contact transmission.

- Most communicable disease can be prevented with immunizations.

DISEASE/VIRUS	SPREAD	INCUBATION	COMMUNICABILITY
Varicella (chickenpox)/varicella-zoster virus	• Direct contact • Droplet • Contaminated objects	14 to 21 days	One day before to 6 days after first lesions appear
Rubella (German measles)/rubella virus	• Direct contact • Droplet	14 to 21 days	7 days before to 5 days after rash
Rubeola (measles)/rubeola virus	• Direct contact • Droplet	10 to 21 days	4 days before to 5 days after rash
Pertussis (whooping cough)/*Bordetella pertussis*	• Droplet	6 to 20 days	Catarrhal stage before paroxysms
Erythema infectiosum (fifth disease)	• Respiratory secretions and blood	4 to 21 days	Unknown
Mumps/paramyxovirus	• Direct contact • Droplet	14 to 21 days	Immediately before and after swelling
Epstein-Barr (EBV) virus (EBV), also known as infectious mononucleosis)	• Direct contact	4 to 6 weeks	Unknown

View Media Supplement:

- Chickenpox (Image)
- Rubella (Image)
- Mumps (Image)

Assessment

- Risk Factors

  o Immunocompromised status

  o Crowded living conditions

  o Poor sanitation

  o Poor nutrition

  o Poor oxygenation and impaired circulation

  o Chronic illness

  o Recent exposure to a known case of a communicable disease

- Subjective and Objective Data

  o Varicella (chickenpox)

    ▪ Headache and irritability

    ▪ Abdominal discomfort

    ▪ Intense pruritus

    ▪ Malaise

    ▪ Decrease in oral intake

    ▪ Fever

    ▪ Lesions beginning as macules, rapidly progressing to papules, and then changing to clear, fluid-filled lesions (vesicles) before crusting over (All stages may be present at one time.)

  o Rubella (German measles)

    ▪ Low-grade fever and mild rash lasting 2 to 3 days

    ▪ Headache and malaise

    ▪ Rash usually beginning on face, spreading down the trunk, and fading in a few days

  o Measles (rubeola)

    ▪ High fever, malaise

    ▪ Sore throat and cough

    ▪ Runny nose

    ▪ Enlarged lymph nodes and conjunctivitis

    ▪ Koplik spots on buccal mucosa (small, bright red spots with a blue-white center that usually appear 2 days before rash)

    ▪ Rash of red maculopapular lesions that begins at hairline and usually spreads down the body, eventually turning brown

- Worsening symptoms that decrease about 2 days after the appearance of the rash
  - Pertussis (whooping cough)
    - Reports of nighttime cough
    - Thick mucus plug that may dislodge with coughing
    - Paroxysm coughing with eyes bulging and tongue protruding
  - Mumps
    - Fever, headache, and malaise
    - Anorexia for 24 hr
    - Earache that increases with chewing
    - Swollen, tender, and painful parotid glands
  - Infectious mononucleosis
    - Headache, malaise, and fatigue
    - Loss of appetite
    - Fever, sore throat
    - Puffy eyes
    - Cervical adenopathy
    - Splenomegaly (tender upper abdomen), which may persist for months
    - Palatine petechiae
    - Pharyngitis/tonsillitis exudate
    - Elevated WBC and atypical lymphocytes detected
    - Possible liver enzymes elevation (AST, ALT) with possible jaundice
  - Conjunctivitis
    - Pain and tearing (foreign body)
    - Purulent drainage and crusted eyelids (bacterial)
    - Watery drainage (viral or allergic)
  - Laboratory Tests
    - CBC
    - Electrolyte panels
    - Mono spot blood test for infectious mononucleosis

Collaborative Care

- Nursing Care
  - Symptomatic treatment
    - Follow airborne, droplet, and contact precautions for a child who is hospitalized.

- Administer an antipyretic for fever. Do not administer aspirin, due to the risk of Reye syndrome.

- Administer analgesics for pain.

- Provide fluids and nutritious foods the child prefers.

- Skin care

  □ Provide calamine lotion for topical relief.

  □ Keep the child's skin clean and dry to prevent secondary infection.

  □ Keep the child cool, but prevent chilling.

  □ Dress the child in lightweight, loose clothing.

  □ Give baths in tepid water, possibly with oatmeal.

  □ Keep the child's fingernails clean and short.

  □ Apply mittens if the child scratches.

  □ Teach good oral hygiene. The child may gargle with warm water for a sore throat.

  □ Change linens daily.

- Provide quiet diversional activities.

- Promote adequate rest with naps if necessary.

- Keep lights dim if the child develops photophobia.

- Keep the child out of the sun.

- Notify the child's school or day care center of the child's infection. Obtain a plan from the school so that the child can continue working on school work at home.

- Notify the health department of infection if necessary (pertussis, mumps, and measles).

- Medications

  ○ Antihistamine – Diphenhydramine hydrochloride (Benadryl) and hydroxyzine (Atarax)

    - Used to controls pruritus

    - Nursing Considerations

      □ Monitor the child's reaction to the medication, because some children may become hyperalert with the administration of a medication from this group.

      □ Monitor the child for drowsiness.

    - Client Education

      □ Educate the family about safety precautions.

  ○ Acetaminophen (Tylenol)

    - Decreases fever

- Nursing Considerations
  - □ Be alert for allergies.
- Client Education
  - □ Teach parents the appropriate dosing for acetaminophen.

- Care After Discharge

  - Client Education

    - Encourage adherence with antibiotic or antiviral therapy.

    - Instruct parents to teach the child to cover her nose and mouth when coughing or sneezing.

    - Instruct parents to wash the child's bed linens daily in mild detergent.

    - Teach parents of children who are immunocompromised to seek prompt medical care if symptoms develop.

    - Encourage adolescents to participate in decision making.

- Client Outcomes

  - The child will experience relief from pruritus.

  - The child will be free from injury.

  - The spread of the disease will be prevented by practicing measures to reduce transmission.

Complications

- Reye syndrome

  - Reye syndrome frequently follows an episode of viral illness (influenza, varicella).

  - Reye syndrome may be associated with the use of aspirin during a viral illness.

  - The best prognosis for Reye syndrome is achieved with prompt diagnosis and aggressive treatment.

  - Nursing Actions

    - Nursing care is provided in the ICU and includes maintaining vital functions, assisting with lumbar puncture, obtaining blood samples, administering IV fluids, performing nasogastric intubation, and inserting an indwelling urinary catheter.

  - Client Education

    - Reye syndrome can be avoided by eliminating the use of aspirin or aspirin-containing products in children.

- Other complications

  - Varicella – Secondary bacterial infections (pneumonia, sepsis encephalitis, scarring, chronic or transient thrombocytopenia)

- o Rubella – Few complications, but there is a teratogenic effect on the fetus of exposed pregnant women

- o Rubeola (measles) – Otitis media, pneumonia, bronchiolitis, laryngitis and laryngotracheitis, and encephalitis

- o Pertussis (whooping cough) – Pneumonia, otitis media, seizures, hemorrhage (caused by forceful coughing), hernia, prolapsed rectum, weight loss, and dehydration

- o Mumps – Epididymo-orchitis in males, hearing loss, encephalitis, meningitis, myocarditis, arthritis, and hepatitis

- o Infectious mononucleosis – Few complications, but ruptured spleen may result from blow to upper abdomen if splenomegaly is present

  - ▪ Participation in contact sports is discouraged.

CHAPTER 36: COMMUNICABLE DISEASES

 Application Exercises

1. A nurse is caring for several children who have communicable diseases. Which of the following communicable diseases may lead to pneumonia? (Select all that apply.)

    _____ Conjunctivitis

    _____ Rubella (German measles)

    _____ Rubeola (measles)

    _____ Pertussis (whooping cough)

    _____ Varicella (chickenpox)

    _____ Mumps

2. A nurse is caring for an adolescent client who has mononucleosis. The nurse assesses fever, fatigue, swollen lymph nodes, sore throat, and a sore upper abdomen. Which of the following instructions should the nurse discuss with the adolescent and her parents? (Select all that apply.)

    _____ Take antibiotics until symptoms subside.

    _____ Drink plenty of liquids.

    _____ Avoid participating in strenuous activities.

    _____ Allow for periods of rest.

    _____ Take aspirin as needed for fever and discomfort.

    _____ Gargle with salt water every 2 to 3 hr.

CHAPTER 36: COMMUNICABLE DISEASES

 Application Exercises Answer Key

1. A nurse is caring for several children who have communicable diseases. Which of the following communicable diseases may lead to pneumonia? (Select all that apply.)

_____	Conjunctivitis
_____	Rubella (German measles)
__X__	**Rubeola (measles)**
__X__	**Pertussis (whooping cough)**
__X__	**Varicella (chickenpox)**
_____	Mumps

Rubeola, pertussis, and varicella may cause pneumonia. The other communicable diseases do not result in pneumonia.

NCLEX® Connection: Physiological Adaptation, Infectious Disease

2. A nurse is caring for an adolescent client who has mononucleosis. The nurse assesses fever, fatigue, swollen lymph nodes, sore throat, and a sore upper abdomen. Which of the following instructions should the nurse discuss with the adolescent and her parents? (Select all that apply.)

_____	Take antibiotics until symptoms subside.
__X__	**Drink plenty of liquids.**
__X__	**Avoid participating in strenuous activities.**
__X__	**Allow for periods of rest.**
_____	Take aspirin as needed for fever and discomfort.
__X__	**Gargle with salt water every 2 to 3 hr.**

Instructions for mononucleosis include drinking liquids to stay hydrated, avoiding strenuous activities, resting, and gargling with salt water to relieve a sore throat. Antibiotics should not be administered for this viral illness unless strep throat is present. Aspirin is not indicated due to the possibility of Reye syndrome. Acetaminophen (Tylenol) is usually recommended for discomfort and fever.

NCLEX® Connection: Physiological Adaptation, Infectious Disease

UNIT 2	NURSING CARE OF CHILDREN WITH SYSTEM DISORDERS
Section	Immune and Infectious Disorders
Chapter 37	Acute Otitis Media

Overview

- Acute otitis media (AOM) is an infection of the structures of the middle ear.

- Otitis media with effusion (OME) is present when there is a collection of fluid in the middle ear but no infection.

- Repeated infections may cause impaired hearing and speech delays.

- Many infections clear spontaneously in a few days.

Assessment

- Risk Factors

  o The eustachian tubes in children are shorter and more horizontal than those of adults. Therefore, children have an increased risk for developing otitis media.

  o Otitis media is most common in the first 24 months of life and again when children enter school (ages 5 to 6). Otitis media infrequently occurs after age 7.

  o Otitis media is usually triggered by a bacterial infection (*Streptococcus pneumoniae, Haemophilus influenzae, Moraxella catarrhalis*) a viral infection (respiratory syncytial virus or influenza), allergies, or enlarged tonsils.

  o There is a lower incidence of otitis media in infants who are breastfed (possibly due to the presence of immunoglobulin A (IgA) in breast milk, which protects against infection.

  o Incidence is higher in the winter months.

  o Exposure to large numbers of children (day care)

  o Exposure to secondhand smoke

  o Cleft lip and/or cleft palate

  o Down syndrome

- Subjective Data

  o Recent history of upper respiratory infection; acute onset of changes in behavior; frequent crying, irritability, and fussiness; inconsolability; tugging at ear; and reports of ear pain, anorexia, nausea, and vomiting.

- Objective Data
  - Physical Assessment Findings
    - AOM
      - Rubbing or pulling on ear
      - Crying
      - Lethargy
      - Bulging yellow or red tympanic membrane
      - Purulent material in middle ear or drainage from external canal
      - Decreased or no tympanic movement with pneumatic otoscopy
      - Lymphadenopathy of the neck and head
      - Temperature (may be as high as 40° C [104° F])
      - Hearing difficulties and speech delays if otitis media becomes a chronic condition
    - OME
      - Feeling of fullness in the ear
      - Orange discoloration of the tympanic membrane with decreased movement
      - Vague findings including rhinitis, cough, and diarrhea
      - Transient hearing loss and balance disturbances
  - Diagnostic Procedures
    - Pneumatic otoscope
      - A pneumatic otoscope is used to visualize the tympanic membrane and middle ear structures. The otoscope also assesses tympanic membrane movement.
      - Nursing Actions
        - Gently pull the pinna down and back to visualize the tympanic membrane of a child younger than 3 years old. For a child older than 3 years, gently pull the pinna up and back.

Collaborative Care

- Nursing Care
  - Provide comfort measures.
    - Position an ice compress over the affected ear.
    - Provide diversional activities.

- Medications
    - Acetaminophen (Tylenol) or ibuprofen (Advil)
        - Used to provide analgesia and reduce fever
        - Nursing Considerations
            - Obtain a liquid preparation.
            - Use age-appropriate techniques to administer medication.
    - Amoxicillin (Amoxil), amoxicillin-clavulanate (Augmentin), and azithromycin (Zithromax)
    - Antibiotics
        - Nursing Considerations
            - Administer in high doses, usually 80 to 90 mg/kg/day in two divided doses.
            - The usual course of treatment is 10 to 14 days in children younger than 6 years of age. The course may be shorter for older children.
        - Client Education
            - Instruct the family that the child should complete the total course of treatment.
            - Observe for signs of allergy to the antibiotic, such as rash or difficulty breathing.
    - Benzocaine (Americaine-Otic)
        - Ear drops for topical pain relief
        - Client Education
            - Instruct the family how to properly administer ear drops.
            - Discourage the use of decongestants or antihistamines.
- Therapeutic Procedures
    - Myringotomy and placement of tympanoplasty tubes may be indicated for the child with multiple episodes of otitis media. This procedure may now be performed by laser treatment.
        - This procedure is performed in an outpatient setting with the administration of general anesthesia. It is usually completed in 15 min.
        - A small incision is made in the tympanic membrane, and tiny plastic or metal tubes are placed into the eardrum to equalize pressure and minimize effusion.
        - Recovery takes place in a PACU, and discharge usually occurs within 1 hr.
        - Postoperative pain is not common and, if present, will be mild.
        - Antibiotic ear drops may be prescribed for a few days.

- ■ The tubes come out by themselves (usually in 6 to 12 months).
- ■ Client Education
  - □ Limit the child's activities for a few days following surgery.
  - □ Instruct parents to notify the provider when tubes come out. This usually does not require replacement of tubes.
- Surgical Interventions
  - ○ Instruct the family to avoid getting water into the child's ears while the tubes are in place. The effectiveness of earplugs is not conclusive. Advise the parents to follow the health care provider's instructions.
- Care After Discharge
  - ○ Client Education
    - ■ Inform the client/parents about comfort measures.
    - ■ Encourage the parents to feed the child in an upright position when bottle or breastfeeding.
    - ■ If drainage is present, clean the external ear with sterile cotton swabs. Apply antibiotic ointment.
    - ■ If possible, each the parents to avoid risk factors if possible (secondhand smoke, exposure to individuals with viral/bacterial respiratory infections).
    - ■ Stress the importance of seeking medical care at initial signs and symptoms of infections (change in child's behavior, tugging on ear).
    - ■ Eliminate exposure to secondhand smoke.
    - ■ Encourage the parents to keep the child's immunizations up to date.
- Client Outcomes
  - ○ The child will be free of infection.

Complications

- Hearing loss and/or speech delays
  - ○ Nursing Actions
    - ■ Assess and monitor for deficits.
    - ■ Refer the child for audiology testing if needed.
  - ○ Client Education
    - ■ Speech therapy may be necessary.

CHAPTER 37: ACUTE OTITIS MEDIA

 Application Exercises

1. A nurse in a clinic is performing a well-child checkup. The child's father tells the nurse that three children in his daughter's day care have developed ear infections, and he wants to know how he can determine if his daughter has developed one. How should the nurse respond?

2. A nurse is caring for a 2-year-old child who has had three ear infections in the past 5 months. The nurse should know that the child is at risk for developing which of the following as a long-term complication?

    A. Balance difficulties

    B. Prolonged hearing loss

    C. Speech delays

    D. Chronic respiratory infections

3. An infant who has signs and symptoms of acute otitis media (AOM) is brought to an outpatient facility by his parent. The nurse should recognize that which of the following factors, if present, place the infant at risk for otitis media? (Select all that apply.)

    _____   The infant is breastfed.

    _____   The infant attends day care.

    _____   The infant is up to date with immunizations.

    _____   The infant was born with a cleft palate.

    _____   The infant's father smokes cigarettes.

CHAPTER 37: ACUTE OTITIS MEDIA

 Application Exercises Answer Key

1. A nurse in a clinic is performing a well-child checkup. The child's father tells the nurse that three children in his daughter's day care have developed ear infections, and he wants to know how he can determine if his daughter has developed one. How should the nurse respond?

   The nurse should tell the father that, if his child develops an ear infection, the child will likely become irritable and difficult to console. The child may then experience disturbed sleeping routines; may pull, tug, or rub on one or both ears; and may develop a temperature, diarrhea, vomiting, and/or loss of appetite. These symptoms may accompany an upper respiratory infection.

    NCLEX® Connection: Physiological Adaptation, Infectious Disease

2. A nurse is caring for a 2-year-old child who has had three ear infections in the past 5 months. The nurse should know that the child is at risk for developing which of the following as a long-term complication?

   A. Balance difficulties

   B. Prolonged hearing loss

   C. Speech delays

   D. Chronic respiratory infections

   Speech delay is a common and serious complication. Balance difficulties and prolonged hearing loss may be present with otitis media, but they are not long-term complications. Chronic respiratory infections are not a complication of otitis media.

    NCLEX® Connection: Reduction of Risk Potential, Potential for Complications From Surgical Procedures and Health Alterations

3. An infant who has signs and symptoms of acute otitis media (AOM) is brought to an outpatient facility by his parent. The nurse should recognize that which of the following factors, if present, place the infant at risk for otitis media? (Select all that apply.)

_____	The infant is breastfed.
__X__	**The infant attends day care.**
_____	The infant is up to date with immunizations.
__X__	**The infant was born with a cleft palate.**
__X__	**The infant's father smokes cigarettes.**

   Infants who attend day care have an increased risk of exposure. Infants born with cleft lip and/or palate are more prone to AOM because microorganisms can more easily move up the eustachian tubes due to reflux of milk. Exposure to secondhand smoke is also a risk factor for AOM. Breastfeeding helps to protect against AOM because breast milk contains secretory Immunoglobulin A. Being up to date with immunizations can help prevent AOM, because it is a complication of some communicable diseases, such as measles.

    NCLEX® Connection: Reduction of Risk Potential, Potential for Complications From Surgical Procedures and Health Alterations

UNIT 2	NURSING CARE OF CHILDREN WITH SYSTEM DISORDERS
Section	Immune and Infectious Disorders
Chapter 38	HIV/AIDS

 Overview

- HIV infection is a viral infection in which the virus infects the T-lymphocytes, causing immune dysfunction. This leads to organ dysfunction and a variety of opportunistic infections in a weakened host. In addition, HIV infections that progress to AIDS place children at risk for developing a variety of malignancies (Kaposi's sarcoma, cranial or Burkitt's lymphoma).

- Children who are born to mothers who are HIV positive or are exposed to HIV from another means usually convert to HIV positive status and develop clinical signs more rapidly than adults.

Assessment

- Risk Factors

  - Having a mother with HIV/AIDs can result in vertical transmission of the HIV virus to the fetus. A woman can also vertically transmit the virus when breastfeeding her infant.

  - Casual contact (visiting the home of a child with HIV, being in the same classroom as a child with HIV) is not a proven mode of transmission.

- Subjective Data

  - Chills

  - Anorexia, nausea, weight loss

  - Weakness and fatigue

  - Headache

  - Night sweats

- Objective Data

  - Physical Assessment Findings and Laboratory Tests

    - HIV infection – Birth to 12 years

IMMUNOLOGIC CATEGORY	LESS THAN 12 MONTHS		1 TO 5 YEARS		6 TO 12 YEARS	
	CELLS/ MEQ/L*	%**	CELLS/ MEQ/L	%	CELLS/ MEQ/L	%
No suppression	1,500 or more	25 or more	1,000 or more	25 or more	500 or more	25 or more
Moderate suppression	750 to 1,499	15 to 24	500 to 999	15 to 24	200 to 499	15 to 24
Severe suppression	less than 750	less than 15	less than 500	less than 15	less than 200	less than 15

*CD4+ T-lymphocyte count = cells/mEq/L

**CD4+ T-lymphocyte percentage of total lymphocytes = %

NOT SYMPTOMATIC	MILDLY SYMPTOMATIC
No signs or symptoms considered to be the result of HIV infection are present, or the child has only one of the conditions listed in the next column.	Two or more of the conditions listed in this column are present, but the child has none of the conditions listed in the next two columns. • Lymphadenopathy • Hepatomegaly • Splenomegaly • Recurrent upper respiratory infections, sinusitis, or otitis media • Dermatitis • Parotitis
MODERATELY SYMPTOMATIC	SEVERELY SYMPTOMATIC
Children with the following conditions are considered moderately symptomatic. • Anemia • Bacterial meningitis, pneumonia, or sepsis (single episode) • Oropharyngeal candidiasis • Cardiomyopathy • Cytomegalovirus infection, with onset before 1 month of age • Recurrent or chronic diarrhea • Hepatitis • Herpes simplex virus (HSV), stomatitis, bronchitis, pneumonitis, or esophagitis • Herpes zoster • Nephropathy • Persistent fever (lasting more than1 month) • Toxoplasmosis • Disseminated varicella	Children with the following conditions are considered severely symptomatic. • Multiple or recurrent bacterial infections (meningitis, septicemia, pneumonia) • Esophageal or pulmonary candidiasis, (bronchi, trachea, lungs) • Cytomegalovirus disease • Pneumocystis jiroveci • HIV encephalopathy with developmental delays • HSV stomatitis, bronchitis, pneumonitis, or esophagitis • Kaposi's sarcoma • Brain or Burkitt's lymphoma • Disseminated or extrapulmonary mycobacterium tuberculosis • Pneumocystis jiroveci pneumonia • Wasting syndrome

- HIV infection – 13 to 20 years (See Adult Medical Surgical Nursing chapter 100)
  - A confirmed case classification meets the laboratory criteria for a diagnosis of HIV infection and one of the four HIV infection stages (stage 1, stage 2, stage 3, or unknown).

STAGE	DEFINING CONDITIONS	CD4+ T-LYMPHOCYTE COUNT	CD4+ T-LYMPHOCYTE PERCENTAGE OF TOTAL LYMPHOCYTES
Stage 1	• None	• 500 cells/mEq/L or more	• 29 or more
Stage 2	• None	• 200 to 499 cells/mEq/L	• 14 to 28
Stage 3 (AIDS)*	• Candidiasis of esophagus, bronchi, trachea, or lungs • Herpes simplex – Chronic ulcers (of more than 1 month's duration) • HIV-related encephalopathy • Disseminated or extrapulmonary histoplasmosis • Kaposi's sarcoma • Burkitt's lymphoma • Mycobacterium tuberculosis of any site • Pneumocystis jiroveci pneumonia • Recurrent pneumonia • Progressive multifocal leukoencephalopathy • Recurrent *Salmonella* septicemia • Wasting syndrome attributed to HIV	• less than 200 cells/mEq/L	• less than 14
Stage unknown	• No information available	• No information available	• No information available

*Documentation of an AIDS-defining condition supersedes a CD4+ T-lymphocyte count of 200 cells/mEq/L or more and a CD4+ T-lymphocyte percentage of total lymphocytes of greater than 14.

- Exposure – Less than 18 months of age and born to a mother who is HIV infected.

Human Immunodeficiency Virus Infection (HIV) (retrieved 3/18/10 from http://www.cdc.gov). To read more about HIV, go to the Web site of the Centers for Disease Control and Prevention (http://www.cdc.gov).

- ○ Diagnostic Procedures
  - Laboratory criteria for diagnosis – 18 months to 20 years
    - □ Positive result from an HIV antibody screening test (reactive enzyme immunoassay [EIA]) confirmed by a positive result from a supplemental HIV antibody test (Western blot or indirect immunofluorescence assay test)
    - □ Positive result or report of a detectable quantity from any of the following HIV virologic (nonantibody) tests:
      - ▸ HIV nucleic acid (DNA or RNA) detection test (polymerase chain reaction [PCR])
      - ▸ HIV p24 antigen test, including neutralization assay
      - ▸ HIV isolation (viral culture)
  - Laboratory criteria for diagnosis – Less than 18 months
    - □ Positive results on two separate specimens (not including cord blood) from one or more of the following HIV virologic (nonantibody) tests:
      - ▸ HIV nucleic acid (DNA or RNA) detection
      - ▸ HIV p24 antigen test, including neutralization assay (for an infant more than 1 month of age)
      - ▸ HIV isolation (viral culture)
  - Liver profile, biopsies, and testing of stool for parasites
    - □ Nursing Actions
      - ▸ Prepare the child for the test.
    - □ Client Education
      - ▸ Inform the child about the details of the test, such as length and what to expect.

Collaborative Care

- Nursing Care
  - ○ Encourage a balanced diet that is high in calories and protein. Obtain the child's preferred food and beverages. Give nutritional supplements.
  - ○ Administer total parental nutrition (TPN) if prescribed.
  - ○ Provide for good oral care and report abnormalities for treatment.
  - ○ Keep the child's skin clean and dry.
  - ○ Provide nonpharmacological methods of pain relief.
  - ○ Assess the child for pain and provide adequate pain management. Use of medications may include nonsteroidal anti-inflammatory drugs (NSAIDs), acetaminophen (Tylenol), opioids, muscle relaxants, and/or a eutectic mixture of local anesthetics (EMLA cream) for numerous diagnostic procedures.

○ Protect/prevent infection using standard precautions.

  ■ Encourage deep breathing and coughing.

  ■ Maintain good hand hygiene.

  ■ Teach the child and parents to avoid individuals who have colds/infections/viruses.

  ■ Encourage immunizations with killed viruses, such as pneumococcal vaccine (PCV) and yearly seasonal influenza vaccine.

  ■ Monitor for signs of opportunistic infections.

○ Administer medications as prescribed for opportunistic infections (acyclovir [Zovirax] for HSV, amphotericin B [Amphocin] for serious fungal infections).

- Medications

  ○ Highly active antiretroviral therapy (HAART) involves using 3 to 4 HIV medications in combination to reduce medication resistance, adverse effects, and dosages.

    ■ Entry/infusion inhibitors – Enfuvirtide (Fuzeon)

      □ This helps to decrease the amount of virus in the body and limit its spread.

    ■ Nucleoside reverse transcriptase inhibitors (NRTIs) – Zidovudine (Retrovir)

      □ These interfere with the virus's ability to convert RNA into DNA

    ■ Non-nucleoside reverse transcriptase inhibitors (NNRTIs) – Delavirdine (Rescriptor) and efavirenz (Sustiva)

      □ These inhibit viral replication in cells.

    ■ Protease inhibitors, such as ritonavir (Norvir), amprenavir (Agenerase), and nelfinavir (Viracept)

      □ These inhibit an enzyme needed for the virus to replicate.

    ■ Nursing considerations

      □ Monitor laboratory results (CBC, WBC, liver function tests). Antiretroviral medications can increase alanine aminotransferase (ALT), aspartate aminotransferase (AST), bilirubin, mean corpuscular volume (MCV), high-density lipoproteins (HDLs), total cholesterol, and triglycerides.

    ■ Client education

      □ Educate about the side effects of the medications and ways to decrease the severity of the side effects.

      □ Educate about the need to take the medication on a regular schedule and to not miss doses.

  ○ Antibiotics

    ■ Trimethoprim-sulfamethoxazole (TMP-SMZ)

      □ Used for prophylaxis treatment of pneumocystis pneumonia (PCP) in newborns of mothers who are HIV infected

- ○ Antibiotics
  - ▪ Trimethoprim-sulfamethoxazole (TMP-SMZ)
    - ☐ Used for prophylaxis treatment of pneumocystis pneumonia (PCP) in newborns of mothers who are HIV infected
  - ▪ Acyclovir (Zovirax)
    - ☐ Used for herpes simplex virus
  - ▪ Amphotericin B (Amphocin)
    - ☐ Used for serious fungal infections
  - ▪ Nursing Actions
    - ☐ Monitor the child for side effects.
  - ▪ Client Education
    - ☐ Teach parents the importance of ensuring that the full dose of the medication is completed.
- Interdisciplinary Care
  - ○ Interdisciplinary care for the child with HIV/AIDS may include social services to help with access to health care and medication acquisition and nutritional support to promote good nutrition.
- Care After Discharge
  - ○ Client Education
    - ▪ Educate the child and parents about the chronicity of the illness and the need for life-long medication administration.
    - ▪ Instruct the parents when to notify the provider. Signs and symptoms requiring medical care include headache, fever, lethargy, warmth, tenderness, redness at joints, and neck stiffness.
    - ▪ Educate the child and parents about transmission of the virus (high-risk behaviors).
    - ▪ Identify stressors that may be affecting the family and make appropriate referrals (school/community response to child, finances, access to health care).
    - ▪ Instruct the child and parents about safe practice when using needles/syringes and administering medications.
- Client Outcomes
  - ○ The child will be free of infection.
  - ○ The child will maintain optimal weight.
  - ○ The child will participate in ADLs.

Complications

- Failure to thrive

  - Nursing Actions

    - Obtain a baseline height and weight and continue to monitor.

    - Promote optimal nutrition. This may require the administration of total parenteral nutrition.

    - Assess growth and development. Monitor for delays.

    - Provide opportunities for normal development (age-appropriate toys, play with children of the same age).

  - Client Education

    - Educate the child and parents about appropriate nutrition and how to meet nutritional needs.

- PCP

  - Nursing Actions

    - Assess and monitor respiratory status, which includes respiratory rate and effort, oxygen saturation, and breath sounds.

    - Administer appropriate antibiotics.

    - Administer an antipyretic and/or analgesics.

    - Provide adequate hydration and maintain fluid and electrolyte balance.

    - Use postural drainage and chest physiotherapy to mobilize and remove fluid from the lungs.

    - Promote adequate rest.

  - Client Education

    - Educate the child and parents about the infectious process and how to prevent infection.

    - Educate the child and parents about the importance of medication and the need to maintain the medication regimen.

CHAPTER 38: HIV/AIDS

(A) Application Exercises

Scenario: A child who is HIV positive is admitted to the emergency department. The child has a high fever; rapid, shallow respirations; a productive cough of white sputum; and crackles heard in the lower lung fields bilaterally. Following assessment by the provider, the child is diagnosed with pneumonia and is admitted to the hospital.

1. Identify interventions the nurse should implement for this child.

2. What information regarding medication administration and preventing infection should the nurse provide to the parent?

3. A parent of a child who has HIV is at risk for disease transmission in which of the following situations? (Select all that apply.)

    _____ Hugging the child

    _____ Being kissed by the child

    _____ Sharing finger food with the child from a central plate

    _____ Cleaning up after the child has a nose bleed

    _____ Wiping the child's tears with a handkerchief when she is crying

    _____ Sharing the child's toothbrush

4. A nurse is caring for a child who is HIV positive. Identify actions the nurse should take to promote good nutrition for the child.

CHAPTER 38: HIV/AIDS

 Application Exercises Answer Key

Scenario: A child who is HIV positive is admitted to the emergency department. The child has a high fever; rapid, shallow respirations; a productive cough of white sputum; and crackles heard in the lower lung fields bilaterally. Following assessment by the provider, the child is diagnosed with pneumonia and is admitted to the hospital.

1. Identify interventions the nurse should implement for this child.

Monitor the child's vital signs and report an increase in temperature.

Anticipate that a chest x-ray and sputum culture may be ordered.

Administer oxygen as prescribed to maintain O₂ saturation at an appropriate level.

Assess the child's lungs and compare to previous findings to determine the effectiveness of treatment.

Administer antipyretics as prescribed.

Encourage oral fluids as tolerated, and provide IV fluids as prescribed.

Administer antibiotics in a timely manner.

Monitor I&O and gastrointestinal function.

NCLEX® Connection: Physiological Adaptation, Infectious Disease

2. What information regarding medication administration and preventing infection should the nurse provide to the parent?

The parent will require written instructions about the name and frequency of the medication dosage. Written instructions should be provided so that the parent understands side effects to observe for with specific medications. The parent should also understand that the child will require periodic blood work monitoring for side effects and that antiviral medications do not make it impossible for the child to infect others. The parent should be instructed on how to monitor the child's temperature and protect the child from others who are ill.

NCLEX® Connection: Physiological Adaptation, Illness Management

3. A parent of a child who has HIV is at risk for disease transmission in which of the following situations? (Select all that apply.)

	Hugging the child
	Being kissed by the child
	Sharing finger food with the child from a central plate
X	**Cleaning up after the child has a nose bleed**
	Wiping the child's tears with a handkerchief when she is crying
X	**Sharing the child's toothbrush**

The only situations posing any risks are cleaning up after the child has a nose bleed and sharing the child's toothbrush. HIV is transmitted by direct contact with blood and body fluids (semen, vaginal secretions). It is important not to share personal hygiene items such as razors or toothbrushes, which could contain blood. None of the other activities should place a person at risk. Even though the virus has been found in small amounts in tears, mucous, and sweat, there is no evidence that transmission has ever occurred unless blood is present.

 NCLEX® Connection: Physiological Adaptation, Infectious Disease

4. A nurse is caring for a child who is HIV positive. Identify actions the nurse should take to promote good nutrition for the child.

The nurse should first assess the child's nutritional status.

Weight and height should be obtained and plotted on a growth chart.

Laboratory values, such as serum protein and electrolyte levels, should be monitored.

The nurse should assess the child's likes and dislikes and assist with menu selection.

If possible, the nurse should group the child with other children of the same age during meals.

The nurse should offer fluids frequently, preferably drinks that are high in calories and protein.

NCLEX® Connection: Physiological Adaptation, Illness Management

UNIT 2: NURSING CARE OF CHILDREN WITH SYSTEM DISORDERS

Section: Neoplastic Disorders

- Organ Neoplasms
- Blood Neoplasms
- Bone and Soft Tissue Cancers

NCLEX® CONNECTIONS

When reviewing the chapters in this section, keep in mind the relevant sections of the NCLEX® outline, in particular:

CLIENT NEEDS: BASIC CARE AND COMFORT

Relevant topics/tasks include:
- Mobility/Immobility
  - Perform a skin assessment and implement measures to maintain skin integrity and prevent skin breakdown.
- Nonpharmacological Comfort Interventions
  - Assess the client's need for palliative care.
- Nutrition and Oral Hydration
  - Manage the client who has an alteration in nutritional intake.

CLIENT NEEDS: PHARMACOLOGICAL AND PARENTERAL THERAPIES

Relevant topics/tasks include:
- Adverse Effects/ Contraindications/Side Effects/Interactions
  - Manage the client experiencing side effects and adverse reactions of medication.
- Expected Actions/ Outcomes
  - Evaluate the therapeutic effect of medications.
- Pharmacological Pain Management
  - Administer and document pharmacological pain management appropriate for client age and diagnoses.

CLIENT NEEDS: REDUCTION OF RISK POTENTIAL

Relevant topics/tasks include:
- Diagnostic Tests
  - Evaluate the results of diagnostic testing and intervene as needed.
- Potential for Complications of Diagnostic Tests/ Treatments/Procedures
  - Monitor the client for signs of bleeding.
- Therapeutic Procedures
  - Provide preoperative care.

Overview

- Wilms' tumor (nephroblastoma) is a malignancy that occurs in the kidneys or abdomen.

  - It most often occurs during the toddler and preschool years.

  - Metastasis is rare.

- Neuroblastoma is a malignancy that occurs in the adrenal gland, sympathetic chain of the retroperitoneal area, head, neck, pelvis, or chest.

  - It occurs before age 10, usually during the toddler years.

  - Most tumors have spread by metastasis at the time of diagnosis.

- Presenting signs and symptoms will vary with the type of cancer.

- Treatment may be a combination of surgery, chemotherapy, and radiation or any combination of these modalities

Assessment

- Risk Factors

  - There is some evidence of genetic predisposition.

- Subjective and Objective Data

  - Wilms' tumor presents as an abdominal swelling or mass that is usually firm, nontender, and unilateral.

  - Neuroblastoma presents as an asymmetrical, firm, nontender mass in the abdomen. This mass crosses the midline.

  - Wilms' tumor and neuroblastoma can cause urinary symptoms (frequency, urgency) with compression on renal structures.

  - Signs and symptoms of metastasis

    - Edema (periorbital) with ecchymosis around eyes

    - Lymphadenopathy (predominantly cervical and supraclavicular in neuroblastoma)

    - Weight loss, anemia, and fatigue

- Hepatomegaly and splenomegaly

- Possible bone pain

- Respiratory involvement leading to shortness of breath, decreased breath sounds, cough, and respiratory distress

- Paralysis that will have varying degrees (neuroblastoma)

○ Laboratory Tests

- Blood studies are used to identify anemia and infection.

- Urine may be evaluated for the presence of breakdown products of catecholamines (vanillylmandelic acid, homovanillic acid, dopamine, norepinephrine) to diagnose adrenal or sympathetic tumors.

- Liver enzyme studies should be obtained to assess the quality of liver function.

○ Diagnostic Procedures

- Chest x-ray, computed tomography (CT) scan, magnetic resonance imaging (MRI), positron emission tomography (PET) scan, and single photon emission computed tomography (SPECT) scans

  □ Used to visualize tumors and metastasis and determine the stage of the cancer

  □ Nursing Actions

    ▸ Assess the child for allergies to dye or shellfish.

    ▸ Assist the child to remain still during the procedure.

    ▸ Instruct the child to drink oral contrast if prescribed.

    ▸ Sedate the child if prescribed.

  □ Client Education

    ▸ Provide emotional support.

- Biopsy

  □ Biopsy may be a local procedure to obtain a sample of tissue for diagnosis. A biopsy can also be obtained during surgery under general anesthesia, possibly in conjunction with excision or resection of the tumor at the same time.

  □ Nursing Actions

    ▸ During the procedure, provide emotional support.

    ▸ Following the biopsy

      ▷ Assess the site for bleeding.

      ▷ Prevent infection at the biopsy site.

      ▷ Provide pain relief.

  □ Client Education

    ▸ Instruct the parents to provide emotional support.

Collaborative Care

- Nursing Care

  - Assess the child and family's coping and support.

  - Assess for developmental delays related to illness.

  - Assess physical growth (height and weight).

  - Provide education and support to the child and family regarding diagnostic testing, treatment plan, ongoing therapy, and prognosis.

  - Monitor for signs of infection.

  - Administer antibiotics as prescribed for infection.

  - Keep the child's skin clean, dry, and lubricated.

  - Provide oral hygiene and keep the child's lips lubricated.

  - Provide age-appropriate diversional activities.

  - Provide support to the child and family.

    - Avoid false reassurance.

    - Listen to the child's concerns.

    - Allow time for the child and family to discuss feelings regarding loss and to grieve.

- Interdisciplinary Care

  - Social services may be of assistance with access to medications and durable medical equipment if needed.

  - A nutritionist may be consulted for development of a diet plan.

- Therapeutic Procedures

  - Treatment for Wilms' tumor

    - Preoperative chemotherapy or radiation to decrease the size of the tumor

    - Surgical removal of the tumor and affected organs

    - Chemotherapy treatment that can last from 6 to 15 months

    - Radiation for children who have recurrent diseases, large tumors, and/or metastasis.

  - Treatment for neuroblastoma

    - Surgical removal of the tumor

    - Radiation in an emergency to decrease the size of a tumor that is compressing the spinal cord

    - Radiation to decrease the size of tumors and palliation for metastasis

- ○ Chemotherapy
  - Chemotherapeutic agents include vincristine (Oncovin), doxorubicin (Adriamycin), cyclophosphamide (Cytoxan), actinomycin D (Dactinomycin) for Wilms' tumor, and cisplatin (Platinol) for neuroblastoma.
  - Medications may be administered orally, intravenously, or locally (such as intrathecally for a CNS tumor).
  - The child may have a long-term central venous access device or a peripherally inserted central catheter (PICC) in place.
  - Nursing Actions
    - □ Handle the chemotherapeutic agents carefully.
    - □ Medicate the child with an anti-emetic prior to administration.
    - □ Allow the child several food choices. Allow the child to choose favorite foods.
    - □ Observe the mouth for mucosal ulcerations.
    - □ Offer cool fluids to prevent dehydration and soothe sore mucous membranes.
  - Client Education
    - □ Educate the child and family about the side effects of chemotherapy (nausea, vomiting, alopecia).
    - □ Educate the child and family about the importance of immunizations and follow-up appointments.
    - □ Educate the child and family about good infection control practices.
- ○ Radiation
  - Radiation is dose calculated and usually delivered in divided treatments over several weeks.
  - Radiation affects rapidly growing cells in the body. Therefore, cells that normally have a fast turnover may be affected in addition to cancer cells.
  - Nursing Actions
    - □ Take care when radiation is in use. Wear lead aprons.
  - Client Education
    - □ Educate the child and family about the procedure and provide support.
    - □ Instruct the child and family not to wash off marks on skin that outline the targeted areas.
    - □ Teach the child and family to wash the marked areas with lukewarm water, use hands instead of a washcloth, pat dry, and take care not to remove the markings. Avoid using hot or cold water.
    - □ Teach the child and family to avoid the use of soaps, creams, lotions, and/or powders unless they are prescribed.

- ☐ Encourage wearing loose cotton clothing.

- ☐ Remind the child and family to keep the areas protected from the sun by wearing a hat and long-sleeved shirts.

- ☐ Instruct the family to seek medical care for blisters, weeping, and red/tender skin.

- Surgical Interventions

  - ○ Tumor debulking

    - ■ Nursing Actions

      - ☐ Preoperative

        - ▸ Avoid palpation of Wilms' tumor.

      - ☐ Postoperative

        - ▸ Monitor gastrointestinal activity (bowel sounds, bowel movements, distention, nausea, vomiting)

        - ▸ Provide pain relief.

        - ▸ Monitor vital signs and assess for any signs and symptoms of infection.

        - ▸ Encourage pulmonary hygiene.

    - ■ Client Education

      - ☐ Provide preoperative teaching to the child and family that includes length of surgery, where the child will recover, and what equipment will be in place (nasogastric tube, IV line, indwelling urinary catheter).

- Client Outcomes

  - ○ The child will consume adequate nutritional intake to maintain an appropriate weight.

  - ○ The child will experience minimal side effects from treatments.

  - ○ The child will be free from infection.

Complications

- Pancytopenia

  - ○ Bone marrow depression resulting in anemia, neutropenia, and/or thrombocytopenia

  - ○ Nursing Actions

    - ■ Monitor vital signs and report them to the health care provider. Report a temperature greater than 37.8° C (100° F).

    - ■ Monitor for signs of infection (lung congestion; redness, swelling, and pain around IV sites) and lesions in the mouth, and monitor the client's wound site and immunization status.

    - ■ Administer antimicrobial, antiviral, and antifungal medications as prescribed.

- Protect the child from sources of possible infection.
  - Use good hand hygiene.
  - Encourage the child and family to use good hand hygiene.
- Encourage the child to avoid crowds while undergoing chemotherapy.
- Instruct the child to avoid fresh fruits and vegetables.
- Avoid invasive procedures (injections, rectal temperatures, catheters). Apply pressure to puncture sites for 5 min.
- Monitor for signs of bleeding.
- Avoid aspirin/NSAIDs.
- Administer filgrastim (Neupogen), a granulocyte colony-stimulating factor that stimulates WBC production, subcutaneously daily.
- Monitor the child for headache, fever, and mild to moderate bone pain.
- Administer epoetin alfa (Procrit) subcutaneously two to three times per week as prescribed to stimulate RBC formation.
- Monitor blood pressure.
- Administer oprelvekin (Interleukin-11, Neumega) subcutaneously daily as prescribed to stimulate platelet formation.
- Encourage the use of a soft toothbrush.
- Use gentle handling and positioning to protect from injury.
- Organize care to provide for rest. Schedule rest periods.
  - ○ Client Education
    - Educate the child and family about infection control procedures at home.
    - Provide support.
- Anorexia, nausea, vomiting
  - ○ These are side effects of chemotherapy and radiation therapy
  - ○ Nursing Actions
    - Avoid strong odors. Provide a pleasant atmosphere for meals.
    - Suggest and assist in selecting foods/fluids.
    - Provide small, frequent meals.
    - Administer antiemetics as prescribed, usually before meals.

- Alteration in bowel elimination

  - Diarrhea is a result of radiation to the abdominal area. Some chemotherapeutic agents may cause constipation. If mobility and nutrition decrease, the child is more likely to develop constipation.

  - Nursing Actions

    - Provide meticulous skin care.

    - Provide a nutritious diet.

    - Determine if certain foods or drinks (high fiber, lactose rich) worsen the child's condition.

    - Monitor intake and output and daily weight.

- Stomatitis and dry mouth

  - Nursing Actions

    - Provide a soft toothbrush and/or swabs.

    - Lubricate the child's lips.

    - Give soft, nonacidic foods. A puréed or liquid diet may be required.

    - Provide analgesics.

  - Client Education

    - Encourage the parents and child to visit a dentist before therapy.

    - Encourage the use of mouth washes, such as 1 tsp salt mixed with 1 pint of water or 1 tsp baking soda mixed with 1 quart of water.

- Alopecia

  - Occurs with chemotherapy and radiation of the head and/or neck

  - Nursing Actions

    - Assess the child's feelings.

    - Discuss cutting long hair.

    - Use gentle shampoos. Gently brush the child's hair.

    - Avoid blow dryers and curling irons.

    - Suggest wearing a cotton hat or scarf.

  - Client Education

    - Suggest that the family purchase a wig.

    - Instruct the child and family to avoid blow dryers and curling irons.

CHAPTER 39: ORGAN NEOPLASMS

 Application Exercises

Scenario: A 3-year-old child with Wilms' tumor of the right kidney is admitted to the pediatric oncology unit. He is to undergo a course of chemotherapy, followed by radiation treatments to shrink the tumor before surgically removing it, along with the kidney and the adjacent adrenal gland. The child will receive additional radiation after surgery.

1. Explain what baseline assessments the nurse should obtain.

2. When completing the child's admission assessment, which of the following components of the abdominal assessment should the nurse avoid?

    A. Auscultation

    B. Palpation

    C. Percussion

    D. Inspection

3. When the child is ready to begin outpatient radiation treatments, what should the nurse teach his parents about this therapy?

4. A primary care provider has prescribed a clear liquid diet for a child who is postoperative following surgical removal of a Wilms' tumor. Which of the following assessment findings requires that the nurse clarify this order?

    A. Abdominal girth 1 cm larger than yesterday

    B. Report of pain at the operative site

    C. Absence of bowel sounds on second postoperative day

    D. Passing of flatus every 30 min

5. When assessing a child who has a neuroblastoma of the adrenal gland, which of the following findings indicate to the nurse that the child has developed metastasis from the primary site? (Select all that apply.)

    _____ Weight gain

    _____ Bone pain

    _____ Varying degrees of paralysis

    _____ Dependent edema

    _____ Hepatomegaly

CHAPTER 39: ORGAN NEOPLASMS

(A) Application Exercises Answer Key

Scenario: A 3-year-old child with Wilms' tumor of the right kidney is admitted to the pediatric oncology unit. He is to undergo a course of chemotherapy, followed by radiation treatments to shrink the tumor before surgically removing it, along with the kidney and the adjacent adrenal gland. The child will receive additional radiation after surgery.

1. Explain what baseline assessments the nurse should obtain.

Vital signs including temperature

Skin to assess for reddened and/or broken areas

Mucous membranes

Last dental visit

Height and weight

Nutritional preferences and normal meal patterns

Activity and mobility levels

Fears and knowledge level of the child and family

(N) **NCLEX® Connection: Reduction of Risk Potential, System Specific Assessment**

2. When completing the child's admission assessment, which of the following components of the abdominal assessment should the nurse avoid?

A. Auscultation
B. Palpation
C. Percussion
D. Inspection

Palpation of the abdomen could rupture the encapsulated tumor. None of the other components of abdominal assessment puts pressure on the tumor.

(N) **NCLEX® Connection: Reduction of Risk Potential, System Specific Assessment**

3. When the child is ready to begin outpatient radiation treatments, what should the nurse teach his parents about this therapy?

> The nurse should explain to the parents that the child will probably have marks on his skin to outline the targeted areas. These should be left in place. The nurse should reinforce information about side effects discussed by the health care provider. The nurse should also teach the parents to wash the marked areas with lukewarm water (using hands), pat dry, and take care not to remove the markings. The use of creams, lotions, and/or powders should be avoided, unless they are prescribed. The areas should also be protected from the sun.

 NCLEX® Connection: Reduction of Risk Potential, Complications of Diagnostic Tests/Treatments/Procedures

---

4. A primary care provider has prescribed a clear liquid diet for a child who is postoperative following surgical removal of a Wilms' tumor. Which of the following assessment findings requires that the nurse clarify this order?

A. Abdominal girth 1 cm larger than yesterday

B. Report of pain at the operative site

C. Absence of bowel sounds on second postoperative day

D. Passing of flatus every 30 min

> The absence of bowel sounds is an indication that gastrointestinal motility is absent. This is an indication that the child should not eat. The increase in girth is probably secondary to edema (it is not significant enough to indicate distention). Pain is normal on the second postoperative day, and the child should be medicated with pain medication. Passing flatus is a positive sign, indicating good bowel motility.

 NCLEX® Connection: Physiological Adaptation, Alterations in Body Systems

5. When assessing a child who has a neuroblastoma of the adrenal gland, which of the following findings indicate to the nurse that the child has developed metastasis from the primary site? (Select all that apply.)

_____	Weight gain
__X__	**Bone pain**
__X__	**Varying degrees of paralysis**
_____	Dependent edema
__X__	**Hepatomegaly**

> Bone pain, varying degrees of paralysis, and hepatomegaly are signs and findings consistent with metastasis. Weight loss, rather than weight gain, and periorbital edema, rather than dependent edema, will be identified.

 NCLEX® Connection: Reduction of Risk Potential, System Specific Assessment

UNIT 2	NURSING CARE OF CHILDREN WITH SYSTEM DISORDERS
Section	Neoplastic Disorders
Chapter 40	Blood Neoplasms

Overview

- Leukemia is the term for a group of malignancies that affect the bone marrow and lymphatic system.

- Leukemia is classified by the type of WBCs that becomes neoplastic and is commonly divided into two groups: acute lymphoid leukemia (ALL) and acute myelogenous or nonlymphoid leukemia (AML/ANLL).

- Leukemia causes bone marrow dysfunction that leads to anemia and neutropenia.

- Leukemia causes an increase in the production of immature WBCs, which leads to infiltration of organs and tissues.

  o Bone marrow infiltration causes crowding of cells that would normally produce RBCs, platelets, and mature WBCs.

    - Deficient RBCs cause anemia.

    - Deficient mature WBCs (neutropenia) increase the risk for infection.

    - Deficient platelets (thrombocytopenia) cause bleeding and bruising.

  o Infiltration of spleen, liver, and lymph nodes leads to tissue fibrosis.

  o Infiltration of the CNS causes increased intracranial pressure.

  o Other tissues may also be infiltrated (testes, prostate, ovaries, gastrointestinal tract).

- Clinical manifestations are related to the area of involvement (bone pain, abdominal pain, neurosensory changes).

Assessment

- Risk Factors

  o Leukemia is the most common cancer of childhood.

  o ALL is the most common form of leukemia in children. There is an increased incidence in Caucasian boys older than 1 year or age, with peak onset being between 2 and 6 years of age.

  o Children with trisomy 21 (Down syndrome) have a greater risk of developing ALL.

- Subjective Data

  - History and physical assessment findings may reveal vague reports (anorexia, headache, fatigue).

- Objective Data

  - Physical Assessment Findings

    - Early manifestations

      - Low-grade fever
      - Pallor
      - Increased bruising and petechiae
      - Listlessness
      - Enlarged liver, lymph nodes, and joints
      - Abdominal, leg, and joint pain
      - Constipation
      - Headache
      - Vomiting and anorexia
      - Unsteady gait

    - Late manifestations

      - Pain
      - Hematuria
      - Ulcerations in the mouth
      - Enlarged kidneys and testicles
      - Signs of increased intracranial pressure

  - Laboratory Tests

    - Complete blood counts

      - Anemia (low blood counts)
      - Thrombocytopenia (low platelets)
      - Neutropenia (low neutrophils)
      - Leukemic blasts (immature WBCs)

○ Diagnostic Procedures

- Bone marrow aspiration or biopsy analysis

  □ Bone marrow aspiration or biopsy is the most definitive diagnostic procedure. If leukemia is present, the specimen will show prolific quantities of immature leukemic blast cells and protein markers indicating a specific type of leukemia. This procedure is performed by an oncologist.

  □ Nursing Actions

    ▸ Assist the health care provider with the procedure.

    ▸ Topical anesthetic, such as a eutectic mixture of local anesthetics (EMLA), may be applied over the biopsy area 45 min to 1 hr prior to the procedure.

    ▸ Unconscious sedation is induced using a general anesthetic, such as propofol (Diprivan).

    ▸ A specimen from the posterior or anterior iliac crest or tibia is obtained by the provider.

    ▸ Postprocedure

      ▷ Apply pressure to the site for 5 to 10 min.

      ▷ Assess vital signs frequently.

      ▷ Apply a pressure dressing.

      ▷ Monitor for signs of bleeding and infection for 24 hr.

  □ Client Education

    ▸ Educate the child and parents about the procedure and postprocedure care.

- Cerebrospinal fluid (CSF) analysis

  □ CSF, obtained by lumbar puncture, is taken to determine CNS involvement (increased intracranial pressure).

  □ Nursing Actions

    ▸ Have the child empty his bladder.

    ▸ Place the child in the fetal position and assist in maintaining the position. Distraction may need to be used.

    ▸ Assist the provider with the procedure.

      ▷ A topical anesthetic (EMLA cream) may be applied over the biopsy area 45 min to 1 hr prior to the procedure.

    ▸ The child may be sedated with fentanyl (Sublimaze) and midazolam (Versed).

- ▸ The provider will clean the skin and inject a local anesthetic.
          - ▸ The provider will take pressure readings and collect three to five test tubes of CSF.
          - ▸ Pressure will be applied after the needle is removed.
          - ▸ Label specimens appropriately and deliver them to the laboratory.
          - ▸ Monitor the site for hematoma or infection.
      - ▫ Client Education
          - ▸ Instruct the child to remain in bed for 4 to 8 hr in a flat position to prevent leakage and a resulting spinal headache. This may not be possible for an infant, toddler, or preschooler.
  - ■ Sonograms
      - ▫ Sonograms are used to detect liver and spleen infiltration, enlargement, and fibrosis.
      - ▫ Nursing Actions
          - ▸ Assist with positioning the child.
      - ▫ Client Education
          - ▸ Educate the child and parents about the procedure.
          - ▸ Provide emotional support.
  - ■ Liver and kidney function studies
      - ▫ These studies are used for baseline functioning before chemotherapy.
      - ▫ Nursing Actions
          - ▸ Draw the appropriate amount of serum.
      - ▫ Client Education
          - ▸ Educate the child and parents about the length of time to receive results.

Collaborative Care

- • Nursing Care
  - ○ Provide emotional support to the child and parents.
  - ○ Encourage peer contact if appropriate.
  - ○ Assess pain using an age-appropriate pain scale.
  - ○ Use pharmacological and nonpharmacological interventions to provide around-the-clock pain management.

- Medications
  - Chemotherapy
    - Chemotherapeutic agents – L-asparaginase, teniposide (VM-26), etoposide (VP-16), bleomycin, cisplatin, vincristine, and cyclophosphamide
    - Chemotherapy is administered in four phases to treat leukemia.
      - Induction therapy – To achieve complete remission or less than 5% of leukemic cells in the bone marrow
      - CNS prophylactic therapy – To prevent invasion of the CNS by leukemic cells
      - Intensification therapy – To destroy any remaining leukemic cells followed by a delayed intensification to prevent any resistant leukemic cells from emerging
      - Maintenance therapy – To sustain the remission phase
    - Nursing Considerations
      - Control nausea and vomiting with antiemetics prior to treatment.
      - Manage side effects of treatment.

SIDE EFFECT	NURSING INTERVENTIONS
Mucosal ulceration	• Provide frequent oral care. • Inspect the child's mouth for ulceration and hemorrhage. • Use a soft-bristled toothbrush or a soft, disposable toothbrushes for oral care. • Lubricate lips with lip balm to prevent cracking. • Offer foods that are soft and bland. • Assist the child to use mouthwashes (such as 1 tsp salt mixed with 1 pint of water or 1 tsp baking soda mixed with 1 qt of water) frequently. • Apply local anesthetics (hydrocortisone dental paste [Orabase], antiseptic mouth rinse [UlcerEase], aluminum and magnesium hydroxide [Maalox]) to mucosa to minimize pain. • Use agents (mouthwashes, lozenges) that are effective against fungal and bacterial infections (chlorhexidine gluconate [Peridex]). • Avoid viscous lidocaine (causes risk of aspiration from depressed gag reflex), hydrogen peroxide (delays healing), milk of magnesia (dries mucous membranes), and lemon glycerin swabs (causes tooth decay and erosion of tissue)

SIDE EFFECT	NURSING INTERVENTIONS
Skin breakdown	• Inspect skin daily. • Assess rectal mucosa for fissures. • Avoid rectal temperatures. • Provide sitz baths as needed. • Reposition frequently. • Use a pressure reduction system.

Neuropathy	• Constipation
	  ○ Encourage a diet high in fiber.
	  ○ Administer stool softeners and laxatives as needed.
	  ○ Encourage fluids.
	• Footdrop
	  ○ Use a footboard in bed.
	• Weakness and numbness of extremities
	  ○ Assist with ambulation.
	• Jaw pain
	  ○ Provide a soft diet.

Loss of appetite	• Monitor fluid intake and hydration status. • Provide small, frequent, well-balanced meals. • Involve the child in meal planning. • Administer enteral nutrition if needed. • Weigh the child daily. • Monitor electrolyte values. • Administer chemotherapy early in the day.
Hemorrhage cystitis	• Encourage fluids. • Encourage frequent voiding. • Administer chemotherapy early in the morning to promote adequate fluid intake and voiding. • Administer mesna (Mesnex) to provide protection to the bladder.
Alopecia	• Prepare the child and parents in advance for hair loss. • Encourage the use of a cotton hat or scarf or a wig if the child is self-conscious about hair loss.

- Client Education
  - Instruct the parents that the use of steroid treatment may cause moon face.
  - Instruct the parents that the child may experience mood changes.
  - Teach the parents to recognize signs of infection, skin breakdown, and nutritional deficiency.
  - Encourage the child and parents to maintain good hygiene.

- □ Teach the child and parents to avoid individuals with infectious diseases.

- □ Instruct the child and parents how to administer medications and provide nutritional support at home.

- □ Instruct the parents in the proper use of vascular access devices.

- □ Instruct the child and parents about bleeding precautions and the management of active bleeding.

- Interdisciplinary Care

  ○ Provide information regarding support services for the child and parents.

- Therapeutic Procedures

  ○ Hematopoietic stem cell transplant (HCST)

    ▪ HCST may be indicated for children who have AML during the first remission and for children who have ALL after a second remission.

    ▪ Nursing Actions

      □ The nurse assists with HCST, which involves high-dose chemotherapy and radiation to destroy tumor cells.

      □ After the tumor cells are destroyed, the child is given donor bone marrow or other stem cells, such as those cells from cord blood. Implantation of new cells may take 2 to 6 weeks.

      □ Implement protective isolation.

        ▸ A private, positive-pressure room

        ▸ At least 12 air exchanges/hr

        ▸ HEPA filtration for incoming air

        ▸ Respirator mask, gloves, and gowns

        ▸ No dried or fresh flowers and no potted plants

    ▪ Client Education

      □ The child is at an increased risk for infection and bleeding until the transfused stem cells grow.

  ○ Radiation therapy

    ▪ To brain and spinal cord

    ▪ Nursing Actions

      □ Assist with positioning.

      □ Provide support to the child and parents.

      □ Manage side effects.

    ▪ Client Education

      □ Educate the child and parents regarding side effects (fatigue, infection)

      □ Encourage adequate rest and a healthy diet.

- Client Outcomes

  - The child will be free of infection.

  - The child will consume adequate nutritional intake to maintain an appropriate weight.

Complications

- Infection

  - Infection can be a complication of myelosuppression.

  - Nursing Actions

    - Provide the child with a private room. The room should be designed to allow for adequate air flow to reduce airborne pathogens.

    - Restrict visitors and health personnel with active illnesses.

    - Adhere to strict hand hygiene.

    - Assess potential sites of infections (oral ulcer, open cut) and monitor temperature.

    - Administer antibiotics as prescribed.

    - Monitor the child's absolute neutrophil count (ANC).

    - Encourage adequate protein and caloric intake.

  - Client Education

    - Educate about infection control practices.

    - Educate the child and parents about sign and symptoms of infection and when to call the health care provider.

    - Avoid all immunizations while the immune system is depressed.

- Bleeding

  - Bleeding can be a complication of myelosuppression.

  - Nursing Actions

    - Monitor for signs of bleeding (petechiae, ecchymosis, hematuria, bleeding gums, hematemesis, tarry stools).

    - Avoid unnecessary skin punctures and use surgical aseptic technique when performed. Apply pressure for 5 min to stop bleeding.

    - Treat a nosebleed with cold and pressure.

    - Administer platelets as ordered.

    - Avoid obtaining temperatures rectally.

- ○ Client Education
  - Encourage/provide meticulous oral care to prevent gingival bleeding. Use a soft toothbrush and avoid astringent mouthwashes.
  - Teach the parents measures for controlling epistaxis.
  - Teach the parents and child to avoid activities that may lead to injury or bleeding.

- Anemia
  - ○ Anemia can be a complication of myelosuppression.
  - ○ Nursing Actions
    - Administer blood transfusions as ordered.
    - Allow for frequent rest periods.
    - Administer oxygen therapy.
    - Administer IV fluid replacement.
  - ○ Client Education
    - Educate the child and parents about foods high in iron.

- Cardiotoxicity
  - ○ Cardiotoxicity is one of the long-term effects of treatment.
  - ○ Nursing Actions
    - Monitor for cardiac dysfunction by checking blood pressure, heart rate, daily weights, capillary refill, and cardiac rhythm disturbances.
  - ○ Client Education
    - Teach the parents to obtain pulse and blood pressure readings.
    - Educate the parents about the need to obtain daily weights.
    - Educate the child and parents about signs and symptoms to report to the health care provider.

- Delayed growth and development
  - ○ Delayed growth and development is one of the long-term effects of treatment.
  - ○ Nursing Actions
    - Assess the child's developmental status.
    - Initiate occupational and physical therapy.
  - ○ Client Education
    - Refer to occupational therapy and/or physical therapy as needed.
    - Provide support.

CHAPTER 40: BLOOD NEOPLASMS

 Application Exercises

1. Match the following conditions with possible manifestations/complications of bone marrow suppression.

_____	Anemia	A. Bruising and nosebleed
_____	Neutropenia	B. Fever and pneumonia
_____	Thrombocytopenia	C. Fatigue and shortness of breath

2. A child who has leukemia is experiencing severe thrombocytopenia. Which of the following actions should the nurse take to prevent complications from thrombocytopenia? (Select all that apply.)

_____ Avoid injections and skin punctures.

_____ Perform frequent hand hygiene.

_____ Limit visitors.

_____ Monitor platelet count.

_____ Avoid obtaining temperatures rectally.

_____ Monitor for fever.

3. A nurse is assessing a child who has leukemia and is undergoing chemotherapy. The child is experiencing weight loss, nausea, and absence of appetite. Identify nursing interventions the nurse should use to promote adequate nutritional intake.

4. A child with leukemia has mucosal ulceration in his mouth and throat due to neutropenia. Which of the following actions should the nurse take? (Select all that apply.)

_____ Swab the mucosa with lemon glycerine swabs.

_____ Apply viscous lidocaine.

_____ Offer soft foods.

_____ Use a soft, disposable toothbrush for oral care.

_____ Encourage gargling with a warm saline mouthwash.

5. An infant diagnosed with rhabdomyosarcoma of the middle ear is to undergo a lumbar puncture. The health care provider tells the nurse that the procedure will be carried out with the infant in a sitting position. Which of the following actions should the nurse take?

A. Cleanse the thoracic area of the infant's back with an antiseptic solution.

B. Apply a eutectic mixture of local anesthetics (EMLA) cream just before the procedure begins.

C. Restrain the infant during the procedure to prevent movement.

D. Position the infant with his head extended and chin raised.

CHAPTER 40: BLOOD NEOPLASMS

 Application Exercises Answer Key

1. Match the following conditions with possible manifestations/complications of bone marrow suppression.

   C   Anemia   A. Bruising and nosebleed

   B   Neutropenia   B. Fever and pneumonia

   A   Thrombocytopenia   C. Fatigue and shortness of breath

With anemia, a decreased number of circulating RBCs causes decreased oxygenation, which manifests itself as fatigue and shortness of breath. Neutropenia, which is a decreased neutrophil count, causes secondary infections, such as pneumonia, and may also result in fever. Thrombocytopenia, which is a decreased platelet count, results in complications such as bleeding and bruising.

NCLEX® Connection: Physiological Adaptation, Pathophysiology

2. A child who has leukemia is experiencing severe thrombocytopenia. Which of the following actions should the nurse take to prevent complications from thrombocytopenia? (Select all that apply.)

   X   **Avoid injections and skin punctures.**

          Perform frequent hand hygiene.

          Limit visitors.

   X   **Monitor platelet count.**

   X   **Avoid obtaining temperatures rectally.**

          Monitor for fever.

The child with thrombocytopenia is at risk for injury due to the high risk for bleeding. The nurse should avoid punctures to the skin whenever possible, monitor the thrombocyte (platelet) count, and avoid obtaining temperatures rectally, which could cause intestinal bleeding. Performing frequent hand hygiene, limiting visitors, and monitoring for fever are interventions to prevent complications from leucopenia (low WBC count).

NCLEX® Connection: Reduction of Risk Potential, Complications From Surgical Procedures and Health Alterations

3. A nurse is assessing a child who has leukemia and is undergoing chemotherapy. The child is experiencing weight loss, nausea, and absence of appetite. Identify nursing interventions the nurse should use to promote adequate nutritional intake.

Involve the child in food selection.

Medicate the child for nausea before meals.

Encourage small, frequent meals.

Encourage high-protein, high-calorie food choices.

Give the child high-protein, high-calorie shakes.

Weigh the child daily to monitor weight loss or gain.

Make food attractive and unusual, such as by cutting a sandwich into a star shape with a cookie cutter.

Allow the parents to bring the child's favorite food from home.

Involve parents in order to learn about the child's usual preferences.

 NCLEX® Connection: Basic Care and Comfort, Nutrition and Oral Hydration

4. A child with leukemia has mucosal ulceration in his mouth and throat due to neutropenia. Which of the following actions should the nurse take? (Select all that apply.)

_____ Swab the mucosa with lemon glycerine swabs.

_____ Apply viscous lidocaine.

__X__ **Offer soft foods.**

__X__ **Use a soft, disposable toothbrush for oral care.**

__X__ **Encourage gargling with a warm saline mouthwash.**

Offering soft foods, using a soft, disposable toothbrush for oral care, and encouraging gargling with a warm saline mouthwash are all effective treatments for mucosal ulceration. Lemon glycerine swabs may cause tooth decay and erosion of tissue, and viscous lidocaine can cause a depressed gag reflex and aspiration.

 NCLEX® Connection: Reduction of Risk Potential, Complications From Surgical Procedures and Health Alterations

5. An infant diagnosed with rhabdomyosarcoma of the middle ear is to undergo a lumbar puncture. The health care provider tells the nurse that the procedure will be carried out with the infant in a sitting position. Which of the following actions should the nurse take?

A. Cleanse the thoracic area of the infant's back with an antiseptic solution.

B. Apply a eutectic mixture of local anesthetics (EMLA) cream just before the procedure begins.

C. Restrain the infant during the procedure to prevent movement.

D. Position the infant with his head extended and chin raised.

The child should be restrained to prevent movement and possible injury during the procedure. The lumbar area of the back, rather than the thoracic area, is where the needle will be inserted. EMLA cream should be applied 60 min prior to the procedure. If the sitting position is to be used, the infant should be positioned with his neck flexed forward and his chin on his chest.

(N) **NCLEX® Connection: Reduction of Risk Potential, Diagnostic Tests**

Overview

- Malignant tumors in bone may originate from all tissues involved in bone growth, including osteoid matrix, blood vessels, and cartilage.

  - Osteosarcoma usually occurs in the metaphysis of long bones, most often in the femur. Treatment frequently includes amputation of the affected extremity as well as chemotherapy

  - Ewing's sarcoma (a primitive neuroectodermal tumor [PNET]) occurs in the shafts of long bones and of trunk bones. Treatment includes surgical biopsy, intensive radiation therapy to tumor site, and chemotherapy, but not amputation.

    - Prognosis depends on how quickly the disease was diagnosed and whether or not metastasis has occurred.

- Soft tissue malignancies arise from undifferentiated cells in any of the soft tissues (muscles, tendons), in connective or fibrous tissue, or in blood or lymph vessels. These malignancies can begin in any area of the body.

  - Rhabdomyosarcoma originates in skeletal muscle in any part of the body, but it most commonly occurs in the head and neck, with the orbit of the eye frequently affected. Treatment consists of surgical biopsy, local radiation therapy, and chemotherapy, rather than radical surgical procedures.

- Children who undergo irradiation for malignancies in or near the pelvic area may experience sterilization and/or secondary cancers.

Assessment

- Risk Factors

  - Osteosarcoma occurs most often in males during puberty, when bone growth is most rapid.

  - Ewing's sarcoma occurs most frequently in individuals 4 years of age and older. It is almost completely confined to those under 30 years of age.

  - Rhabdomyosarcoma occurs more frequently in Caucasian children than in African-American children (the ratio is more than 2:1). The highest incidence is in children younger than 5 years of age.

- Subjective and Objective Data

	SUBJECTIVE DATA	OBJECTIVE DATA
Bone cancers	• Non-specific bone pain that is often mistaken for an injury or growing pains • Temporary relief of pain when extremity is flexed	• Weakness, swelling, or decreased movement of the extremity • Palpable lymph nodes near the tumor • Anemia, generalized infection, or unexplained weight loss

Rhabdomyosarcoma	• May cause pain in local areas related to compression by the tumor (sore throat may occur with tumor of the nasopharynx)
	• Possible absence of pain in some parts of the body, such as in the retroperitoneal area, until the tumor begins to obstruct organs
		• Based on affected area
		  ○ Orbit – Strabismus, exophthalmos, generalized swelling, or color change to conjunctiva
		  ○ Nasopharynx – Palpable area of firm swelling, nasal stuffiness, generalized swelling, palpable lymph nodes, and rhinorrhea
		  ○ Retroperitoneal area – Palpable mass and a urinary or intestinal obstruction

  - Laboratory Tests

    - Alkaline phosphatase –May be elevated in bone malignancies

    - Complete blood count (CBC) and other common tests can help rule out infection, iron deficiency anemia, and other possible causes of findings.

  - Diagnostic Procedures

    - X-rays, CT scans, and magnetic resonance imaging scans

      □ These tests may be used to:

        ▸ Diagnose and evaluate tumor characteristic for types of cancer.

        ▸ Assess soft tissue to tumor boundaries.

        ▸ Determine involvement of blood or nerve tissue.

        ▸ Determine the extent of metastasis (lung, liver).

      □ Bone scan may be performed to evaluate metastasis of bone tumors.

      □ Bone marrow aspiration may be performed to diagnose lung or bone marrow metastasis.

    - Bone marrow aspiration (See chapter 40, Blood Neoplasms.)

    - Cerebrospinal fluid (CSF) analysis

      □ CSF analysis is used for children who have head/neck rhabdomyosarcoma to evaluate for metastasis to the central nervous system. (See chapter 40, Blood Neoplasms.)

Collaborative Care

- Nursing Care

  - Obtain the child's trust by being honest when answering questions and by giving information about the disease and treatment.

  - Allow the child time, usually several days, to prepare emotionally for surgery (especially if amputation is involved) and chemotherapy.

  - Avoid overwhelming the child with information.

- Medications

  - Chemotherapy

    - Various agents used singly or in combination before or after surgery – High dose methotrexate with citrovorum factor rescue, doxorubicin, bleomycin, actinomycin D, cyclophosphamide, ifosfamide, cisplatin, vincristine, ifosfamide, and etoposide

    - Nursing Considerations

      - Control nausea and vomiting with antiemetics prior to treatment.

      - Manage side effects of treatment.

    - Client Education

      - Teach the family to recognize signs of infection, skin breakdown, and nutritional deficiency.

      - Encourage the child and family to maintain good hygiene.

      - Instruct the family in the proper use of vascular access devices.

      - Instruct the child and family about bleeding precautions and management of active bleeding.

  - Amitriptyline (Elavil)

    - A tricyclic antidepressant (TCA) for use with neuropathic pain or phantom pain in adolescents who have amputated limbs.

    - Nursing Considerations

      - Monitor the child for drowsiness, orthostatic hypotension, anticholinergic effects, seizures, mania, and cardiac dysfunction.

    - Client Education

      - Teach the child and family how to manage side effects.

      - Caution the child and parents about taking only the prescribed dosage to prevent toxic reactions.

- Interdisciplinary Care

  ○ Older children and adolescents may benefit from attending a support group for children who have cancer and/or amputations.

  ○ Initiate a referral for mental health counseling to assist the child to resume normal activities.

  ○ Initiate physical and occupational therapy referrals to start while in the hospital and to continue after discharge.

- Therapeutic Procedures

  ○ Localized radiation therapy

    ▪ Radiation therapy may be used in combination with chemotherapy and surgery.

    ▪ Nursing Actions

        ☐ Assist the child with positioning.

        ☐ Monitor for side effects.

    ▪ Client Education

        ☐ Educate the child and family regarding the course of therapy.

- Surgical Interventions

  ○ Surgical biopsy for any of the bone or soft tissue cancers

    ▪ Tumor is biopsied under anesthesia to determine presence and/or tissue type of cancer.

    ▪ Nursing Actions

        ☐ Provide routine pre and postoperative care.

        ☐ Provide for adequate pain relief.

        ☐ Monitor wound for signs of infection.

        ☐ Actions vary with extent and area of surgery, but nursing actions should include pre and postprocedure assessment, including vital signs, medication for pain, and wound care as necessary.

    ▪ Client Education

        ☐ Educate the child and family regarding postoperative care.

  ○ Limb salvage procedure for osteosarcoma

    ▪ This procedure is used only for certain children. It involves a preoperative course of chemotherapy to shrink the tumor and then total bone and joint replacement after the tumor and affected bone are removed.

    ▪ Nursing Actions

        ☐ Administer preoperative chemotherapy.

        ☐ Assist with managing side effects.

- ☐ Provide routine postoperative care.

- ☐ Provide adequate pain relief.

- ■ Client Education

  - ☐ Educate the child and family regarding postoperative care.

  - ☐ Teach the child and family about any expected effects of preoperative chemotherapy, such as hair loss.

- ○ Limb amputation for osteosarcoma

  - ■ Amputation of the affected limb should occur above the joint or 7.5 cm (3 in) above the proximal edge of the tumor. This may include unilateral removal of the scapula and clavicle for tumors of the upper humerus and removal of portions of the pelvis for tumors of the hip. The child may receive chemotherapy both preoperatively and postoperatively.

  - ■ Nursing Actions

    - ☐ Provide routine pre and postoperative care.

    - ☐ Provide emotional support.

    - ☐ Care for the stump as prescribed.

    - ☐ Assess for the presence of phantom limb pain postoperatively and medicate appropriately.

  - ■ Client Education

    - ☐ Prepare the child for fitting of a temporary prosthesis, which may occur immediately after surgery.

    - ☐ Encourage cooperation with postoperative physical therapy.

    - ☐ Work with the child and family to plan for issues such as appropriate clothing to wear with prosthesis.

    - ☐ Role play issues that the child will need to deal with after discharge, such as talking to strangers who ask about the prosthesis.

    - ☐ Assist the family to recognize that the child's emotions, such as anger, are normal grief reactions after amputation, chemotherapy, and other treatments.

- • Care After Discharge

  - ○ Client Education

    - ■ Educate the child and family regarding the importance of follow-up care.

  - ○ Community Services

    - ■ Initiate appropriate referrals to assist the child to resume normal activities (school attendance, physical activities).

- Client Outcomes

  ○ The child will be free of postoperative pain, including phantom limb pain for those children who must undergo amputation.

  ○ The child will learn strategies to manage side effects of radiation and/or chemotherapy.

  ○ The child will express feelings regarding loss.

  ○ The child will participate in age-appropriate activities.

Complications

- Skin desquamation (either dry or moist) with permanent hyperpigmentation and possible damage to underlying structures

  ○ Nursing Actions

    ▪ Assess the site frequently for infection.

    ▪ Assess for damage to underlying structures (nerves, blood vessels) by assessing circulation and movement.

  ○ Client Education

    ▪ Teach the parents methods to prevent additional irritation to the site (use loose-fitting clothing, prevent exposure to sunlight or extremes of temperature).

    ▪ Teach adolescents about risks of sterilization if indicated.

    ▪ Explain the importance of continuing follow-up examinations.

- Myelosuppression

  ○ Elimination of normal blood cells along with cancer cells is a risk with treatment by most chemotherapeutic agents. This may cause infection (reduced leukocytes), hemorrhage (reduced thrombocytes), and anemia (reduced red blood cells).

  ○ Nursing Actions

    ▪ Evaluate laboratory data and assess for symptoms of complications.

      □ Infection – Elevated WBC and fever

      □ Hemorrhage – Blood in urine or stool, bruising, and petechiae

      □ Anemia – Fatigue and decreased hemoglobin/hematocrit

    ▪ Prevent infection

      □ Provide a private room when hospitalized.

      □ Restrict staff/visitors who have infections.

      □ Promote frequent hand hygiene by staff/visitors.

      □ Avoid all live-virus vaccines during periods of immunosuppression.

      □ Ensure that siblings are up-to-date on vaccinations.

      □ Provide a diet adequate in proteins and calories.

- Prevent hemorrhage or injury from bleeding.
  - Use a strict aseptic technique for all invasive procedures.
  - Use gentle technique when providing mouth care.
  - Clean the perineal area carefully to prevent trauma and avoid obtaining temperatures rectally.
  - Infuse platelets as prescribed.
- Prevent anemia or injury from anemia.
  - Provide rest periods as needed.
  - Infuse packed red blood cells as prescribed.
- Client Education
  - Teach family members strategies to recognize complications at home and to prevent damage from infection, hemorrhage, or bleeding.

CHAPTER 41: BONE AND SOFT TISSUE CANCERS

 Application Exercises

1. A nurse is caring for a school-age child who has suspected osteosarcoma. Which of the following laboratory values is likely to be elevated if this diagnosis is correct?

    A. Blood glucose

    B. Hematocrit

    C. Alkaline phosphatase

    D. Serum potassium

2. A nurse in a primary care clinic is assessing a 12-year-old child who reports frequent pain in the left proximal anterior thigh. The health care provider suspects a diagnosis of osteosarcoma. Which of the following assessment findings should the nurse expect if this diagnosis is correct? (Select all that apply.)

    _____ There is visible swelling in the area.

    _____ Pain is temporarily relieved by extending the leg.

    _____ Pain radiates down to the lower leg and up to the hip.

    _____ Pain causes the child to limp at times.

    _____ Lymph nodes in the groin can be palpated.

3. A nurse is caring for a 14-year-old adolescent boy who has been diagnosed with osteosarcoma of the left proximal tibia. The adolescent is 4 days preoperative for an above-the-knee amputation and is admitted to the hospital for preoperative chemotherapy. The adolescent knows about the surgery. Which of the following is the nurse's responsibility in the next 4 days regarding this adolescent's emotional health?

    A. Ensure that the adolescent has a referral for a psychiatrist visit.

    B. Prepare a teaching plan to educate the adolescent in detail about what he should know regarding his diagnosis and treatment.

    C. Spend time with the adolescent to answer any questions he may have.

    D. Perform a mental status examination to assess the adolescent's thought patterns.

CHAPTER 41: BONE AND SOFT TISSUE CANCERS

 Application Exercises Answer Key

1. A nurse is caring for a school-age child who has suspected osteosarcoma. Which of the following laboratory values is likely to be elevated if this diagnosis is correct?

    A. Blood glucose

    B. Hematocrit

    C. Alkaline phosphatase

    D. Serum potassium

    Alkaline phosphatase is made in the liver and in bones. It is likely to be elevated in a child who has a bone malignancy. None of the other values are expected to be elevated in a child who has a bone malignancy, although hematocrit may be decreased.

 NCLEX® Connection: Reduction of Risk Potential, Laboratory Values

2. A nurse in a primary care clinic is assessing a 12-year-old child who reports frequent pain in the left proximal anterior thigh. The health care provider suspects a diagnosis of osteosarcoma. Which of the following assessment findings should the nurse expect if this diagnosis is correct? (Select all that apply.)

    __X__   **There is visible swelling in the area.**

    _____   Pain is temporarily relieved by extending the leg.

    _____   Pain radiates down to the lower leg and up to the hip.

    __X__   **Pain causes the child to limp at times.**

    __X__   **Lymph nodes in the groin can be palpated.**

    Swelling may occur as soft tissue becomes affected, pain may cause the child to limp, and lymph nodes near the tumor may become palpable as the tumor spreads. Pain in osteosarcoma is often relieved by flexing, rather than extending, joints near the area because this relaxes muscles over the affected bone. Pain would also not radiate up and down the entire leg, because the pain of osteosarcoma is localized.

 NCLEX® Connection: Physiological Adaptation, Pathophysiology

3. A nurse is caring for a 14-year-old adolescent boy who has been diagnosed with osteosarcoma of the left proximal tibia. The adolescent is 4 days preoperative for an above-the-knee amputation and is admitted to the hospital for preoperative chemotherapy. The adolescent knows about the surgery. Which of the following is the nurse's responsibility in the next 4 days regarding this adolescent's emotional health?

    A. Ensure that the adolescent has a referral for a psychiatrist visit.

    B. Prepare a teaching plan to educate the adolescent in detail about what he should know regarding his diagnosis and treatment.

    C. Spend time with the adolescent to answer any questions he may have.

    D. Perform a mental status examination to assess the adolescent's thought patterns.

The nurse should be available to answer the adolescent's questions and to listen as he talks about his feelings. None of the other options is indicated. Although it may be helpful for the adolescent to talk to another adolescent who has undergone a similar experience, a referral for a psychiatrist to visit is not indicated. A detailed teaching plan is not useful in this situation, and a mental status examination is not useful for the adolescent's emotional health.

Ⓝ **NCLEX® Connection: Health Promotion and Maintenance, Growth and Development**

UNIT 3: NURSING CARE OF CHILDREN WITH SPECIAL NEEDS

- Pediatric Emergencies
- Psychosocial Issues of Infants, Children, and Adolescents

NCLEX® CONNECTIONS

When reviewing the chapters in this unit, keep in mind the relevant sections of the NCLEX® outline, in particular:

CLIENT NEEDS: HEALTH PROMOTION AND MAINTENANCE

Relevant topics/tasks include:
- Developmental Stages and Transitions
  - Compare the client's development to expected age/developmental stage and report any deviations.
- Health and Wellness
  - Encourage client participation in appropriate behavior modification programs related to health and wellness.
- Health Promotion/Disease Prevention
  - Assist the client in maintaining an optimum level of health.

CLIENT NEEDS: PSYCHOSOCIAL INTEGRITY

Relevant topics/tasks include:
- Abuse/Neglect
  - Identify risk factors for domestic, child, elder abuse/neglect, and sexual abuse.
- Family Dynamics
  - Assess parental techniques related to discipline.

CLIENT NEEDS: PHYSIOLOGICAL ADAPTATION

Relevant topics/tasks include:
- Medical Emergencies
  - Apply knowledge of nursing procedures and psychomotor skills when caring for a client experiencing a medical emergency.

Overview

- Respiratory emergencies

  - Respiratory failure occurs when there is a diminished ability to maintain adequate oxygenation of the blood. A manifestation of respiratory insufficiency is increased work of breathing.

  - Airway obstruction prevents adequate air exchange. Obstruction may lead to respiratory failure or arrest if not corrected.

  - Respiratory arrest occurs when breathing stops completely.

  - When respiratory distress is treated or rescue breathing is started in a timely manner, infants and children are less likely than adults to have cardiac arrest.

- Drowning – Asphyxiation while being submerged in fluid

  - Near-drowning incidents are those in which children have survived for 24 hr after being submerged in fluid.

  - Drowning may occur in any standing body of water that is at least 1-inch in depth (bathtub, toilet, bucket, pool, pond, lake).

- Sudden infant death syndrome (SIDS)

  - SIDS is the sudden, unpredictable, and undetectable death of an infant without an identified cause, even after investigation and autopsy.

  - SIDS is a diagnosis of exclusion that is made only after every other cause of death is discarded. SIDS is not caused by suffocation.

  - SIDS is a major cause of death in infants from 1 month to 1 year of age, and it occurs frequently in the winter months.

  - SIDS is not preventable, but risks may be reduced.

  - Education about reducing the risk of SIDS is increasing.

- Poisoning – Ingestion of or exposure to toxic substances

  - Most poisonings occur in the child's home or homes of relatives or friends.

  - Poisonings may also occur in schools or health care facilities.

  - Acetaminophen (Tylenol) is the most common medication poisoning in children (a toxic dose is 150 mg/kg or higher).

- Toxic substances leading to poisoning are usually ingested, but some may be inhaled.
    - Liquid corrosives cause more damage than granular corrosives.
    - Immediate danger with hydrocarbon ingestion is aspiration.
- It is vital to use methods to prevent poisoning.

Assessment

- Risk Factors
    - Respiratory emergencies (respiratory failure, respiratory arrest)

FUNCTIONAL ALTERATION	POSSIBLE CAUSES
Primary inefficient gas exchange	• Cerebral trauma • Brain tumor • Overdose of barbiturates, opioids, and/or benzodiazepines • Asphyxia • CNS infection (encephalitis)
Obstructive lung disease (increased resistance)	• Aspiration • Infection • Tumor • Anaphylaxis • Laryngospasm • Asthma
Restrictive lung disease	• Cystic fibrosis ○ Pneumonia • Respiratory distress syndrome

- Drowning or near-drowning
    - Age of the child
        - In children over 12 months of age, drowning is a significant cause of accidental death.
    - Gender
        - Males are five times more likely to drown than females.
    - Swimming ability (may be overconfident) or lack of ability
    - Lack of supervision (Children can drown while being supervised.)
    - Boating without life jackets
    - Diving into water

- SIDS
  - Healthy infant
  - Death associated with sleep without signs of suffering
  - Maternal health and behaviors during pregnancy.
    - Age less than 20 years
    - Alcohol, drug, and/or tobacco use
    - Low weight gain during pregnancy
    - Anemia
    - Placental abnormalities
    - Sexually transmitted disease or urinary tract infection
    - Inadequate prenatal care
  - Twins
  - Premature birth
  - Small for gestational age
  - Persistent apnea
  - Bronchopulmonary dysplasia
  - Family history of SIDS
  - Environmental risk factors
    - Low socioeconomic status
    - Crowded living conditions
    - Cold weather
    - Use of soft items in crib (stuffed animals, blankets)
    - Prone sleeping position
    - Sleeping with others
- Poisoning
  - Children who are younger than 6 years of age are more likely to ingest toxic substances due to their developmental level. (Infants explore their environment orally, and preschoolers imitate others.)
  - Medications, household chemicals, plants, and heavy metals are potential sources of toxic ingestion.
  - Lead may be ingested or small particles inhaled during renovations of areas with lead-based paint.
  - Common toxic substances ingested by children include acetaminophen, aspirin, iron, hydrocarbons, corrosives, and/or lead.

- Subjective Data
  - Respiratory emergencies
    - History of illnesses (chronic or acute)
    - History of events leading to respiratory emergency
    - Presence of allergies
  - Drowning/Near drowning
    - History of event including location and time of submersion
      - Salt water or nonsalt water drowning
      - Warm or cold water drowning (bathtub versus cold lake)
  - SIDS
    - History of events prior to finding infant
    - History of illnesses
    - Pregnancy and birth history
    - Presence of risk factors
    - Family coping and support
  - Poisoning
    - History of chronic and acute illnesses
- Objective Data
  - Physical Assessment Findings
    - Respiratory emergencies
      - Color of skin – Central or peripheral cyanosis indicative of hypoxia
      - Heart rate/rhythm – Tachycardia or bradycardia (severe sign of hypoxia)
      - Respiratory effort, depth of respirations, tachypnea or bradypnea (severe sign of hypoxia), expiratory grunting, nasal flaring, and presence of retractions and area noted, such as intercostal (between ribs)
      - Assessment for palpable pulses and capillary refill greater than 2 sec indicates decreased perfusion
      - Ability to talk (sentences or just single words)
      - CNS symptoms ranging from restlessness and lethargy to coma (severe sign)
      - Diaphoresis
      - Signs of choking
        - Universal choking sign (clutching neck with thumb and index finger)
        - Inability to speak
        - Weak, ineffective cough

- ▸ High-pitched sounds or no sounds made while inhaling
- ▸ Dyspnea
- ▸ Cyanosis
- ■ Drowning/Near Drowning
  - ☐ Body temperature for hypothermia
  - ☐ Observation for bruises, spinal cord injury, or other physical injuries
  - ☐ Respiratory assessment for drowning/near drowning – same as above assessment for respiratory emergencies
- ■ SIDS
  - ☐ Blood-tinged fluid is in the mouth.
  - ☐ The infant was found face down in the bed.
  - ☐ Fingers may be clenched.
- ■ Poisoning
  - ☐ List of medications or chemicals that the child may have been exposed to
  - ☐ Number of pills or amount of liquid ingested
  - ☐ Time of ingestion
  - ☐ Physical response
    - ▸ Respiratory rate, rhythm, and effort
    - ▸ Heart rate and rhythm
    - ▸ Level of consciousness
    - ▸ Seizures
    - ▸ Pupil size and response
    - ▸ Swelling of facial area, especially lips and mouth
    - ▸ Color of mucous membranes
    - ▸ Peripheral pulses
    - ▸ Diaphoretic or dry skin
    - ▸ Presence or absence of bowel sounds

SUBSTANCE	CLINICAL MANIFESTATIONS
Acetaminophen	• 2 to 4 hr after ingestion – Nausea, vomiting, sweating, and pallor • 24 to 36 hr after ingestion – Improvement in the child's condition • 36 hr to 7 days or longer (hepatic stage) – Pain in upper right quadrant, confusion, stupor, jaundice, and coagulation disturbances • Final stage – Death or gradual recovery

SUBSTANCE	CLINICAL MANIFESTATIONS
Acetylsalicylic acid (Aspirin)	• Acute poisoning – Nausea, vomiting, disorientation, diaphoresis, tachypnea, tinnitus, oliguria, lightheadedness, and seizures • Chronic poisoning – Subtle version of acute manifestations, bleeding tendencies, dehydration, and seizures more severe than acute poisoning
Supplemental iron	• Initial period (30 min to 6 hr after ingestion) – Vomiting, hematemesis, diarrhea, gastric pain, and bloody stools • Latency period (2 to 12 hr after ingestion) – Improvement of the child's condition • Systemic toxicity period (4 to 24 hr after ingestion) – Metabolic acidosis, hyperglycemia, bleeding, fever, shock, and possible death • Hepatic injury period (48 to 96 hr after ingestion) – Seizures or coma
Hydrocarbons (gasoline, kerosene, lighter fluid, paint thinner, turpentine)	• Gagging, choking, coughing, nausea, and vomiting • Lethargy, weakness, tachypnea, cyanosis, grunting, and retractions
Corrosives (household cleaners, batteries, denture cleaners, bleach)	• Pain and burning in mouth, throat, and stomach • Edematous lips, tongue, and pharynx with white mucous membranes • Violent vomiting with hemoptysis • Drooling • Anxiety • Shock
Lead	• Low-dose exposure – Easily distracted, impulsive, hyperactive, hearing impaired, and mild intellectual difficulty • High-dose exposure – Mental retardation, blindness, paralysis, coma, seizures, and death • Other manifestations – Renal impairment, impaired calcium function, and anemia

- ○ Laboratory Tests
    - ■ Respiratory emergencies
        - □ Arterial blood gases (ABGs) confirm oxygenation level.
    - ■ Poisoning
        - □ Lead levels in blood
        - □ CBC with differential to identify anemia
        - □ ABGs to assess oxygenation status
        - □ Serum iron

- □ Acetaminophen serum levels
- □ Poisoning
  - ‣ Toxicology levels dependent on the type of poisoning.
- ○ Diagnostic Procedures
  - ■ Respiratory Emergencies (including near drowning) – Chest radiographs
    - □ Chest radiographs determine the status of lungs with respiratory distress in cases of near drowning.
    - □ Nursing Actions
      - ‣ Assist with positioning the child.
  - ■ Poisoning – Liver function tests
    - □ Liver function tests should be used to identify liver damage.
    - □ Nursing Actions
      - ‣ Draw the appropriate amount of serum for laboratory tests.
    - □ Client Education
      - ‣ Educate the family on the timing of results.

Collaborative Care

- • Nursing Care
  - ○ Follow the American Heart Association (AHA) guidelines for CPR for respiratory and cardiac arrest.
    - ■ Follow the facility's procedure for activating the emergency response team.
    - ■ Use the current basic life support (BLS) and advanced cardiac life support (ACLS) guidelines for neonates (NALS) and for pediatric clients (PALS).
    - ■ Maintain current BLS and/or ACLS skills
  - ○ Obstructed Airway
    - ■ Responsive victim
      - □ Infants – Use a combination of back blows and chest thrusts.
      - □ Children and adolescents – Use abdominal thrusts
    - ■ Remove any obstruction or large debris, but do not reach into the mouth of an infant to prevent pushing the obstruction farther down the throat.
    - ■ Place the recovered child (one who resumes breathing) into the recovery position (on her side with legs bent at knees to stabilize in place).
    - ■ Use a calm approach with the child and family.
    - ■ Administer oxygen as prescribed.
    - ■ Administer medications, IV fluids, and emergency medications as prescribed.
    - ■ Keep the family informed of the child's status.

- o SIDS
  - Reduction of risk
    - Place infant on back for sleep.
    - Prevent exposure to tobacco smoke.
    - Prevent overheating.
    - Use a firm, tight-fitting mattress in the infant's crib.
    - Remove pillows, quilts, and sheepskins from the crib during sleep.
    - Ensure that the infant's head is kept uncovered during sleep.
  - Death
    - Allow the infant's family an opportunity to express feelings.
    - Provide private time for the family to be with the infant after death.
    - Provide support.
    - Provide home monitoring for those at high risk, such as a remaining twin.
- o Poisoning
  - Assist with intubation if needed, and observe symmetrical movement of the child's chest.
  - Position the child with the head of the bed slightly elevated unless contraindicated.
  - Keep emergency equipment (oral airway, suction catheter) at bedside.
  - Apply a cardiac monitor to the child.
  - Monitor pulse oximetry for infants.
  - Insert an IV and begin administering fluids as prescribed.
  - Insert a nasogastric tube as ordered.
  - Insert an indwelling urinary catheter and attach to urine bag.
  - Monitor Input and output.
  - Administer the specific antidote as prescribed.
  - Keep the family informed of the child's condition and needs.

INTERVENTIONS FOR SPECIFIC SUBSTANCES	
SUBSTANCE	**INTERVENTIONS**
Acetaminophen	• Acetylcysteine (Mucomyst) given orally
Acetylsalicylic acid (Aspirin)	• Activated charcoal • Gastric lavage • Sodium bicarbonate • Oxygen and ventilation • Vitamin K • Hemodialysis for severe cases
Supplemental iron	• Emesis or lavage • Chelation therapy using deferoxamine mesylate (Desferal)
Hydrocarbons (gasoline, kerosene, lighter fluid, paint thinner, turpentine)	• No induced vomiting • Intubation with cuffed endotracheal tube prior to any gastric decontamination • Treatment of chemical pneumonia
Corrosives (household cleaners, batteries, denture cleaners, bleach)	• Airway maintenance • NPO • No attempt to neutralize • No induced vomiting • Analgesics for pain
Lead	• Chelation therapy using calcium EDTA (calcium disodium versenate)

- Medications
  - Obstructed airway
    - Steroids
      - Administer for inflammation.
      - Nursing Considerations
        - Administer as prescribed.
        - Monitor for allergies and effectiveness of the medication.
      - Client Education
        - Educate the child and parents how to administer home doses (scheduling).
    - Bronchodilators – Albuterol (Proventil)
      - Nursing Considerations
        - Monitor respirations and cardiovascular status.

□ Client Education

▸ Educate the child about the importance of using a spacer with the medication if a metered dose inhaler is prescribed.

- Interdisciplinary Care

  ○ SIDS

    ■ Recommend support groups.

    ■ Recommend counseling.

- Therapeutic Procedures

  ○ Intubation may be needed with placement on a ventilator.

    ■ For children with respiratory emergencies, near drowning, and/or poisoning where the airway is unstable and aspiration is likely

    ■ Nursing Actions

      □ Assist with positioning during intubation to reduce the possibility of injury.

    ■ Client Education

      □ Educate the family about the procedure and what to expect when seeing the child.

- Care After Discharge

  ○ Client Education

    ■ Respiratory emergencies

      □ Educate the parents about the risk for obstruction in children. Avoid balloons, small buttons, small candies, hot dogs, and any other foods or objects that may be easily aspirated.

    ■ Drowning

      □ Encourage parents of toddlers to lock toilet seats if their children is at home.

      □ Do not leave the child unattended in the bathtub.

      □ Do not leave the child unattended in a swimming pool, even if the child has had swimming lessons.

      □ Make sure private pools have locking gates to prevent the child from wandering into the area.

      □ Have the child wear a life jacket while boating.

    ■ SIDS

      □ Encourage using a home monitoring system for future infants.

      □ Educate or reinforce proper sleeping position, crib environment, smoke-free environment, and the avoidance of overheating.

- Poisoning
  - Keep the telephone number for the Poison Control Center (PCC) near the telephone.
  - Contact the PCC before taking any action other than maintaining the child's airway.
  - Do not give the child ipecac.
  - Install childproof locks on cabinets containing potentially harmful substances (medications, alcohol, cleaning solutions, mouthwash, outdoor chemicals).
  - Supervise the child when he is taking medications.
  - Do not take medication in front of the child.
  - Discard unused medications.
  - Keep plants out of the reach of the child.
  - Eliminate lead-based paint in the home.
  - Use nonmercury thermometers.
  - Teach children the hazards of ingesting nonfood items.
- Client Outcomes
  - The child will be free of injury.

Complications

- Respiratory arrest
  - Can result from any cause, including drowning, poisoning, and possible SIDS
  - Nursing Actions
    - Initiate CPR.
  - Client Education
    - Encourage the family to attend CPR classes.
- Death
  - Nursing Actions
    - Allow private time for parents to be with the child.
    - Support the parents.

CHAPTER 42: PEDIATRIC EMERGENCIES

 Application Exercises

Scenario: A nurse in an emergency department is caring for the parents of an infant who has just died from SIDS.

1. The parents tell the nurse they found their infant in the corner of the crib blue and not breathing. Which of the following questions should the nurse ask the parents?

    A. "What did you do when you put her down for the evening?"

    B. "Why did you put the blanket in the bed with her?"

    C. "Could you tell me more about how you found her?"

    D. "Didn't you know how to do CPR?"

2. The mother becomes angry and begins yelling at the nurse. How should the nurse react?

3. The nurse returns to the room and is working toward closure with the parents. Explain what intervention is important at this time.

4. Match the following common causes of poisoning in children with the symptoms seen in poisoning with that substance.

    _____ Acetaminophen (Tylenol)   A. Edema of lips, hemoptysis and drooling

    _____ Generic (Aspirin)   B. Mental impairment and blindness

    _____ Lead   C. Liver failure occurring without treatment

    _____ Corrosive substances   D. Nausea/vomiting, ringing in ears and lightheadedness

5. A child who has swallowed paint thinner is brought to the emergency department by her parent. The child is lethargic, gagging, and cyanotic. Which of the following emergency interventions should the nurse implement?

    A. Induce vomiting with syrup of ipecac.

    B. Insert a gastric tube and give activated charcoal.

    C. Prepare for intubation with cuffed endotracheal tube.

    D. Administer chelation therapy using deferoxamine mesylate.

CHAPTER 42: PEDIATRIC EMERGENCIES

 Application Exercises Answer Key

Scenario: A nurse in an emergency department is caring for the parents of an infant who has just died from SIDS.

1. The parents tell the nurse they found their infant in the corner of the crib blue and not breathing. Which of the following questions should the nurse ask the parents?

   A. "What did you do when you put her down for the evening?"

   B. "Why did you put the blanket in the bed with her?"

   C. "Could you tell me more about how you found her?"

   D. "Didn't you know how to do CPR?"

   This is an open-ended question, and its purpose is to obtain information. The other questions are judgmental or accusatory and will serve no purpose.

    NCLEX® Connection: Psychosocial Integrity, End of Life Care

2. The mother becomes angry and begins yelling at the nurse. How should the nurse react?

   The nurse should acknowledge the mother's anger. The nurse should then ensure that a family member is present and leave the room for a few minutes. The nurse should recognize that the mother will shift back and forth in the stages of grief between denial and anger, for at least a few days and that these are normal stages of grieving.

    NCLEX® Connection: Psychosocial Integrity, End of Life Care

3. The nurse returns to the room and is working toward closure with the parents. Explain what intervention is important at this time.

   The nurse should offer the parents the opportunity to hold their infant. The nurse may prepare a box with locks of hair, a blanket, arm bands, or any other personal items belonging to the infant.

    NCLEX® Connection: Psychosocial Integrity, End of Life Care

4. Match the following common causes of poisoning in children with the symptoms seen in poisoning with that substance.

__C__	Acetaminophen (Tylenol)	A. Edema of lips, hemoptysis and drooling
__D__	Generic (Aspirin)	B. Mental impairment and blindness
__B__	Lead	C. Liver failure occurring without treatment
__A__	Corrosive substances	D. Nausea/vomiting, ringing in ears, and lightheadedness

    NCLEX® Connection: Reduction of Risk Potential, System Specific Assessment

5. A child who has swallowed paint thinner is brought to the emergency department by her parent. The child is lethargic, gagging, and cyanotic. Which of the following emergency interventions should the nurse implement?

    A. Induce vomiting with syrup of ipecac.

    B. Insert a gastric tube and give activated charcoal.

    C. Prepare for intubation with cuffed endotracheal tube.

    D. Administer chelation therapy using deferoxamine mesylate.

The emergency treatment for poisoning with hydrocarbons, such as paint thinner, includes intubation to protect the airway before proceeding with gastric decontamination of the stomach. Vomiting should not be induced. Buffering the stomach with activated charcoal is not indicated. Chelation therapy with deferoxamine mesylate is a specific antidote for iron poisoning.

(N) NCLEX® Connection: Physiological Adaptation, Medical Emergencies

UNIT 3	NURSING CARE OF CHILDREN WITH SPECIAL NEEDS
Chapter 43	Psychosocial Issues of Infants, Children, and Adolescents

Overview

- Mental health and developmental disorders in children are not always easily diagnosed, and treatment interventions may be delayed or inadequate. This is because:

    o Children do not have the ability or the necessary skills to describe what is happening.

    o Children demonstrate a wide variety of normal behaviors, especially in different developmental stages.

    o It is difficult to determine if the child's behavior indicates an emotional problem.

- A child's behavior is problematic when it interferes with home, school, and interactions with peers.

    o Behaviors become pathologic when they:

        ▪ Are not age appropriate.

        ▪ Deviate from cultural and societal norms.

        ▪ Create deficits or impairments in adaptive functioning.

- Disorders that may appear during childhood and adolescence

    o Childhood depression, including suicide

    o Anxiety disorders

    o Substance abuse, such as the use of cigarettes, alcohol, and illegal drugs

    o Eating disorders, particularly among girls

    o Behavioral disorders, such as attention deficit hyperactivity disorder (ADHD), oppositional defiant disorder, and conduct disorder

    o Developmental disorders, such as an autistic disorder

- Childhood disorders may have associated comorbid conditions.

- Characteristics of good mental health for children and adolescents

    o Ability to appropriately interpret reality and have a correct perception of the surrounding environment

    o Positive self-concept

    o Ability to cope with stress and anxiety in a healthy and age-appropriate way

- ○ Mastery of developmental tasks

- ○ Ability to express self spontaneously and creatively

- ○ Ability to develop satisfying relationships

Assessment

- • Risk Factors

  - ○ Genetics – The style of behavior (temperament) a child uses to cope with the demands and expectations is thought to be genetically determined. Some developmental disorders may be associated with chromosomal abnormalities.

  - ○ Biochemical – Alterations in the neurotransmitters norepinephrine and/or serotonin

  - ○ Social and environmental – Severe marital discord, low socioeconomic status, large family units and overcrowded conditions, parental delinquency, substance abuse, maternal psychiatric disorders, foster care placement, physical and sexual abuse, and traumatic life events

  - ○ Cultural and ethnic – Difficulty with assimilation, lack of cultural role models, lack of support from the dominant culture

  - ○ Resiliency – The ability to adapt to changes in the environment, form nurturing relationships, distance oneself from the emotional chaos of the parent or family, and use problem-solving skills can help an at-risk child develop normally.

  - ○ Traumatic events in the formative years

  - ○ Familial tendencies

MOOD DISORDERS

Overview

- • Risk factors associated with childhood depression

  - ○ Family history of depression

  - ○ Physical or sexual abuse or neglect

  - ○ Homelessness

  - ○ Disputes among parents, conflicts with peers or family, and rejection by peers or family

  - ○ High-risk behavior

  - ○ Learning disabilities

  - ○ Chronic illness

- • Subjective and Objective Data

  - ○ Feelings of sadness

  - ○ Nonspecific reports related to heath

- ○ Engaging in solitary play or work
- ○ Changes in appetite resulting in weight changes
- ○ Changes in sleeping patterns
- ○ Irritability
- ○ Aggression
- ○ High-risk behavior
- ○ Poor school performance and/or dropping out of school
- ○ Feelings of hopelessness about the future
- ○ Suicidal thoughts

ANXIETY DISORDERS

Overview

- ○ An anxiety disorder exists when:
  - Anxiety interferes with normal growth and development.
  - Anxiety is so serious that the child is unable to function normally in the home, school, and other areas of life.
- ○ Separation anxiety disorder
  - This type of disorder is characterized by excessive anxiety when a child is separated from or anticipating separation from home or parents. The anxiety may develop into a school phobia, phobia of being left alone, panic disorder, or another specific phobia. Depression is also common.
- ○ Posttraumatic stress disorder (PTSD)
  - PTSD may be brought on by experiencing or seeing an extremely traumatic event.
  - Children with PTSD will respond to the precipitating event in a series of phases. The phases begin with an arousal that lasts a few minutes to hours, followed by a period of about 2 weeks in which the child will attempt to deal with the event using defense mechanisms. The last phase, lasting for a period of several months, is when the child may have psychologic symptoms as attempts are made to cope with the event. Failure to cope can lead to obsession regarding the event.
- Risk Factors
  - ○ Anxiety may develop after a specific stressor (death of a relative or pet, illness, move, assault).

- Subjective and Objective Data

  o Children with PTSD may have psychologic symptoms of anxiety, depression, phobia, or conversion reactions.

  o If the anxiety resulting from PTSD is displayed externally, it may be manifested as irritability and aggression with family and friends, poor academic performance, somatic reports, belief that life will be short, and difficulty sleeping.

BEHAVIOR DISORDERS

Overview

  o ADHD

   ▪ Types of ADHD

    □ ADHD combined type (most common)

    □ ADHD predominantly inattentive

    □ ADHD predominantly hyperactive-impulsive

   ▪ Behaviors associated with ADHD must have been present prior to age 7 and must be present in more than one setting for the child to be diagnosed with ADHD. Behaviors associated with ADHD may receive negative attention from adults and peers.

   ▪ Inattentive or impulsive behavior may put the child at risk for injury.

  o Autism spectrum disorder

   ▪ This is a complex neurodevelopmental disorder believed to be of genetic origin with a wide spectrum of behaviors affecting an individual's ability to communicate and interact with others. Cognitive and language development are typically delayed. Characteristic behaviors include an inability to maintain eye contact, repetitive actions, and strict observance of routines.

   ▪ This type of disorder is usually observed before 3 years of age.

   ▪ There is a wide variety of functioning. Abilities may range from poor (inability to perform self-care, inability to communicate and relate to others) to high (ability to function at near-normal levels).

  o Mental retardation

   ▪ Below average intellectual functioning, indicated by an IQ of less than 70

  o Learning disability

   ▪ Group of disorders characterized by difficulty in gaining and using essential skills of listening, speaking, reading, performing math, and writing

  o Communication disorder

   ▪ May be expressive, receptive, or a combination of both

- Subjective and Objective Data

  - ADHD

    - Behavioral problems usually occur in school, church, home, and/or recreational activities.

    - In children with behavior disorders, symptoms generally worsen.

      - Situations that require sustained attention.

      - Unstructured group situations, such as the playground or classroom.

      - Attention deficit hyperactivity disorder (ADHD) involves the inability of a person to control behaviors requiring sustained attention.

    - Inattention, impulsivity, and hyperactivity are characteristic behaviors of ADHD.

    - Inattention is evidenced by a difficulty in paying attention, listening, and focusing.

    - Hyperactivity is evidenced by fidgeting, an inability to sit still, running and climbing inappropriately, difficulty with playing quietly, and talking excessively.

    - Impulsivity is evidenced by difficulty waiting for turns, constantly interrupting others, and acting without considering consequences.

  - Autism

    - Physical difficulties experienced by the child with autism may include sensory integration dysfunction, sleep disorders, digestive disorders, feeding disorders, epilepsy, and/or allergies.

  - Mental retardation

    - Significant limitations in communication, self-care, home living, self-direction, social skills, community use, work, leisure, academic achievement, health, and safety

Collaborative Care

- Nursing Care

  - Obtain a complete nursing history.

    - Mother's pregnancy and birth history

    - Sleeping, eating, and elimination patterns and recent weight loss or gain

    - Achievement of developmental milestones

    - Allergies

    - Current medications

    - Peer and family relationships and school performance

    - History of emotional, physical, or sexual abuse

    - Parents' perceptions and level of tolerance toward the child's behavior

    - Family history, including current members of the household

- Substance use/abuse
  - Tobacco products (cigarettes, cigars, snuff, chewing tobacco) and frequency of use
  - Alcohol, frequency of use, driving under the influence, and family history of abuse
  - Drugs (illegal or prescription) to get high, stay calm, lose weight, or stay awake
- Safety at home and at school
- Actual or potential risk for self-injury
- Presence of depression and suicidal ideation, including a plan, the lethality of that plan, and the means to carry out the plan
- Availability of weapons in the home

○ Perform a complete physical assessment, including a mental status examination.

○ Use primary prevention, such as education, peer group discussions, and mentoring to prevent risky behavior and promote healthy behavior and effective coping.

- Work with the child to help him adopt a realistic view of his body and to improve overall self-esteem.
- Identify and reinforce the use of positive coping skills.
- Employ the use of gun and weapon control strategies.
- Emphasize the use of seat belts when in motor vehicles.
- Encourage the use of protective gear for high-impact sports.
- Provide education on contraceptives and other sexual information, such as transmission and prevention of HIV and other sexually transmitted diseases.
- Encourage abstinence, but keep the lines of communication open to allow adolescents to discuss sexual practices.
- Encourage the child and parents to seek professional help if indicated.

○ Intervene for children who have engaged in high-risk behaviors.

- Instruct the child and family about factors that contribute to substance dependency and tobacco use. Make appropriate referrals when indicated.
- Inform the child and family about support groups in the community for eating disorders, substance abuse, and general teen support.
- Instruct the child regarding individuals within the school environment and community to whom concerns can be voiced about personal safety, (police officers, school nurses, counselors, teachers).
- Make referrals to social services when indicated.
- Discuss the use and availability of support hotlines.
- Perform a depression and suicide assessment. Make an immediate referral for professional care when indicated.

- o Cognitive-behavioral therapy is useful to change negative thoughts to positive outcomes when intervening for depression.
- o Interventions for anxiety disorders
  - ▪ Provide emotional support that is accepting of regression and other defense mechanisms.
  - ▪ Offer protection from panic levels of anxiety by providing for needs.
  - ▪ Increase self-esteem and feelings of achievement.
  - ▪ Assist with working through traumatic events or losses and accepting what has happened.
  - ▪ Suggest group therapy.

- Interventions for behavior disorders
  - o Use a calm, firm, respectful approach with the child.
  - o Use modeling to show acceptable behavior.
  - o Obtain the child's attention before giving directions. Provide short and clear explanations.
  - o Set clear limits on unacceptable behaviors and be consistent.
  - o Plan physical activities through which the child can use energy and obtain success.
  - o Assist parents to develop a reward system using methods such as a wall chart or tokens. Encourage the child to participate.
  - o Focus on the family and child's strengths, not just the problems.
  - o Support the parents' efforts to remain hopeful.
  - o Provide a safe environment for the child and others.
  - o Provide the child with specific positive feedback when expectations are met.
  - o Identify issues that result in power struggles.
  - o Assist the child in developing effective coping mechanisms.
  - o Encourage the child to participate in a form of either group, individual, or family therapy.
  - o Administer medications (antipsychotics, mood stabilizers, anticonvulsants, antidepressants). Monitor for side effects.

- Interventions for an autism spectrum disorder
  - o Initiate referral to early intervention.
  - o Provide for a structured environment.
  - o Consult with parents to provide consistent and individualized care.
  - o Encourage parents to participate and remain at the bedside as much as possible.

- ○ Use short, concise, and developmentally appropriate communication.
- ○ Identify desired behaviors and reward them.
- ○ Role model social skills.
- ○ Role play situations that involve conflict.
- ○ Encourage verbal communication.
- ○ Limit self-stimulating and ritualistic behaviors by providing alternative play activities.
- ○ Determine emotional and situational triggers.
- ○ Give plenty of notice before changing routines.
- ○ Carefully monitor the child's behaviors to ensure safety.

- Medications
  - ○ Medications for children and adolescents include selective serotonin reuptake inhibitors (SSRIs), such as fluoxetine (Prozac); tricyclic antidepressants (TCAs), such as amitriptyline (Elavil); atypical anxiolytics, such as buspirone (BuSpar); CNS stimulants, such as methylphenidate (Concerta, Ritalin SR); and norepinephrine selective reuptake inhibitors, such as atomoxetine HCl (Strattera).

- Interdisciplinary Care
  - ○ Learning disabilities
    - ■ An individualized approach depends on the disorder and is generally treated within the school setting as an interdisciplinary method (special education, speech therapy, physical therapy, and resource teachers).
  - ○ Communications disorder
    - ■ Treated through a variety of modalities (speech and language therapies, adaptive communication devices, hearing aids, sign language)

- Client Outcomes
  - ○ The child has achieved a maximum level of physical, cognitive, and social development.
  - ○ The child is able to communicate effectively.
  - ○ The child and family verbalize the need for information and support.
  - ○ The child verbalizes improved mood.
  - ○ The child has developed realistic goals for the future.
  - ○ The family identifies strategies for managing long-term care of the child.
  - ○ The family identifies strategies for managing disruptive or inappropriate behavior.

MALTREATMENT OF INFANTS AND CHILDREN

Overview

- Maltreatment of infants and children is attributed to a variety of predisposing factors, which include parental, child, and environmental characteristics. Child maltreatment can occur across all economic and educational backgrounds and racial/ethnic/religious groups.

  o Maltreatment of children is made up of several specific types of behaviors.

    ■ Physical – Causes pain or harm to the child (shaken baby syndrome [caused by violent shaking of infants], fractures)

    ■ Sexual – Occurs when sexual contact takes place without consent, whether or not the victim is able to give consent (includes any sexual behavior toward a minor and dating violence among adolescents)

    ■ Emotional – Humiliates, threatens, or intimidates a child (includes behavior that minimizes an individual's feelings of self-worth)

    ■ Neglect – Includes the failure to provide:

      □ Physical care (feeding, clothing, shelter, medical or dental care, safety, education)

      □ Emotional care and/or stimulation to allow normal development (nurturing, affection, attention)

- Failure to thrive (FTT)

  o FTT is also known as growth failure. It is manifested as inadequate growth resulting from the inability to obtain or use calories required for growth. It is usually described in an infant or child who falls below the fifth percentile for weight (and possibly for height) or has persistent weight loss.

    ■ FTT can be the result of an organic (physical) cause, the result of a definable psychosocial cause unrelated to disease, or idiopathic, in which the cause is unknown.

Assessment

- Risk Factors

  o Maltreatment

    ■ The child is under 3 years of age.

    ■ The child is premature, is physically disabled, is the result of an unwanted pregnancy, or has some other trait that makes him particularly vulnerable.

- o FTT
    - Organic causes may include cerebral palsy, chronic renal failure, congenital heart disease, and/or gastroesophageal reflux. However, factors related to nonorganic failure to thrive (NFTT) may include:
        - □ Parental neglect, lack of parental knowledge, or a disturbed maternal-child attachment
        - □ Poverty
        - □ Health or childrearing beliefs
        - □ Family stress
        - □ Feeding resistance
        - □ Insufficient breast milk
- Subjective and Objective Data
    - o Inconsistencies between the parent's report and the child's injuries.
    - o Maltreatment
        - Inconsistency between nature of injury and developmental level of the child.
        - Repeated injuries requiring emergency treatment
        - Inappropriate responses from the parents or child
        - Physical signs such as growth failure, bruises, burns, fractures, poor hygiene, and foul odors or discharge from the genital area
            - □ Assess for unusual bruising on the abdomen, back, and/or buttocks.
            - □ Assess the mechanism of injury, which may not be congruent with the physical appearance of the injury. Many bruises at different stages of healing may indicate continued beatings. Observe for bruises or welts that have taken on the shape of a belt buckle or other objects.
            - □ Observe for burns that appear glove- or stocking-like on hands or feet, which may indicate forced immersion into boiling water. Small, round burns may be caused by lit cigarettes.
            - □ Note fractures with unusual features, such as forearm spiral fractures, which could be caused by twisting the extremity forcefully. The presence of multiple fractures is suspicious.
            - □ Check the child for head injuries. Assess the child's level of consciousness, making sure to note equal and reactive pupils. Also, monitor the child for nausea/vomiting.
        - Inappropriate knowledge of or interest in sexual acts
        - Seductive behavior
        - Avoidance of anything related to sexuality or genitals and the body

- - Withdrawn behaviors or excessive aggression towards others
  - Fear of a particular person or family member
  - ○ Shaken baby syndrome – Shaking may cause intracranial hemorrhage.
    - Assess for:
      - □ Respiratory distress
      - □ Bulging fontanels
      - □ Increased head circumference
      - □ Retinal hemorrhage
    - If bruising is present in an infant before 6 months of age, it should be deemed as suspicious by the nurse.
  - ○ Failure to thrive
    - Less than the fifth percentile on the growth chart for weight
    - Malnourished appearance
    - Signs of dehydration
    - Decreased activity level
    - Developmental delays
    - Negative interactions between the child and parents (no eye contact, irritability, pushing parents away)
    - Difficulty being soothed
  - ○ Laboratory Tests
    - CBC, urinalysis, and other tests that assess for sexually transmitted infections or bleeding
  - ○ Diagnostic Procedures
    - Diagnostics will depend upon the assessment findings and noted findings or injuries. They may include:
      - □ Radiograph
        - ▸ CT scan or magnetic resonance imaging scan

Collaborative Care

- Nursing Care
  - ○ Maltreatment
    - Mandatory reporting is required of all health care providers, including suspected or actual cases of child abuse. There are civil and criminal penalties for not reporting.
    - Clearly and objectively document information obtained in the interview and during the physical assessment.

- ■ Photograph and detail all visible injuries.

- ■ Conduct the interview about family abuse in private.

- ■ Be direct, honest, and professional.

- ■ Use language the child understands.

- ■ Be understanding and attentive.

- ■ Inform the child and parents if a referral must be made to children or adult protective services and explain the process.

- ■ Assess safety and help reduce danger for the victim.

- ■ Use questions that are open-ended and require a descriptive response. These questions are less threatening and elicit more relevant information.

- ■ Provide support for the child and parents.

- ■ Demonstrate behaviors for child-rearing techniques with the parents and child.

  - ○ FTT

    - ■ Obtain a nutritional history.

    - ■ Observe parent-child interactions.

    - ■ Obtain accurate baseline height and weight. Observe for low weight, malnourished appearance, and signs of dehydration.

    - ■ Weigh the child daily without clothing or a diaper.

    - ■ Perform accurate I&O and calorie counts as prescribed.

    - ■ Teach parents to recognize and respond to the infant's cues of hunger.

    - ■ Establish a routine for eating that encourages usual times, duration, and setting.

    - ■ Reinforce proper positioning, latching on, and timing for mothers who are breastfeeding.

    - ■ Encourage parents to:

      - □ Maintain eye contact and face-to-face posture during feedings.

      - □ Talk to the infant while feeding.

      - □ Burp the infant frequently.

      - □ Keep the environment quite and without distractions.

      - □ Be persistent, remaining calm during 10 to 15 min of food refusal.

      - □ Introduce new foods slowly.

      - □ Never force the infant to eat.

- Interdisciplinary Care

  - ○ A team of disciplines may be involved in the care of the child. These may include a dietician, pediatric feeding specialist, physician, and occupational therapist.

  - ○ Initiate appropriate referrals for social services as provided in the community.

- Care After Discharge
  - Client Education
    - Encourage support groups for parents.
    - Encourage attendance at parenting classes.
  - Follow-up
    - Initiate a home health referral.
    - Reinforce the need for follow-up care.

CHAPTER 43: PSYCHOSOCIAL ISSUES OF INFANTS, CHILDREN, AND ADOLESCENTS

(A) Application Exercises

Scenario: The first-time parents of a 3-month-old infant take her to the inpatient pediatric unit. The infant has a medical diagnosis of failure to thrive. She was healthy and in the fortieth percentile for height and weight at birth, but by her 2-month checkup she dropped to the tenth percentile. Today she has dropped below the fifth percentile.

1. Explain what assessments are needed at this time.

2. The mother tells the nurse that the infant is bottle fed. Which of the following feeding techniques should the nurse teach the mother? (Select all that apply.)

_____ Feed the infant in a large common room.

_____ Maintain eye contact with the infant during feedings.

_____ Burp the infant frequently during feedings.

_____ Stop trying to feed the infant after 5 min of refusal.

_____ Develop a structured feeding routine.

3. A nurse in a school health clinic is performing an assessment on an adolescent. Which of the following should alert the nurse to a possible mood disorder? (Select all that apply.)

_____ Psychomotor retardation

_____ Impulsiveness

_____ Changes in sleeping patterns

_____ Difficulty paying attention

_____ Irritability

4. Identify methods of home behavior modification appropriate for a 6-year-old child who has attention deficit hyperactivity disorder (ADHD) and is disruptive in the evenings during dinner.

CHAPTER 43: PSYCHOSOCIAL ISSUES OF INFANTS, CHILDREN, AND ADOLESCENTS

 Application Exercises Answer Key

Scenario: The first-time parents of a 3-month-old infant take her to the inpatient pediatric unit. The infant has a medical diagnosis of failure to thrive. She was healthy and in the fortieth percentile for height and weight at birth, but by her 2-month checkup she dropped to the tenth percentile. Today she has dropped below the fifth percentile.

1. Explain what assessments are needed at this time.

> **The nurse should assess the infant's I&O, daily weight, preparation of formula, feeding patterns, interaction with parents, activity level, and parental concerns.**

 NCLEX® Connection: Reduction of Risk Potential, Potential for Alterations in Body Systems

2. The mother tells the nurse that the infant is bottle fed. Which of the following feeding techniques should the nurse teach the mother? (Select all that apply.)

_____	Feed the infant in a large common room.
X	**Maintain eye contact with the infant during feedings.**
X	**Burp the infant frequently during feedings.**
_____	Stop trying to feed the infant after 5 min of refusal.
X	**Develop a structured feeding routine.**

> **Maintaining eye contact during feedings, burping the infant frequently, and developing a structured feeding routine are all strategies to improve feeding for the infant. The feeding environment should be quiet and have minimal stimulation. Encourage parents to be persistent for at least 10 to 15 min of food refusal.**

 NCLEX® Connection: Physiological Adaptation, Alterations in Body Systems

3. A nurse in a school health clinic is performing an assessment on an adolescent. Which of the following should alert the nurse to a possible mood disorder? (Select all that apply.)

X	**Psychomotor retardation**
_____	Impulsiveness
X	**Changes in sleeping patterns**
_____	Difficulty paying attention
X	**Irritability**

> **Increased sleeping, psychomotor retardation, and irritability are all findings consistent with depression. Impulsiveness and difficulty paying attention are more likely to be signs of attention deficit hyperactivity disorder.**

 NCLEX® Connection: Reduction of Risk Potential, Potential for Alterations in Body Systems

4. Identify methods of home behavior modification appropriate for a 6-year-old child who has attention deficit hyperactivity disorder (ADHD) and is disruptive in the evenings during dinner.

Use a calm, firm, respectful approach with the child.

Use a tangible system the child can actually see or hold, such as a wall chart or tokens that can be turned in for rewards.

Allow the child to have input in planning if possible.

Reinforce with parents the need to be consistent and patient.

Assist parents in setting realistic goals in incremental steps.

Obtain the child's attention before giving directions.

Provide short and clear explanations.

Encourage decreased environmental stimuli when working on behavior modification.

(N) NCLEX® Connection: Physiological Adaptation, Alterations in Body Systems

References

Dudek, S. G. (2007). *Nutrition essentials for nursing practice* (6th ed.). Philadelphia, PA: Lippincott Williams & Wilkins.

Hockenberry, M. J., & Winkelstein M. L. (2009). *Wong's essentials of pediatric nursing* (8th ed.). St. Louis, MO: Mosby.

Lehne, R. A. (2010). *Pharmacology for nursing care* (7th ed.). St. Louis, MO: Saunders.

Pillitteri, A. (2007). *Maternal and child health nursing: Care of the childbearing and childrearing family* (5th ed.). Philadelphia, PA: Lippincott Williams & Wilkins.

Varcarolis, E. M., Carson, V. B., & Shoemaker, N. C. (2006). *Foundations of psychiatric mental health nursing: A clinical approach* (5th ed.). St. Louis, MO: Saunders.

Wilson, B. A., Shannon, M. T., & Shields, K. M. (2010). *Pearson nurse's drug guide 2010.* Upper Saddle River, NJ: Prentice-Hall.

Wong, D. L., Hockenberry, M. J., & Perry, Sl. E. (2007). *Maternal child nursing care.* St . Louis, MO: Mosby.